THE CAMBRIDGE COMPANION TO LITERATURE IN A DIGITAL AGE

Literature has experienced two great medium shifts, each with profound implications for its forms, genres, and cultures: that from orality to writing, and that from writing to printing. Today we are experiencing a third shift: from printed to digital forms. As with the previous shifts, this transformation is reconfiguring literature and literary culture. *The Cambridge Companion to Literature in a Digital Age* is organized around the question of what is at stake for literary studies in this latest transition. Rather than dividing its chapters by methodology or approach, this volume proceeds by exploring the major categories of literary investigation that are coming under pressure in the digital age: concepts such as the canon, periodization, authorship, and narrative. With chapters written by leading experts in all facets of literary studies, this book shows why all those who read, study, and teach literature today ought to attend to the digital.

ADAM HAMMOND is Associate Professor of English at the University of Toronto. He is the author of *The Far Shore: Indie Games, Superbrothers, and the Making of Jett* (2021), *Literature in the Digital Age* (2016), and the coauthor of *Modernism: Keywords* (2014). He is the editor of *Cambridge Critical Concepts: Technology and Literature* (2024). His work has appeared in *Wired* and *The Globe and Mail*, and has been profiled by the BBC and CBC.

A complete list of books in the series is at the back of the book.

THE CAMBRIDGE COMPANION TO LITERATURE IN A DIGITAL AGE

EDITED BY
ADAM HAMMOND
University of Toronto

Shaftesbury Road, Cambridge CB2 8EA, United Kingdom

One Liberty Plaza, 20th Floor, New York, NY 10006, USA

477 Williamstown Road, Port Melbourne, VIC 3207, Australia

314–321, 3rd Floor, Plot 3, Splendor Forum, Jasola District Centre,
New Delhi – 110025, India

103 Penang Road, #05–06/07, Visioncrest Commercial, Singapore 238467

Cambridge University Press is part of Cambridge University Press & Assessment, a department of the University of Cambridge.

We share the University's mission to contribute to society through the pursuit of education, learning and research at the highest international levels of excellence.

www.cambridge.org
Information on this title: www.cambridge.org/9781009349529
DOI: 10.1017/9781009349567

© Cambridge University Press & Assessment 2024

This publication is in copyright. Subject to statutory exception and to the provisions of relevant collective licensing agreements, no reproduction of any part may take place without the written permission of Cambridge University Press & Assessment.

When citing this work, please include a reference to the DOI: 10.1017/9781009349567

First published 2024

A catalogue record for this publication is available from the British Library.

Library of Congress Cataloging-in-Publication Data
NAMES: Hammond, Adam, 1981– editor.
TITLE: The Cambridge companion to literature in a digital age / edited by Adam Hammond.
DESCRIPTION: Cambridge, United Kingdom ; New York, NY : Cambridge University Press, 2024. | Series: CCL Cambridge companions to literature | Includes bibliographical references and index.
IDENTIFIERS: LCCN 2023054694 | ISBN 9781009349529 (hardback) | ISBN 9781009349543 (paperback) | ISBN 9781009349567 (ebook)
SUBJECTS: LCSH: Literature, Modern – 21st century – History and criticism – Theory, etc. | Literature – Study and teaching. | Computational linguistics. | Literature publishing – Technological innovations. | Literature and technology. | Digital humanities.
CLASSIFICATION: LCC PN781 .C38 2024 | DDC 809/.05–dc23/eng/20240102
LC record available at https://lccn.loc.gov/2023054694

ISBN 978-1-009-34952-9 Hardback
ISBN 978-1-009-34954-3 Paperback

Cambridge University Press & Assessment has no responsibility for the persistence or accuracy of URLs for external or third-party internet websites referred to in this publication and does not guarantee that any content on such websites is, or will remain, accurate or appropriate.

Contents

List of Figures		*page* vii
List of Contributors		ix
Chronology		x

	Introduction *Adam Hammond*		1
1	Literary Data *Yohei Igarashi*		12
2	Literary Change *Ted Underwood*		34
3	The Canon *Mark Algee-Hewitt*		47
4	Voice and Performance *Marit J. MacArthur and Lee M. Miller*		66
5	The Archive *Katherine Bode*		89
6	Editions *Claire Battershill, Anna Mukamal, and Helen Southworth*		107
7	Materiality *Dennis Yi Tenen*		125
8	The Literary Marketplace *Tully Barnett*		137
9	Fanfiction, Digital Platforms, and Social Reading *Anna Wilson*		154

10	Narrative and Interactivity *Emily Short*	177
11	Generated Literature *Nick Montfort and Judy Heflin*	194
12	Literary Gaming *Timothy Welsh*	212
13	The Printed Book in the Digital Age *Inge van de Ven*	233
14	Literature's Audioptic Platform *Garrett Stewart*	250
15	Critique *Gabriel Hankins*	273

Index   292

Figures

1.1 and 1.2	Pages from Cooper's "Instructions to Collaborators," Papers of Lane Cooper (MC 045), box 8, folder 9, Special Collections and University Archives, Rutgers University Libraries.	page 26
1.3 and 1.4	Slips from the making of *A Concordance to the Poems of William Wordsworth* (1911), Papers of Lane Cooper (MC 045), box 8, folder 9, Special Collections and University Archives, Rutgers University Libraries.	29
2.1	The probability that a given book is crime fiction, estimated by a model trained on examples of detective, Newgate, and sensation fiction labeled by human readers.	37
2.2	Two discontinuous genres overlap to produce a continuous trend.	38
2.3	Illustration from Ryan Heuser and Long Le-Khac, "A Quantitative Literary History of 2,958 Nineteenth-Century British Novels: The Semantic Cohort Method," *Pamphlets of the Stanford Literary Lab* (2012), 27. Here, "hard seeds" are concrete words.	39
3.1	Diagram of the Literary Field on the axis of popularity (x) and prestige (y). From J. D. Porter, "Popularity/Prestige," *Pamphlets of the Stanford Literary Lab* (2018), 5.	56
3.2	t-sne plot of 100 topic model of Chadwyck-Healey Nineteenth-Century Novel Corpus.	61
3.3	t-sne of 100 topic model of Chadwyck-Healey corpus with select canonical texts labeled.	63
4.1	Pitch contour in Drift. John Ashbery reading "The Painter," ll. 9–10, 92nd St. Y, New York, NY, 1952.	67

4.2	Pitch contour in Drift. Louise Glück reading "The Wild Iris" (1992).	75
4.3	Pitch contour in Drift. Louise Glück reading "The Wild Iris" (1992).	75
4.4	Word duration, pause start and end times, and pause length. Louise Glück reading "The Wild Iris" (1992).	76
4.5	Fundamental frequency every 10 ms in hz. Louise Glück reading "The Wild Iris" (1992).	76
4.6	Harmonics of the fundamental in hz. Louise Glück reading "The Wild Iris" (1992).	77
4.7	Pitch range, speed, and acceleration in sample recordings by seven poets.	82
4.8	Rhythmic complexity of pauses in sample recordings by seven poets (a lower value means a more predictable rhythm).	83
4.9	Words per minute in sample recordings by seven poets.	83
8.1	Robert Darnton's Communications Circuit. Robert Darnton, "What Is the History of Books?," *Daedalus* 111, no. 3 (1982), 67.	139
8.2	Ray Murray and Squires's Digital Publishing Communications Circuit.	144
9.1	Paratextual frame for "Everything Else Is A Substitute For Your Love" by Aria from Archive of Our Own (Archive account-holder view). Image appears with kind permission from the author.	173

Contributors

MARK ALGEE-HEWITT, Stanford University
TULLY BARNETT, Flinders University
CLAIRE BATTERSHILL, University of Toronto
KATHERINE BODE, Australian National University
ADAM HAMMOND, University of Toronto
GABRIEL HANKINS, Clemson University
JUDY HEFLIN, independent scholar
YOHEI IGARASHI, University of Connecticut
MARIT J. MACARTHUR, University of California–Davis
LEE M. MILLER, University of California–Davis
NICK MONTFORT, Massachusetts Institute of Technology and University of Bergen
ANNA MUKAMAL, Coastal Carolina University
EMILY SHORT, independent scholar
HELEN SOUTHWORTH, University of Oregon
GARRETT STEWART, University of Iowa
DENNIS YI TENEN, Columbia University
TED UNDERWOOD, University of Illinois, Urbana–Champaign
INGE VAN DE VEN, Tilburg University
TIMOTHY WELSH, Loyola University New Orleans
ANNA WILSON, Harvard University

Chronology

16th–17th century	The modern binary number system is studied in Europe, systems related to modern binary numbers having already been developed earlier in ancient Egypt, China, and India.
1833	Charles Babbage begins work on the Analytical Engine, a proposed mechanical general-purpose computer.
1843	Ada Lovelace publishes her annotated translation of Luigi Federico Menabrea's description of Babbage's Analytical Engine. She includes a way to calculate Bernoulli numbers using the machine, earning her the title of the world's first computer programmer.
1893	Lucius Adelno Sherman publishes his *Analytics of Literature*, an early data-based approach to literary study.
1911	Lane Cooper publishes *A Concordance to the Poems of William Wordsworth*, compiled using analog data processing techniques.
1936	Alan Turing publishes *On Computable Numbers*, which contains the earliest description of a modern computer.
1943	Work begins on Colossus, the world's first electronic digital programmable computer.
1945	Vannevar Bush describes the Memex, a proto-hypertext device.
1946	Father Roberto Busa begins work on the *Index Thomisticus* project, the first electronic

	concordance, often cited as the first "digital humanities" project.
1957	Josephine Miles's *Concordance to the Poetical Works of John Dryden* is published, the first concordance to be completed using computational methods.
1963	The first edition of the ASCII character encoding standard is released.
	Ted Nelson coins the term "hypertext."
1964	Joseph Weizenbaum begins work on ELIZA, an early natural language processing computer program.
	Frederick Mosteller and David L. Wallace publish their computational analysis of the disputed authorship of *The Federalist Papers*.
1966	*Computers and the Humanities* is founded, the first academic journal in what would become known as the "digital humanities."
1971	Michael S. Hart founds Project Gutenberg, the world's first digital library.
1974	Kurzweil Computer Products, Inc. is founded, a pioneer in optical character recognition (OCR) technology.
1976	Will Crowther releases *Colossal Cave Adventure*, the first text-based adventure computer game.
1982	Robert Darnton publishes his model of the "communications circuit."
1986	The *Women Writers Project* archive is founded.
1987	The Text Encoding Initiative (TEI) project is launched.
1990	Tim Berners-Lee specifies the HTML (HyperText Markup Language) standard, the foundation of the World Wide Web.
1994	Work begins on The William Blake Archive.
1995	The Modernist Journals Project is created.
1996	Brewster Kahle founds the Internet Archive.
1998	FanFiction.net is founded.
1999	The Electronic Literature Organization is founded by Scott Rettberg, Robert Coover, and Jeff Ballowe.

2000	Jay David Bolter's and Richard Grusin's *Remediation: Understanding New Media* is published.
2001	Jerome McGann's *Radiant Textuality: Literary Studies after the World Wide Web* is published.
2002	The Latent Dirichlet allocation (LDA) algorithm for computational topic modeling is released.
2004	The anthology *A Companion to Digital Humanities* is published, coining the term "digital humanities."
	Google Books is announced.
	Facebook is created.
2005	Valve's Steam videogame digital distribution service begins selling third-party titles.
2006	Goodreads is founded.
	Twitter is released.
2007	Amazon releases the first version of its Kindle e-reader.
2008	Apple's App Store digital distribution service is released.
2009	Writing from the Philadelphia MLA convention, William Pannapacker calls digital humanities "the next big thing."
	Chris Klimas releases Twine, an open-source tool for creating interactive hypertext fiction.
2010	Google releases the Google Books Ngram Viewer.
2018	OpenAI releases its first large language model, GPT-1.

Introduction

Adam Hammond

I began my 2016 book *Literature in the Digital Age* with what, in subsequent years, I came to think of as "the parable of the cheese." The story goes as follows.

For their 2013 conference, the organizers of the Modernist Studies Association decided to include their first ever "poster session." Their intention was to showcase the Digital Literary Studies (DLS) research that was then starting to attract attention in the broader discipline. Since I had some work I thought might be of interest – a synoptic digital edition of *To the Lighthouse* that visualized wildly varying interpretations of free indirect discourse in the text – I signed up. One night, we were asked to set up our posters at the wine and cheese reception. Not a single person asked me about my project and no one engaged with the demonstration I had set up on my laptop. At one point, however, a conference-goer in conversation found that they needed both hands to illustrate the point they were making, and so deposited their half-eaten piece of cheese on top of my laptop.

Thus "the parable of the cheese," the upshot of which was that mainstream literary studies was having a difficult time accepting or embracing work in DLS – not out of any hostility or lack of good intentions, but simply because it didn't know what to do with it. Drawing on Virginia Woolf's model of the androgynous mind and Mikhail Bakhtin's "excess of seeing," I presented *Literature in the Digital Age* as a way of showing mainstream literary scholars what to do with digital work: how to grab the mouse and explore the digital exhibit rather than employ it as a convenient surface on which to discard unwanted snacks. As I put it in 2016,

> This book argues that both print and digital literary traditions have something to tell us about each other. Their encounter presents an enormous opportunity to revisit and revise our received methods of reading,

interpreting, and teaching literature – as well as an occasion to adapt traditional literary approaches to the task of explaining and coming to terms with the digital world. Most fundamentally, the encounter of print and the digital presents us with the opportunity to sharpen our sense of what literature is, what it is becoming, and what it is for. But to make the most of this productive encounter, scholars and students trained in print-based approaches need to be able to talk to those steeped in the digital. This book exists to facilitate this conversation.[1]

Sadly, the ensuing years have done little to bring the traditions together. If there is no piece of cheese on the keyboard today, is it most likely because there is no poster session at the conference at all, or because the more traditional literary scholar has learned to take their cheese elsewhere. A decade on from that MSA conference, the indifference of the cheese-depositing academic of 2013 has been largely replaced with a firm and specific disdain for digital work. The conversation I hoped to facilitate has mostly failed to materialize; potential interlocutors now tend to place themselves in different rooms.

This deepening rift was already becoming apparent as my book appeared. In 2016, I was asked to write a "state of the discipline" article for *Literature Compass*, and this time I chose the "hype cycle" for my opening image.[2] Developed by the consulting firm Gartner, the model posits four phases for the adoption of any new technology. During the "technology trigger," expectations are high and investment pours in. After a "peak of inflated expectations," when press turns negative and investors begin to panic, follows a descent into the "trough of disillusionment." Only then can the "slope of enlightenment" be climbed, with steady and modest progress leading to the "plateau of productivity."

In my article, I argued that DLS found itself firmly in the "trough of disillusionment." The "peak of inflated expectations" likely came when William Pannapacker, writing for the *Chronicle of Higher Education* from the 2009 MLA convention, called digital humanities (DH) "the next big thing," capable of delivering public attention, funding, and tenure-track hires to a field deprived of all three. Evidence of a backlash began to emerge shortly afterward.[3] Landmarked by the "Dark Side of the Digital

---

[1] Adam Hammond, *Literature in the Digital Age: An Introduction* (Cambridge: Cambridge University Press, 2016), xvi.
[2] Adam Hammond, "The Double Bind of Validation: Distant Reading and the Digital Humanities' 'Trough of Disillusion,'" *Literature Compass* (1 August 2017): 1–13.
[3] William Pannapacker, "The MLA and the Digital Humanities," *The Chronicle of Higher Education* (December 28, 2009), http://web.archive.org/web/20150908020431/http://chronicle.com/blogPost/The-MLAthe-Digital/19468/.

Humanities" panel at the 2013 MLA, the 2014 *New Republic* piece "Technology is Taking Over English Departments: The False Promise of Digital Humanities" by Adam Kirsch,[4] and the 2016 *LA Review of Books* article "Neoliberal Tools (and Archives): A Political History" by Daniel Allington, Sarah Brouillette, and David Golumbia,[5] a new narrative began to take shape. Inverting Pannapacker's account, DLS was seen to be engaged in a hostile takeover of literary studies, motivated not by core humanities values of nuance, critique, and activism, but rather by the data- and dollar-driven agenda of the neoliberal university. At the same time, many began to question whether digital approaches had produced any genuinely meaningful literary insights – or were even capable of doing so. In his *New Republic* piece, Kirsch concluded a discussion of the digital work of Franco Moretti – at the time, perhaps the most prominent literary scholar to have crossed over into DLS – by arguing that what was "striking" about digital methods was that they were "incapable of generating significant new ideas about the subject matter of humanistic study."[6] In an interview published in the *Los Angeles Review of Books* shortly after, Moretti conceded the point, admitting "our work could have been better" and suggesting that digital literary studies had produced "no great results."[7]

Although I argued in my *Literature Compass* piece that DLS had entered the "trough of disillusionment," the nadir was yet to come. In October 2017 – some eight years after publishing Pannapacker's celebratory report from the 2009 MLA convention – the *Chronicle of Higher Education* published Timothy Brennan's "The Digital Humanities Bust." Following on from the critiques of Kirsch and the concessions of Moretti, Brennan asked what this much-hyped, richly funded field had accomplished. "Not much," he answered, except perhaps to drive a "wedge separating the humanities from its reason to exist – namely, to think against prevailing norms."[8]

---

[4] Adam Kirsch, "Technology Is Taking over English Departments: The False Promise of the Digital Humanities," *The New Republic* (May 2, 2014), https://newrepublic.com/article/117428/limits-digital-humanities-adam-kirsch.

[5] Daniel Allington, Sarah Brouillette, and David Golumbia, "Neoliberal Tools (and Archives): A Political History of Digital Humanities," *Los Angeles Review of Books* (May 1, 2016), https://lareviewofbooks.org/article/neoliberal-tools-archives-political-history-digital-humanities/.

[6] Kirsch, "Technology Is Taking over English Departments."

[7] Melissa Dinsman, "The Digital in the Humanities: An Interview with Franco Moretti," *Los Angeles Review of Books* (March 2, 2016), https://lareviewofbooks.org/article/the-digital-in-the-humanities-an-interview-with-franco-moretti/.

[8] Timothy Brennan, "The Digital Humanities Bust," *The Chronicle Review* (20 October 2017): B12–B14.

Yet the true low point arrived in 2019 with the publication of Nan Z. Da's "The Computational Case against Computational Literary Studies" in *Critical Inquiry*.[9] For months before its publication, rumors circulated among scholars on both sides of the digital-print divide of an imminent "field-killing" essay. (One colleague in my department went so far as to say, in friendly conversation, before either of us had read Da's article, "So I guess you're back to being a modernist now that DH is dead.") What separated Da's article from other landmarks in the "trough of disillusionment" was its method: whereas other attacks had been launched from beyond the castle gates, Da's came from within, using mathematics and statistics to argue its thesis.

Da's fundamental argument was by now a familiar one: that digital literary studies had produced "no great results." Yet it was not only the outcomes of computational literary analysis that she challenged, but also the rigor of the methods. As she put it, "The problem with computational literary analysis as it stands is that what is robust is obvious (in the empirical sense) and what is not obvious is not robust."[10] Da followed with a series of critical close readings of the methods employed in a number of prominent papers in DLS, not only engaging the experimental design and results of the papers but also attempting to replicate their results by running their code. Her conclusion: "the papers I study divide into no-result papers – those that haven't statistically shown us anything – and papers that do produce results but that are wrong."[11]

As predicted (and intended), the article generated significant controversy. *Critical Inquiry* convened a special online forum in which a variety of scholars were invited to comment and reply, including many of those whose work had been attacked in the article. Some applauded: Sarah Brouillette saw Da's article as proving that "DH is a way of doing literary studies without having to engage in long periods of sustained reading, while acquiring what might feel like job skills";[12] to Da's binary taxonomy of DH papers into "no results" and "wrong," Stanley Fish responded "I can only cheer."[13] The scholars whose work had been classified thus were

---

[9] Nan Z. Da, "The Computational Case against Computational Literary Studies," *Critical Inquiry* 45 (Spring 2019): 601–639.
[10] Ibid., 601.   [11] Ibid., 605.
[12] Sarah Brouillette, "Computational Literary Studies: A *Critical Inquiry* Online Forum," *Critical Inquiry* (March 31, 2019), https://critinq.wordpress.com/2019/03/31/computational-literary-studies-a-critical-inquiry-online-forum/.
[13] Stanley Fish, "Computational Literary Studies: Participant Forum Responses, Day 3," *Critical Inquiry*, https://critinq.wordpress.com/2019/04/03/computational-literary-studies-participant-forum-responses-day-3-5/.

naturally less sanguine. Ted Underwood said Da's work was "riddled with material omissions and errors";[14] he and others pointed out that, in seeking to expose mathematical and statistical errors in the work of others, Da had committed several of her own.[15]

Perhaps the most balanced and productive response to Da's provocation came from Katherine Bode, who argued that Da's article was premised on two mistaken assumptions. The first was what Bode called its "constrained and contradictory framing of statistical inquiry." On the one hand, Da accused DLS researchers of employing shoddy methodologies and so failing to achieve rigorous answers to their questions; on the other, Da insisted that literature was sufficiently complex that such statistically rigorous answers were in fact unachievable. As Bode argued, this demand is not only inherently contradictory, but also misrepresents the intentions of the DLS researchers Da takes on, for whom "the pivot to machine learning is explicitly conceived as rejecting a positivist view of literary data and computation in favor of modelling as a subjective practice."[16] Bode's reading of Da's contradictory analysis extended also to Da's project as a whole. The turn of the screw in Da's article is the notion that DLS researchers can be hoisted by their own petards, the inadequacy of their computational approaches demonstrated by their own methods; yet such faith in the absolute truth of statistical claims is precisely the target of her attack. As Bode put it, Da's article "demonstrates the problems it decries."[17]

Bode's second point was that Da's article couldn't possibly "kill" the entire field of DLS because it took on such a narrow slice of it. As Bode wrote, Da's definition of the field – "using statistics, predominantly machine learning, to investigate word patterns" – excluded most of the work Bode would categorize within the field: that which

---

[14] Ted Underwood, "Computational Literary Studies: *A Critical Inquiry* Online Forum." https://critinq.wordpress.com/2019/03/31/computational-literary-studies-a-critical-inquiry-online-forum/.

[15] See Mark Algee-Hewitt, "Computational Literary Studies: A *Critical Inquiry* Online Forum." https://critinq.wordpress.com/2019/03/31/computational-literary-studies-a-critical-inquiry-online-forum/; Andrew Piper, "Do We Know What We Are Doing?" *Cultural Analytics* (April 1, 2019): 1–13; Fotis Jannidis, "On the Perceived Complexity of Literature: A Response to Nan Z. Da," *Cultural Analytics* (July 17, 2019): 1–13. Da conceded certain points; see Nan Z. Da, "Computational Literary Studies: Participant Forum Responses, Day 2," *Critical Inquiry* (April 2, 2019), https://critinq.wordpress.com/2019/04/02/computational-literary-studies-participant-forum-responses-day-2/.

[16] Katherine Bode, "Computational Literary Studies: A *Critical Inquiry* Online Forum," *Critical Inquiry* (March 31, 2019), https://critinq.wordpress.com/2019/03/31/computational-literary-studies-a-critical-inquiry-online-forum/. See also Piper, "Do We Know What We Are Doing?" and Ted Underwood, "The Theoretical Divide Driving Debates about Computation," *Critical Inquiry* 46 (Summer 2020): 900–912.

[17] Bode, "Computational Literary Studies."

employs data construction and curation as forms of critical analysis; analyzes bibliographical and other metadata to explore literary trends; deploys machine-learning methods to identify literary phenomena for noncomputational interpretation; or theorizes the implications of methods such as data visualization and machine learning for literary studies.

Taken together, the two parts of Bode's argument make a crucial point. Da's article, seeking to take down an entire field, aimed only for the statue's feet, as it were – and also missed the mark. Yet Bode's argument can be taken further, as this collection aims to demonstrate.

It is not only that DLS as a field is richer and more varied than its critics have assumed; the broader argument of *The Cambridge Companion to Literature in a Digital Age* is that DLS should not be conceived as a separate field at all. Rather than approaching the digital in terms of *what it has achieved as distinct discipline*, it is more productive and enlightening to approach it in terms of *how it is transforming the discipline of literary studies*. Rather than speaking of DLS as if it existed outside of "traditional" literary studies, this book explores the broad impact that digital technology is exerting on all facets of literary production, reception, and analysis.

Literature has experienced two great medium shifts, each with profound implications for its forms, genres, and cultures: that from orality to writing, and that from writing to printing. Today we are experiencing a third such shift: from printed to digital forms. As with the previous shifts, the current transformation is reconfiguring literature and literary culture at the same time as it is altering the methods and materialities of literary research. Many literary texts are today composed, edited, distributed, marketed, consumed, and discussed in digital formats. Born-digital forms such as interactive fiction, generated poetry, and videogames are expanding and challenging the conventional boundaries of the literary. Literary research, itself increasingly conducted in digital forms, has begun to engage digitized literary texts and archives, employ computational analysis, and study the shifting institutional and professional configurations of the digital literary sphere. Yet far from superseding their analogue predecessors, digital forms and methods exist alongside them in complex relationships of competition, admiration, and adaptation.

This *Companion* is organized around the question of what is at stake for literary studies in this latest transition. Rather than dividing its chapters by methodology or approach (distant reading, computational analysis, book history, or electronic literature), it proceeds by exploring the major categories of literary investigation that are coming under pressure in the digital age: concepts such as the canon, periodization, authorship, and narrative. Whereas direct focus on DLS makes for stirring polemics, it offers little to students and scholars interested in the transformative stakes of digitization for literary studies. Rejecting the prevailing model of for-or-against, *The Cambridge Companion to Literature in a Digital Age* shows why all those who read, study, and teach literature today ought to attend to the digital.

The volume opens with "Literary Data," in which Yohei Igarashi argues that, despite recent arguments that position "data" as anathema to its identity, academic literary studies has long embraced it. Considering cases such as Lucius Adelno Sherman's *Analytics of Literature* (1893), Igarashi shows how, in a formative moment for literary studies around the turn of the twentieth century, professional scholarship distinguished itself from amateur or *belles lettres* precisely because of its reliance on "data." The early history of literary studies reveals not only a long-standing engagement with data, Igarashi demonstrates, but also the "specificity and idiosyncrasies" of what data has meant to literary scholars.

In "Literary Change," Ted Underwood investigates how computational research is reshaping the notion of literary periods. To date, Underwood argues, accounts of literary history have been delivered in the form of *narratives*, which privilege radical transformations carried out by particular events, authors, and works. Whereas narratives struggle to represent gradual change, quantitative approaches excel in doing so; as Underwood argues, computational attempts to understand literary history tend to represent literary history not as radical breaks but as gradual processes extending over long timelines. At this juncture, Underwood argues, "[i]t appears likely that there is an error somewhere in our understanding of the past": either "quantitative researchers have failed to measure the most important aspects of literary change," or else narrative-based "period concepts are less inevitable than our existing histories imply."

In "The Canon," Mark Algee-Hewitt explores how the digital age is reorienting our approach to classic texts. In the early days of DLS, a utopian belief prevailed whereby unlimited, free, and instant access to digital copies of all literary texts might abolish the canon. Yet, because even vast digital archives reflect selection biases and tend to reinforce the canon, Algee-Hewitt proposes more modest means by which computational analysis might intervene. On the one hand, when canonical texts cluster together in large-scale analysis, this makes more evident the groups of noncanonical texts and reveals the underlying decisions that helped form the canon. On the other, when noncanonical and canonical texts cluster together, such analysis prompts reflection on why one text rather than another is elevated to such exalted status. In both cases, Algee-Hewitt argues, the provisional findings of large-scale computational analysis must be verified by close readings of unfamiliar, even unknown texts. In other words, such analysis sends us beyond the canon.

The next chapter, "Voice and Performance," shows how digital forms and methods are leading scholars to question the fundamental modalities of literature. Drawing on sound studies, voice studies, and the neuroscience of speech perception, Marit J. MacArthur and Lee M. Miller describe a new method for studying literary recordings. Such approaches – able to push beyond the canon by focusing on large numbers of recordings, while also avoiding "older methods of impressionistic generalizing" – not only provide new insights into the nature of literary performance, but also serve to reground literature *as* performance.

A series of chapters follows on how the digital age is impacting the materials and materiality of literature and literary research. Katherine Bode's "The Archive" pushes back against the widespread conception of digital archives as passive "backgrounds for research" rather than "active shapers of literary knowledge." Bode explores the ways in which scholars are using media-specific approaches to adapt philological and media archaeological methods to build a picture of the complex and interdependent relationships between literary knowledges, technologies, and infrastructures. As she argues, approaching digital archives as "interpretive constructs" requires that we "recognize that our concepts have always been bound to and formed by technologies, and vice versa."

In "Editions," Claire Battershill, Anna Mukamal, and Helen Southworth build on this notion to argue that the digital age demands a rethinking of the concept of an "edition." Placing them within a broader and longer tradition of textual scholarship, book history, and scholarly editions, they show how digital editions have extended and challenged existing paradigms and practices. "Old definitions drawn from print materialities will no longer suffice," they argue; instead, we must "detach our understanding of textual choices from their material instantiations in type and attach them instead to a new digital materiality."

The latter is the subject of the next chapter, Dennis Yi Tenen's "Materiality." Yi Tenen begins with a postulation – "ideas take shape in matter" – and a question: "What is a book, really?" He pursues the "thinginess" of books in the digital age through the example of "a crisp, 'pirated' copy of Russell's *Power: A New Social Analysis*" purchased in a small shop in Lahore. Tracing the book's history from the shop, to online retail, to his own bookshelf, Yi Tenen shows the process by which ideas become objects, emphasizing the fact that the affordances of the object – what can be done with it, how, and where – powerfully affect our practices of interpretation.

Tully Barnett's "The Literary Marketplace" adopts a materialist approach to investigate the means by which digital technologies are transforming the ways that books are produced, published, distributed, and experienced. In the midst of this transformation, Barnett outlines a variety of responses: from those who believe that the digital marketplace is democratizing literary publishing, to those who lament the loss of the quality of an age without gatekeepers, to those who bemoan the fate of authors who, in an age of hyperabundant literature, must spend as much time marketing themselves as they do writing. Yet, noting the decent decline in e-book sales and the ongoing resurgence of literature in print form, she concludes that the current state of the literary marketplace can be defined only by flux itself: "the development of new complications of the notions of production, distribution and reception."

The next group of chapters focuses on the ways that digital-native literary forms are challenging central pillars of literary theory. It has long been argued that digital textuality fundamentally alters familiar conceptions of literary authorship. Beginning in the 1990s, critics such as Jay David Bolter, George Landow, and Mark Poster articulated a conception whereby the interactive affordances of digital textuality would level the playing field between author and reader; rather than consuming the text passively, the reader would become a "coauthor," actively creating a unique narrative through their interactions and narrative choices. While these bold prophesies may not have materialized, digital textuality has worked in subtler ways to challenge the model of individual authorship.

In "Fanfiction, Digital Platforms, and Social Reading," Anna Wilson traces the origins of fanfiction to the premodern period, providing a literary history of collective authorship. Wilson shows how fan sites such as FanFiction.net and Archive of Our Own are putting pressure on conventional means of evaluating literary excellence – most notably, by challenging conceptions of originality and distinctiveness. She considers how another facet of digital reading – social reading, as practiced on sites like Goodreads – is creating new feedback loops between authors and readers, facilitating the development of new "interpretive communities" and thus working to undermine the centrality of the solitary genius and the solitary reader to conceptions of literary production and reception.

Building on Wilson's investigation of authorship, Emily Short's chapter on "Narrative and Interactivity" assesses the challenges that interactive forms of digital literature pose to print-based assumptions about narrative. Speaking from her perspective as a highly regarded author of interactive and choice-based literature, Short draws on a variety of interactive digital forms to demonstrate the ways in which they challenge print-bound assumptions about narrative: "the reader does not write any of the text," "the text is finite and bounded," and "the external circumstances of reading have no effect on content."

In their chapter on "Generated Literature," Nick Montfort and Judy Heflin survey the long history of computer-generated literary art, from the 1950s to the 2020s. Focusing on the figure of the "author/programmer," who engages the codes of both human and machine language, they argue that generated literature provides insight into machine voices and computer cognition – topics that, in the age of AI, are increasingly salient. Montfort and Heflin further argue that, with the rise of opaque and proprietary text generation systems such as ChatGPT, the social role of the literary author/programmer is to investigate and make legible processes that are increasingly locked inside black boxes.

Timothy Welsh's "Literary Gaming" begins from the observation that videogames, arguably the dominant narrative form of our time, "occupy a cultural role once held by literature." Like novels in the nineteenth century, games are today widely perceived as "unproductive, idle, and possibly dangerous." Yet Welsh argues that literary *criticism* has an important role to play both in reshaping and in redeeming the value of videogames. Just as twentieth-century literary criticism and theory was focused on "decentering, queering, politicizing, and generally reading against ... colonizing, normalizing trajectories," so too can literary studies help us avoid a "crass commercialist future" for videogames by teaching us how to "read – or play – our games differently."

The volume closes with a group of chapters that consider – and demonstrate – the transformations that the digital age has brought to the most traditional corners of literary studies. In "The Printed Book in the Digital Age," Inge van de Ven explores the way that the printed codex has adapted and revived in the time of its widely prophesied death. Examining a series of "Renaissances" in twenty-first century analog literary practices – in book art, book design, and the forms and subjects of literary fiction – van de Ven argues that "the digital has brought the book, and the novel as the literary art form bound by the book, into sharper focus."

Garrett Stewart's chapter on "Literature's Audioptic Platform" is at once a meditation and an exhibition. On the one hand, it sets out to reconsider the relationship between text and image in the age of computer graphics, proposing the generative rubric of "IMAGEdTEXT" to describe the operation of the "audiovisual engine" of literary texts by authors from George Eliot and Henry James to Marcel Proust and Richard Powers. On the other hand, the chapter demonstrates the ways that familiar modes of literary criticism – especially close reading – can be energized through contact with digital forms, methods, and theories.

The concluding chapter, "Critique" by Gabriel Hankins, brings the volume's concerns full circle. Returning to some of the debates and controversies I have surveyed in this introduction, Hankins argues for a self-reflective mode of digital literary theory and practice informed by the long intellectual and political history of critique. Providing a genealogy of the origins of critique in early modern textual criticism and eighteenth-century disputes over autonomous criticism, Hankins calls for a mode of critique that "recognize[s] ... the contradictions of intellectual work that engages the struggle against an age of digital instrumentalism, data science solutionism, and pervasive surveillance ... from *within* surveillance capitalism, not some point outside it." In so doing, he makes the case not only that digital approaches *can* be aligned with critique – an alliance forbidden in so many polemical accounts – but that they *must* be brought together if our discipline is to continue to engage with and challenge the contemporary world.

In the end, my aim for this collection is identical to that of my 2016 book: I hope that it facilitates a conversation between scholars and students of literature who tend to find themselves on opposite sides in the polemics that animate discussion of literary scholarship. Although the chapters of this volume can model this mode of conversing – drawing together methods, theories, and texts from a variety of print and digital traditions to show how each challenge and enrich the other – the real conversation begins with you, the reader. May you find the voices in this book worthy interlocutors.

CHAPTER I

Literary Data

Yohei Igarashi

1.1 Literary Data Processing, Part I

We have evidently been living through a data revolution. Datafication is everywhere, subjecting everyone and everything. What, then, is this specialized concern, *literary* data? Is it a distinct, meaningful category? Literary data evokes, among other things, recent computation-driven literary scholarship, but even in that context other terms have been the subject of more commentary, while the term "data" tends to be invoked as a matter of course. The unglamorous preparatory data work that goes into such scholarship and the longer history of literary data have received much less reflection.[1] This chapter addresses the latter, with a close look at the former as it pertained to literary data circa 1910. Dipping into some earlier chapters in a would-be history of data in literary study, the chapter shows what literary data looked like in the past – the materials and techniques

---

[1] Other kinds of "literary data" include, of course, bibliographic data and metadata, as well as earlier practices of literary indexing. Regarding the former, see, for example, the discussion of "data-rich literary history" in Katherine Bode, *A World of Fiction: Digital Collections and the Future of Literary History* (Ann Arbor: University of Michigan Press, 2018), especially 37–58; on the latter, see, for example, Robin Valenza, "How Literature Becomes Knowledge: A Case Study," *ELH* 76 (2009): 215–245.

Some exceptions to the lack of discussion on the concept of literary data, almost all of them quite brief, include the following: Alan Liu, *Friending the Past: The Sense of History in the Digital Age* (Chicago: University Chicago Press, 2018), 3–5; and the 2014 Stanford Arcade colloquy, "What Is Data in Literary Studies?" (https://arcade.stanford.edu/content/what-data-literary-studies-1) convened by James English, and featuring brief essays by David Alworth, Eric Hayot, Heather Houser, Lauren Klein, Peter Logan, and Scott Selisker. Andrew Goldstone attributes some forms of literary data analysis to social scientific content analysis; see his "The Doxa of Reading," *PMLA* 132.3 (May 2017): 638. Goldstone also gives a helpful account of teaching a practical graduate course on "literary data": see "Teaching Quantitative Methods: What Makes It Hard (in Literary Studies)," in *Debates in the Digital Humanities 2019*, ed. Matthew K. Gold and Lauren F. Klein (Minneapolis: University of Minnesota Press): https://dhdebates.gc.cuny.edu/read/untitled-f2acf72c-a469-49d8-b e35-67f9ac1e3a60/section/620caf9f-08a8-485e-a496-51400296ebcd#ch19. Yet, on the whole it remains the case that, in English's words, "we as literary scholars have not really given much thought to the concept, or made much of an effort to understand its relationship to our discipline" (qtd. in "What Is Data in Literary Studies?").

involved before electronic computing – as well as how the concept was used by literature scholars to signal a commitment to a certain epistemological framework that was opposed to other methods for knowing and reading in the academic field.

Literary data today conjures a digital instantiation or representation of a set of information that is abstracted from literary works. Literary data might be represented in spreadsheet files containing verbal and numerical information obtained by processing literary works: to give two rudimentary examples, novel titles in one column and their publication years in the next, or the 100 most frequently appearing words in a long poem in one column and each of their frequencies in the next. This representation is prior to what might eventually become scholarly claims, prior also to re-representations of that same information in the form of graphs or tables. Literary data come after – are abstracted from – literature and the research questions that determine what gets categorized and collected as data in the first place. But the data come before – are potential evidentiary grounds for – any knowledge claim.[2]

That is a simplified sketch of how literary data might be instantiated today, but it suffices as a starting point from which to look at the colorful backstory of literary data, and to notice the differences and continuities between past and present. The notion of "literary data" has been around since the early years of literary study in American universities, but it first achieved some prominence – at least by that name – in the mainstream of the discipline in the 1960s. The work of Stephen Parrish gives us a helpful place to begin. In 1957, Parrish, with the help of IBM collaborators, used existing data processing routines for scientific computation to make a concordance to Matthew Arnold's poetry – the first computer-assisted literary concordance ever made. (A concordance is a type of reference work: an alphabetized index of the words used by an author or found in a text, listing the locations of each word's appearance and usually providing a contextualizing snippet of the sentence in which the word occurs; we will return to concordances in greater detail later in the chapter.)[3] In the following years, Parrish gave a series of talks, wrote several articles, and

---

[2] See Howard S. Becker, *Tricks of the Trade: How to Think About Your Research While You're Doing It* (Chicago: University of Chicago Press, 1998), 47–50; and Bruno J. Strasser and Paul N. Edwards, "Big Data Is the Answer... But What Is the Question?," *Osiris* 32 (2017): 329–330.

[3] For good accounts of concordances, see Andrew Abbott, "Googles of the Past: Concordances and Scholarship," *Social Science History* 37.4 (Winter 2013): 427–455, and Daniel J. Rosenberg, "An Archive of Words," in *Science in the Archives: Pasts, Presents, Futures*, ed. Lorraine Daston (Chicago: University of Chicago Press, 2017), 287–291.

organized a conference, all pertaining to what he called "literary data processing."[4] A 1965 *PMLA* article heralds a new era of literary study wherein electronic computing will "help us to be better critics... [and] to be better scholars" relative to the ideal or fantasy of "objective criticism." Better yet, literary data processing promised consilience: to join literary scholars with computer scientists, even to bring together the two cultures so that humanists would one day be as comfortable with "quantitative measurement" as biologists and psychologists.[5] Such enthusiasm corresponded to an "interdisciplinary bonanza" that peaked at around this time, but it was also personally motivated by Parrish's wartime experience in computer-assisted cryptanalysis, which gave him the requisite expertise and a penchant for computational approaches to language and literature.[6]

At the same time, Parrish acknowledged the pervasive "psychological resistance to automation in the humanities." "Literary 'data,'" he admitted, putting the latter word in quotes and dwelling on the strangeness of the phrase, is what he had "come with some misgivings to call the poems, plays, and novels that we read and study" when they are processed by "mechanical and electronic devices." Just as troubling as computers themselves, he anticipated, would be the use of unfamiliar methods on literary works – methods that raised questions about qualitative versus quantitative evidence, subjectivity and objectivity, the emotional elements of criticism,

---

[4] See, for example, "Preface," in *A Concordance to the Poems of Matthew Arnold*, ed. Stephen Maxfield Parrish (Ithaca: Cornell University Press, 1959), vii–xxi; "Problems in the Making of Computer Concordances," *Studies in Bibliography* 15 (1962): 1–14; "Computers and the Muse of Literature," in *Computers for the Humanities?* (New Haven: Yale University Press, 1965), 53–63; "Summary," in *Literary Data Conference Proceedings*, ed. Jess B. Bessinger, Jr., Stephen M. Parrish, and Harry F. Arader (White Plains: IBM Data Processing Division, 1964), 3–10; "Literary Data Processing," *PMLA* 80.4, part 2: Supplement (September 1965): 3–6. Although Parrish was anticipated by Paul Tasman, who wrote on "literary data processing" in 1957 in describing Roberto Busa's concordance to St. Thomas Aquinas, Parrish is significantly more knowledgeable about the implications for literary study. On Tasman and Busa, see Steven E. Jones, *Roberto Busa, S. J., and the Emergence of Humanities Computing: The Priest and the Punched Cards* (New York: Routledge, 2016), 62.

[5] "Literary Data Processing," 4–6; "Computers and the Muse of Literature," 55.

[6] On interdisciplinarity, see Andrew Abbott, *Chaos of Disciplines* (Chicago: University of Chicago Press, 2001), 133. As Parrish recounted, during World War II and the Korean War, "I was assigned to the National Security Agency, or its forerunners, where I engaged in various kinds of language analysis, much of it computer-assisted (mainly Japanese, Russian, and Chinese)"; see "Biographical Sketch" in his NSF Proposal for "Computer Concordance to the Writings of Sigmund Freud" (Cornell Special Collections, Stephen Parrish papers, Box 3, Folder 11). Parrish is another instance of the historical link between literary scholarship and cryptanalysis that can be seen also in Edith Rickert's *New Methods for the Study of Literature* (Chicago: University of Chicago Press, 1927), which also precedes the age of electronic computing and is similarly influenced by codebreaking. On this link, see Brian Lennon, *Passwords: Philology, Security, Authentication* (Cambridge, MA: Harvard University Press, 2018).

and the very aims of literary study. The concept of literary data also raised unsettling ontological questions about one of the discipline's main objects of study, literature: something "especially disturbing" happens when "poems and novels and plays are ... converted into 'literary data.'"[7] After all, Parrish and his collaborators saw literary data in a sequence of transformed manifestations: from an authoritative printed edition of Arnold's poetic text, to a different symbolic representation of that text on punch cards, which then got transferred to magnetic tape readable by an IBM 704 Data Processing Machine, to preliminary printouts, to the published concordance.[8] All the while, it hardly mattered that what was being processed was literature. From a data processing standpoint, literary language is essentially the same kind of linguistic data as that which could be obtained from other records written in natural language. The adjective "literary" might indicate the research questions or a goal (like a poetry concordance), the kinds of documents in the corpus, and/or the specialty of the scholars involved, but not any quiddities of a particular kind of data nor a special category of writing.

Parrish answered all this anxiety by offering a different perspective. The concept of literary data could be viewed not (or not only) as a sign of the coming "automation in the humanities," a bad kind of interdisciplinarity, or a perversion of literariness, but as fundamental to disciplinarity, literary study being no exception.[9] The very emergence of "English literary history and criticism" as an academic subject involved thinking about literary works as data to some degree. One could trace a line beginning with foundational kinds of scholarly work, through a dominant kind of twentieth-century literary criticism, and up to literary data processing of the 1960s, because they all shared something like a data mindset:

> Significant advances were the sharply improved standards of textual editing that began to prevail just after the turn of the century... [and] the immense thrust forward given to the tactics of analytical bibliography [which was followed by] the New Criticism, which has stubbornly attempted to focus our critical attention on the literary text, to standardize criteria of objective judgment, and to reduce or suppress the subjective, purely emotional responses that always precede or accompany the act of criticism.[10]

---

[7] "Problems in the Making of Computer Concordances," 2; "Literary Data Processing," 4; "Computers and the Muse of Literature," 54.
[8] See "Preface," vii–xii.
[9] See also Lisa Gitelman and Virginia Jackson, "Introduction," in *"Raw Data" Is an Oxymoron*, ed. Lisa Gitelman and Virginia Jackson (Cambridge, MA: MIT Press, 2013): 3.
[10] "Literary Data Processing," 3.

Literature taught and studied academically involved such practices as the following: "textual editing," so that there were standard editions of literary works – in other words, shared data that made possible collective inquiry; a scholarly discourse that prioritized data, facts, and information; a kind of literary criticism ("the New Criticism") that believed that rigorous analysis could approach the ideal of "objective judgment" by suppressing "emotional responses" to literary texts; and an ongoing collective inquiry into epistemological questions about data, evidence, objectivity, and the validity of critical judgments and scholarly claims.[11] In sum, around sixty years ago, Parrish looked back more than sixty years before then to later nineteenth-century precedents for thinking about literary study in terms of data, as a subject area that in principle, if not in practice, oriented itself to an ideal of objective knowledge.

1.2 Early Meanings of Literary Data

When one looks to that earlier era, one finds discussions of literary data – for example, in William Morton Payne's *English in American Universities* (1895), a compilation of reports from twenty American colleges and universities, each describing how English is being taught at that institution. *English in American Universities* is a significant document for histories of literary study because it gives a snapshot of English departments at a formative moment a couple of decades after the establishment of the first departments in the United States in the 1870s. Payne's polemical introduction states that the reports taken together "establish beyond question the claims of English as a proper subject of university instruction."[12] But the question of what actually made up the university subject of "English," and especially the role of *literature* in it, were far from settled. To make a long story short, departments of English were initially dominated by philologists, who were professional scholars credentialed in the academic study of languages – hence "English," which continues to be the name of most departments today. Philologists studied literary works among other written documents, but literature was not their main focus. In the 1890s, as literature became a popular undergraduate and graduate subject, philologists continued to teach literature in a scientistic manner: their teaching, like their research, focused on fact-oriented activities such as

---

[11] See Lorraine Daston and Peter Galison on working objects and collective empiricism in their *Objectivity* (New York: Zone Books, 2010), 19–27.

[12] William Morton Payne, "Introduction," in *English in American Universities*, ed. William Morton Payne (Boston: D. C. Heath & Co., 1895), 20.

"obtaining exterior information, hunting down quotations, dates, and allusions, surveying a poem by the rod and line of a technical phraseology, [and] detecting parallels."[13] Opposing these philologists was a group of teachers who also taught literary works in the same departments, but who focused on a set of other subjects that were closely related among themselves: primarily *belles lettres* ("fine letters"), which focused on the appreciation and evaluation of literary works, but also on the subjects of rhetoric and composition.[14] Both modern-day expository writing and creative writing courses descend from this latter set of subjects, which were aligned against the paradigm of scientific research adopted and adapted by philologists.[15] Belletrist critics lamented that philology – the "science of linguistics" – led to a Gradgrindian literary pedagogy that fixated on facts and deadened student interest. Philologists such as Albert Stanburrough Cook answered that philology joined the intellectual analysis of language to a passion for literary art – philology "enlists the head in the service of the heart" – insinuating the lack of rigor and a feminine emotionalism in appreciationist approaches.[16]

Thus, data in literary study was initially *philological* data, shaped by how philologists imagined linguistic and literary knowledge. "Data" meant *any* preliminary facts or information sought, collected, and analyzed in the course of study. Unlike our contemporary associations with the word "data," these data more often than not concerned nonnumerical facts, although they could be numerical information too (for example, dates).

---

[13] Payne, "Introduction," 19.
[14] Payne identifies three different component subjects in many English departments: the study of English literature, flanked by two older subjects, "the science of linguistics" (philology) and "the art of rhetoric," usually closely associated with a fourth subject: composition (26). Similarly, the University of Pennsylvania's report subdivides "English" into four subjects: composition, the closely related subject of forensics (rhetoric), English literature, and English language and philology (*English in American Universities?*, 130). The foregoing, simplified account draws on useful histories of this era of literary study and related questions, including John Guillory, "Literary Study and the Modern System of the Disciplines," in *Disciplinarity at the Fin de Siècle*, ed. Amanda Anderson and Joseph Valente (Princeton: Princeton University Press, 2001), 31–37; Deidre Shauna Lynch, *Loving Literature: A Cultural History* (Chicago: University of Chicago Press, 2015); Michael Warner, "Professionalization and the Rewards of Literature, 1875–1900," *Criticism* 27.1 (1985), 1–11; Gerald Graff, *Professing Literature: An Institutional History* (Chicago: University of Chicago Press, 2007), 55–118; Gerald Graff and Michael Warner, "Introduction," in *The Origins of Literary Studies in America: A Documentary Anthology*, ed. Gerald Graff and Michael Warner (New York: Routledge, 1989), 4–8; D. G. Myers, *The Elephants Teach: Creative Writing Since 1880* (Chicago: University of Chicago Press, 1996), 15–34; James Turner, *Philology: The Forgotten Origins of the Modern Humanities* (Princeton: Princeton University Press, 2014), 254–273.
[15] Myers, *The Elephants Teach*, 26–34.
[16] Albert S. Cook, "The Province of English Philology," in *The Higher Study of English* (Boston: Houghton, Mifflin & Co., 1906), 32.

Literary data in a philological sense can be further broken down into several uses. Data was invoked to differentiate graduate and professorial research from undergraduate study. This is from the University of Pennsylvania's report:

> Neither in literature nor in philology do we set undergraduates to what is sometimes called in the English of catalogues "original research," preferring to devote these years to the laying of such foundation stones as we may, rather than to the amateurish collection of unimportant *literary data* or the perfunctory compilation of unnecessary indices.[17]

Such "literary data" could be "literary" in the sense of focusing on imaginative writing: for example, the data could concern the degree to which loan words appeared in Thomas De Quincey's writing, the recurrence of poetic invocations to personified "Sleep" in Renaissance poetry, the influence of Dante on some English poets, or facts about a poem's meter.[18] All of these are based on, and are themselves, data. A related, slightly later instance of "literary data" denotes a source: Lane Cooper (more on him later in the chapter) writes that "[Edmund] Spenser's careful investigation of Irish ways and traditions convinces him of their value as *literary data*, and their right to conscientious treatment [in his *A View of the Present State of Ireland* (1596)]."[19] This is a minor sense of "literary data," but it has a major implication: the world itself can be thought of as providing "data," as in material, for literature. Another minor sense of data appears in the same University of Pennsylvania report to characterize, in a philological idiom, an introductory sort of literary-historical knowledge gained by undergraduates: "When the student has begun to note literary phenomena with some degree of ease, we direct his attention to the relation subsisting between the various phenomena noted, still demanding that he increase his *data* by constant reading of literature and frequent exercises."[20] Compared to the data collected for graduate-level "original research," these data are more epistemologically basic, closer to the observed object – in this case,

---

[17] *English in American Universities*, 134, my emphasis.
[18] These examples, as well as the "inveigle" example later in the chapter are the results from searching through the journal *Modern Language Notes*: Albert S. Cook, "Native and Foreign Words in De Quincey," *Modern Language Notes* 1.2 (February 1886): 15–16; Albert S. Cook, "The Elizabethan Invocations to Sleep," *Modern Language Notes*, 4.8 (December 1889): 229–231; Oscar Kuhns, "Dante's Influence on English Poetry in the Nineteenth Century," *Modern Language Notes* 14.6 (June 1899): 176–186.
[19] Lane Cooper, *Methods and Aims in the Study of Literature: A Series of Extracts and Illustrations* (Boston: Ginn and Company, 1915), 161–162, my emphasis. Given the scope of this chapter, I do not attempt to take up the problem of Spenser and Ireland.
[20] *English in American Universities*, 132, my emphasis.

literary works treated as natural objects for scientific observation, as "literary phenomena."[21] Today we would probably just say that an undergraduate student increases her familiarity with literary history, rather than increases her "data."

Though the University of Pennsylvania's report appears to contradict itself – undergrads do and do not deal with literary data – the report in fact attests to different facets of the concept of literary data in circulation during these early years. Above all, philological literary data often indicated *nonliterary* information of the kind for which philology was routinely criticized: data as in facts surrounding a literary work, including those about "antiquities, history, geography, etymology, phonetics, the history of the English language, and general linguistics."[22] The etymology of the word "inveigle" would be an example of this kind of philological, nonliterary literary data.[23] Either way, whether literary data focused on literary texts or "exterior" facts, there was a general perception by nonphilologists that the philological approach – literature as "phenomena" to study for facts – was missing the whole point of literature.

In most contexts, most of the time, data can mean something like "information" or "evidence." But in literary study, historically, to invoke "data" was also to signal an epistemological perspective – a real or desired affiliation with objectivity and scientific authority – that was always in relation to, or against, other perspectives. In the earlier, philological moment, literary data marked two differences: it distinguished undergraduate and "amateurish" study from the work of graduate students and professors, and philological research from *belles lettres* and related subjects. Moreover, even as English pursued legitimacy as a university discipline, and as teachers disagreed among themselves about how best to teach literature, scholars invoked data to project an ideal of disciplinary cohesion and tradition. The more "minute" or precise the scope of the "original research," the more valuable it was: literary data were discrete pieces of information that served as evidentiary building blocks for such research

---

[21] The report describes how undergraduates began with contemporary or recent literary prose works and then gradually worked backward toward more linguistically complex and historically remote works, to older "periods such as that of Chaucer or that of Shakespeare" (132), ultimately to learn literary history. In certain respects, and oddly enough, the nineteenth-century curriculum's reverse chronology and graduated philological-linguistic-historical difficulty make more sense than the structure of present-day English majors, where Chaucer or Spenser can precede the most readable and most recently published works, including those aimed at children.
[22] *English in American Universities*, 89.
[23] Hans C. G. von Jagemann, "The Etymology of Inveigle," *Modern Language Notes* 1.2 (February 1886): 18–19. See also note 18 (this chapter).

(which, in turn, were data for other scholars to build on), and every researcher was understood to make modest contributions to the larger disciplinary effort of cumulative inquiry and knowledge.[24] Finally, we should pause to note that "data" in literary study was more or less synonymous with *fact* and *information*. This is not the case today or in other domains. For example, in information science, data can be distinguished from and prior to information, and occupies the lowest conceptual place in the so-called DIKW (data, information, knowledge, wisdom) hierarchy or pyramid; moreover, a datum is arguably distinguishable from, and prior to, a fact.[25] A hierarchy of data, fact, information, knowledge, and wisdom can theoretically be transposed to literary study. But while all disciplines negotiate with data in one form or another, there are also disciplinary specificities or idiosyncrasies: "data" has been interchangeable with terms such as "facts" and "information" because *all* of these terms indifferently symbolized an approach to literature that was counterbalanced by a humanism exemplified early on by *belles lettres*, the discourse of criticism, and the writing subjects.[26] This other perspective had its own set of terms signifying the values associated with literary culture: appreciation, art, emotion, enjoyment, genius, pleasure, and spirit. Aspects of this perspective remain with us most conspicuously in creative writing pedagogy, with its preoccupations with the role of craft, voice, performance, and sound, but no teaching of literature and literary history can do entirely without them either.[27] This constellation of values also defines what David Simpson has called the "academic postmodern," with its emphases on storytelling, the conversational, the personal, the local, and so on.[28] Belletrism's metonym for style and writing in general is the same as the

---

[24] See Graff, *Professing Literature*, 57–59, and Daston and Galison, *Objectivity*, 22.
[25] See Daniel Rosenberg, "Data before the Fact," in *"Raw Data" Is an Oxymoron*, ed. Gitelman and Jackson, 18. As Rosenburg points out in his essay, in theory, "when a fact is proven false, it ceases to be a fact," whereas "false data is data nonetheless," although we have seen this distinction erode since then in public discourse, as misinformation, disinformation, and propaganda have proliferated.
[26] See Lynch, *Loving Literature*. Lynch brilliantly argues that it is impossible to understand English studies without acknowledging appreciation and affective labor, which have always attended, and continue to shape, our work.
[27] See Lynch, *Loving Literature*. Myers identifies this as a kind of "constructivism" in *The Elephants Teach*, 9. On creative writing's phonocentrism, see Mark McGurl, *The Program Era: Postwar Fiction and the Rise of Creative Writing* (Cambridge, MA: Harvard University Press, 2009), 234–238. For a memorable reaction against the cult of craft, see Elif Batuman, "Introduction," in *The Possessed: Adventures with Russian Books and the People Who Read Them* (New York: Farrar, Straus and Giroux, 2010), 18–20, which details her "disillusionment with the transcendentalist New England culture of 'creative writing'" (18).
[28] David Simpson, *The Academic Postmodern and the Rule of Literature: A Report on Half-Knowledge* (Chicago: University of Chicago Press, 1995).

long-standing metonymic euphemism for social agency, political representation, and identity, all being matters of *voice*. Even if such different kinds of voice are conflated more often than their actual meanings and relations are pondered, the overlapping metonyms make for a potent combination in the dominant strains of literary and cultural studies today.

During the transitional period captured by *English in American Universities*, some departments still taught literature in a predominantly philological way, as we have seen, while other departments viewed literature in a more belletristic way, placing an emphasis "not so much on reading *about* the author as on familiarity with the author himself" and on vocal recitation and appreciation.[29] Still others sought to reconcile philological and belletristic approaches, blending the "linguistic" and the "literary."[30] Lucius Adelno Sherman's *Analytics of Literature: A Manual for the Objective Study of English Prose and Poetry* (1893) is a scholarly work that pursues a version of this last approach, and exemplifies this era's discourse of literary history.[31] Sherman's stylometric study brings us to a final important early example of literary data. But first, here he is on literary study in general:

> In our literary laboratory there is no talk about *elements*. Organic compounds are taken for granted and treated as ultimate phenomena, without much recognition that there may be "inorganic" or less complicated forms of the same kind, as well as ultimate elements whose presence in new proportions and new combinations make up all differences observed. It is as if there had once been, or should be, an effort to teach Chemistry without recognition of the unlike molecular constitution, we will say, of spring water and coal tar. In other words, Chaucer and Shakespeare are considered simply as Chaucer and Shakespeare, with no reference to the fact that there must be in both common constituents and factors which, in different frequency and degrees of potency, make up the very diverse effects of their respective poetry. The same must be also true of our prosaists.... The difference between the style of Newman and De Quincey can be analyzed out [*sic*] through inventorying all points of sentence structure, as also each element or item in the character of their respective terms, phrases, and figures.[32]

---

[29] *English in American Universities*, 114. Hiram Corson is the figure most identified with "vocal culture" because of his teaching and his various writings on the subject: see, for example, his report in *English in American Universities*, 60–64, which concentrates on recitation and altogether omits an account of philology, and Warner, "Professionalization and the Rewards of Literature, 1875–1900," 8–12.

[30] The motif of harmonizing the study of linguistics and of literature can be found in several of the departmental reports; see, for example, *English in American Universities*, 43 and 46.

[31] See Guillory, "Literary Study and the Modern System of the Disciplines," 32–33.

[32] L[ucius] A[delno] Sherman, *Analytics of Literature: A Manual for the Objective Study of English Prose and Poetry* (Boston: Ginn and Company, 1893), ix–x. Sherman can be credited with referring to a "literary laboratory" more than a century in advance of today's Stanford Literary Lab; Amherst College also conceived of their English curriculum as partly based on "the laboratory method,"

Sherman's view of his object of study was closer to the spirit of *belles lettres* than philology: he lamented that the "philologic" method asked students to "memorize observations from text-books about literature, or biographies of authors, or circumstances under which masterpieces have been composed" or teachers' opinions about books, at the expense of studying "literature itself." But Sherman's scientific method was consistent with philology and anti-belletristic; he lamented that *belle lettres* taught authors as auratic monoliths or mere names ("Chaucer and Shakespeare are considered simply as Chaucer and Shakespeare"), rather than analyzing them by the common denominator of language, and, more particularly, by the unit of the word.[33] Just as a chemistry student breaks down a given substance into constituent parts, so literary scholars should take apart Chaucer, Shakespeare, De Quincey, or Newman into commensurate "elements" in order to reveal their stylistic differences in a manner that Sherman (as his study's title suggests) considered more "objective." As Sherman puts it, "all the *data* are present in the pages of the author himself."[34]

Moreover, *Analytics of Literature* was concerned to show the "data" purportedly "in the pages of the author himself" in the form of *numerical* information, with Sherman providing ample statistics arranged in tables and represented in graphs.[35] The study's most well-known contribution might be its data on sentence simplification. Sherman wanted to demonstrate a shift in prose style from the Renaissance to the nineteenth century: namely, that there was, over the centuries, a decrease in predication, and therefore in overall sentence length as measured by words per sentence. For example, some passages from Spenser's prose have sentences that average nearly fifty words per sentence, whereas some of Ralph Waldo Emerson's sentences average only twenty. Even lay readers could probably intuit such a shift in prose style, if only from their preference for more readable contemporary writing, but Sherman was intent on providing copious data as part of a larger effort to reorient literary study: "there is no good reason," Sherman writes, "why aesthetics ... should not have the material

---

partly "aimed as to get at the spirit of literature" (*English in American Universities*, 114). For useful background on Sherman and related studies, see Benjamin Morgan, *The Outward Mind: Materialist Aesthetics in Victorian Science and Literature* (Chicago: University of Chicago Press, 2017), 233–238.

[33] Sherman, *Analytics of Literature*, vii–viii. It seems appropriate, then, that Sherman's *Analytics of Literature* acknowledges his indebtedness to *both* Albert Cook and Hiram Corson.

[34] Sherman, *Analytics of Literature*, vii, ix (emphasis added). As Graff points out, that New Critical mantra of "the text itself" "had already been formulated by the mid-nineties" (*Professing Literature*, 123), even if the main interpretive protocols of literary criticism were still to come.

[35] Sherman, *Analytics of Literature*, xv; 304.

aid of facts and statistics."[36] In *Analytics of Literature*, Sherman brings us much closer to some instantiations of literary data today – that is to say, numerical information accompanied by graphs. Then again, this older period actually had much broader and more variegated ways of understanding literary data, recognizing that in literary study, there were sets of information categorizable as data at every step of the way, from the real-world material that inspired the literary work to the text itself to "original research" to what might be retained in students' minds about literary history.

1.3 Literary Data Processing, Part II: The Case of Lane Cooper's *A Concordance to the Poems of William Wordsworth* (1911)

What did the process of dealing with literary data look like in these years before electronic computing? Sherman's and others' studies (including those by some of his students) arguably foreshadow today's works of quantitative literary history, but their work did not lead to a surge of this kind of statistical scholarship in the early twentieth century.[37] Nor did Sherman and others leave detailed accounts of how they did their "analytics," as far as I am aware. But there was a collaborative project, informed by Sherman's work, that gives us a vivid portrait of the techniques involved in literature data processing around this time: The Concordance Society. The Society was founded at the Modern Language Association meeting in December 1906 by Albert Cook, the philologist. According to Cook, what literary study needed was a scholarly collective devoted to producing concordances, especially for vernacular poets. Here is his reason why:

> The student is as powerless before a huge aggregate of conglomerate facts as the refiner before a hundred-ton mass of gold ore. The student, like the refiner, is in search of something which to him is precious; but before he can obtain it from the enormous bulk before him, rich perhaps with various metals, it must first be broken up, and eventually comminuted.... What we need is more works which shall contain ... the ordered materials from which the elements ... can be extracted. In other words, we need more indexes and concordances.[38]

---

[36] Sherman, *Analytics of Literature*, 256–262; xiii.
[37] Nevertheless, the early scholarly epistemological emphasis on objectivity feeds into literary criticism; one illustration of this would be William Empson's observation that "there are two sorts of literary critic, the appreciative and the analytical; the difficulty is that they have all got to be both"; see William Empson, *Seven Types of Ambiguity* (New York: New Directions, 1966), 249.
[38] Albert S. Cook, "The Concordance Society," *Modern Language Notes* 22.2 (February 1907), 33.

Cook knew Sherman's *Analytics of Literature* and similarly viewed literary works as objects needing to be broken down and then analyzed in order to extract objective-seeming "facts."[39] Where Sherman used a chemical conceit to describe literary analysis, Cook turned to mining imagery, unintentionally presaging the practice of text mining. We can begin to see why later scholars who engaged in similar "objective" or numerical investigations – for example, Parrish, but also Josephine Miles – acknowledged that the roots of this mode of analysis go back to the work produced by the Society, and especially Lane Cooper's *A Concordance to the Poems of William Wordsworth* (1911).[40]

The Society was quite short lived. Although it existed in name until the late 1920s, it was really only active from 1906 until the beginning of World War I. And although it gave out subventions toward the publication of other concordances until around 1928, it put out only three concordances officially under its auspices: *A Concordance to the English Poems of Thomas Gray* (1908), edited by Cook himself; Cooper's Wordsworth concordance; and *A Concordance to the Poems of Edmund Spenser* (1915), edited by Charles Grosvenor Osgood.[41] But the Society was enormously influential, shaping virtually all later concordances made in the first half of the twentieth century until the electronically made ones of Roberto Busa and Parrish. For one thing, the Society came to function as an information hub to which concordancers would report, and to which prospective concordancers would send inquiries in order to make sure a particular author was not already being worked on.[42] Moreover, the Society widely disseminated the techniques Cook and Cooper devised in order to make concordances by hand. It was Cook who thought up much of the method in his correspondence to Cooper in 1907–8, as he drew on the experience of making the Gray concordance and as he urged on Cooper to take on Wordsworth's poetry.[43] But it was Cooper who described and codified the method in

---

[39] Cook had done a similar statistical analysis of De Quincey's prose (see note 18); see also note 33.
[40] For example, see Parrish, "Computers and the Muse of Literature," 57–58, and Miles's review of Parrish and others' concordances in Josephine Miles, "*Concordance to the Poems of Matthew Arnold* by Stephen M. Parrish; *Concordance to the Poems of W. B. Yeats* by Stephen M. Parrish; Concordance to the Poems of Wallace Stevens by Thomas F. Walsh," *Victorian Studies* 8.3 (March 1965), 290–291. On Miles, see Christopher Rovee, "Counting Wordsworth by the Bay: The Distance of Josephine Miles," *European Romantic Review* 28.3 (2017): 405–412.
[41] "Circular letter of the Concordance Society circa February 1928, Lane Cooper Papers (14-12-680), box 6, folder 6, Division of Rare and Manuscript Collections, Cornell University Library.
[42] As Chris Rovee pointed out to me in conversation, Lane Cooper's correspondence is full of such inquiries. See, for example, Lane Cooper Papers (14-12-680), box 7, folder 10, Division of Rare and Manuscript Collections, Cornell University Library.
[43] See Cook's letters to Cooper in Lane Cooper Papers (14-12-680), boxes 3a and 3b, Division of Rare and Manuscript Collections, Cornell University Library.

a document called "Instructions for Collaborators," which gave meticulous directions to the many volunteers or "collaborators" who would help him put together the concordance; the document is an unrecognized but veritable landmark in literary data processing (see Figures 1.1 and 1.2). What the "Instructions" dictate in unvarnished form was incorporated into Cooper's later accounts of the process. Cooper received requests for his "Instructions" from concordancers from all over the United States, England, and elsewhere, and he readily mailed copies of it to them, into the 1940s. The concordances for Keats, Chaucer, Herrick, Coleridge, and Wyatt were all made using Cooper's "Instructions."[44]

For the Wordsworth concordance, Society members recruited forty-six collaborators (twenty-three men and twenty-three women), several of them Cooper's colleagues in the Cornell English department and their wives, but many others who were located all over the United States and worked remotely.[45] Cooper's concordance belonged to the tradition of biblical concordances and humanist scholarly practices like excerpting, and was also indebted to more recent Victorian concordances, but he also adopted the dominant, paper-based data-processing techniques of his time.[46] At the center of the process, coursing through it as its lifeblood, was the 3 × 5 inch blank slip (also called a "thesis slip"), the size of an index card, but made of very lightweight paper.[47] These belonged to the same species of slips and cards that the enterprising Melvil Dewey – of Dewey Decimal System fame – was getting all sorts of organizations to adopt for their information management needs around 1900: most obviously libraries (for card catalogues), but also banks, insurance companies, and hospitals.[48] At this time, "no area of data processing remain[ed] untouched by card indexes."[49] As demonstrated by the Society's reliance on this paper format, or Parrish's later embrace of techniques that existed for scientific computation, or distant reading today which borrows methods developed for other contexts, literary data processing has consistently drawn on

---

[44] "Instructions to Collaborators," Papers of Lane Cooper (MC 045), box 8, folder 9, Special Collections and University Archives, Rutgers University Libraries. Cooper also recounts the process in Lane Cooper, "The Making and the Use of a Verbal Concordance," *The Sewanee Review* 27.2 (1919), 188–206, and "Preface," in *A Concordance to the Poems of William Wordsworth* (London: Smith, Elder & Co., 1911), v–viii.

[45] The collaborators are listed in Cooper, "Preface," v–vi.

[46] See, for example, Ann M. Blair, *Too Much to Know: Managing Scholarly Information before the Modern Age* (New Haven: Yale University Press, 2010), 38–41.

[47] Cooper, "Instructions to Collaborators."

[48] Markus Krajewski, *Paper Machines: About Cards & Catalogs, 1548–1929* (Cambridge, MA: MIT Press, 2011), 90–106.

[49] Krajewski, *Paper Machines*, 97.

CONCORDANCE TO THE POETICAL WORKS OF WILLIAM WORDSWORTH

INSTRUCTIONS TO COLLABORATORS

The fundamental requisites in this undertaking are thoroughness and accuracy. To make his work of any value, each collaborator must strictly observe the following directions. Work which does not conform to them means time thrown away.

1. TEXTS. The text to be used is the Oxford Edition of Wordsworth's Poetical Works, one volume, 1906. No other text may be employed. A sufficient number of partially prepared texts will be furnished to each collaborator. He should set one of these aside for reference, and immediately proceed to utilize five others -- or six or more others, when the number of concordance-words to a line happens at any point to exceed five in his section of the work.

2. GENERAL PROCEDURE. First, he should delete in all these texts all the numerals referring to foot-notes. Then, having made a very liberal estimate of the number of concordance-words (see below, No. 7) on a given page -- presumably the first page -- of his portion of text, he should take an equal number of thesis-slips of the required size and weight (see below, No. 4), and in the upper right-hand quarter of each slip should record with a rubber stamp or a pencil the number of the page. Thus for page 3 of the Oxford text he should stamp or write the number 3 in the upper right-hand quarter of, say, 325 slips. The number of concordance-words on a full page of text seems to run from

Figures 1.1 and 1.2 Pages from Cooper's "Instructions to Collaborators," Papers of Lane Cooper (MC 045), box 8, folder 9, Special Collections and University Archives, Rutgers University Libraries.

4

The addition of the line-number to the concordance-title completes the work on the individual slip.

3. CONCORDANCE-TITLES. A prepared list of titles of Wordsworth's poems, as these are to be cited in the Concordance, will be furnished to each collaborator for his section of the text. No other titles may be employed. An asterisk (*) before a title indicates that the title is derived from the first words of a poem; a dagger (†) that the poem is by the poet's sister or wife, etc.

4. THESIS-SLIPS. All the work of recording is to be done upon white, unruled thesis-slips, exactly three inches by five. Sample slips will be sent to the collaborators, who are then requested to procure each the requisite number for himself. The general editor will nevertheless furnish the necessary slips to collaborators who do not feel ready to obtain them otherwise. No other kind or size of slips may be used.

5. ARABIC NUMERALS. Under no circumstances may Roman numerals be used in the work of recording. Arabic numerals must be employed throughout. (See the examples below, No. 8.)

6. RUBBER STAMPS. It is imperative that the work of recording begin immediately. As the work progresses, collaborators are urged to employ rubber stamps for convenience and accuracy in recording page-numbers, concordance-titles, and the like, that are often repeated. Such stamps should be obtained from Arthur D. Perkins, 13 Center St., New Haven, Conn. Ask for an Office Printing Outfit, No. 2, costing $1.00 at retail (postage extra), and mention the Wordsworth Concordance.

7. PARTICLES, ETC. TO BE OMITTED. A quotation consisting of one line of poetry is to be excerpted for every occurrence of

Figures 1.1 and 1.2 (cont.)

techniques from other disciplines and domains. In any case, each collaborator obtained for herself, or was sent by Cooper, thousands of such slips. They were also equipped with multiple copies of sections from unbound copies of the *Oxford Wordsworth* (1907); a stamp set with movable rubber types (Cooper insisted that collaborators buy a particular stamp set from a specific stationary store in New Haven); and a pencil, scissors, and paste.[50]

The project ran on the assumption that there were around eight to ten words per line of verse, but that only around five words would be of interest, to be recorded ("concordance words"). Cooper's "Instructions" provided a list of stop words or words collaborators were to ignore, or rather to scan visually but not record: the list included many of the words omitted by earlier concordances, including most function words and other high-frequency words like pronouns, but Cooper made an exception for first-person pronouns and pronominal adjectives ("I," "me," "mine," "my") in consideration of Wordsworth's egotistical sublime.[51] As a first step, a collaborator would stamp the top right corner of about 300 slips with the *Oxford Wordsworth* page number in question (say, "756"), then stamp the bottom center of every slip with the poem's shortened title as prescribed in the "Instructions" ("*Excursion*"), and then, if applicable, stamp or write a book or poem number ("1" for Book 1 of *The Excursion*). The collaborator then began visually scanning a poetic line, recording each head word. Let us look at lines 7 and 8 of Book I of *The Excursion*:

> Determined and unmoved, with steady beams
> Of bright and pleasant sunshine interposed;

The collaborator would have written "Determined" on the slip already conveniently labeled for line 7 of *The Excursion*, and proceed to do the same for "unmoved," "steady," and "beams" (ignoring "and" and "with"), and the same for the following line. Next, the collaborator would use her scissors to cut out the poetic line in question from her copies of the *Oxford Wordsworth* and paste it onto the middle of all of the appropriate slips: this contextualizing snippet would come to be known as a "key word in context," or "KWIC" for short. Cook and Cooper chose the method of cutting and pasting in order to avoid transcription errors from hand-copying and for speed. In our example, the collaborator would have needed

---

[50] Cooper, "Instructions to Collaborators."
[51] Cooper, "The Making and the Use of a Verbal Concordance," 191; Cooper, "Preface," vi.

four cut-outs of line 7 – one for each slip featuring a head word from that line, although she would have had up to eight copies of this section of the *Oxford Wordsworth* in case there were eight concordance words in a line. Then the collaborator turned to line numbers. In the bottom right corner of her four slips for line 7, she could stamp or write "7," then "8" on the next four slips, and so on (see Figures 1.3 and 1.4).

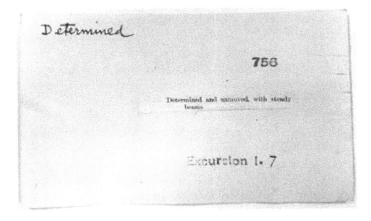

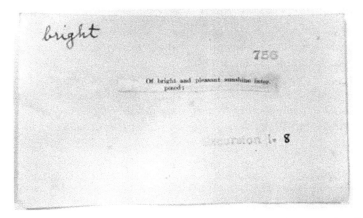

Figures 1.3 and 1.4 Slips from the making of *A Concordance to the Poems of William Wordsworth* (1911), Papers of Lane Cooper (MC 045), box 8, folder 9, Special Collections and University Archives, Rutgers University Libraries.

Cook and Cooper's method prescribed routinized, repetitive tasks for the sake of efficiency, transforming the collaborators into cyborg-like processors (of visual information on the printed page and on the slips), inscribers, cutters, pasters, and stampers. Though it is conceivable that the work was fun at times, one still imagines the process as an arduous, sped up, and mechanized version of scrapbooking.[52] The "psychological resistance to automation in the humanities" later diagnosed by Parrish takes on a new cast, since we are looking at a longer history of automated humans in the production of reference works – not to mention the fact that the faculty wives in this case remind us of when "computers" meant women.[53] All this done, the collaborator would mail every hundred or so finished slips to Cooper for his review. When all of the poems had been treated this way – the *Oxford Wordsworth* has about 900 pages of poetic text – a full, alphabetized set of slips was sent off to the publisher.

The group managed to complete the concordance in seven months, between November 1908 and May 1909, in the end compiling 210,994 slips, each one containing a word occurrence from Wordsworth's poetry.[54] Parrish would later note the greater ease and speed of literary data processing in the 1960s in contrast to the painstaking work of Cooper and his collaborators, and we might do the same given today's computing technology. But the manual versus electronic computer comparison prevents us from recognizing the Concordance Society's work against the backdrop of how literary data was imagined leading up to it – from early philological conceptions to Sherman's literary analytics. The comparison also does not do justice to the unlikely speed of the Wordsworth concordance, the number of participants the Society was able to recruit, or the overall coordination achieved by means of mail and Cooper's "Instructions." Above all, the manual–computer distinction makes it difficult to appreciate the data processing techniques that drove the project. Each slip, originally unlined and blank, also became a standardized form for filling with data and metadata: head word, page number, book and line number, poem title, and the line of verse. The slips had predetermined fields at fixed

---

[52] Cooper, "Instructions to Collaborators"; Cooper, "The Making and the Use of a Verbal Concordance," 191–196. On the Renaissance practice of cutting and pasting paper slips for the purpose of compiling, see Blair, *Too Much to Know*, 210–229. Cook and Cooper's method resembles, and arguably incorporates techniques from, the culture of scrapbooking; the variety of media on any given thesis slip is also like that on the pages of such albums. See Deidre Lynch, "Paper Slips: Album, Archiving, Accident," *Studies in Romanticism* 57.1 (Spring 2018): 87–119.
[53] See Jennifer S. Light, "When Computers Were Women," *Technology and Culture* 40.3 (July 1999): 455–483.
[54] Cooper, "The Making and the Use of a Verbal Concordance," 195.

spots, and it was imperative, according to Cooper, that each slip was "uniform."[55] Any given set of such "uniform" slips – whether the sets of 100 that each collaborator sent off to Cooper, or the final bundle of nearly 211,000 sent off to the publisher – was basically a database. They were sortable alphabetically by word or by poem title, or by page number in the *Oxford Wordsworth*, and searchable once sorted.

Although the 1908–9 concordance project looks like a quaintly predigital instance of literary data, even the analogue–digital distinction is not so simple. Bruno J. Strasser and Paul N. Edwards observe in their discussion of the idea of "digital data" that there is a key difference between converting truly analogue data (for example, continuous sound) into digital form and transcribing one set of discrete symbols into another set of discrete symbols. In the latter case, both are arguably already digital. The word "digital" is distinct from "electronic," and originally denoted numerical or nonnumerical symbolic representations "based on a finite set of discrete elements." Such symbolic representations include, of course, script systems like the alphabet.[56] Viewed in this light, one recognizes that the relative quickness with which one of Cooper's collaborators could rubber stamp a single page number ("756") on 300 slips was because the page number in the *Oxford Wordsworth* was digital data in symbolic numeric form, as was the number repeatedly imprinted by the rubber stamp: in fact, they were digital data of the same kind. In other words, it is possible to categorize *A Concordance to the Poems of William Wordsworth* (1911) as a significant digital literary data project when one works with a broader understanding of data and a better understanding of digitality.

1.4 *A Return to* Belles Lettres

It is intuitive to think that literary study has only recently come to confront data. But, as we have seen, that is not the whole story. It has been observed, for example, that thinking in terms of data is "not always a comfortable framework" in the humanities, but humanists are now "beginning to think in terms of data, metadata, standards, interoperability, and sustainability."[57] According to that narrative, due to the digital technologies that drive scholarly practices – from our everyday reliance on search engines and digitized archives to sophisticated computation-based studies in the

---

[55] Cooper, "The Making and the Use of a Verbal Concordance," 193.
[56] Strasser and Edwards, "Big Data is the Answer," 332–334.
[57] Christine L. Borgman, *Big Data, Little Data, No Data: Scholarship in the Networked World* (Cambridge: MIT Press, 2015), 162.

humanities – nearly all humanities scholars, including literary scholars, are increasingly aware of the data "framework" within which knowledge is produced today. A related narrative is that literary scholars have recently come to embrace the quantitative methods of sociology and other social sciences; by this argument, literary studies is turning to these other disciplines to figure out how to scale up its analyses of literature, culture, and history.[58] These accounts are valid too. But it also turns out that since the study of literature became an academic subject, scholars have been dealing with data – perhaps even digital literary data – in a variety of senses, instantiations, media, and formats.

This historical background can be a useful reminder, especially in response to polemics against computational approaches to literary study or to a persistent "psychological resistance to automation in the humanities" that Parrish presciently described long ago. The point, though, is not that literary data is old news. The earlier history of literary data puts into relief the specificity and idiosyncrasies of what data has meant within the context of literary study, even as literary study resembles other disciplines in necessarily having techniques for dealing with data, different kinds of evidence, and so on, all in the course of arriving at knowledge and in teaching. But even if we all necessarily work with data, we do not all like to say that a student learning about literary history is "increas[ing] his data," or think about literature as metals needing to be "comminuted," or embrace statistical studies of literature. Within the disciplinary field, to invoke data is to disclose one's view of literary knowledge under certain historically specific conditions against an array of different ways of understanding and experiencing literature. If, in the episodes we have considered, a data-centric approach was an expression of a desire for objectivity and disciplinary legitimacy, what does the approach symbolize now? What are the *other* ways of pursuing knowledge about literature to which the data mindset is a contrast – more pointedly, to what extent is today's interest in data in some quarters of literary study a function of the academic postmodern and its aftermath?[59] Instead of discussing yet again

---

[58] James F. English and Ted Underwood, "Shifting Scales: Between Literature and Social Science," *Modern Language Quarterly* 77.3 (September 2016): 277–295. But see also Andrew Piper, *Enumerations: Data and Literary Study* (Chicago: University of Chicago Press, 2018), 5, on the reliance on methods from computational linguistics and information science.

[59] Of course, to return to the historical groups I have focused on, there can be found, among the philologists, the more belletristic-minded and the less so; likewise, among the belletrists, there can be the more philologically inclined and the less so; and those subgroups can continue to divide further along similar lines. One contemporary example of this would be algorithmic or generative creative composition. On the repeating, fractal-like bifurcations into which a discipline can be divided, see

a return to philology – a scholarly commonplace – we might ask: What is the return to *belles lettres*, or, what is belletrism today? Whatever it may be – perhaps an autobiographical vocalism, a vocal autobiographism – that is among the epistemological positions most remote from the data framework, and, far more than customarily named affiliates and alternatives to computational literary study, allows us to locate by opposition literary data's place in the disciplinary field, like south from north. And yet, at the same time, today's belletrisms and philologies both share an interest in the practices of abstracting and modeling, the former in the process of literary creation and the latter in the process of datafication. Better belletrisms recognize fully the differences between the model – the literary work – and the world from which that model is derived; better philologies recognize fully the differences between the data and the literary works from which that data are derived. Observing such differences – of mediatedness and representedness, of what escapes or confounds datafication – is prelude to a better science of signifying systems in the realm of verbal art.

Abbott, *Chaos of Disciplines*, 3–33. Finally, I wish to record my gratitude to Anna Lindemann, Yuka Igarashi, Chris Rovee, and Allen Riddell for their conversations on this topic and their many insights as I wrote this in 2019–20.

CHAPTER 2

Literary Change

Ted Underwood

Marc Bloch memorably called history "the science of change,"[1] and the description could apply to literary history as well. Whether they are identifying works that shaped a decade or tracing a genre across a century, literary historians describe and explain change. They describe change primarily, of course, by organizing sensitively described details into a persuasive narrative. But in recent decades quantitative analysis has begun to play an ancillary role as well. This chapter will consider the difference numbers make, emphasizing three topics where they are providing a new kind of leverage on the past.

2.1 Measuring Continuous Change

To grasp what quantitative representation can add to literary history, we need to start by thinking about the prevailing alternative, historical narration. Narrative is a flexible medium, but it does have specific strengths and weaknesses. In general, historical narratives organize discrete events in a sequence that is at once chronological and implicitly hierarchical. At the bottom of the hierarchy are particular historical actors and actions – say, William Wordsworth and the publication of *Lyrical Ballads*. At a higher level, those actions get organized into patterns that are themselves events in a larger story. *Lyrical Ballads* may be presented as part of the ballad revival, for instance, which in turn forms part of a larger story about representation of the past in Romanticism. This structure excels at several important things – especially, articulating causal connections, and the relationship of individual actors to broader social patterns. But it is not a structure designed to illuminate comparative questions of degree. Nor is it good at describing processes of transformation that don't divide neatly into events.

---

[1] Marc Leopold Benjamin Bloch, *Strange Defeat: A Statement of Evidence Written in 1940* (New York: W. W. Norton, 1986), 117.

These blind spots have allowed many obvious questions about literature to go unasked, especially questions that require measuring degrees of difference and similarity. For instance, the world represented in literature has a particular shape: some cities, technologies, or household appliances loom larger than others. We might ask how similar this fictional world is to the real social world. Does fiction immediately reflect recent changes in the social world at the time of publication, or does it tend to lag behind social history? And if there is a lag between social change and fiction, how long is the lag? A decade? A generation? It is a simple question, but one that could illuminate many other dimensions of literary history since it tells us something about the tightness or looseness of the mediations that bind literature to other aspects of society.

Matthew Wilkens has investigated "literary attention lag" by comparing the prominence of cities in nineteenth-century American fiction to their real populations at different points in the century. He finds evidence of a thirty-year lag. For instance, the closest fit to the distribution of literary attention in 1862 comes from the real population distribution in 1832. Another way to put this is that, on average, the world represented in literature looks like the world authors would have encountered "at age 12."[2]

The pattern in Wilkens's nineteenth-century evidence is strikingly clear, but it may be too early to generalize it to other periods and other kinds of social change. For instance, Alexander Manshel discovered a slightly different picture when he investigated representations of technology in twentieth- and twenty-first-century fiction. The average pattern is not entirely different from the one Wilkens discovered: adoption of a new technology in fiction often seems to lag ten to thirty years behind its adoption in American homes. But the details vary a great deal. Best sellers are quicker to reflect technological change than the books that win literary prizes. And there are some technologies, like computing, that appear in fiction well before writers would have encountered them at home.[3]

In measuring the closeness of fit between arcs of change in fiction and reality, the importance of numbers is not purely to enlarge the number of books a scholar can consider. One could investigate the changing prominence of different cities, for instance, by skimming hundreds of books and taking notes on paper. Gathering evidence would be more work without a computer, but it wouldn't be impossible. On the other hand, it would be

---

[2] Matthew Wilkens, "Literary Attention Lag," *Work Product*, January 13, 2015, https://mattwilkens.com/2015/01/13/literary-attention-lag/.
[3] Alexander Manshel, "The Lag: Technology and Fiction in the Twentieth Century," *PMLA* 135.1 (2020): 40–58.

hard to draw any conclusion from this evidence without drawing a trend line or measuring the gap between two curves. Numbers become indispensable for questions of this kind, not because they constitute "big data," but because they allow historians to measure change as a continuous quantity.

2.2 Looking for Discontinuities

While numbers excel at representing continuous change, they needn't force us to ignore moments of discontinuity. Admittedly, quantitative methods haven't yet revealed a lot of sharp ruptures in literary history. But even one example suffices to show that it is, in principle, possible to make this sort of discovery. For instance, in modeling crime fiction I found that 160 years of the genre could be described by a single model. The linguistic patterns that distinguish Robert B. Parker's detective stories from fiction in other genres are also legible in Dorothy Sayers, and stretch all the way back to Edgar Allan Poe's short stories of the 1840s. A model trained on a random sample of detective fiction can recognize any of these authors as belonging to the same genre. But if we try to stretch the model twenty years further to cover "Newgate" fiction of the 1820s and '30s, something breaks (see Figure 2.1).[4] Although we might lump *Oliver Twist* and "The Purloined Letter" together as "crime fiction" – and critics sometimes do – a linguistic model doesn't recognize them as very similar.

The break around 1840 is not surprising, since Poe's stories are often mentioned as prototypes of the detective genre. Their influence is too clear to need confirmation. The point of this experiment is rather to confirm that quantitative methods are flexible enough to notice discontinuities when they occur. Critics often worry that numbers will inherently, and almost by definition, level the irregularities of history to produce an artificial smoothness. Benjamin Mangrum suggests, for instance, that distant reading produces a new picture of the past by constructing an "aggregate population" and redefining the object of inquiry as "the averaged arc of generational shifts."[5] So, it is important to confirm that quantitative methods are capable of noticing significant outliers and

---

[4] Ted Underwood, *Distant Horizons: Digital Evidence and Literary Change* (Chicago: University of Chicago Press, 2019), pp. 50–52.
[5] Benjamin Mangrum, "Aggregation, Public Criticism, and the History of Reading Big Data," *PMLA* 133.5 (2018): 1212, 1209.

Literary Change

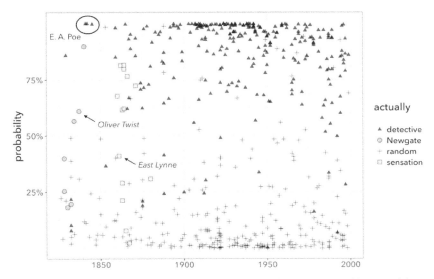

Figure 2.1 The probability that a given book is crime fiction, estimated by a model trained on examples of detective, Newgate, and sensation fiction labeled by human readers.

sudden shifts when they do occur – as when Poe's "The Murders in the Rue Morgue" effectively inaugurates a new genre.

More generally, it is important to check that our representations of average trends don't erase discontinuities between individual cases. A sharp break between older and newer literary forms might well appear gradual if we attended only to the aggregate trend. Even if there were in reality no intermediate forms, the apostles of an older form might, after all, die or retire one by one. So, the aggregate average of literary practice could appear to change gradually when the change was actually discontinuous. Figure 2.2 represents an imaginary case of this kind, where the novel of ideas is slowly replaced by popular thrillers, producing a shift toward concrete diction that appears gradual, even though the two market niches are in reality sharply distinct.

I used imaginary data for Figure 2.2 because literary historians haven't encountered many patterns of this kind. But we could still encounter them, so it is good practice to plot individual volumes and examine the full distribution of the data, not just an average trend. When researchers do that, they more commonly see patterns such as that shown in Figure 2.3,

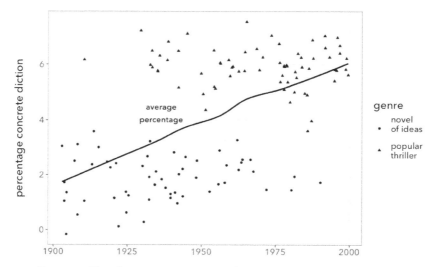

Figure 2.2 Two discontinuous genres overlap to produce a continuous trend.

drawn from real research on concrete diction at the Stanford Literary Lab.[6] Here, individual works cluster around the mean value for any given year, and the whole distribution moves together in the direction of concreteness.

When Ryan Heuser and Long Le-Khac first published Figure 2.3 in 2012, it was surprising not only because change appeared continuous, but also because the pace of change was so constant. This simple, straight, century-long trend does not closely resemble prevailing narratives of literary history, which tend to be organized around discrete literary periods and movements. For instance, many accounts of descriptive language in nineteenth-century fiction might imply some shift of emphasis between Romanticism and the Victorian realist novel, and perhaps another course adjustment between realism and naturalism. But if those shifts do take place, they make no difference for the direction of the trend in Figure 2.3.

In fact, the familiar outlines of periods and movements are invisible in all of the graphs produced thus far by quantitative literary scholarship. Like all negative evidence, this absence is hard to interpret. But it still deserves reflection. It appears likely that there is an error somewhere in our understanding of the past. Either quantitative researchers have failed to measure

---

[6] Ryan Heuser and Long Le-Khac, "A Quantitative Literary History of 2,958 Nineteenth-Century British Novels: The Semantic Cohort Method," Stanford Literary Lab Pamphlet Series, May 2012, https://litlab.stanford.edu/LiteraryLabPamphlet4.pdf.

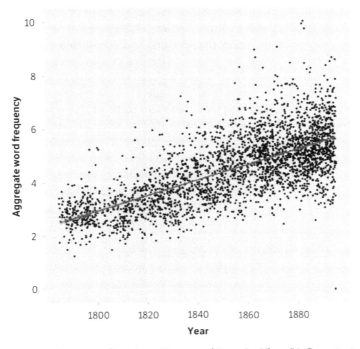

Figure 2.3 Illustration from Ryan Heuser and Long Le-Khac, "A Quantitative Literary History of 2,958 Nineteenth-Century British Novels: The Semantic Cohort Method," *Pamphlets of the Stanford Literary Lab* (2012), 27. Here, "hard seeds" are concrete words.

the most important aspects of literary change, or period concepts are less inevitable than our existing histories imply. Or, perhaps likeliest of all, both things are true at once.

It is almost certain that quantitative literary scholars have failed to measure important aspects of the past. Figuring out what to measure is a basic problem in this field, and not a solved one. For instance, Figure 2.3 was produced by constructing a list of concrete words and measuring their frequency in novels. But concreteness might simply be the wrong thing to inquire about if we want to understand the significant phases of nineteenth-century literary history. We could of course choose a different topic. But if we want a full picture of the pace of literary change, perhaps we should try to consider all topics at once.

For instance, instead of focusing on a select group of concrete words, we could ask generally how authors' diction changes, by representing each work as a distribution across the lexicon, and measuring the difference between distributions. If we imagine diction as a geometric space, this would be like measuring the distance between two points in that space. Of course, diction is just one aspect of language. If we believed that word order was more important, nothing would prevent us from also representing the sequential relationships between words (for instance, as a matrix of probabilities) and measuring the distance between those matrices. Some scholars have tried to measure change in this more encompassing way, grouping all the novels in a decade and measuring the linguistic distance between one decade and the next. Similar experiments have been pursued to measure the pace of change in popular music.[7]

These experiments do reveal significant fluctuations in the pace of change. But when scholars try to measure all aspects of language at once, a new set of interpretive problems emerges. The decision not to emphasize any particular aspect of language is still a decision about emphasis, and it may not necessarily be the correct one. For instance, if we count the replacement of "will not" by "won't" as a significant difference, we might be measuring linguistic drift rather than *literary* change; it would seem strange to interpret a broadly shared shift in usage (like the rise of contractions) as an acceleration of change in literary genres specifically. There is, in any case, little evidence so far that the pace of change in poetry or fiction (however we measure it) corresponds to our received ideas about the boundaries of periods and movements.

The interpretive problems produced by trying to measure all aspects of language at once suggest that it might be more fruitful to move in the other direction. Perhaps a linguistic concept like "concreteness" fails to reveal the discontinuities we might expect in literary history because it is defined too loosely. If we could isolate the individual tropes and techniques that actually define fiction, perhaps we would start to see the jumps we expect between Romanticism, realism, naturalism, and so on. In support of this theory, one might observe that when quantitative methods do reveal clear historical discontinuities, it is almost always because the experiment has been designed to measure something quite specific. For instance, as I remarked earlier, a model trained to recognize detective fiction notices a clear break around the year 1840. A model of this kind may use, at

---

[7] Ben Lambert, Georgios Kontonatsios, Matthias Mauch, et al., "The Pace of Modern Culture," *Nature Human Behaviour*, January 20, 2020, www.nature.com/articles/s41562-019-0802-4.

bottom, the same sort of evidence used in Figure 2.3 – the frequencies of individual words. But because the model is "supervised" (that is, trained to match the pattern seen in known examples of detective fiction), it can look for a pattern of diction specific to a particular literary institution rather than a general metric of "concreteness."[8]

One could carry out a similar experiment with a movement like "naturalism" – training a model on works commonly treated as emblematic of the movement, and then using the model to measure the similarity of other works that have been characterized as precursors or descendants. If we find that similarity to naturalism drops off relatively abruptly as we move backward or forward in time, we will have some evidence that literary history can make sudden jumps and shifts of direction. If the gradient of similarity is smooth, it might lend support to a theory of continuity. Experiments of this kind may eventually give literary scholars a better grasp of what they mean when they write words like "naturalism" and "modernism." Are we gesturing at social phenomena that are relatively compact, or quite diffuse?[9] But it is difficult to imagine that any experimental outcome would lead literary scholars to abandon periodization entirely. Our use of period terms is not currently premised on a belief that they represent real cultural formations divided by accelerated periods of change. Eighty years ago, to be sure, that view was prevalent. René Wellek and Austin Warren influentially defined a literary period as "a time section dominated by a system of literary norms, standards, and conventions." For Wellek, and for many other twentieth-century scholars, these systems were realities rather than critical conventions. Tracing their emergence and dissolution was "the central task of literary history."[10]

Defining literary periods today would be a harder task. Fredric Jameson, for instance, has considered the possibility "that period concepts finally correspond to no realities whatsoever."[11] Not everyone agrees: David James

---

[8] If we want to include more complicated syntactic evidence, we can certainly do that by training a neural network. But researchers have so far found little evidence that neural models improve significantly on bag-of-words methods for classification of book-length documents.

[9] To be clear, traditional historical methods already support a great deal of reflection on topics like this, and it will be hard to improve on existing work, because the task is not really as simple as tracing a gradient. A word like "modernism" has multiple senses, and articulating the relation between them is a philosophical challenge more than a question of measurement. See, for instance, "Modern, Modernism," in *Modernism: Keywords*, ed. Melba Cuddy-Keane, Adam Hammond, and Alexandra Peat (Hoboken: John Wiley and Sons, 2014), 139–146. Smaller movements like imagism and naturalism may conceivably be more tractable.

[10] René Wellek and Austin Warren, *Theory of Literature* (New York: Harcourt, Brace, and Jovanovich, 1977), 265, 261.

[11] Fredric Jameson, *Postmodernism; or, The Cultural Logic of Late Capitalism* (Durham: Duke University Press, 1991), 282.

and Urmila Seshagiri have defended the years 1890 and 1940 as durable and meaningful boundary markers for modernism.[12] Somewhere between those two poles, Melba Cuddy-Keane has called for a "flexible periodization," where a period term evokes "not a coherent formation but multiple patterns."[13] But there is in practice a great deal of common ground between these positions. The important thing is that everyone continues to use period terms, untroubled by disagreement about their ontological status. Even Jameson's speculation that period concepts correspond to "no realities whatsoever," for instance, is drawn from a book titled *Postmodernism*. Elsewhere, he remarks that period concepts are "as indispensable as they are unsatisfactory."[14] The practical impossibility of dispensing with these concepts is widely conceded in the humanities. "[P]eriods are necessary," one historian has explained, "not as immutable landmarks but as conventional divisions which help to give history a structure."[15]

Why is the practice of periodization so much more durable than the theory? I noted earlier that historical narrative works by organizing discrete events in an implicit hierarchy. Actors are grouped into a school or movement; then movements are pitted against each other to define the characteristic struggle of a period; finally, periods are connected to outline a narrative arc. The names of movements and periods are indispensable because they provide the rhetorical bones and muscles that articulate this strategy. In other words, literary historians don't tell a story about movements and periods because they have found evidence that those formations exist. Rather, they posit that periods exist because they need to tell a story. As long as historians tell stories, labels of this kind will remain useful.

So, there is little need to worry that quantitative research will undermine periodization by proving that period concepts don't correspond to anything real. That would be in the first place quite difficult, because it is hard to prove a negative thesis. We can try to measure the breaks between periods and fail to do so, but it will always remain possible to interpret

---

[12] David James and Urmila Seshagiri, "Metamodernism: Narratives of Continuity and Revolution," *PMLA* 129.1 (2014): 91.

[13] Melba Cuddy-Keane, "Crossing the Victorian/Modernist Divide: From Multiple Histories to Flexible Futures," in *Beyond the Victorian/Modernist Divide: Remapping the Turn-of-the-Century Break in Literature, Culture, and the Visual Arts*, ed. Anne-Florence Gillard-Estrada and Anne Besnault-Levita (New York: Routledge, 2018), 35.

[14] Fredric Jameson, *The Political Unconscious* (London: Methuen, 1981), 28, qtd. in Lawrence Besserman, *The Challenge of Periodization: Old Paradigms and New Perspectives* (New York: Garland, 1996), 4.

[15] Gordon Leff, "Models Inherent in History," in *The Rules of the Game: Cross-Disciplinary Essays on Models in Scholarly Thought*, ed. Teodor Shanin (London: Tavistock, 1971), 151.

our failure as proof that the real differences between periods are too evanescent to be captured by numbers. Like belief in God, belief in periodization can survive a lot of silence. But, more fundamentally, it is already clear that proving period boundaries unreal would do nothing to stop the practice of periodization. That practice doesn't depend on any ontological consensus; rather, it is sustained by rhetorical and institutional imperatives.

If quantitative methods challenge periodization, they will do so indirectly: not by proving periods unreal, but by providing a different way to represent change. Figure 2.3, for instance, reveals an important fact about the history of the novel without invoking periods even in a nominalistic, rhetorical way. Because numbers allow us to position books on a continuum, we can describe the growing concreteness of nineteenth-century fiction without needing to stabilize ideal types or draw boundaries. We can, so to speak, trace the course of a stream of change instead of carrying the water in discrete containers. This is not an objection to periodization, just an alternative to it. But since periodization persists more as a practice than an argument, alternatives might prove more important than objections.

2.3 Interpreting and Explaining Change

It's clear, then, that quantifying literary history makes it easier to represent literary change as a continuous process. But can a continuous process produce the kind of meaning literary historians are seeking? There are good reasons to be doubtful. Historical narrative makes change meaningful in part by crystallizing it in agents. These agents don't have to be individual people; they could be social classes, literary schools, or famous debates. The web of relations between agents can still take a form that we recognize as "explanation." A line on a graph doesn't illuminate change in the same way; it describes a trend without explaining agency.

Even scholars who work with computational models often feel that describing trends is not enough. For instance, Franco Moretti and Oleg Sobchuk have certainly used numbers to trace trends. But they argue in a recent article that this approach has become too dominant. At first, perhaps, the trend line produced a new kind of meaning, subsuming the crises and generational struggles of traditional historiography in a larger pattern – and making the pattern visible. But the impersonal slope of a trend line can also make change seem "inevitable." Moretti and Sobchuk suggest that this approach has become hegemonic in digital humanities: "our exaggerated reliance on trends has *de facto* banished conflict from DH research." Along with conflict, they suggest, we are losing our ability to produce the "in-depth explanations" that would come from understanding underlying causes in detail.[16] One way to restore explanation, of course, would be to steer back toward the sort of narrative that crystallizes agency in particular writers, movements, and publications. But Moretti and Sobchuk propose, as an alternative, Darwin's model of natural selection as a branching tree. This model would neatly resolve the apparent conflict between continuous change and causal narrative by reframing the causal forces in literary history as *processes* of struggle, selection, and adaptation.

In effect, Moretti and Sobchuk are arguing for a closer connection between the humanities and a subfield of social science that pursues evolutionary explanation of cultural change. This connection has been proposed more than once, but literary historians have circled the evolutionary metaphor warily.[17] For many scholars, the differences between cultural transmission and natural selection are more salient than the similarities. Christopher Prendergast suggests that "whereas biological life is governed by proliferation, differentiation and divergence, cultural life is governed by amalgamation, anastomosis and convergence."[18] Contemporary social scientists who work on this topic acknowledge that their analogy to natural selection is imperfect, and tend to frame cultural evolution not as passive selection but as a process of imitation and learning (which may sometimes be convergent). Alberto Acerbi, for instance, describes the remixing and transmission of culture online as a process mediated by "wary learning."[19] Of course, digital media provide an ideal test case for theories of transmission, since faithful digital copies blaze a clear trail for researchers. It remains to be seen whether evolutionary models will be equally illuminating for print media, where there is no "retweet" button and transmission can be a muddy process stretching over many years.

Evolutionary models are not, of course, the only way to move from quantitative description to deeper understanding. Scientists have traditionally done this by studying the strength of the statistical association between different phenomena. This is how we learned, for instance, that smoking

---

[16] Franco Moretti and Oleg Sobchuk, "Hidden in Plain Sight: Data Visualization in the Humanities," *New Left Review* 118 (2019): 95–96, 113.
[17] For an ambivalent survey, see Brian Baker, "Evolution, Literary History and Science Fiction," in *Literature and Science*, ed. Sharon Ruston (Cambridge: Cambridge University Press, 2008), 131–150.
[18] Christopher Prendergast, "Evolution and Literary History," *New Left Review* 34 (2005): 56.
[19] Alberto Acerbi, *Cultural Evolution in the Digital Age* (Oxford: Oxford University Press, 2019).

and lack of exercise correlate with heart disease. Some philosophers would argue that statistical models of this kind are in themselves a kind of explanation.[20] But, if so, the explanation they provide is not necessarily an account of causes. Even in sciences like medicine, where it is possible to perform controlled, randomized experiments, variables that look like causes can turn out to be proxies for hidden factors. (Perhaps some patients failed to exercise because they were already in poor health.) So proving causation often requires more than a statistical connection. To be confident, we might need to understand, for instance, exactly how exercise strengthens the heart.

Models of cultural (and literary) history are even harder to interpret than epidemiological ones. Works of art and literature are hard to represent concisely; to model them, researchers may need thousands of variables (for instance, a variable for each word in the text), which tends to diffuse explanatory significance across an array of factors. Frustration with this aspect of text analysis lies behind Nan Z. Da's critique that textual models reveal mere symptoms (of genre, for instance) rather than the forces that "actually drove the genre differences."[21] The machine learning algorithms capable of grappling with thousands of variables can also be opaque. It may be hard to point to the particular part of a neural network that produced a literary judgment. But this purely technical obstacle to explanation is well publicized and perhaps in danger of being exaggerated. In practice, it's usually possible to open so-called black boxes. The machine learning algorithm that produced Figure 2.1, for instance, tells us that detective stories are distinguished by references to *crime*, *murder*, and *investigation* – which is not exactly a dark riddle.

The bigger problem with modeling literary history is a long-familiar one. Historians can rarely intervene in their object of study to perform an experiment. With a few interesting exceptions, our evidence about the past is observational, and it is difficult to extract causal conclusions from observational evidence.[22] Since researchers can't cut the connection between variables by randomly assigning writers to different groups, we are left with a web where every variable is potentially connected to every other one. In a web of that

---

[20] Wesley Salmon, *Statistical Explanation and Statistical Relevance* (Pittsburgh: University of Pittsburgh Press, 1971).
[21] Nan Z. Da, "Computational Case against Computational Literary Studies," *Critical Inquiry* 45 (Spring 2019): 622.
[22] For an interesting example of a "natural experiment," see Elliott Ash, Daniel L. Chen, and Suresh Naidu, "Ideas Have Consequences: The Effect of Law and Economics on American Justice," June 26, 2017, available at SSRN: https://ssrn.com/abstract=2992782. Thanks to Richard Jean So for this lead.

kind, patterns can still be recognized, but it may be difficult to trace them to a causal origin. But this should not come as a surprise. Similar problems confront traditional approaches to literary history. The causal stories we tell about history have always been speculative – interwoven with arguments about chickens and eggs. As a result, our understanding of literary-historical change can often be improved by things that fall well short of a strictly causal explanation. A correlation between writers' social background and their critical reception, for instance, might be very illuminating, even if we couldn't prove that the first variable directly caused the second.

In some cases, we don't even need to test correlations: mere description of literary change can sometimes reveal illuminating patterns. For instance, much of the evidence that Moretti and Sobchuk use to argue for a theory of "branching processes" in cultural history comes from the descriptive method they are proposing to transcend. They point out, for instance, that researchers who set out simply to plot trends in film and literature have often ended up producing graphs that look like a branching tree, because the trend lines representing different genres or market segments turn out to diverge over time.[23] Moretti and Sobchuk are right to recognize this pattern, and right that we need a deeper theoretical understanding of it. We need to ask, more systematically, whether literary change is shaped by general processes of differentiation and specialization. But if quantitative description has motivated this theoretical question, it also follows that merely plotting trend lines can after all lead us toward a deeper understanding of change.

***

In short, quantitative methods are creating a new picture of literary history. These methods have not yet provided much evidence to refute (or support) periodization as a theoretical claim about the literary past. But they are doing something that might be more important, by giving scholars an alternative to periodization as a rhetorical practice. Text analysis and data visualization make it possible to represent literary change as a continuous process. This approach has some clear disadvantages: historical narrative is still usually better at foregrounding agency, conflict, and causality. But quantitative methods can complement those strengths of narrative by supporting inquiry about the trends, relationships, differences of degree, and processes of transmission or selection that have shaped literary culture.

---

[23] Moretti and Sobchuk, 108–110. They point, for instance, to the visualizations in Ted Underwood and Jordan Sellers, "The Emergence of Literary Diction," *Journal of Digital Humanities* 1.2 (Spring 2012): https://web.archive.org/web/20200727222119/http://journalofdigitalhumanities.org/1-2/the-emergence-of-literary-diction-by-ted-underwood-and-jordan-sellers/.

CHAPTER 3

The Canon

Mark Algee-Hewitt

For scholars working on computational approaches to literature, the demise of the canon is always just around the corner. Among the utopian early promises of the digital humanities (DH) was an easy exit to the so-called "canon wars" of the late twentieth century. This, it was imagined, could be attained not through a radical and contentious rethinking of what books deserve to be taught and read, but simply because the notion of a canon would become obsolete through a methodology that, for the first time, was capable of analyzing everything. Literary studies would finally become "comprehensive and definite" as computational models could study everything written during a given period.[1] This shift in scale, from the hundreds or thousands of texts that a single reader can bring to bear on a question to the hundreds of thousands of texts that a computational analysis can mobilize, even suggested the possibility that period distinctions themselves would disappear. At the same time, the storage and communication capacity of our digital infrastructure enabled the creation and dissemination of archives that could meet the hungry demand of these analyses. A century's worth of print, which even thirty years ago would occupy floors of libraries, can be copied, traded, and loaded into memory, giving more readers and scholars access to more materials at their fingertips than at any point in human history. If the canon is a technology of selection, then once we no longer need to make that selection the canon can disappear.

The problem is that the canon's demise has been just around the corner for the past twenty years. Despite the efforts of computationally driven literary scholarship, the canon persists in DH as well as in the greater field of literary study. As it turns out, neither the availability of large, digitized archives of textual material, nor the new methods of computational

---

[1] Matthew Jockers, *Macroanalysis: Digital Analysis & Literary History* (Champaign: University of Illinois Press, 2013), 31.

analysis that have been applied to them, can erase the organizing principle of the canon. Both aspects of computational study carry with them unresolved challenges that, either by accident or by design, recenter the canon in their analysis of the literary field. Our new digital archives of texts vastly increase the scale of what is available to scholars and students outside of private, hard-to-access, library collections. Yet, as historical artifacts themselves, they are not unbiased representations of the period or literature that they claim to represent. Instead, the biases of both the period they reflect and the method of their assembly are coded into the texts that they contain, even while their scale serves to convince us of the ways that they improve the canon-centered collections of traditional literary scholarship.[2] Similarly, while the expense of travelling to collections of texts previously erected barriers to the kinds of scholarship that digital archives promised to make universally possible, the purchase price of these collections has created a new set of economic barriers.

Even the methods that we use to analyze these collections at scale have not permitted us to abandon the canon altogether. While computational models can take into account both commonly read texts and those that have rarely been opened since their initial printing, allowing both to inform the analysis, this new equality falls apart at the interpretive step. As we explore large-scale models of literary periods and genres, we are tasked with making sense of the computational results in a way that reflects our understanding of literary scholarship. Often in this crucial step we turn back to the canon to aid us in explaining the model such that we can register its findings within the body of knowledge that literary criticism has assembled over the past two centuries.[3] Yet this relationship between the new technologies of DH and the old technology of the canon leaves both changed. While computational approaches to literary study have not yet

---

[2] Questions of representativeness have been at the center of recent debate in the field, most notably between Ted Underwood, who, in *Distant Horizons*, offers perspectival modeling as a potentially effective computational way of accounting for biases in a corpus, and Katherine Bode who, in her review of Underwood's book, argues that the only solution is to assemble a well-sourced corpus with a rich bibliography and acknowledge its limits. Catherine D'Ignazio and Lauren Klein also interrogate the ways that methods of corpus assembly can bias what they contain in chapter 4 of *Data Feminism*. Ted Underwood, *Distant Horizons: Digital Evidence and Literary Change* (Chicago: University of Chicago Press, 2019), 36–38; Katherine Bode, "Why You Can't Model Away Bias," *Modern Language Quarterly* 81.1 2020: 95–124, 100–101; Catherine D'Ignazio and Lauren Klein, *Data Feminism* (Cambridge: The MIT Press, 2020).

[3] Scholars working with computation often pull canonical examples to serve as an explanation of their results. Underwood, for example, uses Charlotte Bronte and George Eliot to focalize his results on gender dimorphism, while Andrew Piper, in *Enumerations*, discusses topics in relation to Goethe. Underwood, *Distant Horizons*, 129; Andrew Piper, *Enumerations: Data and Literary Study* (Chicago: University of Chicago Press, 2019), 75–83.

been successful in erasing the canon, and its pernicious influence, from scholarship, the use of computational methods has forced a mutual evolution to take place in how the canon is used to make sense of the literary field. While not as utopian in its possibilities as our original belief in the canon's coming obsolescence, we can now reimagine how we might harness the canon to change the way that we understand the study of literature.

3.1 The Evolving Canon

The canon itself is a technology of literary study. Although ideas of valuation and greatness have adhered to writing since at least the classical period and the theater of Athens, the contemporary concept of a canon is, in many ways, a response to the European deluge of printed material in the eighteenth century.[4] With the increasing number of printed copies of books, selection on the part of readers, rather than mere availability, began to play a role in what was read. This shift in reading practice required a way of distinguishing what *should* be read from what *could* be read. Since there was far more text available than a single reader could consume within a lifetime, it became important to distinguish the works that were worth reading (a subject that authors of the time were not neutral on). The problem became acute with respect to contemporary authors. Whereas the simple fact of historical survival could retroactively demonstrate the greatness of a Chaucer or a Shakespeare, for readers seeking to read the best of the literature produced by their own cultural milieu, the task of sorting between the vast quantity of writing available was daunting at the least. The proliferation of aesthetic theory (and its attendant focus on matters of "taste") demonstrates the perceived need for a system to sort through the sea of writing that threatened to drown the public reading sphere.[5]

By the nineteenth century, in the minds of the European and American cultural elite, the need for a mechanism to sort between "good" and "bad"

---

[4] The formation of a new reading public during the eighteenth century, in both England and continental Europe, is intimately tied to the numerical increase in the number of printed books. In Rolf Engelsing's study of German print culture, he notes that there were both more books and more readers to consume them. Rolf Engelsing, *Der Büger als Leser: Lesergeschichte in Deutchland 1500–1800* (Suttgart: Metzler, 1974).

[5] See, for example, Denise Gigante's reading of Milton's take on the proliferation of print in his *Areopagitica* and the ways that taste connects to virtue: "That the 'good' book is a means to taste, as well as to virtue, is an idea that reverberates through the Century of Taste." Denise Gigante, *Taste: A Literary History* (New Haven: Yale University Press, 2005), 42.

literature had become acute. The tide of print had continued to rise and the task of selecting the "right" sort of literature had taken on new significance. In *Culture and Anarchy* (1869), Matthew Arnold joined the earlier task of literary selection to his project of cultural advancement. By studying and understanding what he called "the best that has been thought and said," Arnold argued, a citizen would not only improve their own mind but would also serve as a bulwark against the forces of anarchy threating to debase British culture.[6] So-called "low" cultural objects (including popular literature and what would come to be called "genre fiction") were no longer a passive waste of paper; they actively threatened the political and cultural stability of the nation. In the nineteenth century, the ethical imperative that was always implicit in ideas on taste and judgment surfaced in the work of Arnold and his contemporaries to create the limited list of culturally approved works that we have inherited as the canon. That the works on this list were written almost exclusively by white and overwhelmingly by male authors was simply part of the imperial nature of the cultural project that the canon supported.

This is not to suggest that the canon was exclusively assembled top-down by self-appointed cultural authorities. Market forces and, more importantly, cultural institutions also worked to reinforce the canon from the ground up. John Guillory has written persuasively about the role that school curricula played in establishing the literary canon: repeated instruction in a limited set of texts (of the type that were also approved by Arnold) reinforced the idea among generations of students that these so-called "great works" *were* English literature.[7] The system perpetuated itself: the more that a work was taught, studied, and read, the more likely it was that it would be taught studied and read in the future. At the same time, the nascent field of literary study also worked to reify the canon. As new theories combined formal complexity with aesthetic judgment, literary critics reached for the known and widely read books of the canon to illustrate their points, implicitly (and often explicitly) connecting their theories to highly valued works. Whether it was Bakhtin's "heteroglossia,"

---

[6] "The whole scope of the essay is to recommend culture as the great help out of our present difficulties; culture being a pursuit of our total perfection by means of getting to know, on all the matters which most concern us, the best which has been thought and said in the world." Matthew Arnold, *Culture and Anarchy: An Essay in Political and Social Criticism* (London: Smith, Elder and Co., 1869), viii.

[7] "What does have a concrete location as a list, then, is not the canon, but the syllabus, the list of works one reads in a given class, or the curriculum, the list of works one reads in a program of study." John Guillory, *Cultural Capital: The Problem of Literary Canon Formation* (Chicago: University of Chicago Press, 1993), 30.

Empson's "ambiguity," Brooks's "complexity," or even Barthé's "writerly texts," literary theorists have long located these values in the canon, often arguing (in the case of Empson and Brooks) that these works were valuable *because* they evidenced these phenomena.[8]

It is telling that the critiques of the canon that emerged in the late twentieth century centered on its limited principles of selection. Emerging scholars, recognizing that the canon contained mostly white and male authors, sought to *expand* it by adding additional authors from historically marginalized groups, rather than doing away with the system of the canon altogether.[9] At the same time, however, a turn toward archival studies refocused literary attention, particularly among younger scholars, on the authors who had slipped between the cracks of history. Reclamation projects sought to rehabilitate authors on the margins of the canon or, better yet, recover authors who had been entirely forgotten for a new audience.[10] This combination of canon reformation and archival recovery, therefore, set the stage for some theorists of the canon to embrace new forms of digital epistemology that held the potential for moving us outside of the canon altogether, effectively replacing the canon (a technology of selection) with computational analysis (offered as a technology of comprehension).

Two technologies paved the way for this transformation. First, the push to move archival records online offered both private companies and nonprofit organizations an alternative to distributing their material through physical media (books, for example, or microfiche that required both storage space and specialized equipment). Large archives of literature suddenly became available to scholars at participating institutions, with the most massive opening up tens or hundreds of thousands of texts, which

---

[8] Mikhail Bakhtin, *The Dialogic Imagination: Four Essays*, ed. Michael Holquist. Trans. Caryl Emerson and Michael Holquist (Austin: University of Texas Press, 1981), 326; Cleanth Brooks. *The Well Wrought Urn: Studies in the Structure of Poetry* (London: Denis Dobson, 1947), 188; William Empson. *Seven Types of Ambiguity* (London: Chatto and Windus, 1949), 29; Roland Barthes, *S/Z*, trans. Richard Miller (Oxford: Blackwell Press, 1990), 3–4.

[9] While it is largely true that efforts to reform the canon in the late twentieth century focused primarily on expansion, some did argue that any principle of selection introduced problematic hierarchies into art and that therefore we should do away with the author-centric canonical approaches that define our anthologies. Michelle Levy and Mark Perry, "Distantly Reading the Romantic Canon: Quantifying Gender in Current Anthologies," *Woman's Writing*, 22.2, 2015: 132–155, 134.

[10] While largely welcomed by scholars interested in diversifying literary study, the expansion of the canon was not without its attendant dangers. Scholars interested in Black literature, for example, expressed concern that including Black writers in the largely white canon would lead to their homogenization. Gail Low and Marion Wynne-Davies. "Introduction," in *A Black British Canon?* (New York: Palgrave, 2006), 1–13, 4.

were fully indexed and retrievable through a simple search query.[11] While the change in format did nothing to alter the ability of literary critics to read through the archive (if anything, the online interfaces made actually reading the text more difficult), the accessibility of these collections as *digital* artifacts made them available to the second emerging technology of literary study: computational analysis. Moving beyond stylometry and other frequency-based methods of analyzing literature, large-scale modeling techniques such as topic modeling, word embeddings, or, recently, contextual embeddings now *required* the massive amount of text contained in the archive to operate at all.[12] While the canon was never small on the scale of a single reader, the hundreds of texts that it contained were only a fraction of the billions of words needed to unlock the full potential of these methods.

Scholars – both those working within and those outside of computational literary analysis – suddenly saw the potential for a seismic shift, not just in how research could operate outside of the canon, but also, and more importantly, in the ways that we thought about what lay in the domain of the noncanonical. As long it was confined to physical archives and libraries, the vast collection of writing that did not belong to the canon remained outside of the scholarly perceptions of literary criticism. Through the sudden availability of these collections on individual researchers' computers, as well as a set of methods could account for the sheer amount of text they contained, the archive became thinkable for the first time as a single object. When Margaret Cohen, building on the work of Franco Moretti's *Graphs, Maps, and Trees*, in her 2009 article "Narratology in the Archive of Literature" names the archive "the great unread," she also renders it legible: a vast potential repository of unread literature that not only may contain forgotten classics, but also holds an unprecedented

---

[11] Among the many collections that have transformed computational study in the humanities are the *Eighteenth Century Collections Online* and the *Nineteenth Century Collections Online* archives published by Thomson Gale, and the *Early English Books Online* collection published by ProQuest, which also hosts the Chadwyck-Healey Collection that I use later in this article. An important alternative to these for-profit collections is HathiTrust, a massive archive housed at the University of Illinois at Champagne-Urbana that is available (with limits) to most university-affiliated scholars. Companies holding the rights to these platforms benefited both in that they no longer had to store the books themselves and also in that the digital subscription platform meant that they no longer needed to ship physical media, loosening the restrictions on the potential upper bounds of the size of collections.

[12] The foundational paper on word representations in vector space makes clear, from the outset, that these new methods function only with corpora that number in the billions of words. Thomas Mikolov, Kai Chen, Greg Corrado, and Jeffrey Dean, *"Efficient Estimation of Word Representations in Vector Space"* (ICLR Workshop, 2013): https://arxiv.org/abs/1301.3781.

bounty of culturally and historically relevant material.[13] With the archive now available along with methods that could aid scholars in parsing it, the new technologies of DH were set to supplant the technology of the canon.

The fact that they failed to do so is testament both to the resiliency of the technology of the canon and, perhaps more importantly, to three inherent problems in the newly available digital archive. First, although the digital repositories were advertised as democratizing access to archival materials, the for-pay and subscriber-based models introduced by their publishers simply shifted the associated costs from transportation to subscription. Only the wealthiest institutions could afford the full range of digital platforms, and even nonprofit collections were restricted in terms of how much in-copyright material they could make available.[14] Secondly, far from solving the issues of bias and underrepresentation in the canon, the newly available digital archives enhanced these problems. While the canon remains a deeply imperfect record of literary writing, at least its biases and exclusions have become visible through decades of study. The newly available "great unread," by virtue of being unread, hides its biases in the sheer volume of material that it contains. If we cannot account for what is in the archive, we cannot account for what is missing.[15] Moreover, the size of the archive amplifies any misrepresentations that may exist: not only do the 18,200 novels of the Gale *American Fiction* collection suggest, by virtue of the collection name, that they represent nineteenth-century American fiction as a whole, the sheer scale of the archive encourages us to understand it as comprehensive. Although this collection is based on a bibliographic source, it is one that only represents novels that were published through traditional venues: novels by minor publishing houses, regional novels, and those circulated only in manuscript (which are disproportionately written by women authors and people of color) are vastly underrepresented. Finally, although the "great unread" promised a wealth of new findings, analyses conducted on this literature failed to turn up any forgotten classics: rather, even their large-scale results echoed the findings that had already been produced with canonical samples.[16] Faced with a growing awareness of these difficulties, many scholars working in

---

[13] Margaret Cohen, "Narratology in the Archive of Literature," *Representations*, 108.1, 2009: 51–75, 59.
[14] Access to even HathiTrust requires that a scholar's university have a partnership agreement with the organization.
[15] Bode, "Why You Can't Model Away Bias," 101–102.
[16] For example, in *Macroanaysis*, Jockers explores language denoting "Irishness" and "Englishness" in a corpus of ~5,000 nineteenth-century novels, finding that Jane Austen and Anthony Trollope are among the most stylistically English authors, while Oscar Wilde and Bram Stoker are among the least stylistically Irish of the nationally Irish authors. Jockers, *Macroanalysis*, 116.

computational criticism turned away from these kinds of large-scale analyses designed to obviate the canon and toward considering the canon itself as an object of study.

3.2 The Canon as Object

Implicit in the history of the canon that I have outlined is the question of what makes a work of literature "great" – the most centrally expressed criteria of canonization. This question, however, is highly contingent on whether we understand the canon itself to be an effect of sociological forces or of the formal features of the texts themselves. In other words, is a text "successful" because it is the right text, at the right place, at the right time, or because there is something about canonical texts of any era that sets them apart from the bulk of literature produced? These formal mechanisms underpin the technology of the canon, and yet we have only a hazy understanding of exactly how they work. Our ability to predict which texts will be canonized from contemporary literature has not improved over the past 300 years. The kinds of quantitative analysis made possible by cultural analytics, however, showed promise in their ability to grapple with this question at new scales of analysis. If we could use a computational model to uncover a set of formal differences (in vocabulary or grammar) that reliably differentiated canonical texts from the works of the archive, then we could begin to both predict the future canonicity of contemporary texts and explain the existence of the canon with reference to those textual differences. If, however, we assume that the canon owes its existence to an ever-changing set of social or cultural practices, then we can use the methods of computational analysis to probe the specifics of this history. Either way, these methods give us new purchase on the question of the canon itself. Perhaps if we could not shake off the prescriptive technology of the canon by radically increasing our corpus size, we could turn our computational critical lens on the object itself to try and understand where it came from.

Attempts to define the canon sociologically often build on the foundations laid by Pierre Bourdieu who, in his later work, sought to map the "literary field."[17] Diagramming the popularity of various forms of aesthetic writing against their cultural cachet, Bourdieu sought to recover the specific social pressures that divide the literary field into its various

---

[17] Pierre Bourdieu, *The Field of Cultural Production: Essays on Art and Literature* (New York: Columbia University Press, 1993), 49; Pierre Bourdieu, *The Rules of Art: Genesis and Structure of the Literary Field* (Stanford: Stanford University Press, 1996), 122.

substrata (high art, popular art, etc.). Although Bourdieu's work does not immediately address the canon as an object in and of itself, the positions on his diagrams mark out the different factors through which writing is canonized. Balancing economics against audience and age against prestige, Bourdieu's works reminds us of the complexity of canonization and the different kinds of forces that push works out of the archive and into the canon. By assigning specific roles to different social strata, moreover, Bourdieu makes explicit the canon's connection to traditional metrics of literary success, whether it is measured by economic or social capital. Works sit on a dual axis of consecration (works that are older or more intellectually prestigious) and autonomy (the degree to which the work depends on the market). While Bourdieu understands his work as describing the social forces around the reception of art, the diagrams he draws suggest the socially prescriptive tendency of the canon.[18] The two axes represent the poles of literary, or artistic, success and the placement of works on them indicates not just the sector of the reading public to whom they belong, but also the status of the high-ranking members of each genre (symbolist poetry, the naturalist novel, the psychological novel). Although Bourdieu's work is focused on the French literary tradition, his conclusions have been transportable to other literary contexts.

Although they are effective at theorizing the social space of canonical and noncanonical literature, Bourdieu's diagrams are schematic at best: his metrics are imprecise and he lacks the capacity to measure the social reception of literature at scale, particularly in the contemporary book marketplace. Taking the canon itself as their object of study, numerous computational approaches have sought to pick up where Bourdieu left off. J. D. Porter's work in the Stanford Literary Lab, for example, reorients Bourdieu's diagram to place individual authors on the axes of popularity and prestige (Figure 3.1). Measuring prestige as the number of times an author appears as a subject of a paper indexed by the MLA bibliography (an admittedly academically focused metric), and popularity as the number of times the author was reviewed on the online reading community "Goodreads," Porter argues that these two metrics define the canonicity of a given author. On the graph, the works at the top right are high in both measurements: this, Porter argues, is the space of "hypercanonical" authors: those that are indisputably part of the canon. Yet the diversity

---

[18] For the purposes of this chapter, the two diagrams are less important for the specifics of their layout (where the genres of literary production are placed), than the attempt to place them at all on these axes.

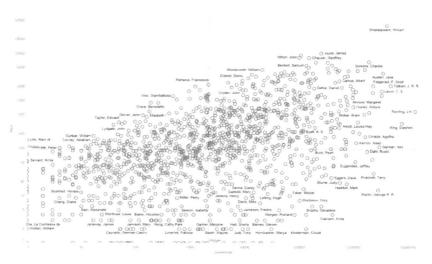

Figure 3.1 Diagram of the Literary Field on the axis of popularity (x) and prestige (y). From J. D. Porter, "Popularity/Prestige," *Pamphlets of the Stanford Literary Lab* (2018), 5.

of authors here suggests a more complicated understanding of the mechanisms of canonicity than we typically adopt. Alongside such traditionally hypercanonical authors as Shakespeare, Jane Austen and Charles Dickens, we also find J. R. R Tolkien and J. K. Rowling. Such authors traditionally lie outside of the institutional canon (at least as it is understood by the academy); however, these results ask us to reconsider what we mean by canon, particularly when it comes to recent authors. These findings suggest that there are multiple paths to canonicity. Like Bourdieu's diagram, there are different spaces of the canon, each representing an alternative configuration of the forces of popularity and prestige. Here, however, the sharp contrast between the two metrics used (books read widely by the public versus books read widely by academics) becomes more meaningful, even as it assumes less structural importance. While books high on the prestige axis echo the definition of the institutionalized canon that academics are familiar with, those high on the popular scale also manage to make it into the hypercanonical space. This suggests a deep correlation between the two metrics: books high in prestige sell more copies, while bestselling books often receive more critical attention as their popularity grows. Porter's work is therefore able to push back on Bourdieu's binary between the prestigious, but poorly selling, works of "high art," and the popular appeal of "lower" art forms by constructing a dynamic *continuous* relationship between popularity and prestige that alters the status of reception on both axes for a work high on either one.

Such computational approaches to investigating the canon as a socially prescriptive literary space frequently run up against definitional limits. For older texts, mere survival is often enough to indicate membership in the canon. These, however, come with their own limitations; for example, it is difficult to accurately assess the "popularity" of a text published centuries ago and most frequently read as part of a school curriculum.[19] In studies of contemporary novels, however, the problem lies in predicting this survivorship and guessing which books will be canonized through the institutions of reading and criticism. Researchers therefore frequently turn to current metrics of literary prestige as a proxy for contemporary canonicity. Literary prizewinners, for example, have informed a number of studies concerned with contemporary writing, as the high social prestige of the prize can serve as a predictor as to which books will be accessioned to the canon.[20] As these studies have indicated, however, such proxies for canonicity are subject to the same social forces that are under investigation: the logic behind which books are selected for different prizes (each with their own set of criteria), and which will eventually be canonized are not necessarily identical. If, for example, Porter is right and canonicity is a joint function of popularity *and* prestige, then prizewinning books that sell fewer copies may not be ideal candidates for canonization even if they occupy an important place in an imagined literary field. Features shared by books that win literary prizes at a given moment may be subject to a different set of immediate selective pressures than the long-term social forces that result in the formation of the canon.[21] At stake in this debate is the question of *representation*: does the

---

[19] Different theorists have sought to tackle this problem through innovative means. Researchers at the Stanford Literary Lab used the number of reprints and translations as an indicator of popularity in the "Canon/Archive" pamphlet. Ted Underwood and Jordan Sellers, for their work on "The *Longue Durée* of Literary Prestige," found contemporaneous reviews of novels. The unavailability of sales figures, either because they are lost in the case of historical works or because they are closely guarded trade secrets among contemporary publishers, has seriously hampered research in this area. Mark Algee-Hewitt, Sarah Allison, Marissa Gemma, et al. "Canon/Archive: Large-Scale Dynamics of the Literary Field," *Pamphlets of the Stanford Literary Lab* (Stanford: 2016), 4; Ted Underwood and Jordan Sellers, "The Longue Durée of Literary Prestige," *Modern Language Quarterly* 77.3, 2016: 321–344, 322–323.

[20] Jim English lays the groundwork for this approach in his book *The Economy of Prestige*. His subsequent work with the Price Lab has brought computational methods to bear on his study of prizewinning fiction. James English, *The Economy of Prestige: Prizes, Awards, and the Circulation of Cultural Value* (Cambridge: Harvard University Press, 2008).

[21] For example, Alexander Manshel argues that recent prizewinning fiction is much more likely to be set in the past than the present. It remains to be seen if this historical turn among prizewinning

canon reflect the larger literary milieu from which its works emerge? Or is the canon a biased sample of elite reading practices within a given historical period? The overall whiteness of the canon, and the lack of gender diversity among the authors it contains, argues against its representativeness; however, as the work on the social prescriptions for canonicity has demonstrated, the question of what is consecrated as canonical is a much more complex question – one equally as imbricated with historical readerships and publishing practices as it is with elite literary culture.

Whether their focus is on historical or contemporary literature, computational approaches have demonstrated the socially prescriptive nature of the canon. The complexities of the sociological forces at play, however, have prevented them from accounting for the specific logics through which any given text may be canonized. In other words, such analyses can describe the cultural forces that were at work in creating an extant canon, but the level of resolution through which these factors can be studied is not yet sufficient to explain the rationale behind the canonization of a single text. Some analyses, then, turn from the social features that Bourdieu outlined to the internal, formal, features of the texts themselves in the hopes of gaining a better purchase on the rationale of the canon. New modeling practices hold the promise of revealing the formal commonalities that are shared among canonical works. For example, researchers can begin with a preclassified training corpus (in this case, a group of canonical novels and a group of noncanonical novels), as well as a set of formal features (word frequencies, parts of speech), and train a supervised model to differentiate between the two groups. If such formal differences do exist, then the resulting model should not only be able to predict the membership of any given novel in either the canonical or noncanonical groups, but it would also be able to reveal the rationale behind its selections, thereby giving us an entirely new theoretical schema on which to base our understanding of the canon. In reality, while such analyses have been able to identify new aspects of canonicity, they have also been unable to offer a comprehensive supervised model of the category that can consistently and accurately divide the field between the canonical and noncanonical.[22] Not only are the underlying

---

fiction will register in the texts that are eventually canonized from the late twentieth and early twenty-first centuries. Alexander Manshel, "The Lag: Technology and Fiction in the Twentieth Century" *PMLA* 135.1, 2020: 40–58, 52–53.

[22] This depends, to some degree, on the operative definition of "canonical." Underwood uses word frequencies from a corpus of nineteenth- and twentieth-century poems to predict contemporaneous prestige (in his formulation, whether or not the poem or volume was reviewed in a periodical) The relatively high accuracy of the model, at 79.5%, hints at the possibility of such predictive formal

commonalities between canonical texts equally as difficult to parse as the social pressures above, but also given the geographic breadth and historical diversity of the canon, archival and canonical texts from a single period are more like each other than they are like the other members of their respective categories from different periods. Either the formal cohesion of the canon is weak enough that it still resists our best efforts, or, more likely, the social factors involved in canon production are diverse enough that there is not a single set of formal features shared by canonical texts across periods, geographies, or even genres.

3.3 The Persistence of the Canon

Despite our efforts to move outside of the canon, either by scaling up our analyses to the level of the archive or by studying the canon itself as a historical, social, or formal object, it, however unfortunately, remains a critical tool for computational literary criticism. While there are ongoing efforts in the field to reassess texts, genres, or even literatures that have been overlooked as part of the archive, most work still centers on canonical texts.[23] Even equipped with models that can reveal the underlying patterns in corpora of thousands of texts, our examples gravitate to familiar authors. For example, Jane Austen's *Pride and Prejudice* has been central both to computational literary analyses and the methods that enable them: Austen's text is a favorite among computational linguists seeking to train Natural Language Processing models.[24] What hold does the canon continue to have on the imagination of computational analyses of literature? Are these new methods simply being subsumed into the traditional modes of literary analysis, or is there something different at work in our continued interest in the canon?

We have seen how the canon became a prescriptive force, not only circumscribing the number and kind of works that we can read and study, but also by applying social and formal pressures on authors eager to ensure

---

features of canonicity; however, many books were reviewed and then subsequently forgotten. Underwood, *Distant Horizons*, 77–78.

[23] For example, Matt Erlin et al. move outside of the canon to explore the degree to which "minor" world literatures are more focused on issues of nationality in "Cultural Captials." Matthew Erlin, et. al., "Cultural Capitals: Modeling 'Minor' European Literature," *The Journal of Cultural Analytics* 2, 2021: 40–73.

[24] Bamman et al., for example, used *Pride and Prejudice* as one of the key sets of training data for the first version of their literature-minded NLP annotation software, BookNLP. David Bamman, Ted Underwood, and Noah A. Smith, "A Bayesian Mixed Effects Model of Literary Character," in *Proceedings of the 52nd Annual Meeting of the Association for Computational Linguistics* (Volume 1; Baltimore: Long Papers, 2014).

the success of their work. Coupled with its lack of diversity, the canon became a tool of exclusion, prefiguring the type of work that could be analyzed or even written. But because of its centrality to the field (a centrality that we can attribute to its coercive power), the canon also contains a common set of texts shared among scholars that can act as a shorthand for the broader horizons of the literary field. The titles and authors of the canon are a *lingua franca* among readers and scholars. The canon can therefore aid us in explaining the often incomprehensible patterns that we uncover through our computational work. This is not to suggest that we should treat the canon as representative of the literature of a given period: institutions, publishers, and readers alike used the canon to enforce exclusionary policies in literature and criticism. The continuing lack of authors of color, or women, in the canon is evidence of its ability to enforce the larger social norms of its current cultural milieu. Assuming, however, that we remain carefully attentive to who is excluded from the canon and why, we can still provisionally make use of it in order to situate ourselves, and our analyses, within a larger literary context. Where before the canon was a *prescriptive* technology, limiting the things that could be studied, interpreted, or written, it has become a *descriptive* technology, anchoring the vast literary field of the archive to a common set of texts that not only allows but encourages us to move beyond them.

This is a crucial function of the canon and one that has particular importance for the use of computational analysis in literature. For example, Figure 3.2 shows a graph of the topical relationships between nineteenth-century novels in the United Kingdom, Ireland, and the United States.[25] The image displays the result of a *topic model* – an unsupervised model that seeks to identify the "topics" (the repeated patterns of words that occur across multiple texts) that make up the system of similarities and differences among a corpus of texts.[26] Each text is assigned a number of topics, which, in

---

[25] The novels in this example were all drawn from ProQuest's Chadwyck-Healey collection, which contains 3,516 individual novels written in English and published in England, Scotland, Ireland, and the United States during the nineteenth century. The core of this collection is hypercanonical (canonicity was the criteria for the initial collection of ~500 novels); however, as the corpus has expanded, a much greater variety of authors and texts have been added. Given the numbers involved, it would be hard to suggest that there are 3,516 canonical novels from the nineteenth-century. It is, however, important to acknowledge that this collection echoes the biases of both the period it represents and the prescriptively canonical forces of collection criteria. While the corpus does contain many female authors (although still fewer in number than male authors), the overwhelming majority are white. Again, this reflects both the disparity in access to publishing and book markets by authors of color, and the pervasive forces of the canon.

[26] The topic model in this analysis was created with the open-source software Mallet. The topic model I discuss in this paper is a 100 topic model of the corpus, with common words (stopwords) excluded

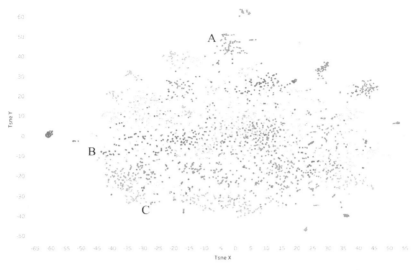

Figure 3.2 t-sne plot of 100 topic model of Chadwyck-Healey Nineteenth-Century Novel Corpus.

turn, are made up of words from the corpus organized so that the words with the highest probability of belonging to the topic have the most weight in defining that topic. The similarities and differences between texts can thereby be measured in terms of shared topics: two texts that share multiple topics are typically similar in their vocabulary and subjects, while two texts that do not share any topics in any meaningful way are understood as dissimilar across these dimensions. In the visualization, each dot represents a novel from the corpus, and its position within the various clusters can be interpreted from its location relative to the other points on the graph: two dots, or clusters, that are close together represent two texts that share a significant number of topics, while two dots that are on opposite sides of the graph indicate that they share few topics.[27] Each work is shaded for its most probable topic: dots of the same shade were judged by the model to share similar topics. From such a graph, then, we can see a large, although

---

from the analysis. Andrew Kachites McCallum, "MALLET: A Machine Learning for Language Toolkit" (www.cs.umass.edu/~mccallum/mallet; 2002).

[27] This visualization was produced with a t-stochastic neighbor embedding (t-sne) algorithm, which uses an iterative process to arrange the multidimensional similarities and differences within a two-dimensional space that preserves as much of the variation as possible.

not comprehensive, slice of the nineteenth-century Anglophone literary field, as represented by this corpus, as a single set of relationships.

The advantages of such a visualization are immediately apparent: rather than compare a handful of texts to each other, we can see how each text fits into a local neighborhood of similar texts, and, by extension, how that neighborhood fits into a larger picture of nineteenth-century literature (although one still bound by the limits of the corpus). The challenges of this method, however, are equally as apparent. Faced with a dizzying array of thousands of texts, abstracted into clusters of dots, how can we begin to make sense of their arrangement? The topics themselves can be useful in this process. The model not only estimates the topical composition of documents within the corpus (creating the feature set that can be used to plot them in relation to each other), it also estimates the lexical composition of each topic. By looking at the words that make up a shared topic on the graph, we can gain insight into that topic. For example, the texts in cluster A in Figure 3.1 all share a topic headed by the words ship, captain, sea, boat, men, deck, man, water, board, vessel. Although we may not know any of the individual novels in the cluster, we can intuit, based on these terms, that the texts may have something to do with the sea, a popular genre in nineteenth-century literature. Similarly, texts in cluster B share a topic with the words castle, count, father, baron, night, convent, lady, door, mind, chamber. While individually these are not quite as legible as the words belonging to the sea topic, taken together they suggest that the texts might be familiar to an expert reader who could recognize this cluster as one containing Gothic novels.

Although the apparatus of the topic model can help us interpret the meaning behind some of the clusters, others are far more resistant. For example, cluster C is formed from texts whose shared topic includes till, time, present, immediately, made, idea, long, thought, moment, person. These words include aspects of time and cognition, but within the novel, these are among the most prevalent concepts. Even a scholar familiar with the genres of nineteenth-century literature would encounter difficulty establishing an interpretable commonality from these words alone. Most topics, moreover, look much more like the one linking cluster C than the easily legible nouns that make up the Gothic and sea topics. Even with the topics in hand, the graph remains largely impenetrable to a casual reader.

If, however, we leverage the technology of the canon, the graph becomes much easier to navigate. Although the canon is in no way representative of the diversity and complexity of the archive, it remains embedded within

The Canon

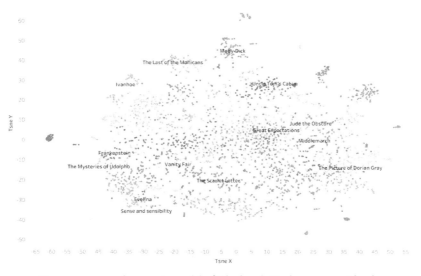

Figure 3.3 t-sne of 100 topic model of Chadwyck-Healey corpus with select canonical texts labeled.

the various genres and clusters that make up the theoretical literary field. By superimposing just a few hypercanonical titles as labels on the graph, Figure 3.2 immediately becomes more legible (see Figure 3.3). The placement, for example, of *Moby Dick* within the cluster we have already identified as sea fiction offers a shorthand for the same information as the topic words in a much more condensed form. In the same way, the Gothic nature of cluster B is revealed by the inclusion of *The Mysteries of Udolpho* and *Frankenstein*. Cluster C, whose topic words remained largely unidentifiable, now is labeled by both Frances Burney's *Evelina* and Jane Austen's *Sense and Sensibility*, identifying it as a cluster of social novels of manners. The history of research work and close reading of the canon can be translated into the nuanced complexities of the graph. From a quick glance, we can tell the difference between the cluster containing Scott's *Ivanhoe* and that with Cooper's *Last of the Mohicans*. Both mark clusters of historical novels, but the one containing *Ivanhoe* features texts set in the medieval period, primarily by British authors, and the one containing Cooper's text is primarily made up of frontier novels written by American authors. Even at a broad scale, the presence of many early nineteenth-century works on the left-hand side of the plot and later nineteenth-century novels on the right reveals the important structuring role that time plays in the topicality of the novel. This is the technology of the canon at work: it makes the graph readable to field experts in the nineteenth-century novel in a way that nothing else can. Far from being simply a set of prescriptive rules for which texts are worth studying (or writing), the canon here becomes a descriptive methodology, orienting us within the broader literary field so that we can move beyond the canonical to the archive with some knowledge of the areas that we should investigate.

Of course, such an approach is still not without substantial dangers. By letting the canon guide our understanding of the archive, we risk replicating its acknowledged biases within a much broader context. Dominated by authors who are white and male (particularly in the nineteenth century), including the canon in our analyses can have the effect of suppressing works by authors with different identity positions, either effacing them within their clusters in favor of labeling the canonical authors or directing our attention away from the parts of the graph where they cluster. If, however, we remain attentive to these biases, there are two advantages to using the canon for researchers interested in identifying noncanonical authors and texts. First, while the canon marks out known areas of the literary field, it also reveals, through its absence, entire neighborhoods that are left out of our account of nineteenth-century literature. For example, the two outlying clusters of texts on the top right of the graph remain unlabeled as they contain no canonical works. By remaining unmarked, they invite closer inspection: both have the potential to reveal aspects of nineteenth-century literature that are new to scholarship simply by virtue of their lack of canonical texts. Secondly, even areas of the graph identified by their canonical inclusions can serve as a crucial prompt for further investigation. The cluster near the top of the graph labeled with Stowe's *Uncle Tom's Cabin* contains a wealth of lesser-read abolition literature of which Stowe's novel is only the tip of the iceberg. By using the cluster's identification with Stowe's novel as a prompt for further investigation, we can direct our attention to a critical area of nineteenth-century writing whose members can now be easily recognized by their proximity to Stowe and to each other.[28] In both cases, we must treat the canon as the starting point of a deeper investigation rather than the endpoint of a shallow analysis.

---

[28] Such a move echoes the recent movement in literary study to use canonical works as a platform for introducing noncanonical authors, typically authors of color or women, to a broader audience. See David Damrosch, "World Literature in a Postcanonical, Hypercanonical Age," in Haun Saussy (Ed.), *Comparative Literature in an Age of Globalization* (Baltimore: Johns Hopkins University Press, 2006: 43–53).

3.4 Conclusion

This final turn, in which the canon is transformed from a prescriptive set of rules about what can be taught, studied, and written into a technology of description, is an effect of the ways in which computational criticism can harness the technology of the canon. The inclusion of computational analysis into literary studies has opened up the possibility for reforming the canon in a number of ways – from what it contains to how it can be used to assist us in understanding the larger archive that it represents. Although not without some significant risks, the use of the canon can help literary scholars to interpret the results of computational analyses and even prompt new investigations by identifying domains of writing that lie outside of the canon's limited representational capacity. At the same time, the interaction between these new methods of study and the canon has already led to significant changes in our understanding of the canon itself. If we continue to put pressure on the canon, and if we adopt it not as a comprehensive explanation but as a beginning point for further research and acknowledge and think through its biases, the canon has the potential to become an important tool of computational analysis. While research in DH has failed to make the canon obsolete, it nevertheless holds the potential to substantially transform both the canon itself and the ways in which we understand it as a historical and literary technology.

CHAPTER 4

Voice and Performance

Marit J. MacArthur and Lee M. Miller

4.1

All speech is performative (to some degree), and any text can be performed. Many have been, and we have digital access to numerous audio and video recordings of such performances. This fact of access, along with new tools for analyzing recordings, is driving fundamental changes in the interpretation and reception of literature.

Which aspects of speech capture our attention when we listen to – and study – these recordings? When speech happens so fast? When tone of voice matters as much, if not more than, semantics?

I'm not angry! The young woman insisted.[1]

When we listen to a speaker, we guess at the speaker's mood and identity, we weigh semantics against tone – "her tone of meaning ... without the words" in Robert Frost's phrasing[2] – and interpret accordingly. How far can we trust our ears? How do our brains process a voice? How do we filter a voice through our personal history of listening experiences, and our expectations for a particular style or genre of performance, however much we intend to listen with an open mind?

Scientific approaches, from phonetic linguistics and the neuroscience of speech perception, offer some answers but, as a rule, they have avoided the cultural, aesthetic, historical, and political questions that humanists like to ask. And they have rarely taken, as their object of study, something like a poetry recording. If they do, they aren't likely to bring knowledge of literary or performance history, or Erving Goffman's concept of frame

---

[1] This example of a phrase in which the speaker's intonation, volume, etc., may contradict the semantic meaning is taken from Jody Kreiman and Diane Sidtis, *Foundations of Voice Studies: An Interdisciplinary Approach to Voice Production and Perception* (New York: Wiley, 2011), 306.
[2] Robert Frost, "Never Again Would Birdsong Be the Same," in *Collected Poems, Prose and Plays* (New York: Library of America, 1995), 308.

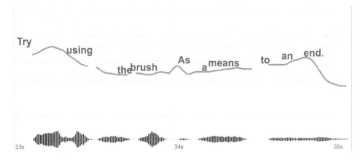

Figure 4.1 Pitch contour in Drift. John Ashbery reading "The Painter," ll. 9–10, 92nd St. Y, New York, NY, 1952.

analysis,[3] to bear on an individual performance of a literary or dramatic text for a particular audience. Not only that, the software tools used by linguists are not designed for the noisy, older recordings common in the audio archive of, for instance, poetry readings. Few humanities scholars, moreover, are trained in audio signal processing or linguistic analysis.

Sound studies in general, and voice studies in particular, do not dominate digital humanities scholarship and probably never will, amid our overwhelmingly visual and textual culture (no matter that we are living in the Golden Age of the Podcast). In practical terms, this means that the software tools available to digital humanists who want to study performative speech are less familiar and less developed for our uses. The user base is also much smaller than for text mining or network analysis. These are all challenges we have faced in choosing from the available tools for our research in voice studies, and in developing new digital tools. But the digital study of literary recordings has advanced in the last decade, and its future looks bright.

4.2

Before we discuss our research on poetry recordings, some theoretical framing of our approach to digital voice studies is in order. Close listening remains an inspiring concept that, through the influence of Charles Bernstein's *Close Listening: Poetry and the Performed Word*,[4] has generated

---

[3] Erving Goffman, *Forms of Talk* (Philadelphia: University of Pennsylvania Press, 1981).
[4] Charles Bernstein (Ed.), *Close Listening: Poetry and the Performed Word* (New York: Oxford University Press, 1998).

considerable scholarship on poetry recordings. Despite the fact that Bernstein cofounded and codirects one of the largest online archives of poetry audio, PennSound, close listening, when practiced in published scholarship, has often maintained distance from actual recordings of poetry reading. Cantankerous old-school scholars used to complain about theoretical readings of literature that fly "10,000 feet above the text." Much work in sound and voice studies is still, to our frustration, visual and textual: published in print form, without audio recordings embedded in the work, maintaining and enforcing a distance from the audio by failing to make interaction with it an essential part of scholarship about it.[5] When published electronically, work in sound studies does increasingly embed audio and allow for interaction with it,[6] but there is a long way to go to make this the norm in the field.

In *The Audible Past: Cultural Origins of Sound Reproduction*, Jonathan Sterne advances a persuasive critique of conventional assumptions about hearing versus vision, which he calls "the audiovisual litany," including the notions that "hearing tends toward subjectivity, vision tends toward objectivity" and "hearing is a temporal sense, vision is primarily a spatial sense."[7] Of course, vision is no more objective than hearing, and both hearing and vision function spatially and temporally. A child looking for her mother, for instance, can call out "Where are you?," and the mother can simply say "In here" because she knows the child can tell where in the house her voice is coming from. Nevertheless, a photograph stays still when we study it. And the words of a poem by Emily Dickinson, even as we recognize that it is not an authoritative version of itself, hold still on the page while we study them. A recording of the same words does not, nor do our impressions of what we heard. Perhaps we liked the performance, or we didn't, or we liked some things about it, and we try to explain why. Perhaps we mistrust ourselves, and feel we need to listen again.

Why does this matter to the study of poetry and poetry performance? Because poetry is an oral form, and scholarly work on poetry performance and other performative speech is still in its impressionistic infancy. When we listen to a voice, feeling is first (with nods to E.E. Cummings and

---

[5] While it isn't possible to embed audio files in this article, we do provide URL links in this article and stable links at zenodo.org via a related piece, "Slow Listening: Digital Tools for Voice Studies," *Digital Humanities Quarterly* 17.2, (2023). www.digitalhumanities.org/dhq/vol/17/2/000688/000688.html.

[6] See the publishing platform at Fulcrum.org, and the Soundbox project, developed at Duke University: http://soundboxproject.com.

[7] Jonathan Sterne, *The Audible Past: Cultural Origins of Sound Reproduction* (Durham: Duke University Press, 2003), 15.

Lauren Berlant), and our inchoate feelings about voices bear scrutiny. As we have written elsewhere,[8] the complexity of our perceptions of voices highlight the fact that poetry is, after all, stylized communication. It calls on deep, evolutionarily old neural pathways that support language as speech, but not language as written. Writing is a recent kludge, an add-on, not a deep, inevitable function of the human brain like speech – and even deeper and older are the vocal elements that create the tone of a voice.

What are often called paralinguistic elements of the voice – the pitch, the intensity (volume), the tempo, and so forth – are also pre-linguistic, preceding our knowledge and development of language, and triggering emotional responses that have little or nothing to do with the semantics of words. As such, the tone of voice exerts a direct emotional impact that is wordless, as when we hear a baby's cry, or when we hear a speaker's angry tone of voice conflicting with the semantic meaning of her words, as in the example cited earlier: *I'm not angry!* We cannot ignore these elements if we really want to understand the experience of poetry, or of any performative speech.

Studying performative speech should also mean listening to ourselves listening, like the proverbial recursively self-conscious ethnographer. In her recent book, *The Race of Sound: Listening, Timbre and Vocality in African American Music*, musicologist Nina Sun Eidsheim discusses the question we ask when we listen to a voice: "Who is this?"[9] We ask this question of an unknown caller when we answer the phone. Indeed, we ask it when we hear any disembodied voice, anywhere, as we try to pin down the speaker's identity – and thus radically reduce that voice's individuality to conform to or be rejected by our expectations. Eidsheim calls "Who is this?" *the acousmatic question*, after Pierre Schaeffer, who "derive[s] the ... root [of acousmatic] from an ancient Greek legend about Pythagoras's disciples listening to him through a curtain," and she argues that it relies on fundamental misunderstandings of the human voice and our own listening practices, particularly in regard to vocal timbre.[10]

Accordingly, she argues that the acousmatic question is impossible to answer and that it is, in fact, the wrong question to ask. She offers three

---

[8] Marit MacArthur, and Lee M. Miller, "After Scansion: Visualizing, Deforming and Listening to Poetic Prosody," in Stanford ARCADE Colloquy Series: Alternative Histories of Prosody (December 13, 2018). https://arcade.stanford.edu/content/after-scansion-visualizing-deforming-and-listening-poetic-prosody.
[9] Nina Eidsheim, *The Race of Sound: Listening, Timbre and Vocality in African American Music* (Durham: Duke University Press, 2019), 9.
[10] Eidsheim, *The Race of Sound*, 26.

correctives to it: (1) "Voice is not singular; it is collective"; (2) "Voice is not innate; it is cultural"; and (3) "Voice's source is not the singer; it is the listener."[11] That is, everyone is trained throughout their lives, whenever they vocalize and someone makes comments about their voice, to then adjust it to match the culture's expectations of how they should sound, in Foucauldian fashion – "as a condition of participation in a culture." Scholarship on poetry readings and performative speech too often tends toward confident judgments about performance styles, with little acknowledgment of the complexity of listening, or of the influence of the listener's own aesthetic, cultural, and ideological biases and preferences in regard to performance style.[12]

As Eidsheim paraphrases James Baldwin, one is always "hearing one's voice through the ears of others."[13] And we are always listening to others' voices through the ears of others, wondering "Would others agree with my judgments about this voice?" We listen to other voices through the ears of others; just as we never simply use our natural voices because there is no such thing as a natural voice unaffected by cultural training, nor do we listen in a way that is free of cultural training. There is no such thing as a neutral, singular, objective listener. What we can do, following Eidsheim, is acknowledge the role of the larger culture in cocreating our voices and our listening habits, the ways we speak and the ways we hear one another in different contexts.

What follows is a critical narrative of our developing method and tools, with some highlights of the resulting research and its implications for literary study in the digital age. Digital tools can enable humanist scholars to practice *slow listening* in the study of performative speech, to refine and test our impressionistic understandings of a given recording. Slow listening involves (1) repeated listening; (2) scrutiny of our listening habits, assumptions, implicit biases, and expectations, based on information about authorial identity, media formats, venues, and so forth; (3) sound

---

[11] Eidsheim, *The Race of Sound*, 9.
[12] See our discussion of Raphael Allison's *Bodies on the Line: Performance and the Sixties Poetry Reading* (2014) in Marit MacArthur, Georgia Zellou, and Lee M. Miller, "Beyond Poet Voice: Sampling the Performance Styles of 100 American Poets," *Journal of Cultural Analytics* (April 19, 2018). https://culturalanalytics.org/article/11039-beyond-poet-voice-sampling-the-non-performance-styles-of-100-american-poets. See also Leslie Wheeler, who asserts that contemporary American poets, as observed at the 2006 Associated Writers Conference, typically do not "display emotions at their readings but instead tend ... to manifest intellectual detachment, if not in the poem's words then through carefully neutral delivery" (Lesley Wheeler, *Voicing American Poetry: Sound and Performance from the 1920s to the Present* [Ithaca: Cornell University Press, 2008], 140.) This may sound intuitively accurate, but what does neutral delivery mean? Might the display of some emotions come across as vocal restraint? And so on.
[13] Eidsheim, *The Race of Sound*, 269.

visualization; and (4) quantification of sonic patterns in recorded voices as physical phenomena.

In this approach, we make an analogy to the practice among some musicians of slowing down a musical recording – say, a piano or saxophone piece with a very fast tempo – to understand and practice a technique, often by transcribing it. (Thanks to Alexander Ullman for alerting us to the term for this practice: *slowdown[ing]*.) This is not precisely what we are doing, but performative speech, like music, rewards scrutiny with insight. Such scrutiny can illuminate (there's the hegemony of the visual for you!) our listening habits and perceptions, and trends in particular genres of performative speech over time. This is particularly true when we find ourselves questioning our perceptions and impressions, and when sound visualizations and data about, say, pitch, timing and intensity (volume), derived from signal processing of a speech recording, do not neatly match up with our impressionistic perceptions of a recording or a body of recordings.

4.3

Our collaboration in testing and developing tools for digital voice studies emerged from an effort to visualize and quantify what is popularly known as "Poet Voice." We hoped to confirm whether it exists, and if it does, to capture it in the wild, and at a larger scale – that is, to find examples not only by listening with our own ears, but by searching for particular pitch and timing patterns in poetry recordings that we and other listeners might agree sound like Poet Voice.

I know it when I hear it, many listeners might say confidently about Poet Voice, echoing Supreme Court Justice Potter Stewart's insistence that, although he could not define hardcore pornography, he could recognize it on sight.[14] In the case of pornography or obscenity, we know that cultural background and personal experience influence what viewers find offensive. But what about a poetry performance style that no one admits to liking, which no one wants to admit to using, and yet seems to be so widely employed that any poetry lover – or NPR listener – can recognize it?

Early on, without any digital tools to augment perception, one of us defined Poet Voice, or monotonous incantation, as speech employing a repeated cadence within a narrow range of pitch, and imposing that

---

[14] *Jacobellis* v. *Ohio*, 378 US 184 (1964).

cadence on each line of a poem, regardless of the mood or semantics of the words spoken.[15] A few key points about speech perception: **pitch and timing** are fundamental to the perception of tone of voice. Is a speaker's voice especially high or low? How much do they vary their pitch, and for what apparent semantic or affective reasons? Do they speak quickly? Slowly? At a moderate, predictable pace? Do they pause often? Briefly? Long and awkwardly? Suspensefully? And so on.

We began our collaborative research with a few samples of Poet Voice by Natasha Trethewey[16] and Louise Glück[17] – two poets who are often thought to use it – and, by considering only measures in pitch and timing discussed herein, found other poets apparently using it as well in a study of sample recordings of 100 American poets.[18] These poets included Cecilia Llompart reading "Omens"[19] and Matthew Zapruder reading "When It's Sunny They Push the Button."[20] In the case of Llompart, we were not familiar with her work before we sampled it for the study. In the case of Zapruder, whom one of us counts as a pleasant acquaintance, we were a bit chagrined to learn that, by our measures, he seemed to use Poet Voice in this recording, and didn't quite want to believe it. Speaking impressionistically, Zapruder's reading voice has some affinities with the likes of singer Bill Callahan, whose voice music critic Amanda Petrusich describes as "a heavy baritone that is somehow both entirely affectless and drenched in feeling."[21] Why is it that we might appreciate low or flat affect in male poets or singers, perceived as such through a narrow pitch range, yet readily criticize examples of similar intonation patterns, when used by female poets, as Poet Voice?

Might this suggest an element of unreflective sexism, in our own and others' perceptions of Poet Voice? Are we more likely to use Poet Voice as a critical term about women poets? Do women poets use it more often than

---

[15] Marit MacArthur, "Monotony, the Churches of Poetry Reading, and Sound Studies," *PMLA* 131.1 (January 2016), 38–63.
[16] Natasha Trethewey, "Monument (Audio Only)," recorded 2006, *Poets.org,* streaming audio, https://poets.org/poem/monument-audio-only.
[17] See Louise Glück, "The Wild Iris (Audio Only)," recorded [no date], *Poets.org,* streaming audio, https://poets.org/poem/wild-iris-audio-only.
[18] See MacArthur, Zellou, and Miller, "Beyond Poet Voice."
[19] Cecilia Llompart, "Omens," recorded 2016, *Poets.org,* streaming audio, https://poets.org/poem/omens.
[20] Matthew Zapruder, "When It's Sunny They Push the Button," recorded 2009, Wavepoetry/Soundcloud, streaming audio. https://soundcloud.com/wavepoetry/when-its-sunny-they-push-the.
[21] Amanda Petrusich, "'Domestic Arts,' Rev. of Bill Callahan's Shepherd in a Sheepskin Vest," *The New Yorker* (June 2019), 88–89.

men? Or do we expect men but not women to sound low-affect, if that's what Poet Voice even is? Listeners might well disagree on whether a given sample of apparent Poet Voice displays intense yet restrained affect, or insincere affect, or simply low or no affect. Sentiment analysis, performed, for instance, by openSMILE (open-source Speech and Music Interpretation by Large-space Extraction), might seem to promise an answer, but AI is ultimately based on human perception of sentiment.[22] Perhaps we just don't want to believe that our friends might use Poet Voice, even if they don't use it all the time, because we are used to hearing it as a critical term, if not an insult? Interestingly, in a popular rant against Poet Voice, poet Rich Smith complains about contemporary poets using Poet Voice (including Glück, Trethewey, and Gregory Orr), but claims that "Poet Voice is an effective and affecting style" when practiced by, for instance, William Butler Yeats.[23] Allen Ginsberg also uses a very monotonous speaking style in "Howl,"[24] yet, as with Yeats,[25] the effect seems to us more sermonic than Poet Voice. Do we have trouble accepting women poets using a sermonic style?

To fully appreciate our analysis, we encourage readers to take a moment to listen to the samples of Glück, Trethewey, Llompart, Zapruder, Yeats, and Ginsberg – available via audio links noted on first reference in this article, and directly linked in a related piece in *Digital Humanities Quarterly*[26] – to discover whether they agree that the poets are using a similar performance style. For contrast to the earlier cited samples of Poet Voice, we also considered a sample from Rae Armantrout,[27] a conversational poet who uses comparatively contrastive pitch, less regular rhythm, and a wider pitch range.

In using digital tools to analyze and visualize acoustic signals, we treat neither the tools nor the resulting data as supremely objective and

---

[22] audEERING, *openSMILE* v 3.0 MacOS, Android. GitHub 2022. www.audeering.com/research/opensmile/.

[23] Rich Smith, "Stop Using 'Poet Voice,'" *CityArts*. Encore Media Group (July 2014). www.cityartsmagazine.com/stop-using-poet-voice/.

[24] Allen Ginsberg, "Howl," recorded 1956, KPFA Pacifica Studio, PennSound, streaming audio. https://writing.upenn.edu/pennsound/x/Ginsberg.php.

[25] William Butler Yeats, "The Lake Isle of Innisfree," recorded 1937, PennSound, streaming audio. https://media.sas.upenn.edu/pennsound/authors/Yeats/Yeats-WB_Lake-Isle-of-Innisfree_1937.mp3.

[26] Marit J. MacArthur and Lee M. Miller, "Slow Listening: Digital Tools for Voice Studies," *Digital Humanities Quarterly* 17.2 (2023). www.digitalhumanities.org/dhq/vol/17/2/000688/000688.html.

[27] Rae Armantrout, "Heart of It," recorded 1998, Double Happiness, New York, PennSound, streaming audio. https://media.sas.upenn.edu/pennsound/authors/Armantrout/Segue-98/Armantrout-Rae_16_Heart-Of-It_Segue-Series_Double-Happiness_11-14-98.mp3.`

corrective, but rather use them to complement and sometimes refine or check our own, inevitably idiosyncratic, aural perceptions and impressions. Beyond Poet Voice, we were, and are, interested in exploring trends and changes in performance styles over time, and changing tastes in performance styles, not only in poetry recordings but also in other genres of performative speech, such as political addresses, sermons, and radio broadcasts.

To visualize, interpret, describe, and quantify patterns in pitch and timing for our research on poetry performance, we needed one or more open-source, user-friendly tool that could easily and accurately visualize pitch contours, or intonation patterns, with the text aligned beneath the contours. We wanted these tools to be user friendly for the humanist: not requiring much, if any, programming skills to use. Yet, we also wanted to enable users to apply them with some basic knowledge about speech production and perception, and about signal processing. Additionally, we wanted these tools to provide numerical values measuring pitch (in hz) and timing (in seconds) for further analysis, and possibly other data about the voice, including intensity (volume), breathiness, nasality, and so on.

There is a long history to the hope that, by tracking pitch, we might measure patterns of expression. In 1853, Edouard-Leon Scott de Martinville began creating what he called phonautograms: "a visual record of the pitch of someone's voice, how loudly he spoke, and with what emphasis." He felt that this represented "our living speech," our essential character even, and he "regarded Edison's invention of the phonograph, in 1877, as pointless, because it reproduced sound instead of writing it."[28]

As we have written elsewhere,[29] pitch has long been neglected in the study of prosody in poetry, despite much interest in its role among prominent poetry scholars such as I. A. Richards, who wrote in 1926 that "more serious omission is the neglect by the majority of metrists of the pitch relations of syllables ... that a rise and fall of pitch is involved in metre and is as much a part of the poet's technique as any other feature of verse, as much under his control also, is indisputable."[30]

This neglect in 1926 was understandable due to the lack of tools for pitch analysis. Yet today there are many commercial software packages for

---

[28] Alec Wilkinson, "A Voice from the Past," *The New Yorker* (May 2014), www.newyorker.com/magazine/2014/05/19/a-voice-from-the-past.
[29] MacArthur and Miller, "After Scansion."
[30] I. A. Richards, *Principles of Literary Criticism* (New York: Psychology Press/Routledge Classics Series, 1926/2001), 128–129.

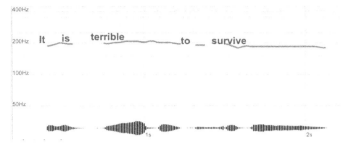

Figure 4.2 Pitch contour in Drift. Louise Glück reading "The Wild Iris" (1992).

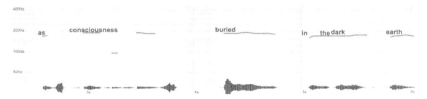

Figure 4.3 Pitch contour in Drift. Louise Glück reading "The Wild Iris" (1992).

tracking pitch and performing other speech analyses. For qualitative and quantitative analysis in linguistics, available tools for analyzing pitch and timing variables are called *pitch-trackers* and *forced aligners*. A pitch-tracker samples a speaker's pitch, called the fundamental frequency, or f0, at certain intervals (e.g. every 10 milliseconds). A forced aligner takes a transcript of a speech recording and aligns it with the recording, delivering timing information. Figures 4.2 and 4.3 show the pitch contour for Louise Glück reading a few lines from "The Wild Iris" visualized in Drift.[31] Figures 4.4 and 4.5 show word and pause length data in CSVs for the same recording from Gentle,[32] an open-source forced aligner that Drift works with, and the fundamental frequency for every ten milliseconds in hz for two words, "It is," from Drift.

The pitch contour of Glück's voice shows the fundamental frequency: the vibration rate of the vocal folds per second. (To better understand how

---

[31] Drift is an open-source pitch-tracker, including alignment of text with pitch contours, whose development we have supported. See Robert Ochshorn, Max Hawkins, Hannan Walliulah, and Sarah Yuniar, Drift v4.0, MacOS, GitHub, 2022, https://drift4.spokenweb.ca.

[32] Robert Ochshorn and Max Hawkins. Gentle v1.0, MacOS, GitHub, 2017, http://lowerquality.com/gentle/.

A	B	C	D	E
Transcript	Lexicon	Start Time	End Time	Pause Length
It	it	0.35	0.49	
is	is	0.49	0.67	0
terrible	terrible	0.67	1.23	9.992E-16
to	to	1.23	1.42	0
survive	survive	1.42	2.28	0
as	as	2.56	2.82	0.28
consciousnes	consciousnes	2.85	3.93	0.03
buried	buried	4.2	4.89	0.27
in	in	5	5.17	0.11
the	the	5.17	5.27	0
dark	dark	5.27	5.71	0
earth	earth	5.78	6.15	0.07

Figure 4.4 Word duration, pause start and end times, and pause length. Louise Glück reading "The Wild Iris" (1992).

Time	Pitch	Word	Phoneme
0.4	185.07	It	ih_B
0.41	185.07	It	ih_B
0.42	185.07	It	ih_B
0.43	190.49	It	ih_B
0.44	190.49	It	t_E
0.45	190.49	It	t_E
0.46	190.49	It	t_E
0.47	196.07	It	t_E
0.48	196.07	It	t_E
0.49	201.82	It	
0.5	201.82	is	ih_B
0.51	201.82	is	ih_B
0.52	201.82	is	ih_B
0.53	196.07	is	ih_B
0.54	196.07	is	ih_B
0.55	196.07	is	ih_B
0.56	196.07	is	ih_B

Figure 4.5 Fundamental frequency every 10 ms in hz. Louise Glück reading "The Wild Iris" (1992).

the human voice generates the fundamental frequency, we recommend watching a video of the vocal cords vibrating; there are many on YouTube.) Glück's voice maintains a narrow pitch range, starting off at 185 hz, rising to 207 with "terrible," and so on; the Gentle data also shows that Glück pauses for almost a third of a second after "survive" and "buried," lingering on the suffering involved.[33]

The harmonic frequencies of the fundamental frequencies – which follow the formula f1 = 2 × f0, f2 = 3 × f0, and so forth, as they resonate through the vocal tract – give a voice its unique timbre and distinguish different vowels regardless of the pitch.[34] The spectrograph shown in Figure 4.6 illustrates the fundamental frequency of Glück's voice, saying

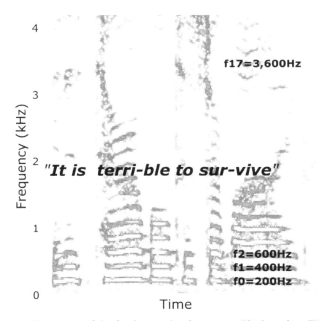

Figure 4.6 Harmonics of the fundamental in hz. Louise Glück reading "The Wild Iris" (1992).

---

[33] An average frequency for male voices is 125 Hz, and 225 Hz for female voices, though this can vary by language, region, and many other variables; by "male" and "female" in this context, we mean biological sex assigned at birth. See Carlos Gussenhoven, *The Phonology of Tone and Intonation* (New York: Cambridge University Press, 2004), 3.

[34] While linguists typically refer to the fundamental frequency as f0, there is some disagreement about whether to start counting at 0 or 1.

"It is terrible"; again, the fundamental frequency is around 200 hz; the second harmonic (f1) is at 400 hz, the third (f2) at 600 hz, and so on, all the way up the seventeenth harmonic at 3,600 hz.

As a rule, more expressive speakers use a relatively wider range of pitch. However, it is also important to note that "pitch perception is not linear"; an octave is a logarithmic relation, twice or half a given frequency.[35] For instance, an octave above 120 hz is 240 hz (a difference of 120 hz); an octave below is 60 hz (a difference of only 60 hz). This means we do not perceive women as having a wider vocal range than men, although they use a wider range of pitch as measured in hz. The same holds for notes on a piano: the octave between C3 and C4 uses a wider pitch range than between C2 and C3, but we hear it as the same interval. This makes interpreting linear graphs of pitch a challenge, and thus we have moved toward the more perceptually relevant logged pitch values, as with the pitch contour in Drift of Glück's voice cited earlier.

In analyzing the pitch of human speech, we could in theory base our approach on articulation, perception, or acoustics. Measuring articulation – especially, for pitch, the vibration of the vocal folds, but also the movements of the tongue, lips, jaw, and so forth – is not usually possible. As humanists, we often work from recorded speech audio, and/or lack the requisite instrumentation to objectively measure vocal fold vibration. Measuring perception would be impractical, even though pitch *is* perceptual. As phonologist Carlos Gussenhoven explains in *Phonology of Tone and Intonation*, "Unfortunately, listeners lack the appropriate conceptualizations and vocabulary to report their sensations, and are typically incapable of saying even whether a given pitch change represents a fall or rise." Since individual perception is largely a "black box" process, it may be impossible to say *why* different individuals report pitch differently, or *why* they make certain errors (e.g. whether pitch is rising or falling).[36]

Moreover, the fuzziness and subjectivity of perceived pitch can be an impediment to research because of individual and cultural differences. Our descriptions of pitch, not to mention what pitch range we feel is appropriate for a given speaker in a given context, also varies according to culture – for example, the same woman might speak at a higher average pitch and use a wider pitch range in her native Japanese than in American English. Dutch speakers describe pitch as "high" or "low," whereas the same vocal quality is characterized as "thin" or "thick" in Farsi.[37] And so on.

---

[35] Ilse Lehiste, *Suprasegmentals* (Cambridge, MA: MIT Press, 1970), 65.
[36] Gussenhoven, *Phonology of Tone and Intonation*, 6, 5.
[37] Sarah Dolscheid, Shakila Shayan, Asifa Majid, and Daniel Casasanto, "The Thickness of Musical Pitch: Psychophysical Evidence for Linguistic Relativity," *Psychological Science* 24.5 (2013), 613–621.

Consequently, the best and most established approach to pitch estimation relies on computational analysis of speech acoustics. Drift, the pitch-tracker we use, samples the fundamental frequency of a recorded voice every 10 milliseconds, and is designed to avoid errors as much as technically possible, even with noisy recordings.[38] We strongly advocate this approach because (1) the algorithms approximate perception, in that they rely on similar acoustical features as human listeners do when estimating pitch; (2) computational approaches developed, practiced, and vetted by a large number of expert researchers in acoustic analysis are comparatively objective in the sense of being unaffected by a researcher's personal biases about pitch, or by codifying biases explicitly; (3) the techniques can be used on arbitrarily large datasets with minimal additional resources; (4) they are usually reproducible, so results can be replicated within or across research groups, a matter of increasing importance in any field aspiring to rigorous empirical scholarship; and (5) the algorithms themselves can be shared openly, compared, and queried when they yield errors or fail, which they inevitably do sometimes with real data.

In parallel with using Gentle and Drift, we have also built an open-source free toolbox called Voxit,[39] to enable greater ease of data exploration and in-depth analysis (or manipulation) of vocal characteristics. To date, Voxit has been a sort of feature-rich, developmental sandbox for large-scale quantitative analysis to complement the simpler and user-friendly Drift and Gentle, which are best for qualitative, visual, and small-scale quantitative analysis. It allows us to consider other vocal prosodic measures that have perceptual importance for speaking style, context, and so on, such as pitch range (in octaves), pitch speed (in octaves per second), pitch acceleration (in octaves per second squared), and rhythmic complexity of pauses (roughly, the predictability of the rhythm). To better understand how the two approaches can work, and work together, we encourage users to read "Beyond Poet Voice: Sampling the (Non-)Performance Styles of 100

---

[38] We refer anyone interested in a technical discussion of pitch tracking and vocal analysis, and the specific software we have used and helped develop (Gentle, Drift and Voxit, cited earlier), to the related piece, "Slow Listening: Digital Tools for Voice Studies." Our research was supported in 2018 and 2019 by a National Endowment for the Humanities Digital Humanities Advancement grant project, "Tools for Listening to Text in Performance." The tools continue to be supported by a seven-year grant project, "The Spoken Web: Conceiving and creating a nationally networked archive of literary recordings for research and teaching," with funding through 2025 from the Social Sciences and Humanities Research Council (SSHRC) of Canada through the SpokenWeb project.

[39] Lee M. Miller, Voxit v1.0, MacOS and PC, GitHub, 2020, https://github.com/MillerLab-UCDavis/Voxit.

American Poets," which illustrates the applications of the Voxit toolbox; "After Scansion: Visualizing, Deforming and Listening to Poetic Prosody," which walks users through applications of Drift and Gentle with fifteen sample poetry recordings; and "101 Black Women Poets in Mainly White and Mainly Black Rooms," which applies our analytical approach and tools to 203 poetry recordings.[40]

As we have learned, collaboration is not just an ideal for this sort of research. It may be a prerequisite. Our own collaboration honors the fact of disciplinary expertise: the skill of Robert Ochshorn, developer of Gentle and Drift, and his knowledge about interface design, object-oriented programming, and audio signal processing are complemented by MacArthur's intimacy with poetry as an oral form and capacity to pose good questions about poetry performance and literary history, and by Miller's understanding of speech production and perception, audio signal processing, and quantitative analysis. The years of training and experience that each of us brings to collaboration cannot be underestimated. In digital humanities, of course, it is not unusual that the technical expertise is provided by men (Ochshorn and Miller), though they do not provide only that, nor that the female humanist in the collaboration (MacArthur) has acquired new technical knowledge in order to carry out the research.

In "An Information Science Question in DH Feminism," Tanya Clement writes:

> In digital humanities, the technology of mastering technology has been considered a productive means of combating what is considered the general "degree of ignorance about information technology and its critical relevance to humanities education and scholarship" [McGann 2005, 71] ... There has been much debate in DH about whether designing and building tools gives one an indispensable knowledge of its processes and whether or not women and people of color (and others) are precluded from these activities for a variety of very real and very situated reasons. In this sense, the rhetoric of "mastery" over technology can be intellectually prohibitive since it threatens an advancement of knowledge production from other perspectives.[41]

---

[40] MacArthur and Miller, "After Scansion"; MacArthur, Zellou, and Miller, "Beyond Poet Voice"; Marit MacArthur, Howard Rambsy, Xiaoliu Wu, Qin Ding, and Lee M. Miller, "101 Black Women Poets in Mainly White and Mainly Black Rooms." August 27, 2022, *Los Angeles Review of Books*. https://lareviewofbooks.org/article/101-black-women-poets-in-mainly-white-and-mainly-black-rooms/.

[41] Tanya Clement, "An Information Science Question in DH Feminism," *Digital Humanities Quarterly* 9.2 (2015). www.digitalhumanities.org/dhq/vol/9/2/000186/000186.html.

Voice and Performance 81

While we agree that, on the one hand, requiring – much less fetishizing – technical mastery in DH research can lead to the exclusion of valuable and novel perspectives, we also have practical objections to the requirement of technical mastery, or, to be more precise, the expectation that collaborative researchers will become masters of one another's disciplinary expertise. Beyond the political and economic problems with asking graduate students and scholars in the humanities, whatever their identity or cultural background, to master digital technologies or acquire advanced coding skills – which must inevitably take time away from the primary study of, for instance, literary history – it is practically inefficient *not* to collaborate across disciplines on the development of tools such as Gentle and Drift and Voxit, and in research applying them to literary recordings.

At the same time, it would be all too easy for a literary scholar with no background in linguistics, data visualization, or quantitative analysis to misunderstand or misuse Gentle and Drift and the data they provide. Thus, our approach in developing these tools, training users to apply them, and developing tutorials and documentation has been to emphasize ease of use and access to data while also educating users on the basics of speech production and perception, audio signal processing, and quantitative analysis.

The pitch contour in Drift at the outset of this article visualizes the intonation of John Ashbery's voice, in a 1952 reading of his sestina "The Painter" at the 92nd Street Y in New York.[42] The painter described in the poem wants to paint the sea; eventually he gives up and leave the canvas blank. The line shown in the pitch contour is the advice of the "people who lived in the buildings" to the painter: "Try using the brush / As a means to an end. Select, for a portrait, / Something less angry and large, and more subject / To a painter's moods."[43] "The Painter" almost too neatly thematizes Ashbery's poetic ambitions – not only to represent, but to enact the big impossible subject of consciousness unfolding in time, here symbolized by the changing face of the sea, as it constantly moves and shifts. This is not a bad figure for the experience of listening in real time. Sound, and the human voice in particular, elude our perceptual grasp as much as the sea slips through our fingers, to mix metaphors. But slow listening, with tools such as Gentle, Drift, and Voxit, can extend the possibilities for reading and listening to literature more slowly and thoughtfully.

---

[42] See Marit MacArthur, "John Ashbery's Reading Voice," *The Paris Review Online* (October 29, 2019). www.theparisreview.org/blog/2019/10/29/john-ashberys-reading-voice/.
[43] John Ashbery, "The Painter," in *The Mooring of Starting Out: The First Five Books of Poetry* (New York: Ecco Press, 1997), 40–41.

4.4

To return to Poet Voice, when we analyzed sample recordings of 100 American poets, we found that other pitch and timing patterns – in addition to a slow pace and narrow pitch range – are also important in the perception of this style of reading poetry.[44]

Voices that sound, at least to us, like they are using Poet Voice tend to read relatively slowly, with a predictable rhythm, in terms of tempo and pauses, compared to poets we might hear as more expressive or conversational, which tend to exhibit less predictable rhythmic patterns. They also tend to change pitch slowly, as well as using a relatively narrow range of pitch, again compared to more expressive or conversational speakers. Figures 4.7–4.9 show some of these variables for recordings of these poems in their entirety: Natasha Trethewey's "Monument," Louise Glück's "The Wild Iris," Cecilia Llompart's "Omens," Matthew Zapruder's "When It's Sunny They Push the Button," William Butler Yeats's "The Lake Isle of Innisfree," Rae Armantrout's "Heart of It," and the first 2:45 of Allen Ginsberg's "Howl." In this set, Armantrout and Ginsberg are the only poets who do not sound, to us, as if they are using Poet Voice.

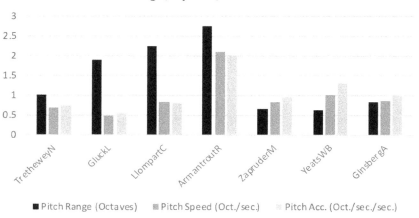

Figure 4.7 Pitch range, speed, and acceleration in sample recordings by seven poets.

---

[44] See MacArthur, Zellou, and Miller, "Beyond Poet Voice."

Voice and Performance 83

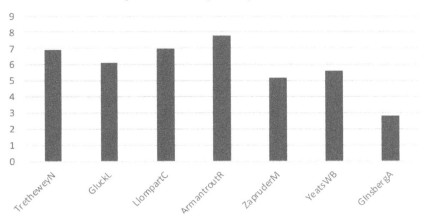

Figure 4.8 Rhythmic complexity of pauses in sample recordings by seven poets (a lower value means a more predictable rhythm).

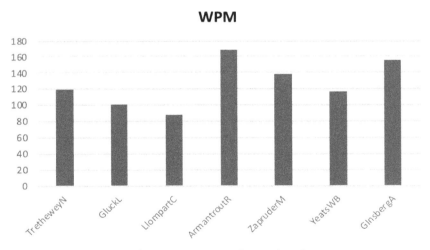

Figure 4.9 Words per minute in sample recordings by seven poets.

From these few samples, we conclude that, when some listeners hear poets read with even just one or two of these characteristics – slow pitch speed, slow pitch acceleration, narrow pitch range, low rhythmic complexity, and/or slow speaking rate – they hear Poet Voice.[45] In other words, if we don't particularly enjoy the way a poet reads, we listen selectively and use fuzzy inference, seeking at least one reason, or apparently objective vocal quality, to support or justify that displeasure. But Poet Voice is not a monolithic manner of reading poetry. It is collectively constructed, at least in part, in the ears of listeners, as Eidsheim might say.

What is potentially transformative about slow listening research, as our work on Poet Voice suggests, is that the tools provide a nuanced empirical and quantitative perspective on the intuitions we have developed as, respectively, a poetry scholar, poet, and amateur singer with years of experience attending poetry readings and listening to and teaching with poetry recordings (MacArthur), and a neuroscientist of speech perception and amateur musician with more than a casual interest in vocal performance, speech, and song (Miller). This perspective is not infallible, but it is a very useful complement. Both of us are fascinated by (and opinionated about!) what makes for compelling speech, in teaching, in academic lectures, and in US culture at large. Yet we recognize, and these tools have helped us appreciate further, that in testing and refining our own biases and intuitions in terms of speech perception, we need all the help we can get.

Today there is just no reason for scholars to rely solely on older methods of impressionistic generalizing about a performance, without incorporating audio clips, and without recourse to digital tools or computational analysis of the audio. In other words, if we're studying audio, let's help readers actually listen to it—slowly. This has been the typical approach of close listening. This is not to criticize Bernstein, who has encouraged our research every step of the way; indeed, his former student Chris Mustazza,

---

[45] The insight provided by such slow listening is a far cry, we hope, from the oversimplifications of snap judgments about voices, exemplified in the game of telephone that occurred when our research on our research briefly went viral. One of the last stops was aggregator Newser's URL description: www.newser.com/story/258972/science-proves-boring-poet-voice-exists.html, for a story by Arden Dier, "Poems May Be Great, But 'Poet Voice' Is the Pits," *Newser*, May 8, 2018. Newser misconstrued an article by Cara Giamo, who interviewed MacArthur, for *Atlas Obscura*, "An Algorithmic Investigation of the Highfalutin' 'Poet Voice,'" on May 1, 2018 (www.atlasobscura.com/articles/cultural-analysis-poet-voice), which in turn brought attention to but oversimplified some aspects of our longer article ("Beyond Poet Voice," published in *The Journal of Cultural Analytics*). The *Atlas Obscura* article took its title not from anything we wrote, but from a quotation from poet Rich Smith's popular polemic about Poet Voice (quoted earlier), which appeared in *City Arts*.

now codirector of PennSound, characterizes the new approaches we and others are using as "machine-aided close listening."[46] The rich intuitions of scholars form an excellent starting point for research on poetry performance, which can benefit enormously from these methods. Indeed, it was heartening when Bernstein wrote about our work in 2017 "You are certainly doing the work I had hoped might be done."[47]

And we are not alone. In recent years, a small but growing number of literary and humanities scholars have begun to apply digital sound studies tools to the analysis of speech recordings. Some of this work is led by other fields with more training in the human voice, media history, and/or digital tools. For instance, *The Oxford Handbook of Voice Studies*, which focuses mostly on voice in song, oral history, and political speech, includes pieces by comparative literature scholar Tom McEnaney on the timbre of NPR voices, Dan Wang on "cinematic speech," and Jennifer Fleeger on robot speech in film.[48] The *Journal of Cultural Analytics* and *Digital Humanities Quarterly* welcome work on the study of sound in literary recordings, though both are understandably dominated by computational analysis of text and image. *The Journal of Interdisciplinary Voice Studies*, founded in 2016, has also hosted some scholarship on literary recordings.

Two research projects, funded by the National Endowment for the Humanities, have particularly advanced digital approaches to the study of literary recordings. The first was HiPSTAS (High Performance Sound Technologies for Access and Performance),[49] directed by Tanya Clement from 2012 to 2017, followed by Tools for Listening to Text-in-Performance,[50] directed by MacArthur and Neil Verma from 2018 to 2019. A highlight of the research emerging from HiPSTAS shows that research on literary audio does not mean limiting the analysis to speech or text. Clement, in collaboration with Stephen McLaughlin, used machine learning to find, visualize, and measure instances of applause in the vast PennSound audio archive of poetry readings, "as a discovery point for

---

[46] Chris Mustazza, "Machine-Aided Close Listening: Prosthetic Synaesthesia and the 3D Phonotext," *Digital Humanities Quarterly* 12.3 (2018), www.digitalhumanities.org/dhq/vol/12/3/000397/000397.html.
[47] Charles Bernstein, email to Marit MacArthur, June 13, 2017.
[48] Nina Eidsheim and Katherine Meizel, eds., *The Oxford Handbook of Voice Studies* (New York: Oxford, 2019).
[49] Tanya Clement, *"White Paper: High Performance Sound Technologies for Access and Scholarship."* University of Texas, Austin, January 25, 2016, https://hipstas.org/2016/01/25/hipstas-neh-institute-final-white-paper/.
[50] Text In Performance: https://textinperformance.soc.northwestern.edu/.

considering how a poet interacts with an audience in a particular poetry culture."[51]

Tools for Listening to Text-in-Performance involved a team of twenty user-testers on Drift and Gentle from across the United States, representing the disciplines of communications, literary studies, film studies, performance studies, media and radio history, comparative literature, science and technology studies, theater, and media preservation, including media historian Patrick Feaster (cofounder of FirstSounds.org). Initial results illustrate the exploratory potential of this research for all sorts of speech in performance. Tools can be applied in new ways, and yield surprising insights, depending on the scholar's interests. For instance, Jacob Smith used it to explore vocal stereotypes in vaudeville recordings before cinema.[52] The PodcastRE archive and research group at the University of Wisconsin-Madison, also funded by a NEH grant, used Drift to consider "different genres of podcasts and radio ... to analyze potential differences in tone and delivery." They also used Gentle "to see if different genres of podcasts have different conventions of duration and WPM [words per minute, or speaking rate]."[53] In an application we did not anticipate, they also used Gentle's ability to create rough transcripts to search for particular vocabulary in podcasts, as a tool to explore which podcasts to study more closely. Adam Hammond and Jonathan Dick have used both tools to analyze different speakers' performances of T. S. Eliot's *The Waste Land*, finding that

> timing and pitch data from Gentle and Drift ... can reveal something to a human listener (very familiar with the recordings) that they didn't already know ... [O]ur example was Eliot's reading of *The Waste Land*, which the prosodic measures position as one of the most internally varied of the readings we've heard, despite most [human] listeners' sense that he's among the most monotonous.[54]

---

[51] Tanya Clement and Stephen McLaughlin, "Measured Applause: Toward a Cultural Analysis of Audio Collections," *Journal of Cultural Analytics*, May 24, 2016. https://culturalanalytics.org/article/11058-measured-applause-toward-a-cultural-analysis-of-audio-collections.

[52] Jacob Smith, "The Courtships of Ada and Len: Mediated Musicals and Vocal Caricature Before the Cinema," in *The Oxford Handbook of Cinematic Listening*, ed. Carlo Cenciarelli (New York: Oxford University Press, 2021), 68–89. https://doi.org/10.1093/oxfordhb/9780190853617.013.4.

[53] See Jacob Mertens, Eric Hoyt, and Jeremy Wade Morris, "Drifting Voices: Studying Emotion and Pitch in Podcasting with Digital Tools," in *Saving New Sounds: Podcast Preservation and Historiography*, ed. Jeremy Wade Morris and Eric Hoyt (Ann Arbor: University of Michigan Press, 2021), 154–178.

[54] Adam Hammond and Jonathan Dick, *"They Do the Police in Different Voices: Computational Analysis of Digitized Performances of T. S. Eliot's The Waste Land"* (presentation, Association for Computation in the Humanities, Pittsburgh, PA, June 2019).

Another signal of serious academic interest in the intersection of sound studies and literature is a special section of *PMLA* in March 2020 devoted to aurality and literacy, curated by Matthew Rubery, author of *The Untold Story of the Talking Book* (2016), and Christopher Cannon. Though it did not involve much direct application of digital tools to literary recordings, one particular piece in that issue articulates both the need for and some of the obstacles to this sort of research on literary audio. As James English argues in "Teaching the Novel in the Audio Age," the success of the audiobook, "the market for [which] is dominated by literary works, and specifically by novels, which comprise nearly three quarters of all sales," necessitates new pedagogies that incorporate audio versions of literary texts into teaching, as much as the texts themselves. For English, "[e]very vocal performance of a novel is an interpretation, a reading as well as a reading out loud" and "[n]one stands outside what [Matthew] Rubery calls the 'politics of narration.'" Thus concerns arise, with the voices of different characters and narrators, about vocal stereotyping according to race, gender, sexuality, (dis)ability, and so forth. Yet, he concludes that these concerns should not be a focus in teaching audio books:

> The novel is a dialogic form, and even those written in the first person (a distinct minority, by the reckoning of Ted Underwood and his collaborators) incorporate lots of reported speech. Except in the rare case of full-cast audio dramatizations, audiobooks require a vocal performer capable of rendering multiple voices. Conveying social distinctions between characters through faked accents and other tricks of the voice is a skill fundamental to performative work in the medium. Some degree of stereotyping is inescapable.
>
> The issues around vocal stereotyping can of course be embraced as teachable controversies. But that shifts time and attention away from other interpretative concerns, other teaching that we might have in mind for a class. It also requires of us some new proficiencies with classroom technology.[55]

Those proficiencies, for English, mostly come down to preparing audio segments from audiobooks for listening and discussion, accepting the time commitment required, being prepared for the technical difficulties that may arise for both students and instructors – and then "contend[ing] with our discipline's entrenched anti-audio prejudices."

---

[55] James English, "Teaching the Novel in the Audio Age," *PMLA* 135.2 (March 2020), 422–423, https://doi.org/10.1632/pmla.2020.135.2.419.

However, from our point of view, the real work begins when such conditions are already met – when we have easy access to audio and tools for analysis, and have committed to studying it. The methods of slow listening outlined herein, including attention to implicit bias, can be usefully applied to audiobooks and other intentionally performative recordings of literature – not to reduce the analysis to finger-pointing about vocal stereotypes, but to help students and instructors alike to think more deeply about the politics of performance and identity, so central to both the dramatization and interpretation of literature, and to the role of individual and collective listening experiences and habits.

Acknowledging in our pedagogy and scholarship that the aural/oral dimensions of literature are just as important as the text – and, indeed, directly affect the reception and interpretation of the text – extends a long and necessary movement away from New Critical assumptions about the text's primacy. While digital tools are not objective, they can augment our listening. Friedrich Kittler observed that "[t]he phonograph does not hear as [trained] ears [do] . . . it registers acoustic events as such." Media scholars have long argued that new technologies transform performance. In the development of Method Acting, for instance, Jacob Gallagher-Ross argues that "the unpredictable terrain revealed by the tape recorder's unbiased hearing" caused actors and playwrights to reconsider what they previously had considered "realistic" ways of writing and performing dialogue. The use of digital tools applied to literary audio, in both teaching and research, can direct an analogous paradigm shift in how we study literature in performance. Though digital analysis cannot eliminate bias, it can refine our listening experience, help reveal listening habits we might not know we had, and also, perhaps, give us new insights into the performative choices we ourselves make, as de facto performers of literature in the classroom.

CHAPTER 5

The Archive

Katherine Bode

In the extensive discussion of the role and impact of digital technologies in literary studies, far more attention is paid to the methods for analyzing and visualizing literary data than to the digital archives with which literary data are predominantly constructed. As Ryan Cordell says of digitized historical text collections, "in a very real sense we do not see the digital object, but instead a facsimile or worse, a surrogate of the print object from which it is derived."[1] When discussed, digital archives are often marveled at – or viewed suspiciously, or even denounced – for their size and the access to literary documents they enable. Yet such apparently divergent commentary often shares a perception of digital archives as entirely different from nondigital ones, and as passive: that is, as novel and enabling (or disabling) settings or backgrounds for research rather than as active shapers of literary knowledge. This understanding produces abstract critiques and leads foundational contributions to computation literary analysis to mistake events and trends in the histories of the literary data they investigate with events and trends in literary history. By contrast, an emerging group of media-specific explorations of digital archives recognizes their continuities with as well as departures from nondigital collections. They respond by adapting traditional philological or media archaeological approaches to explore the complex and interdependent relationship between literary knowledges, technologies, and infrastructures, and the multiple and substantial ways in which the histories and compositions of digital archives affect what can be known with them.

Most critics of digital approaches to literature, if they discuss digital archives at all, simply note the profound change they signify for literary studies. Yet there are exceptions: critics who express discomfort with – or object outright to – the size of digital archives as being in conflict with essential qualities of literary meaning and value. Referring to Franco Moretti's analysis of 7,000 British novel titles, Katie Trumpener associates

---

[1] Ryan Cordell, "'Q i-jtb the Raven': Taking Dirty OCR Seriously," *Book History* 20 (2017): 192.

his "large-scale database" with "processing literature by the ton" and argues that this approach "violate[s] the individuality" and aesthetic qualities of these literary works.[2] Haun Saussy aligns digital archives with contemporary flows of information and neoliberalism, presenting them as incompatible with literary value and meaning. For Saussy, the "world according to Google" offers a "flat" "intellectual landscape." Although that landscape is "vast (and getting vaster all the time, now that whole libraries are being scanned into its database)," it limits us to asking questions "of preestablished categories narrowing down to pre-established subcategories."[3] Saussy instead affirms close reading and print literature as "relic[s] of an earlier, data-poor, low-bandwidth era of communications" that "frustrate the economy of information in which more data and faster access is always better."[4] Whatever the negative consequences of the "Googlization" of knowledge,[5] as a critique of digital literary studies such arguments are blunted by a lack of specificity. Reducing digital archives to a question of scale, and, in Saussy's case, conflating all of them with Google, obscures their status as critical artifacts with distinct histories and contemporary manifestations as well as varied affordances, limitations, and implications.

These accounts might appear quite different from those of proponents of computational approaches, who advocate the capacity of digital archives to expand the scope and insights of literary studies. Yet many of the field's foundational arguments also approach digital archives as passive sites for – rather than active contributors to – literary knowledge. In *Distant Reading*, Moretti identifies "digital databases and automatic data retrieval" as the reason why the current quantitative turn in literary studies "is probably going to be different" from previous, short-lived ones.[6] He celebrates the scale and affordances of this shift, looking forward, just "a few years," to when "we'll be able to search just about all novels that have ever been published and look for patterns among billions of sentences."[7] Yet Moretti ultimately understands these "new, much larger archives" as static and complete: "there to stay" and

---

[2] Katie Trumpener, "Critical Response I. Paratext and Genre System: A Response to Franco Moretti," *Critical Inquiry* 36.1 (2009): 168, 171, 160.
[3] Haun Saussy, "Exquisite Cadavers Stitched from Fresh Nightmares: Of Memes, Hives, and Selfish Genes," in *Comparative Literature in an Age of Globalization*, ed. Haun Saussy (Baltimore: Johns Hopkins University Press, 2004), 33.
[4] Saussy, "Exquisite," 32, 33.
[5] Siva Vaidhyanathan, *The Googlization of Everything (And Why We Should Worry)* (Berkeley: University of California Press, 2011).
[6] Franco Moretti, *Distant Reading* (London: Verso, 2013), 212.   [7] Moretti, *Distant*, 181.

"important but not intellectually exciting."[8] In explaining his method of "macroanalysis," Matthew Jockers, similarly conceives of digital archives as precritical and defined by scale. For Jockers, digital archives allow "for investigations at a scale that reaches or approaches a point of being comprehensive. The once inaccessible 'population' has become accessible and is fast replacing the random and representative sample."[9] In calling for "the literary equivalent of open-pit mining or hydraulicking," he presents digital archives as akin to natural resources, awaiting "the trommel of computation to process, condense, deform and analyse the deep strata from which these nuggets were born" and "unearth, for the first time, what these corpora really contain."[10] Like the critics of computational approaches to literature discussed earlier, these proponents of such methods, in viewing digital archives as there-to-stay or ready-and-waiting, overlook their status as material practices and arrangements. Accordingly, they do not recognize the multiple people (librarians, scholars, information scientists, digitization laborers, managers) and technological systems (optical character recognition [OCR], search algorithms, database management systems) that variously sample, translate, and transform the documentary record. This understanding also minimizes the dynamism of digital archives: the multiple ways in which they change through time, whether as a result of new additions, technological developments, or institutional and economic shifts.

Most proponents of computational approaches to literature don't describe digital archives in these reductive terms. Yet, the same sense of them as precritical and passive is suggested by three features of that research. The most obvious is an emphasis on the number of documents analyzed, over or instead of information about the characteristics and potential limitations of the resulting dataset. As Cordell writes: "Descriptions of source data in computational text analysis [are] often ... accounts of the size of the data in works, in words, or in gigabytes, but offer little account of provenance."[11] While the number of documents investigated is material to such analyses and thus important to note, foregrounding scale implies that digital archives provide access to previously obscured knowledge, by virtue of their size alone.

---

[8] Franco Moretti, "The Bourgeois: Between History and Literature; Review and Interview by Karen Shook," *Times Higher Education*, June 27, 2013, www.timeshighereducation.co.uk/books/the-bourgeoisbetween-history-and-literature-by-franco-moretti/2005020.article.
[9] Matthew L. Jockers, *Macroanalysis: Digital Methods and Literary History* (Champaign : University of Illinois Press, 2013), 7.
[10] Jockers, *Macroanalysis*, 9, 10.   [11] Cordell, "'Q i-jtb," 215.

Two further, related tendencies in quantitative literary research are the treatment of data visualizations as primary and transparent objects of analysis coupled with the failure to publish the data on which visualizations are based. This approach to data visualization has been effectively critiqued,[12] and computational arguments are increasingly expected to be accompanied by data publication (due, in large part, to the influence of forums such as the *Journal of Cultural Analytics* and the *Post45 Data Collective*).[13] Yet even some very recent digital literary research persists in these tendencies. For instance, in "Popularity/Prestige," J. D. Porter bases his argument that the archive and canon are defined by fractal patterns largely on a single data visualization: "At the center of this argument is Figure 1. The rings represent 1,406 authors, their names assembled over the course of Pamphlet 11 from a disparate combination of sources."[14] In a footnote, Porter indicates that these sources include Eighteenth-Century Collections Online (ECCO), the Raven-Garside-Schöwerling bibliography, the Chadwyck-Healey Nineteenth-Century Fiction corpus, the Internet Archive of the University of Illinois, Stanford University's list of PhD exam texts, and a Stanford Literary Lab dataset of twentieth-century "best-of" lists. Although he states that the resulting dataset "is not designed to be comprehensive,"[15] in combining data from these diverse digital archives in a single visualization – with no mention or discussion of their diverse histories or contemporary manifestations, and without making either the originally derived datasets or the composite one available – Porter disregards what must inevitably be multiple differences in their histories, ontologies, definitions, and assumptions. He treats digital archives as if they make no difference, as if they simply provide access to – as opposed to mediating and fundamentally shaping – the documentary record.

Approaching digital archives as if they are concurrent with literature that existed and circulated in the past creates two main problems, the first being a tendency to ascribe unrealistic exactitude to the findings of computational literary research. Returning to the foundational computational arguments mentioned earlier, Moretti proposes that analyzing bibliographic data "can tell us when Britain produced one new novel per

---

[12] See, for example, Johanna Drucker, *Graphesis: Visual Forms of Knowledge Production* (Cambridge, MA: Harvard University Press, 2014).
[13] *Journal of Cultural Analytics*, https://culturalanalytics.org/; *Post45 Data Collective*, https://data.post45.org/.
[14] J. D. Porter, "Popularity/Prestige," *Stanford Literary Lab Pamphlet* 17 (September 2018): 9.
[15] Porter, "Popularity," 10.

month or week or day, or hour for that matter."[16] As well as obscuring differences between the multiple bibliographies of British novels he uses, this statement ignores the inevitable and variable gaps that exist in and between all bibliographies and the publishing contexts to which they refer. A second outcome of this understanding of digital archives as windows onto the past is the treatment of basic bibliographical information (such as dates of first book publication or authors' nationalities) as if it encapsulates the meanings of, and relationships between, literary works. Although datasets of this type can be – and have been – used effectively to address questions about trends in new literary production, they do not answer all questions about literary history. In particular, they do not account for the complex ways in which literary works exist and relate to one another in particular, historical contexts. Using this basic data model, Jockers conceives of literary history in a dematerialized and depopulated way, with literary works exerting influence equally and chronologically from their first date of book publication, regardless of actual conduits of influence (which require availability to readers who buy, borrow, and sometimes write literature). While Moretti explores the relationship of literary to social phenomena, his arguments often rely on interpreting information about publication as both expressive of and explicable in terms of reading habits. For instance, he attributes the common shape of the growth in novel publications, in five national contexts, to what we might call a law of novel reading, wherein readers at first gradually, then rapidly, increase the rate at which they consume such fiction. Whatever the feasibility of this argument, basing it on this dataset requires that only (and all) new titles by authors of particular nations are available to, and read by, only (and all) readers of those nations.[17]

Even researchers who recognize that digital archives are selections from and interpretations of the literature that circulated and was read in the past can be inattentive to the consequences of this situation for their arguments. For instance, Hoyt Long and Richard Jean So's transnational study of the diffusion of stream of consciousness narratives – from avant-garde to popular Anglophone works, and from Anglophone nations to Japanese literature – is based on a detailed model of thirteen formal features characteristic of such works (for instance, average sentence length, the proportion of sentences without verbs). Yet they train and test this detailed model on a dataset comprised of available digital copies of the 10,000 titles

[16] Franco Moretti, *Graphs, Maps, Trees: Abstract Models for Literary History* (London: Verso, 2005), 9.
[17] Moretti, *Graphs*, 5.

most commonly held by American libraries.[18] This dataset would seem bound to work against their comparative intention, given that American libraries are more likely to collect American (and, to a lesser extent, British) novels than works from other Anglophone nations.

In their study of gender trends in fiction, Ted Underwood, David Bamman, and Sabrina Lee take steps to counteract a potential bias in the main digital archives they use, noting that HathiTrust Digital Library and Chicago Text Lab corpus offer "evidence ... shaped by the book-buying practices of academic libraries (with additional contributions from the Library of Congress and the New York Public Library)."[19] Although brief, this comment is important, and it's worth pausing to consider its grounds and implications. Contrary to the common view of digital archives as radically different from nondigital ones, it acknowledges that the former are predominantly created with the latter, typically with the collections of major university libraries and cultural institutions. Even the largest digital libraries, such as Google Books and HathiTrust – although often understood as global literary records – privilege the holdings of a relatively small and select group of American and British university and major public libraries. Because these institutional collections are more likely to hold literature by canonical authors and from dominant literary traditions, without a radical interrogation of such frameworks in the process of digitization, these aesthetic and national selections – and the gendered, linguistic, racial, and other differences they involve – will be embedded into the infrastructure used for digital literary studies. In other words, Underwood, Bamman, and Lee's comment recognizes Élika Ortega's point that both "analog ... [and] digital archives impose forms of discursive authority, shape their reading and navigation, grant access to their holdings and obfuscate their deficiencies, give some rein to peruse them freely, but ultimately shape the knowledge that can be extracted out of them."[20]

In an effort to counteract potential biases in HathiTrust and the Chicago Text Lab corpus, these authors test their findings about gender trends against those in "a less academic sample drawn from *Publishers'*

---

[18] Hoyt Long and Richard Jean So, "Turbulent Flow: A Computational Model of World Literature," *Modern Language Quarterly* 77.3 (2016): 345–367.
[19] Ted Underwood, David Bamman, and Sabrina Lee, "The Transformation of Gender in English-Language-Fiction," *Journal of Cultural Analytics*, February 13 (2018): https://culturalanalytics.org/article/11035-the-transformation-of-gender-in-english-language-fiction.
[20] Élika Ortega, "Archives, Libraries, Collections, and Databases: A First Look at Digital Literary Studies in Mexico," *Hispanic Review* 86.2 (2018): 233.

Weekly." Based on the academically oriented datasets, they identify "an eye-opening, under-discussed decline in the proportion of fiction actually written by women, which drops by half (from roughly 50% of titles to roughly 25%) as we move from 1850 to 1950."[21] This decline in authorship – which continued until the 1970s, before a return to women writing around half of titles in the latter part of the twentieth century – was concurrent with a reduction in descriptions of women characters. The *Publishers' Weekly* data indicates somewhat higher rates of women authorship in the late nineteenth and early twentieth centuries, but shows an even more dramatic fall in women's writing and female characterization in the middle of the twentieth century. Underwood, Bamman, and Lee argue that this comparison confirms that the decline in women writers (and with them, women characters) was not "produced merely by library purchasing patterns" but "impact[ed] on every aspect of literary life."[22]

Digital literary studies requires more such attempts to recognize effects of the histories of digital archives and to accommodate them. But even these authors do not adequately account for these histories. For instance, while *Publishers' Weekly* incorporates multiple popular genres that do not feature in academic collections, it doesn't index the most prominent and prolific popular romance fiction publisher of twentieth century: Mills and Boon. The omission of popular romance fiction – a genre where women authors and characters predominate – stands in contrast to the inclusion of male-oriented genres, such as crime fiction and thrillers, in *Publishers' Weekly*'s lists, and suggests that the selection of fiction for this periodical was shaped (among other factors) by a gendered perception of women's writing as less worthy of attention than men's. Given that the heyday of popular romance fiction publishing was precisely in the period where Underwood, Bamman, and Lee identify declines in women authors and descriptions of women characters – that is, from the 1950s to the 1970s – it seems likely that at least some (perhaps a significant) part of these trends was due to the absence of popular romance fiction from both academic and popular datasets.

These studies by Long and So, and Underwood, Bamman, and Lee, carefully deploy computational methods to make nuanced arguments about the past. Their analyses – in attending to the influence, in literary history, of the nation state and gender, respectively – are also politically attuned in a way that is increasingly common, but still sorely needed in,

---

[21] Underwood, Bamman, and Lee, "Transformation," np.
[22] Underwood, Bamman, and Lee, "Transformation," np.

digital literary studies.[23] Long and So's work, in particular, contests the overwhelming Anglophone-orientation of digital literary studies. Although inherited from predigital literary studies and the analog archives that have long enabled the discipline, this orientation is amplified by multiple aspects of digitization, as discussed later in the chapter. Nevertheless, ensuring that these important political interventions investigate the dynamics of literature in the past, rather than the selection effects of digital archives in the past and present, requires researchers to prioritize investigation of the histories of these collections, including aspects of those histories that work against the very questions they seek to address.

A key reason for the lack of attention to such issues in digital literary studies is the long-standing abstraction of archives in literary studies generally. Over the last few decades, many commentators have identified an "archival turn" in the humanities and social sciences, characterized by a "move from archive-as-source to archive-as-subject," particularly of social and political power.[24] But if archives are a prominent topic in literary studies, they have long been a relatively abstract and abstracted one. In the 1970s and 1980s, for instance, Marxist, feminist, and postcolonial literary scholars encouraged and conducted archival research into previously neglected working-class, women, and nonwhite authors. But such research generally discussed inequalities in the contemporary canon by referring broadly to the operations of discourse and power in "the archive." Relatively rare were studies that explored specific people, practices, beliefs, and decisions responsible for the prominence or exclusion of particular authors or groups of authors.[25] Such abstraction continued in subsequent paradigms. The New Historicism considered particular documents in particular archives, but based its revisionist agenda on a metaphoric conception of archives as coincident with history, such as in Louis Montrose's insistence on the "textuality of history and the historicity of texts."[26] More recently, the post- or

---

[23] For recent exceptions see articles by Sarah Bruno and Jessica Marie Johnson; Long Le-Khac, Maria Antoniak, and Richard Jean So; Laura B. McGrath; Matt Warner; and others in the special double issue of *New Literary History* on "Culture. Theory. Data," ed. Ted Underwood, Laura McGrath, Richard Jean So, and Chat Wellmon, 53.4–54:1 (2022–2023).

[24] Ann Laura Stoler, "Colonial Archives and the Arts of Governance," *Archival Science* 2 (2002): 87–109, 87; for an overview of the "archival turn," see Marlene Manoff, "Theories of the Archive from Across the Disciplines," *portal: Libraries and the Academy* 4.1 (2004): 9–25.

[25] For an exception, see Jane Thompkins, *Sensational Designs: The Cultural Work of American Fiction, 1790–1860* (Oxford: Oxford University Press, 1985).

[26] Louis A. Montrose, "Professing the Renaissance: The Poetics and Politics of Culture," in *The New Historicism*, ed. H. Aram Veeser (London: Routledge, 1989), 20.

transnational turn in literary studies has been concurrent with a shift, in historical research, away from a notion of archives as "enclosed, static, and discrete" – typically limited to a particular time and place – to a global archive conceived as "the product of the constant circulation of information and the heavy intertextuality of many forms of knowledge."[27] This is no doubt a selective history; but it suffices to show that the abstract framing of archives did not begin with digital literary studies.

At the same time, multiple features of digital archives likely exacerbate the abstractions and inequalities of this inheritance. The false – though common – perception of digital text as immaterial resonates with and reinforces the view of digital archives as idealized (or demonized) sites of global information flow, rather than discrete collections with particular affordances and limitations. Ubiquitous computing, and its conception of "user-friendly" interfaces as invisible ones, compounds such idealization by "effac[ing] our capacity to read, let alone write, the interface" of digital archives, and "turning us into consumers rather than producers of content."[28] Relevance ranking algorithms for searching digital archives can reproduce and intensify existing hierarchies. For instance, when they return to the top of search results authors and titles that have been searched for most often in the past, these algorithms increase the likelihood that canonical authors and prominent national literatures will become better known, while lesser known authors and literatures are even less likely to be considered.

Methods of digitization and computational text analysis further increase the likelihood that historical inequalities embodied by nondigital archives will be reinforced in the creation of digital ones. The presence of Anglophone literatures in digital archives tends to be amplified by historical and contemporary factors that make certain texts more suitable for digitization than others; these range from historical unevenness in the distribution of printing technologies to the terms of contemporary copyright laws.[29] Methods used to create digitized text (such as OCR) were typically developed for use with English-language texts, with techniques for generating and investigating non-English language corpora, particularly for non-Latin scripts, lagging behind. The use of web scraping as the

---

[27] Tony Ballantyne, "Rereading the Archive and Opening up the Nation-State: Colonial Knowledge in South Asia (and Beyond)," in *After the Imperial Turn: Thinking with and through the Nation*, ed. Antoinette Burton (Durham: Durham University Press, 2003), 113.
[28] Lori Emerson, *Reading Writing Interfaces: From the Digital to the Bookbound* (Minneapolis: University of Minnesota Press, 2014), 2.
[29] Lara Putnam, "The Transnational and the Text-Searchable: Digitized Sources and the Shadows they Cast," *American Historical Review* 121.2 (2016): 389.

basis for creating large language models such as GPT-3 reinforces this English-language orientation of textual technologies. Finally, while the accessibility of digital archives is often asserted and celebrated, such access is not inevitable. Factors such as the growing costs of subscriptions to online repositories owned by companies like Elsevier or ProQuest, restrictions on computational access to the contents of such collections, or the capacity for companies such as Google to begin charging for the availability of their collections make it possible that digital archives could become (or may, for some disadvantaged groups, already be) less accessible than nondigital ones.

What, then, should be done about the abstraction of digital archives and the negative consequences of this approach for computational literary studies? Indeed, what can be done about the broader challenge of the corporate ownership and shaping of digitized records? For many years, textual scholars such as Jerome McGann have argued that the future of literary studies as a whole – and of digital literary studies in particular – relies on overcoming a long-standing division of the discipline: between literary criticism, on the one hand, and literary scholarship, on the other. Where literary critics interpret and evaluate literary works, literary scholars investigate and intervene in the forms in which those literary works are encountered, especially by analyzing their transmission in the past and present, and by creating technologies or infrastructures – such as bibliographies, scholarly editions, or translations – to ensure their survival and intelligibility in the present and into the future. As McGann argues, this division is also a hierarchy, with many literary critics regarding literary scholarship as "narrowly technical" even as their arguments are reliant upon and safeguarded by such practices, forms, and structures.[30]

Computational analyses of literature do not currently benefit from an equivalent scholarly infrastructure, though this is not because there are no digital scholarly projects. Indeed, much of the history of what was once called humanities computing is both philological and literary, from the concordances created by Josephine Miles, Father Roberto Busa, and others to the authorship attribution studies that dominated computational research in the humanities for many decades. Many early digital humanities projects were likewise (literary and) scholarly, including large-scale digital bibliographies such as the Women Writers Project

---

[30] Jerome McGann, *A New Republic of Letters: Memory and Scholarship in the Age of Digital Reproduction* (Chicago: University of Chicago Press, 2014), 2.

and The Orlando Project.[31] The richly annotated, single-author archives that were among the most high-profile early digital humanities projects – such as The Rosetti Archive,[32] The Whitman Archive,[33] and The William Blake Archive[34] – were also scholarly: explicitly modeled on, even as they aimed to extend, the tradition of the printed scholarly edition.

Beyond employing some of the archives and methods devised by these early, scholarly enterprises, current computational approaches to literature have relatively little to do with the scholarly tradition in humanities computing and digital humanities. Both Roopika Risam and Shawna Ross have commented on this disconnection, though they make contrasting claims as to its cause and effects. For Risam, the scholarly tradition in digital humanities is marked by its focus on "the writing of dead white men . . . individuals unlikely to be forgotten in Anglophone literary history even if these projects did not exist."[35] By contrast, as Moretti originally articulated the method of "distant reading," computational literary studies aims to progress an anticanonical form of literary history, devoted to analyzing the "lost 99 percent of the archive" that had been excluded from literary history.[36] Ross reverses this situation, describing recent computational approaches to literature as having a masculinist orientation that has overwhelmed an earlier, feminist scholarly tradition. In Ross's words, the focus in digital literary studies on "the coolness of one's tool, the bigness of one's data, or the goodness of one's intentions" both obscures the history of and contributes to a current decline in politically oriented digital humanities projects, such as the bibliographies of women's writing mentioned earlier.[37]

More pragmatically, the disconnection between scholarly practices in digital humanities and computational literary inquiries should be understood in the context of a shift in digitization, in the early 2000s, from a predominantly researcher-driven activity to an institutional and, more particularly, a corporate one. From this time, on a far larger scale than for

---

[31] Women Writers Project. Northeastern University, 1999–2016: www.wwp.northeastern.edu; Susan Brown, Patricia Clements, and Isobel Grundy, directors. The Orlando Project: Feminist Literary History and Digital Humanities, www.artsrn.ualberta.ca/orlando/.
[32] Jerome McGann, ed. Rosetti Archive: www.rossettiarchive.org/.
[33] Ed Folsom and Kenneth M. Price, eds., The Walt Whitman Archive, http://whitmanarchive.org/.
[34] Morris Eaves, Robert Essick, and Joseph Viscomi, eds., William Blake Archive, www.blakearchive.org/.
[35] Roopika Risam, "Beyond the Margins: Intersectionality and the Digital Humanities," *Digital Humanities Quarterly* 9.2 (2015): www.digitalhumanities.org/dhq/vol/9/2/000208/000208.html.
[36] Moretti, *Graphs*, 77.
[37] Shawna Ross, "Toward a Feminist Modernist Digital Humanities," *Feminist Modernist Studies* 1.3 (2018): 212.

earlier, scholar-led digitization projects, research institutions, and multinational corporations undertook mass-digitization programs that, in some cases, now encompass millions of texts across multiple centuries, geographic regions, genres, and publishing formats. Archives created with mass-digitization – including Google Books, the Internet Archive, HathiTrust, and Europeana, as well as nationally oriented ones such as the Bibliotheque nationale de France's Gallica, the British Library's British Newspaper Archive, and the National Library of Australia's Trove database – are the ones that computational studies of literature predominantly investigate. Especially in the case of corporate entities, these digitization projects often have a vested interest in concealing information about the construction of these archives, whether to protect the value of proprietary data and infrastructure or to maintain the perceived value of their product by concealing problems with the collections.

For this reason, and due to the sheer scale of these mass-digitized collections, developing scholarly frameworks for them is no small task. Nevertheless, and though in its early stages, a growing body of work is beginning to devise practices, systems, and concepts to understand and manage the complexities of extensive digital archives. This scholarly work goes by various names, including "digital bibliography,"[38] "philology in a new key,"[39] "comparative textual media studies,"[40] "digital book history,"[41] "critical infrastructure studies,"[42] and "forensic materiality."[43] What these approaches share is a media-specific orientation and a conception of literary works and collections as vast and distributed assemblages of material documents, rather than as collections of single texts, stable in place and time.

In recent years, a growing number of scholars have thus insisted on the "pressing if rarely acknowledged need to know more about the digital infrastructure underpinning humanistic scholarship."[44] To progress this

---

[38] Cordell, "Q i-jtb." [39] McGann, *New*.
[40] N. Katherine Hayles and Jessica Pressman, eds., *Comparative Textual Media: Transforming the Humanities in the Postprint Era* (Minneapolis: University of Minnesota Press, 2013).
[41] Liza Daly and Whitney Trettien, *Digital Book History*, https://digitalbookhistory.com/.
[42] Alan Liu, "Toward Critical infrastructure Studies: Digital Humanities, New Media Studies, and the Culture of Infrastructure," University of Connecticut. February 23, 2017, https://alanyliu.org/citation/toward-critical-infrastructure-studies-digital-humanities-new-media-studies-and-the-culture-of-infrastructure-u-connecticut/.
[43] Matthew Kirschenbaum, *Mechanisms: New Media and the Forensic Imagination* (Cambridge, MA: MIT Press, 2008).
[44] Christopher N. Warren, "Historiography's Two Voices: Data Infrastructure and History at Scale in the *Oxford Dictionary of National Biography* (*ODNB*)," *Journal of Cultural Analytics*, November 22, 2018: https://culturalanalytics.org/article/11031-historiography-s-two-voices-data-infrastructure-and-history-at-scale-in-the-oxford-dictionary-of-national-biography-odnb.

aim, researchers have offered detailed histories of particular mass-digitized collections – including Gale's *British Nineteenth-Century Newspapers*,[45] ProQuest's *Early English Books Online*,[46] and the *Oxford Dictionary of National Biography*[47] – exploring the conditions of their construction, the assumptions those collections manifest, and how all of this affects the types of arguments that digital archives can support. As one of the earliest, and most theoretically rich, of these studies, Bonnie Mak's analysis of *EEBO* has been especially influential. Mak develops an archaeological approach to exploring "the ontological rift that separates digitizations from their exemplars" by investigating how past medial, institutional, and historical phenomena are "embedded as part of what might be called the infrastructure of the EBBO database."[48] Her analysis – which ranges across phenomena as various as the *English Short Title Catalogue*, the nature of manual text transcription, and funding decisions to support the postwar growth of American universities – explores both the historical construction of EBBO and the digitized documents themselves as "palimpsests" that transmit "clues in [their] very instantiation about the circumstances of [their] manufacture and dissemination." Confirming the difficulty of analyzing proprietary mass-digitized collections, Mak also demonstrates how corporations deliberately efface such "intersecting temporalities" in an effort to present their digital archives as authoritative and comprehensive.[49]

Other researchers use philological frameworks, developed by the field of textual studies, to inquire into mass-digitized archives. Cordell makes a compelling case that a media-specific bibliographical approach could be used to account for mass-digitized collections as new forms of evidence in literary studies. Like Mak, he maintains that digitized historical texts and text collections bear traces of the documents from which they are derived and of the "series of decisions over decades or centuries about documentation, collection, access, and preservation."[50] Rejecting myths of mass-digitized collections as surrogates or replacements for print documents, Cordell uses a bibliographical framework to reconceive them as "assemblages of new editions, subsidiary editions, and impressions of historical sources," arguing that all of "these various parts

---

[45] Paul Fyfe, "An Archaeology of Victorian Newspapers," *Victorian Periodicals Review* 49.4 (2016): 546–577.
[46] Bonnie Mak, "Archaeology of a Digitization," *Journal of the Association for Information Science and Technology* 65.8 (2014): 1515–1526.
[47] Warren, "Historiography's," np. [48] Mak, "Archaeology," 1515, 1517.
[49] Mak, "Archaeology," 1515. [50] Cordell, "Q i-jtb," 213.

require sustained bibliographical analysis and description."[51] Cordell also outlines a program for describing these assemblages that attends to previous documentary remediations as well as to documentary metadata and multiple paratexts (including grant applications, digitization guidelines, and project reports). In so doing, Cordell suggests that a bibliographical approach might qualify the claims we make in analyzing existing, mass-digitized collections and "instruct our efforts to build more democratic and representative historical collections."[52]

This effort to construct a scholar-built interpretation of a mass-digitized collections was one I undertook, with bibliographer Carol Hetherington, in our work to uncover fiction in the pages of the National Library of Australia's digitized historical newspapers.[53] Rather than simply using the resulting data for literary history, I drew on the theoretical frameworks and technological systems of scholarly editing to frame a selection of approximately 10,000 extended works of nineteenth-century fiction as a "scholarly edition of a literary system."[54] While many people perceive scholarly editions as especially accurate or detailed versions of literary works, in contemporary textual studies they are understood as "embodied arguments about textual transmission"[55] or "hypothetical platform[s]" for historical inquiry.[56] In other words, scholarly editions present an argument – historical, critical, and technical – about the nature of the literary work, made with reference to the remaining (often contested and conflicting) documentary evidence of it.

Building on this practice, my scholarly edition of a literary system sought to investigate and model relationships between literary texts that were published, circulated, and read – and thereby accrued meaning – in a specific historical context, with respect to the practices and processes by which these texts were transmitted through collections over time so as to be accessible in the present. In both cases, this argument about the constitution of the literary work or system is pursued through a critical apparatus (exploring the history of transmission by which the available documentary evidence is constituted) and a curated text or dataset (offering – in a stable,

---

[51] Cordell, "Q i-jtb," 190.   [52] Cordell, "Q i-jtb," 213.
[53] Katherine Bode and Carol Hetherington, eds., *To Be Continued: The Australian Newspaper Fiction Database*, http:cdhrdatasys.anu.edu.au/tobecontinued/.
[54] Katherine Bode, *A World of Fiction: Digital Collections and the Future of Literary History* (Ann Arbor: University of Michigan Press, 2018).
[55] Paul Eggert, *Securing the Past: Conservation in Art, Architecture and Literature* (Cambridge: Cambridge University Press, 2009), 177.
[56] Jerome McGann, "From Text to Work: Digital Tools and the Emergence of the Social Text," in *The Book as Artefact: Text and Border*, ed. Anne Hansen, Roger Lüdeke, Wolfgang Streit, Cristina Urchueguía, and Peter Shillingsburg (Amsterdam: Rodopi, 2005), 203.

historicized, and publicly accessible form – the outcomes of that enquiry for use by any literary scholar, whether for computational or noncomputational research). Although I still find the scholarly edition useful as a framework for interpreting and managing the documentary uncertainty of digital archives, increasingly I wonder if the "heavy ... associations" it carries "from print culture" might ultimately constrain rather than enable such investigation.[57] Where print conventions maintain the ontological priority of literary works, digital archives might be more usefully conceived in ways that question and explore a broader range of connections between literary documents, the platforms on which they are made available, and the organizations that create those platforms.

Another way in which the philological tradition is increasingly brought into conversation with digital archives and literary data is by reference to translation. Andrew Piper, for instance, links linguistic translation with the transition from words to numbers in digital literary studies.[58] Jenny Bergenmar and Katarina Leppanen extend this idea, noting in reference to digitization that any translation is inevitably an adaptation to culture and language.[59] As these researchers imply, potential exists for nonmechanistic understandings of translation to inform conceptions of digital archives, such that digitization (like translation) is seen as "something more than delivery systems for content ... as having a weight and resistance of its own" that is intrinsic to the production of meaning.[60] Digital literary scholars might build, for instance, on the work of translation scholar Lawrence Venuti, who conceives of translation as having ethical and political effects as well as a performative relationship to the receiving culture and its dominant resources and ideologies.[61]

In this vein, Venuti's focus on the centrality and invisibility of translators to translation might suggests ways of extending analyses of labor and power relations in digitization and digital archives,[62] while at the same time

---

[57] Kenneth M. Price, "Edition, Project, Database, Archive, Thematic Research Collection: What's in a Name?" *Digital Humanities Quarterly* 3.3 (2009): www.digitalhumanities.org/dhq/vol/3/3/000053/000053.html.
[58] Andrew Piper, *Enumerations: Data and Literary Study* (Chicago: University of Chicago Press, 2018), x.
[59] Jenny Bergenmar and Katarina Leppanen, "Gender and Vernaculars in Digital Humanities and World Literature," *NORA – Nordic Journal of Feminist and Gender Research* 25.4 (2017): 239.
[60] Saussy, "Exquisite," 14.
[61] See Lawrence Venuti, *The Translator's Invisibility: A History of Translation* (London: Routledge, 1995) and Lawrence Venuti, *Scandals of Translation: Towards an Ethics of Difference* (London: Routledge, 1998).
[62] Warren, "Historiography's," np.

signaling critically productive tensions between translation and digitization. While the figure of the translator is an established one in literary culture, we might ask "Who is the digitizer?" Is it the librarian or literary scholar who selects the text; the worker (often a woman and/or a person of color) who conducts the scanning; or even the OCR algorithm that transforms image into text? What might be the political – and epistemological – implications of this role of digitizer being distributed among different actors, human and nonhuman? As Brad Pasanek writes, "The digital humanities presides over decades of transcriptive labor and hours of web design, not to mention server maintenance" that we have barely begun to mention, let alone to theorize. Could ethical frameworks in translation theory offer a way to recognize, and respond effectively to, the "alienations" held within the "ready-to-hand corpora" of the large digital collections that digital literary studies relies upon?[63] Alternatively, we might adapt Venuti's terminology for translation to imagine what it would mean to create a "foreignizing" digitization: one that remains legible while disclosing the digitized status of the text and the digitizer's intervention. Current scholarly approaches challenge the idea that digitization reproduces the same text and offer nuanced insights into the conditions of production of digital archives. Translation theory might help in understanding the nature of that difference, including with respect to always emergent conditions of reception.

An important figure and guide to the future of digital archival scholarship is Matthew Kirschenbaum, who emphasizes the ways in which digital technologies are transforming archives and archiving. While analog archives are written and read by humans, the "vast majority of what is written to and from computational storage media is neither written by or intended to be read by humans."[64] This shift has two main effects: first, digital archives are inscribed with the "instrument of [their] own composition"; second, they are dispersed "across multiple supports," ranging from "various kinds of magnetic media" to server farms. Where the first effect provides valuable clues to media archaeologists or philologists in exploring the materiality of archived documents, the second requires new forms of material analysis that recognize and respond to the fact that a digital archive is rarely, if ever, "an explicitly differentiated

---

[63] Brad Pasanek, "Extreme Reading: Josephine Miles and the Scale of the Pre-Digital Digital Humanities," *ELH* 86.2 (2019): 372.
[64] Matthew Kirschenbaum, "The Transformissions of the Archive: Literary Remainders in the Late Age of Print," Rosenbach Lectures 2016. University of Pennsylvania, www.youtube.com/watch?v=6TuA4dkRegQ.

object that is the essential unit of attention."[65] Archivists have been known to object to the term "digital archives," arguing that it collapses an important distinction between collections (which gather disparate material based on subject or interest) and archives (which preserve the original contexts of creation and use of documents with respect to the records' provenance). Kirschenbaum's point is not only that this distinction is lost in digital contexts, but that archives and archiving have come to mean the opposite of what they once did: to connote duplication rather than uniqueness.

Alan Liu is another influential theorist of digital archives and their consequences for literary studies. For Liu, digital infrastructure is now so fundamental to culture that cultural studies has become a mode of critical infrastructure studies.[66] Imagining the future of digital scholarship in this context, Liu proposes that digital archives be constructed in "N + 1" dimensions, by which he means that they should embrace the generative messiness that results from collisions of "different media classificatory ontologies, and social-political-economic values."[67] In *Friending the Past*, Liu widens the scope of this argument to propose that the "*rhetoric-representation-interpretation*" regime in which the humanities have always operated is now destabilized by an emerging regime of "*communication-information-media*."[68] The earlier one is "shaky and hollowed out," unable to make sense of fundamental forms of contemporary knowledge, including data and technology as well as models and infrastructure. But the emerging regime is "infirm in its own way,"[69] with the abstractness and opacity of its terms serving, at best, to "mask the fact that we don't really know what we are doing, let alone signifying, when speaking and listening, writing and reading, and so on."[70] In effect, digital literary studies faces the challenge of devising practices, forms, and structures with which to interpret and manage the digital archives that are increasingly central to our discipline, at the same time as we struggle to understand – or even find the words for – the nature and effects of what we are trying to build.

Since the time of Liu's writing, this challenge has been compounded by the accelerated development of large language models, which use

---

[65] Kirschenbaum, "Transformissions," np.   [66] Liu, "Toward," np.
[67] Alan Liu, "N + 1: A Plea for Cross-domain Data in the Digital Humanities," in *Digital Humanities: The Expanded Field*, ed. Lauren F. Klein and Matthew K. Gold (Minneapolis: University of Minnesota Press, 2016), np.
[68] Alan Liu, *Friending the Past: The Sense of History in the Digital Age* (Chicago: University of Chicago Press, 2018), 3 (emphasis original).
[69] Liu, *Friending*, 4.   [70] Liu, *Friending*, 5.

(large parts of) the Internet for training data and as the archival basis for the text they generate. Though the rate of change makes the challenge more acute, the technologies with which we interpret the documentary record have always shaped that record, not just our capacity to know it. In this respect, literary studies has substantial experience and a tradition to draw on in exploring the ways our practices transform what they interpret, and our infrastructures constitute the conditions of our discipline and the literary knowledge it enables.

Moretti's confident assertion that "one thing's for sure, digitization has completely changed the literary archive" is thus true, but not in the way that Moretti seems to mean it.[71] Digital archives do not provide instant and unmediated access to the literary past. To the contrary, documents in digital archives, and their organization, are largely inherited from analog archives and from the views of the world, and of literary value, that such infrastructure embodies. Approaching digital archives as interpretive constructs, and understanding their continuities with and departures from analog archives, requires interventions that are simultaneously technological and theoretical; or perhaps, more particularly, it requires us to recognize that our concepts have always been bound to and formed by technologies, and vice versa. While the requirements of this task are still emerging, useful ways forward are suggested by media-specific approaches, whether these look to philological frameworks in the history of the discipline or to archaeological perspectives in media studies. These fields help in understanding the complex ways in which the findings of digital literary studies are entangled with its knowledge infrastructures. As a consequence, they provide a basis for approaches that are critically attuned to the implications, for their arguments, of the digital archives on which their analyses are based, as well as the digital methods employed in such investigations.

---

[71] Franco Moretti, "Patterns and Interpretation," *Stanford Literary Lab Pamphlet* 15 (September 2017): 1.

CHAPTER 6

Editions

Claire Battershill, Anna Mukamal, and Helen Southworth[1]

A quarter-century ago, book historian Robert Darnton lamented the constraints of the printed, codex-bound scholarly work:

> Any historian who has done long stints of research knows the frustration over his or her inability to communicate the fathomlessness of the archives and the bottomlessness of the past. If only my reader could have a look inside this box, you say to yourself, at all the letters in it, not just the lines from the letter I am quoting. If only I could follow that trail in my text just as I pursued it through the dossiers, when I felt free to take detours leading away from my main subject. If only I could show how themes criss-cross outside my narrative and extend beyond the boundaries of my book.[2]

His proposed solution in 1999: to structure a radically new kind of book, one "in layers arranged like a pyramid," with the top layer constituting "a concise account of the subject, available perhaps in paperback" and subsequent layers containing "expanded versions of different aspects of the argument, not arranged sequentially as in a narrative, but rather as self contained units that feed into the topmost storey." Both the book's form and function would be altered; as Darnton presages, "the appropriate texts could be printed and bound according to the specifications of the reader. The computer screen would be used for sampling and searching, whereas concentrated, long-term reading would take place by means of the conventional codex."[3] In Darnton's vision of scholarly reading, the computer screen functions as a mediating device with the capacity to create unique codices tailored to the particular uses and needs of each reader – the book could assume different forms for different functions. The major features of digital editions have to some extent been informed by spatial and textual

---

[1] The authors would like to acknowledge the generous feedback and advice of Alice Staveley, Nicola Wilson, Cillian O'Hogan, and Elaine Treharne.
[2] Robert Darnton, "The New Age of the Book," *The New York Review of Books*, March 18, 1999, 75.
[3] Ibid., 76–77.

imaginaries that sought to enhance the reading and research experience as the material and cost constraints of print editions ceased to matter. That is, the kinds of imagined navigability Darnton envisages are precisely those that give rise to large-scale digitization projects that make historical records available to a broader public.

The landscape of critical and scholarly editions today includes print editions, their digital equivalents, and new innovations in digital editing that attempt to fulfill Darnton's vision of a form that captures more of the "fathomlessness of the archive" and the "bottomlessness of the past" that researchers encounter and seek to harness for readers. Assuming, like Darnton, that the digital scholarly edition should and does try to do something different in *kind* from the print edition, we outline here the affordances offered by digital editions, tracing the debates, metaphors, and considerations that arise when scholarly print editions go digital. We divide these affordances into three basic categories: networked structure and the "capacious edition," interactive reading, and multimodality. We explore some of the experiments in alternative textual forms that have arisen from the technological shift away from the printed codex as the material symbol for, and primary vehicle of, knowledge production. Throughout the chapter we consider the various types of digital editions (from app to XML) and examine what they do. We focus here less on mass-market e-books and other commercially produced digital texts (which have their own attendant contemporary debates and critical literatures) and more on editions with an academic dimension, whether for classroom teaching, research, or generally interested readers looking for some annotation or augmentation of a historical text. As Katherine Bode notes in her chapter in this volume on digital archives, scholarly editions have a specific function; unlike digitized texts without scholarly apparatus, they "present an argument – historical, critical, and technical – about the nature of the literary work, made with reference to the remaining (often contested and conflicting) documentary evidence of it."[4] Sometimes they also present digitized mediations of that documentary evidence for the user's perusal, thereby offering some glimpse, however partial, into the "bottomless" archive that Darnton imagined.

In 2002, the Modern Language Association (MLA) Ad Hoc Committee on Scholarly Publishing noted that print scholarly editions were increasingly time- and cost-intensive to produce[5] – a development arising from,

---

[4] See Bode, Chapter 5 in this volume, p. 102.
[5] MLA Ad Hoc Committee on Scholarly Publishing, "The Future of Scholarly Publishing," *Profession* (2002): 172-186. www.mla.org/content/download/3014/80410/schlrlypblshng.pdf.

and also prompting, increased experimentation in the domain of digital editions. As digital editions, and the broader category of digital projects, became increasingly institutionalized in university contexts, Peter Robinson argued in 2013 that "the time for theoretical innocence is over."[6] But, as Matthew James Driscoll and Elena Pierazzo have more recently put it, we have yet to decide if digital scholarly editing is "a new discipline or a new methodology" – as they aptly ask, "Are we simply putting 'old wine in new bottles,' or are we doing something which has never been done – indeed, never been doable – before?"[7] When considering the thorny semantic territory involved in actually characterizing a digital edition, it becomes immediately clear that old definitions drawn from print materialities will no longer suffice. The bibliographic definition of a specific "edition" as a book printed substantially from the same set of type (a new edition, therefore, requiring a resetting of the type) must change with more iterative digital editions that don't require lead sorts to be locked into place and altered only rarely at significant cost. If a new edition no longer requires a new setting of type, and indeed can be subject to continual revision, then what exactly *is* it?[8] The very idea requires that we detach our understanding of textual choices from their material instantiations in type and attach them instead to a new digital materiality and to the implicit arguments that such new forms make about the text and its associated historical record. What is lost in the world of scholarly editing when we move away from the codex? How do we take into account what Jerome McGann calls our "textual inheritance" in building an "understanding [of] the structure of digital space"?[9] As reading continues to be diversified, still including the traditional print codex, but also increasingly various kinds of screens, what role does the digital edition play in scholarly reading today?

Amy A. Earhart's important study *Traces of the Old, Uses of the New: The Emergence of Digital Literary Studies* explores how "the centrality of the digital edition form that emerged from . . . textual studies transferred key ideas regarding texts and materiality to digital literary studies." Putting the scholarly print edition at the vanguard of the digital print revolution, she argues along with Kenneth Price that digital editions, as "some of the most

---

[6] Peter Robinson, "Towards a Theory of Digital Editions," *The Journal of the European Society for Textual Scholarship* 10 (2013): 106.
[7] James Driscoll and Elena Pierazzo, "Introduction: Old Wine in New Bottles?," in *Digital Scholarly Editing: Theories and Practices*, ed. Matthew Driscoll and Elena Pierazzo (Cambridge: Open Book Publishers, 2016), 3.
[8] On the problems and opportunities of versioning, see Paul A. Broyles, "Digital Editions and Version Numbering," *Digital Humanities Quarterly* 14.2 (2020).
[9] Jerome McGann, *Radiant Textuality* (New York: Palgrave Macmillan, 2001), xi.

visible early digital projects in digital literary studies," are "the primary form of the first generation of the field."[10] As digital editions become increasingly prevalent, the MLA has made efforts toward standardizing the field, emphasizing five key tenets of digital editorial practice: accuracy, adequacy, appropriateness, consistency, and explicitness, this latter term meaning that the editorial policy is explicitly stated and followed.[11] These principles, which indicate an interest in preserving scholarly standards as material forms become more divergent, affirm Bode's contention that articulating the edition's approach or argument must remain one of its central definitional features.

6.1 Networked Structures and the Capacious Edition

The major features of digital editions have to some extent been informed by spatial and textual imaginaries that sought to enhance the reading and research experience. The goal of McGann's groundbreaking Rossetti Archive (completed in 2008), for example, was to include "high-quality digital images of *every* surviving documentary state of [Dante Gabriel Rossetti]'s works: all the manuscripts, proofs, and original editions, as well as the drawings, paintings, and designs of various kinds, including his collaborative photographic and craft works ... transacted with a substantial body of editorial commentary, notes, and glosses."[12] McGann opted for the term "archive" over "edition" for Rossetti, as have many subsequent digital humanists, presumably to reflect the more capacious nature of his project, which is "built so that its contents and its webwork of relations (both internal and external) can be indefinitely expanded and developed."[13] In the digital editorial context, the terms of "archive" and

---

[10] Amy A. Earhart, *Traces of the Old, Uses of the New: The Emergence of Digital Literary Studies* (Ann Arbor: University of Michigan Press, 2015), 11. See also Kenneth Price, "Edition, Project, Database, Archive, Thematic Research Collection: What's in a Name?" *Digital Humanities Quarterly* 3.3 (2009).

[11] Earhart classifies "digital editions" as those projects which meet the MLA Guidelines for Editors of Scholarly Editions. This set of comprehensive guidelines, last updated in 2022, is an invaluable rubric for editors of scholarly editions, including an annotated bibliography of key works in the theory of textual editing. The guidelines, not specific to digital editions, are nonetheless helpful efforts towards standardization in the field. See MLA Committee on Scholarly Editions, "Guidelines for Editors of Scholarly Editions," Modern Language Association, revised 4 May 2022, www.mla.org/Resources/Guidelines-and-Data/Reports-and-Professional-Guidelines/Guidelines-for-Editors-of-Scholarly-Editions. For the MLA's specific response to the digital context, see MLA Committee on Scholarly Editions, "MLA Statement on the Scholarly Edition in the Digital Age," Modern Language Association, May 2016, www.mla.org/content/download/52050/1810116/rptCSE16.pdf.

[12] "The Complete Writings and Pictures of Dante Gabriel Rossetti: A Hypermedia Archive," Rossetti Archive. www.rossettiarchive.org/. Emphasis added.

[13] McGann, *Radiant Textuality*, 69.

"edition" have complex and unsettled relations to their paper or material equivalents. Paul Eggert proposes visualizing "a horizontal slider or scroll bar running from archive at the left to edition at the right," or, we might propose, a spectrum of engagement between text and extratextual materials.

Darnton's envisioning of the future of the book, or the book of the future, echoes McGann's 1995 assertion that editing texts for the digital medium would follow the "rationale of hypertext,"[14] which is to say pieces of text connected to one another by hyperlink.[15] McGann emphasizes that "unlike a traditional book or set of books, the hypertext need never be 'complete' – though, of course, one could choose to shut the structure down if one wanted, close its covers as it were." In other words, the hypertext's "specific material design" is infinitely iterable: "unlike a traditional edition, a hypertext is not organized to focus attention on one particular text or set of texts . . . but rather to disperse attention as broadly as possible."[16] This breadth allows editors to forego some of the selection and curation that concerns Darnton when he worries about the reader missing out on the "boundlessness" of the past. If you can include more documents in a linked, networked structure, then the reader can open at least some of the metaphorical archival boxes that have led an editor to their conclusions. Indeed, the possibility of including much more material is precisely what sometimes turns "editions" into "archives" – a slippage that would seem unimaginable in the material codex world.

With this capacious notion of digital scholarship, Darnton and McGann revised the long-dominant Greg-Bowers approach to textual criticism, which attempted to reconstruct a single ideal text among various instantiations of it by hewing as closely as possible to the author's intentions.[17] For instance, in *Critique of Modern Textual Criticism* (1983) and *The Textual*

---

[14] The OED defines hypertext as "Text which does not form a single sequence or which can be read in various orders; *spec.* text and graphics (usually in machine-readable form) which are interconnected in such a way that a reader of the material (as displayed at a computer terminal, etc.) can discontinue reading one document at certain points in order to consult other related matter." "hypertext, n.," *OED Online*, Oxford University Press. www.oed.com/view/Entry/243461?redirectedFrom=hypertext#eid.

[15] Manuel Portela, "Designing Digital Editions," *MatLit: Materialidades de Literatura* 4.2 (2016): 284. McGann's "The Rationale of HyperText" – evoking W. W. Greg's 1950 essay "The Rationale Of Copy-Text" – argues that the digital fundamentally changes the way scholars would conceive (and thereby present in an edition) different instantiations of a text. See Jerome McGann, "The Rationale of HyperText," *Text* 9 (1996), 31–32. The article was later reprinted in McGann's *Radiant Textuality*. Sherman Young, in turn, characterizes hypertext as "the creation of non-linear texts that allow users to create their own pathways through a narrative of sorts." See Sherman Young, *The Book Is Dead (Long Live the Book)* (Sydney: University of New South Wales Press, 2007), 129–130.

[16] McGann, *Radiant Textuality*, 71.

[17] Fredson Bowers, and then G. Thomas Tanselle, expanded W. W. Greg's "rationale of copy-text" after Greg's death in 1959.

Condition (1991), McGann advocated what has been called "social text criticism," arguing that "the meaning [of a text] is in the use, and textuality is a social condition of various times, places, and persons."[18] Precisely because "no single editorial procedure – no single 'text' of a particular work – can be imagined or hypothesized as the 'correct' one," an edition should aim to expose readers to the text's socially embedded process of becoming rather than (in his view erroneously) attempting to reconstruct an "ideal text" that never actually existed.[19] George Bornstein develops this idea in *Material Modernism: The Politics of the Page* (2001), reinscribing McGann's concept of "bibliographic code" as "the semantic features of [a text's] material instantiations," in addition to its linguistic code, or its words.[20] With this formulation, McGann et al. point us toward an expansive, proliferative concept of the edition that, though still involving and including books, goes beyond the edges and borders of the physical book.

All of the strands of textual studies that emphasize a user-oriented, multivalent, profligate textual future thus seem to anticipate the "network culture" in which present-day scholarly editions are embedded.[21] They also variously maintain, augment, and reimagine the spatial and epistemological structures of the codex even as they imagine its future. For instance, as Earhart notes, many early digital editions sought to "reinstate lost sections of the text," therefore counterintuitively using technology to heighten attention to the material manuscript.[22] The adjectival descriptor "digital" does not, then, necessarily dispense with the printed page as we've known it, since the text technology of the codex made the printed book the dominant mode of reading. Instead, the codex-bound history of textual criticism and scholarship undergirds our contemporary definitions of, and experiments in creating, digital editions.

These imaginings of new textual forms drawn from the disciplines of editorial and textual studies anticipate some ways in which the spatial metaphors that characterize our thinking about the edition begin to loosen

---

[18] Jerome McGann, *Critique of Modern Textual Criticism* (Princeton: Princeton University Press, 1983); *The Textual Condition* (Princeton: Princeton University Press, 1991), 16.
[19] Ibid., 62.
[20] Ibid., 100. George Bornstein, *Material Modernism: The Politics of the Page* (Cambridge: Cambridge University Press, 2001), 6.
[21] "Network culture" is a term for contemporary information structures and cultures theorized and defined by Tiziana Terranova as "a cultural formation ... that seems to be characterized by an unprecedented abundance of informational output and by an acceleration of informational dynamics." See Tiziana Terranova, *Network Culture: Politics for the Information Age* (London: Pluto Press, 2004), 1.
[22] Earhart, *Traces of the Old, Uses of the New*, 25.

themselves from the codex in acts of metaphorical and literal unbinding. Despite the proliferation of new editions and scholarship on scholarly editing practice since Darnton, McGann, and Bornstein's visions of the 1990s and early 2000s, the ideal or even usual form of digital scholarly editions is still far from settled. The expansive spatial metaphors that augment and provide alternatives to the codex – including hypertexts, networks, and webs – highlight the potential of digital editions to be more inclusive, more capacious, and just generally *more* than print editions. Indeed, in 1996, textual studies scholar Peter Shillingsburg presciently argued that the electronic scholarly edition provides us with more efficient ways to do what a print concordance or edition allowed, including searching for all occurrences of a phrase or featuring "reproductions of the covers and title pages and facsimiles of the texts or significant historical editions; ... [or] having the explanatory notes with the possibility of several levels of detail and pictures to go with descriptions of buildings, people, and places."[23] Anticipating Darnton, he continues,

> This vision of an electronic scholarly edition begins to resemble an archive of editions with annotations, contexts, parallel texts, reviews, criticism, and bibliographies of reception and criticism. In effect it is really a library we want ... In the digital age, if we follow out, in the way of texts broadly defined, what we would like to have as scholars and critics and readers of literary texts, we very soon outstrip the printed scholarly edition's capacity to accommodate us.[24]

This idea of an "archive of editions" emphasizes multiplicity and invites a comparative approach: between versions of a text (as in the now-completed Modernist Versions Project, which presents several different variants of *Ulysses*), or, indeed, between types of media. Capacious, or inclusive, digital editions feature nonlinear "browsing paths"[25] more prominently than the print edition, partly out of necessity: the more material included, the more complex its navigation becomes. Nowhere is this more evident than in The William Blake Archive, which, as Adam Hammond notes, presents Blake's idiosyncratic production method "in fully embodied form"[26] by presenting many and often every single surviving

---

[23] Shillingsburg's essay, "Textual Criticism and the Text Encoding Initiative," is collected in Richard J. Finneran, ed., *The Literary Text in the Digital Age* (Ann Arbor: University of Michigan Press, 1996), 24.
[24] Ibid., 24–25.
[25] Patrick Sahle, "What Is a Scholarly Digital Edition?," in *Digital Scholarly Editing – Theories and Practices*, ed. Matthew Driscoll and Elena Pierazzo (Cambridge: Open Book Publishers, 2016), 27.
[26] Adam Hammond, *Literature in the Digital Age* (Cambridge: Cambridge University Press, 2016), 62.

copy of Blake's hand-colored works. As Hammond argues, the Blake Archive is an instance in which the digital archive goes beyond not only what a printed facsimile could offer, but also what a single scholar could hope to do with the original plates in physical libraries, since the resource allows the viewer to compare the plates directly to each other even if they are housed in different locations. Similarly, for example, the Samuel Beckett Digital Manuscript Project aggregates digital facsimiles held in different libraries to better enable genetic criticism.[27] This increased "browsability" in turn grants the reader more agency, a feature Shillingsburg had already noted in 1996: "Display of materials to a passive observer is not the only goal. The user must have liberty to navigate the materials at will."[28] As Patrick Sahle argues, this reconceptualization of the phenomenological experience of the book iteratively modifies our understanding of the book (or object of knowledge) itself: "A printed edition can be read. A digital edition is more like a workplace or a laboratory where the user is invited to work with the texts and documents more actively."[29] This is not to say that the printed codex does not (always) already possess interactive, laboratory-like qualities (as the existence, practice, and habit of marginalia shows, an idea we'll return to in the following section when we discuss features of interactivity). But the digital has the capacity to amplify these qualities, thereby facilitating an expansion of reading pathways and meaning-making experiences.

Of course, from one perspective this proliferation of pathways undermines what we might call a manageable reading experience, connoting both linearity and a sense of how one is intended to engage. Acknowledging that there are different kinds of readers *and* different ways in which a given reader engages with a text (depending on their varying purposes), Krista Stinne Greve Rasmussen theorizes a distinction between *readers* and *users* of a text. We hasten to emphasize that, in our view, the reader-as-reader and reader-as-user are not necessarily (maybe even ever) different people; rather, the practice of reading to read and reading to use or study are not only co-occurring, but also mutually reinforcing. The concept is most helpful, then, when cast as less a distinction than a dialectic. Because it creates many paths through the components of a text (or collection of texts and objects), the digital edition might, to the inconvenience of the reader-as-reader, be more advantageous

---

[27] See "Samuel Beckett Digital Manuscript Project." www.beckettarchive.org/home.
[28] Shillingsburg, "Textual Criticism and the Text Encoding Initiative," 33.
[29] Sahle, "What Is a Scholarly Digital Edition?" 30.

for the reader-as-user seeking to understand various mechanisms of textual production and reception. As Greve Rasmussen puts it,

> a knowledge site is a locus for continuous knowledge enhancement, much like a library or an archive. The same is true for digital editions that regularly publish new works. Research and reception are always in progress, a fact that may be relevant for the reader-as-user.[30]

Here the ideal function of the "knowledge site" is generatively compared to that of the digital edition. As Bode has similarly argued, a scholarly edition of a literary system is "intended not to conclude but to enable various forms of investigation, including those that move between the single literary work and the system in which it existed and operated," a concept clearly genealogically linked to McGann's social text criticism.[31]

Even before the pervasiveness of digital textuality there were various attempts to conceptualize editions beyond the codex in order to visualize many things at once. Collation, even in the service of the "ideal text" model advocated by Bowers in 1959, requires a spatial layering, a textual multiplicity, and a kind of double vision. To facilitate this way of seeing many things at once, in 1984 Randall McLeod invented a portable collator that uses mirrors to allow the viewer to "see" two editions simultaneously and note the differences between them – a mechanical solution prefiguring digital tools such as Juxta that highlight textual variants between digitized texts.[32] Much earlier, Early Modern book wheels or carousels were designed as a mechanical mobilization of texts that allowed a stationary reader to easily access several volumes without leaving their seat.[33] Rotating wheels, parallel texts, and other nonlinear conceptualizations of editions allowed for comparison of codex to codex even before digital devices facilitated comparative, multitextual edition making and computational analysis at various scales from large corpus to individual word or even letterform. Portela summarizes this idea of varying layers of textual engagement: "Taking advantage of the modularity of the digital medium, the modelling [sic] of bibliographic and

---

[30] Krista Stinne Greve Rasmussen, "Reading or Using a Digital Edition? Reader Roles in Scholarly Editions," in *Digital Scholarly Editing – Theories and Practices*, ed. Matthew Driscoll and Elena Pierazzo (Cambridge: Open Book Publishers, 2016), 132.

[31] Katherine Bode, "The Equivalence of 'Close' and 'Distant' Reading; or, Toward a New Object for Data-Rich Literary History," *Modern Language Quarterly* 78.1 (2017): 101.

[32] Simon McLeish, "Library Machines," The Conveyor: Research in Special Collections at the Bodleian Libraries, The Bodleian Libraries, 3 September 2010, https://blogs.bodleian.ox.ac.uk/the conveyor/library-machines-the-mcleod-collator/.

[33] Agostino Ramelli, "Le diverse et artificiose machine del capitano Agostino Ramelli" ("The Various and Ingenious Machines of Captain Agostino Ramelli, 1588"), Science History Institute. https:// digital.sciencehistory.org/works/4b29b614k.

linguistic codes can happen at various levels of granularity: from the macro-textual level of literary form and bibliographic unit to the micro-textual level of word and character."[34] Digital editions often take advantage of these levels of engagement, imagining deeper investigations into the particularities of a text or broader contexts, histories, and comparisons than offered by the codex's bound form. Despite experimentation in the digital realm and emphasis on hypertext and other nonlinear structures, however, most current digital editions still evoke the paradigm of the printed page and employ "skeuomorphic" design features that imitate physical books, such as the page-turning functions in the International Image Interoperability Framework (IIIF) viewer.[35] Such features that draw on the epistemology and aesthetic of the codex signal that digital reading always exists in a dialectic with print reading.

6.2 Interactive Reading

The 2016 MLA's Committee on Scholarly Editions' statement on the Scholarly Edition in the Digital Age[36] outlines several other key affordances of digital editions vis-à-vis their print counterparts: harnessing the edition's data and metadata for other research purposes at different scales; supporting more interactive features such as user annotation; and facilitating exploration of the edition's space such that the user is mobilized to become a sort of contingent editor.[37] Each of these suggests a reorientation of the reader toward the edition, usually with the goal of increasing their participation in creating and mobilizing the edition's meaning.

Reading on a screen, and particularly in a web browser, demands participatory navigation from the reader. For Andrew Piper, what is at stake in the debates about the impact of the digital on reading practices is the change in the *formal structure* of reading; as he argues, "only when we reconceptualize the page as the basic unit of reading are we truly entering into new conceptual

---

[34] Portela, "Designing Digital Editions," 285.
[35] Skeuomorphism refers in design theory to an object retaining as aesthetic features the structural or material attributes of another version of a similar artifact even though there is no material requirement that they be retained – in other words, the "conversion of originally necessary features into purely decorative patterns." See "skeuomorph, n.," *OED Online*, Oxford University Press. www.oed.com/view/Entry/180780?redirectedFrom=skeuomorph#eid.
[36] See MLA Committee on Scholarly Editions, *MLA Statement on the Scholarly Edition in the Digital Age*.
[37] This last imperative, of course, evokes Darnton's theorization of the pyramidal book, whereby the user uses the digital to curate and collate documents, assembling their own codex. See Darnton, "The New Age of the Book," 76–77.

terrain."[38] The constant shifting of the page as seen in web browsers – whereby the content "could always be otherwise" simply by scrolling slightly down – necessarily prompts a different kind of reading engagement *with* that page, since "where we 'curl up' with a book, we 'roam' across a plane" in a web browser.[39] While the print codex's perceived "closedness" – the fact that it can be "grasped as a totality" – has been seen as "integral to its success in generating transformative reading experiences," digital editions by contrast "are radically open in their networked form. They are marked by a very weak sense of closure."[40] This structural difference – the destabilization of the page in a digital text – alerts us "more consciously, perhaps more critically, [to] the nature of our interconnected textual universe."[41] Sherman Young takes this point even further in his discussion of the potentiality of "networked books," which – like, and as an extension of, McGann's social text criticism – decenter the ultimate authority of the author in favor of creating "a model for a new (virtual) object that relies on building a relationship between the author and her readership ... allow[ing] readers to contribute to an evolving text" which is more about process than product.[42]

Reader contributions and annotations therefore constitute one key affordance of the digital edition. While adding marginalia to a printed book was always possible, digital editions allow multiple users and groups to annotate works together, and some projects, such as COVE (Collaborative Organization for Virtual Education) Electronic Editions, promote digital annotation as a way of encouraging engaged critical reading.[43] Similarly, web annotation tools like hypothes.is allow multiple users to annotate any webpage and share their annotations as a group.[44] The pedagogical implications of such tools are obviously significant: one only has to imagine being able to pass around a single copy of a text to an entire class of students to recognize that these sorts of digital interfaces and tools will allow reader interactions of a nature, kind, and scale that are impractical in print. The use of these kinds of annotation platforms also formalizes and reframes the once-taboo act of producing marginalia. As H. J. Jackson notes, marginalia in physical books has a long history of being considered "irresponsible, weak, or transgressive."[45] Without the

---

[38] Andrew Piper, *Book Was There: Reading in Electronic Times* (Chicago: University of Chicago Press, 2012), 48.
[39] Ibid., 55.   [40] Ibid., 14.   [41] Ibid., 56.   [42] Young, *The Book Is Dead*, 133–134.
[43] See "COVE Editions." https://editions.covecollective.org/.
[44] See "Hypothes.is." https://web.hypothes.is/.
[45] Heather Jackson, *Marginalia: Readers Writing in Books* (New Haven: Yale University Press, 2001), 74.

materiality of defacement that occurs in books, however, digital annotation is more likely to be encouraged and invited by digital editors, especially since it can often be turned on and off (as in the case of hypothes.is) so as not to affect other readers' experiences when that is not desirable. This is also true in the production of scholarly monographs that undergo open digital peer review and use annotation platforms to solicit feedback that will eventually inform both the print and digital versions of the scholarly text.[46]

While annotation and navigation are two ways of interacting with digital texts, another important scholarly interaction that digital texts specifically facilitate is computational textual analysis. Texts are now of course read by machines as well as by humans. Digitized editions and digital archives may or may not engage with textual encoding that renders the text machine-readable and computationally tractable. Machine readability may be achieved through the very straightforward process of plain text encoding or through the much more complex process of textual markup. One early and longform attempt to set protocols and standards for digital scholarly editing using markup is the Text Editing Initiative (TEI), which originally established guidelines in 1994 for encoding texts in a digital form.[47] The TEI was founded in 1987 by The Working Committee on Text Encoding Practices of the Association for Computers and Humanities. The TEI increases consistency and interoperability among digital editions, but encoding is a slow process which often requires extensive training. The primary practical drawback for many projects is therefore that TEI is extremely labor intensive. It remains, however, one of the only systematic protocols for digital textual editing.

An early literary example of such an encoding project is *Odour of Chrysanthemums: A Text in Process*, which uses transcriptions to explore textual variants of D. H. Lawrence's short story in a digital environment. It is important to note, however, that much analytic work that happens in digital literary studies does not regularly rely upon the use of digital scholarly editions. Digitized versions of text with no new attendant scholarly materials, such as the plain texts provided by Project Gutenberg or the digitized page images provided by Google Books, can provide texts for analysis without specific deliberate digital editorial intervention. While

---

[46] See, for example, Catherine D'Ignazio and Lauren Klein, "Data Feminism and the Open Peer Review Process." https://datafeminism.io/blog/2020/07/19/data-feminism-and-the-open-peer-review-process/.

[47] The TEI guidelines have "been taken up as a standard or norm for digital archival production by the MLA (Committee on Scholarly Editions 2011) and granting agencies." See Laura Mandell, *Breaking the Book: Print Humanities in the Digital Age* (New York: Wiley Blackwell, 2015), 180–181.

those sources undoubtedly have their myriad uses (and, indeed, increasingly plain text versions of literary works in particular are desirable for computational analytic purposes), scholarly editions are those that retain some of the character of the long-standing discipline of textual studies in which the intensive labor of the scholarly editor(s) produces a reading experience enriched by new apparatuses. Editions encoded in TEI position XML encoding itself as an editorial practice: one that makes transparent the editor's textual choices and enables advanced analysis that is often shaped by an editor's decisions about metadata.

6.3 Multimodality: Image, Sound, and Video

While affordable printed scholarly editions are nearly always freshly typeset in a format uniform with the rest of the works in the series, digital editions often use copious images to explicitly retain many of the aesthetic features of the historical first edition or primary document, such as typography and illustration. The printed precedent to these kinds of digitized editions would perhaps have been the facsimile edition, but digital archives tend to offer something genuinely new and newly ambitious, including not only page images but also extensive apparatuses and annotations in a variety of media. Returning to Shillingsburg's capacious "archive of editions" discussed in the first section, multimodality helps capture and recreate the historical materials that digital editions might now, as never as fully before, include.

Even as digital editions have aimed to construct such a networked library of texts, objects, and other media relevant to "the book" broadly construed, what Sahle and others have called "the page paradigm" still persists. One of the reasons why "the page" remains important, and at the same time why multimodality is a crucial element of many successful digital editions, is that the presence of sound, video, color image, and other media difficult to reproduce in print compensates for some of the loss of tactile sensory experience that occurs in the transition from page to screen. As a notable benefit of this continuation, "the replication of print in a digital form is designed to increase access to materials and aid examination of aspects of the original (illustrations, typography, etc.) that is rarely possible in modern reprints."[48] Good examples of this include the two Emily Dickinson-related archives hosted by Harvard and Amherst.[49]

---

[48] Earhart, *Traces of the Old, Uses of the New*, 12.
[49] See "Emily Dickinson Archive." www.edickinson.org/, and "About: Dickinson Electronic Archives." www.emilydickinson.org/about.

Despite the impact and power of images in well-executed digitizations, especially of unusual manuscript works like Dickinson's that are beautiful to begin with (and written on materials that are difficult to reproduce in print), there is a risk to indefinitely continuing the page paradigm. In other words, though digitization does increase access to sometimes rare historical materials, merely reproducing the page paradigm of the print edition does not fully harness the digital edition's epistemological power.

One potential explanation for the page paradigm's continued dominance is that reproducing the format/structure of the print codex in digital form is one way of safeguarding against the discrete "losses" or "drawbacks" of transcending the codex. Skeptics of the digital turn have long lamented what they perceive to be the loss of tactility or materiality inherent in digital reading; as Piper puts it, "the more screenish our world becomes, the more we try to reinsert tactility back into it," because – as the charge goes – "digital texts lack feeling."[50] Similarly, Young, approaching the question from the media and cultural studies perspective, argues that the print book provides its reader with a sort of haptic feedback that a digital edition cannot.[51]

When we approach this issue in a very different context – for example, the digitization of medieval manuscripts – the loss becomes even clearer. Elaine Treharne acknowledges that "[t]he digital medium has unprecedented benefits for accessibility and for the virtual reconstruction of medieval libraries."[52] The digital enables scholars to see things not visible to the naked eye; for example, work underway at the University of Texas at Austin magnifies eighteenth-century handmade paper to show watermarks, chain lines, and other details that help to identify the documents' situatedness in history.[53] At the same time, Treharne argues that "[t]here is always, inevitably, loss in the provision of the virtual; this loss is the inability to fulfill the interpretive potential of the [superordinate] TEXT," which she defines as "the whole fleshy body of the book" or

---

[50] Piper, *Book Was There: Reading in Electronic Times*, 16, 15. Another aspect of materiality is the cost of producing the physical printed book versus the e-book. Young also cites industry/manufacturing figures to argue that e-books are less damaging to the environment to produce and to enable potential readers to consume. While print books require both dead trees and the environmental cost of shipping across the world, e-books – though requiring the environmental costs associated with the production of an electronic reading device – are still more sustainable. See Young, *The Book Is Dead*, 158.

[51] Ibid., 108.

[52] Elaine Treharne, "Fleshing Out the Text: The transcendent manuscript in the digital age," *Postmedieval: A Journal of Medieval Cultural Studies* 4.4 (2013): 466.

[53] Other projects and institutions have also used sophisticated imaging technologies to examine the deep structures of old bindings and other materials. See Alex Gillespie, "Old Books New Science," Old Books New Science (OBNS) Lab. https://oldbooksnewscience.com/.

"the whole object in its complexity." How can one capture in digital form, Treharne asks, the "codicological architexture" of a text like The Eadwine Psalter, for Treharne "an Edifice of Letters" – that is, the different versions, translations, drawings, "the texture of the folios, the *ex libris*, the mark of ownership, the binding, its weight of something like 30 pounds, it *aura*, its value"?[54] Of course, a printed facsimile would suffer from similar if not even greater obstacles to the representation of "the whole fleshy body" of a medieval manuscript. The Benjaminian aura that Treharne evokes is likewise lost when a piece of parchment is reproduced on a piece of woodpulp paper and digitally printed rather than written by hand. As G. Thomas Tanselle argues, "computerization is just the latest chapter in the long story of facilitating the reproduction and alternation of texts; *what remains constant is the inseparability of recorded language from the technology that produced it and made it accessible.*"[55] And that accessibility, while it comes at the potential cost of a specific type of sensory encounter with the original, can offer different multimodal sensory experiences.

With regard to multimodality, McGann insists on "organizing a hyperediting project in hypermedia form":[56]

> [Although] hypereditions built of electronic text alone are easier to construct ... they can only manipulate the semantic level of the original work. Hypermedia editions that incorporate audial and/or visual elements are preferable since literary works are themselves always more or less elaborate multimedia forms.[57]

The ability of digital editions to harness and remediate some of this inherent multimediality is one of the great strengths of the multimodal digital edition. In other words, in order to take full advantage of the digital form, multimodality is essential. In this vein, some scholars are already arguing that "the prominence of initiatives like the Modernist Journals Project" – which reproduces full-text, high-quality digital scans and metadata of hard-to-find periodicals published from 1890 to 1922 – "obscures the need to go beyond making digital editions and engage in truly multimodal digital scholarship."[58] In their view, multimodality entails deeper engagement with media elements such as audio, video, and functions which harness metadata to dynamically generate data visualizations.

---

[54] Treharne, "Fleshing Out the Text," 468. Emphases original.
[55] Thomas Tanselle, qtd. in Earhart, *Traces of the Old, Uses of the New*, 20, emphasis added.
[56] McGann, "The Rationale of HyperText," 16. [57] McGann, *Radiant Textuality*, 58.
[58] Shawna Ross, "From Practice to Theory: A Forum on the Future of Modernist Digital Humanities," *Modernism/modernity Print Plus* 3.2, https://modernismmodernity.org/forums/practice-theory-forum. See also "Modernist Journals Project," Brown and Tulsa Universities, https://modjourn.org/.

Multimodal editions are also more amenable to diverse learning styles and modes of textual engagement. Thus, audio files can animate poetry in ways that print editions never could; for example, "The Waste Land" app includes audio recordings of contemporary poets and actors – as well as Eliot himself – reading and performing the poem. Similarly, the Moby Dick Big Read offers "an online version of Melville's magisterial tome: each of its 135 chapters read out aloud, by a mixture of the celebrated and the unknown, to be broadcast online in a sequence of 135 downloads, publicly and freely accessible."[59] More recently, the Canterbury Tales App features audio recordings of the poem read in Middle English alongside an edited text, manuscript images, and a modern English translation.[60] Images and sound – such as those found at The Whitman Archive, which includes "a 36-second wax cylinder recording of what is thought to be Whitman's voice reading four lines from the poem 'America'" – can enhance a reader's multisensory experience of a work. As these examples illustrate, multimodal digital scholarly editions offer "major epistemological and methodological benefits," increasing accessibility by expanding the ranges of possible semiotic modes of engagement with a text. Yet because multimodal editions are "composites of distributed data sources" often collaboratively built in an interinstitutional "networked paradigm," they have a high "maintenance load" of costs, both computational and (inter)institutional. To counteract eventual obsolescence, scholars, IT specialists, librarians, and archivists must therefore collaborate to implement new and creative solutions to ensure their ongoing accessibility as technology evolves.[61]

6.4 Conclusion

When a scholar, collaborative team, or publisher makes a digital edition, they are doing something different in kind from their editorial predecessors. Digital editions afford new praxis, impelling renewed consideration of the imbrication of editing and pedagogy and thereby usefully complicating seemingly settled terms. Yet while the digital environment has considerable potential to reshape scholarly enquiry, as McGann et al. noted many years ago and others have consistently affirmed, it remains true that "there has

---

[59] See "Moby Dick Big Read." www.mobydickbigread.com/.
[60] See "General Prologue." https://apps.apple.com/us/app/general-prologue/id1480038830. Note that this app is designed for iPhone or iPad.
[61] Joris J. van Zundert and Peter Boot, "The Digital Edition 2.0 and The Digital Library: Services, Not Resources," *Bibliothek und Wissenschaft* 44 (2011): 1-2, 6.

been more promise than delivery so far" in digital editions and that print editions remain the dominant form in most classrooms.[62] Given the clear potential for digital scholarly editions not to replace, but certainly to complement print editions, why are many scholars slow to engage in this kind of work? How can we better harness both the labor of creating and the experience of using the digital scholarly edition in order to complement more traditional scholarly work?

We hypothesize that the challenges to development in the area of digital scholarly editions result from a combination of the following, which often constitute barriers to entry: labor costs; questions about prestige, remuneration, and institutional support (including leave time and technical infrastructure); and expertise. In its initial stages at least, a digital scholarly edition, like its conventional print counterpart, lacks the revolutionary potential of a well-received monograph. Yet in the case of a successful digital edition with longevity, it does invariably constitute a more "living" resource, one that can grow and change, being both made by and utilized by audiences its original creators might not have envisioned. Like conventional scholarly print editing, digital scholarly editing requires collaboration and long-term commitment, in terms of both labor and financial resources, the digital perhaps even more costly in the end than the conventional. Although the technology of the codex remains a central animating feature of our bibliographic imaginations, as we have argued throughout this chapter the longevity of digital standards, interfaces, and tools is much less certain. Rosselli Del Turco outlines two problems: the relatively short life span of software and issues of compatibility as technology rapidly advances; and long-term sustainability with respect to the web server(s) in which the digital edition is housed, a problem compounded by differing (and potentially dynamic, as with Brexit) international copyright laws.[63] The May 2016 statement on Scholarly Editions in the Digital Age by the MLA Committee on Scholarly Editions particularly emphasizes the need for the digital scholarly edition to "include consideration of how the edition can circulate and function as a scholarly resource over time," stressing that "addressing this challenge involves infrastructural, financial, and data representation issues."[64] These

---

[62] Paul Eggert, *The Work and the Reader in Literary Studies: Scholarly Editing and Book History* (Cambridge: Cambridge University Press, 2019), 2.
[63] Roberto Rosselli Del Turco, "The Battle We Forgot to Fight: Should We Make a Case for Digital Editions?," in *Digital Scholarly Editing – Theories and Practices*, ed. Matthew Driscoll and Elena Pierazzo (Cambridge: Open Book Publishers, 2016), 228–229.
[64] See MLA Committee on Scholarly Editions, *MLA Statement on the Scholarly Edition in the Digital Age*.

issues remain largely unsettled, and the long-standing publishing infrastructures that continue to support nondigital editions often flounder when faced with the digital transition (one only has to encounter the wide variety and high variability of e-reading interfaces for academic books to see that this is so).[65]

Despite some of the authenticity costs of the digital edition, it arguably makes more manifest than the printed codex that a given text is always already situated in a larger, networked sociological structure.[66] Multimodality enhances readers' experiences of this structure by providing non- or extratextual engagements. Invitations to interact, annotate, and analyze texts enliven the networks that come with new modalities. This network functions on multiple levels, from the ability to see many instantiations of a text in a digital edition to the capacity to foster collaboration between the text's "author" and its readers. As Shillingsburg argued more than two decades ago, "we need a webbing or networking of cross-references connecting variant texts, explanatory notes, contextual materials, and parallel texts," and the digital edition clearly offers this affordance which was once only a scholarly wish.[67] As we have shown, both of these ideas are indebted to McKenzie's "sociology of texts."[68] The digital edition embedded in a richly social reading community has the capacity to transform the relationship between reader and user, author and reader, text and commentary. The sociology of the scholarly digital edition, therefore, as a community of praxis founded on collaboration, open-endedness, and capaciousness of vision, continues to hold promise despite the practical challenges that always attend the production and circulation of texts.

---

[65] See, for example, Stanford University Press's "Publishing Digital Scholarship" initiative. www.sup.org/digital/.

[66] This idea harkens back to Darnton's famous essay, "What Is the History of Books?," in which he proposes a general model for analyzing the way books come into being and move through society. See Robert Darnton, "What Is the History of Books?," *Daedalus* 111.3, Representations and Realities (1982): 65-83.

[67] Shillingsburg, "Textual Criticism and the Text Encoding Initiative," 28.

[68] D. F. McKenzie, *Bibliography and the Sociology of Texts* (Cambridge: Cambridge University Press, 1999), 13, 12.

CHAPTER 7

Materiality

Dennis Yi Tenen

The interpretation of texts is complicated by the fact that ideas take shape in matter. My words thus reach you within a specific medium – paper, audio file, or an electronic text – which serves as a conduit for the transmission of information. Aristotle, in his *Poetics*, similarly differentiated between the objects or content of art, its medium, and the mode of mimesis. Prose describing the way a bird sings, for example, finds its object of imitation in actual bird songs, further expressed in the medium of written language.[1] Charlie Parker's style of playing imitated birds musically, through his saxophone, whilst the American ornithologist John James Audubon painted his birds in watercolor. Sound moves through air, its medium. Light, ink, and paper mediate painting.

Yet even this distinction between media fails to capture the difference in the modality of perception (and comprehension also). Of the mode Aristotle mentions only the contrast between an author "speaking in one's own person" and speaking with "other people engaged" in mimesis. Consider, for example, a film actor turning to the camera to address their audience, thus shifting the interpretive perspective from an intradiegetic vantage to an extradiegetic one. Sit still, our actor says. The directive plays with conventional theater-going habits. Contemplated in the somber silence of an art house theater it gains philosophical significance, though I would prefer to watch it amongst the clamor of a movie night at a local pub. Though in both places the film remains the medium of cinema, the modality of my comprehension changes with the change in venue. So does the meaning. A somber drama in a theater may become the object of ridicule in a crowded pub.

Some of you might similarly prefer to read a novel in the comfort of your own home, while others enjoy the sense of community and deep discussion that happens in book clubs, online, or in class. However we

---

[1] Aristotle, *Poetics*, trans. Richard Janko (Indianapolis: Hackett, 1987), 93.

read, texts in their abstract sense must pass into print to become reified objects – book things. They will take shape on paper or on a digital screen, and once again rarefy into thought (in our minds) by diffusion into their physiological and social contexts. At first, we simply wanted to read a book. But in practice, we now must discuss the modality of where and when it is to be understood. "Where and when" matter in a way that prevents us from talking about meaning in the abstract. Meaning, one might say, is always situated in its material context.

The material conditions of a thought can often be disregarded in favor of its ideational content. It bears asking, however: What kind of stuff is designated under a single title?[2] When we refer to Zora Neale Hurston's collection of African American folklore published under the title *Mules and Men* in 1935, we denote equally the numerous editions of the work published since then.[3] Under a single title, this allocation usually excludes the related notes and manuscripts, available in parts at the American Folklife Center in the Library of Congress; at the Beinecke Rare Book and Manuscript Library, Yale University; and in the P. K. Yonge Library of Florida History at the University of Florida.

Once these additional documents come into view, they assert an inexorable pull on the content of the published work. Our awareness of the auto-ethnographic method at work in Hurston's prose irrevocably changes our perception of the novel. Rather than seeing it as one thing, we can now perceive a number of related publications, notes, drafts, and manuscripts, which in their overlapping totality comprise the general field of the work. Matter ultimately asserts itself through the idea. We are reminded at once of its palpable effects on abstraction and of its shape-giving influence on the foundations of any thought.

Methodologically, a materialist approach, and especially historically inflected materialism, would insist on the often inconvenient intrusion of the physical world into the realm of the ideal. I would prefer to sit back in my armchair and just read Hurston, heeding neither New Haven nor Gainesville. I would rather forego the messiness of conflicting manuscript witnesses, editorial interventions, and international editions of the work which have, over the years, altered and normalized Hurston's language to better accord to publishing standards. It is easier to "just read," without a thought for Harlem Renaissance, Hurston's problematic stance toward

---

[2] On textual genesis see Jerome McGann, *The Textual Condition* (Princeton: Princeton University Press, 1991).
[3] Zora Neale Hurston, *Folklore, Memoirs, and Other Writings* (New York: Library of America, 1995).

it, her time at Columbia University spent with Franz Boas and Margaret Mead, her literary patronage, her sometime poverty, the socioeconomic realities of black publishing, or, in her own words, "what white publishers won't print" (the title of an essay she published in the *Negro Digest* in 1950).

These contexts disturb the surface of the text, as they do my mind and posture. They force me to stand and travel in an effort to read. They fracture the unity of meaning. Where I presumed to interpret and to explain, instead I find a multiplicity of competing possibilities, errors, and emendations along with my own various limits and conditions, incommensurate to the lived, written experience of another. It's not that I can ever recreate Hurston's contexts. I'm just not free of my own materialities. To reach content I must pass though the physical world – mine here and now, and hers, extended through history.

A materialist method thus entails a practice of interpretation radically embedded and embodied. To think in one's head is insufficient for understanding: we must also walk, touch, make, and be unsettled.

7.1 Bertrand Russell in Lahore

In March of 2018, our research group traveled to Lahore, Pakistan, under invitation of the Archives and Libraries Department in the Government of the Punjab and the Punjab Information Technology Board. We were there to present on "Architectures of Knowledge," a topic that for me meant engagement with the material culture of print: the study of online book-sharing communities, do-it-yourself book scanning technology, and pirate archives. As part of the week's program, we toured the Civil Secretariat complex which houses the Punjab Archives in the storied Tomb of Anarkali – a solid, octagonal building that witnessed the Mughal Empire, colonial rule, and the partition.

The Punjab Archives contain records related to the socioeconomic and political history of the region, from the nineteenth and twentieth centuries. On location, we observed library staff treat a stack of fragile materials in a giant metal autoclave chamber, filled with poisonous gas to destroy mold and insects. Bundles of government records were packaged in large, white sacks labeled in red and blue ink as "Persian Records," "General Medical," and "Revenue Agriculture." Ribboned file folders signaled their provenance in a mixture of print and cursive, indicating such government agencies as the Punjab Civil Secretariat and the Home Department. An exhibition of rare books and manuscripts was arranged around the tomb itself. An archive official ushered us into a tall, tiered room where balconies, ladders, and metal scaffolding framed several neat rows of small, square storage compartments extending several stories upward to the ceiling.

I was invited ostensibly as an expert in the digitization of records, to advise on things like document scanning, optical character recognition, and sustainable digital preservation practices. But I was also in a sense trespassing, arriving with no relevant language skills and having only a cursory familiarity with the region's history. Therefore, I listened and observed with a naïve heart. Lahore's rich intellectual traditions encompassed multiple variegated topographies. The city reminded me that the belief in the radical embeddedness of thought prevents us from making universal generalizations. Specific material contexts necessitate the understanding in situ, where the hardware of intellectual infrastructure meets the software of ideational content. Here as elsewhere, such sites are located not only in institutional libraries, but also in coffee shops, home kitchens, and outdoor book markets.

At one such location, next to the King Edward Medical University, we met with a book seller whom I will call Bilal, the proprietor of Bilal Old Books, a small shop specializing in "medical, engineering, English, Urdu, and Islamic literature." Judging by the extensive inventory of medical textbooks, his clientele consisted largely of local medical students. The volumes, many of them in English, were inexpensive though high-quality reproductions of cutting-edge medical literature published originally in Europe and the United States. Such textbooks are either not otherwise available in Pakistan or prohibitively expensive there. The alley leading to Bilal's shop was one of several connecting a small network of translators, printers, binders, and specialty book sellers who, together, support the publishing needs of their community.

A wall of shelves unlike the others inside the shop caught my attention. Here, a patron could find the complete works of Bertrand Russell: his *Basic Writings* published by Routledge Classics, his autobiography, his *Unpopular Essays* and *History of Western Philosophy*. Bilal, as it turned out, was a serious reader of the British philosopher. Although these works did not sell well, he maintained a well-stocked corner of the store in hopes of promoting Russell's thought.

On the way out, after thanking Bilal for his time and hospitality, I purchased a crisp, "pirated" copy of Russell's *Power: A New Social Analysis*, clearly designated on the cover as a "Special Indian Edition."[4] Such editions serve a twofold function for the publisher. First, the British- or American-specific English lexicon may be substituted for its

---

[4] Bertrand Russell, *Power A New Social Analysis* [Special Indian Edition] (London: Routledge, 2010).

equivalent in International English. Changes like these could also involve editorial suggestions specific to the region, such as the substitution of imperial for metric units of measurement. The second function is economic. Routledge and other publishers sell their wares at a lower price in the South Asian market, creating a cost disparity in relation to their North American and Western European counterparts. To prevent resale and reuse across regional boundaries, publishers subsequently introduce arbitrary differences into their international editions. A "Special Indian Edition" of a textbook on organic chemistry, for example, could be repaginated slightly, so as to make weekly reading assignments given by an American university instructor difficult to follow. There was no way of knowing whether my "Special Indian Edition" contained any such changes without comparing it to other similar volumes.

The US Supreme Court considered a case related to special international editions in 2012, when the British-based publisher John Wiley & Sons Inc. brought a suit against Supap Kirtsaeng, a citizen of Thailand.[5] Then a student at the University of California, Kirtsaeng had his textbooks sent from home. He then resold them locally to recoup costs. The case hinged on the question of whether the doctrine of the "first sale" could be limited geographically by countervailing copyright claims. If Kirtsaeng bought his materials in Thailand lawfully, could he not subsequently sell them in the United States on the used market? The judgment in favor of the defendant explained that Section 106 of the US Copyright Act granted copyright owners (John Wiley, in this case) "certain exclusive rights," including those of exclusive original sale. However, these rights were also limited by the doctrines of "fair use" and "first sale." Fair use, according Section 107 of US Copyright Law, does not infringe on copyrights, "for purposes such as criticism, comment, news reporting, teaching (including multiple copies for classroom use), scholarship, or research." The "first sale" principle in Section 109 grants "the owner of a particular copy," the right to "sell or otherwise dispose of the possession" provided it was "lawfully made under this title."[6] We can thus imagine owning a vinyl copy of a recent hit record, in a case where the artist and their music label own the general rights for distribution, but where an individual also has the right to dispose of this one, specific record in their possession on the second-hand market. The first party can be said to own the right to the work of art in the abstract (and hence to its first sale), and the second, to a singular object of art, and thereafter to its second sale.

[5] *Kirtsaeng* v. *John Wiley & Sons Inc.*, 568 US 519 (2013).
[6] *Copyright Law of the United States, Title 17, US Code* (2022).

In light of the aforementioned statues, we may surmise that Kirtsaeng had second sale rights to his property. But what happens when resale goes global? Wiley argued that the principle of first sale did not in fact extend to copies purchased outside the United States. On that view, the phrase "lawfully made under this title" implied a geographic as well as a legal restriction. In their interpretation, the defendant bought the books lawfully but not under the US jurisdiction. The court ultimately ruled in Kirtsaeng's favor, with the majority opinion affirming a nongeographic understanding of the clause. The ruling conceded that its consequences would make the division between foreign and domestic markets through discriminatory pricing more difficult, if not impossible. However, it also argued that the US copyright law did not especially entitle geographic price discrimination in the first place. Subsequent to the ruling, international students were free to continue reselling their books.

I don't know whether Bilal's photocopied editions of Russell's work would be considered legal copies under the US copyright law. The question is likely irrelevant to Pakistani students in the pursuit of a quality education. Our discussion concerns the material life of intellectual works, which, in this case, have passed through the halls of Trinity College in the United Kingdom, to Routledge's international offices in New Delhi, and onto a side street of printers and booksellers in Lahore. We followed the book's path.

The situated nature of such custody chains prevents us from treating anything like a "literary work" as a universal construct. Meaning, at stake in reading, depends on the environment. It further transforms in circulation. Multiple communities – in this case, authors, students, teachers, book sellers, stockholders, and multinational publishers – diverge in their goals, charters, practices, socioeconomic conditions, and histories. Diverse communities differ in their understanding of the work, in a way that cannot be reconciled neatly into a singular Russell's *Power*, true for all time and everywhere. Literary scholars sensitive to diverging material contexts aim to read Russell on their own universally ideational terms and, simultaneously, to retrace the passage of Russell's thought as an object, through its specific, physical instantiations.

The story of this book, now on my bookshelf, reminds me of my own superfluous presence in Pakistan. The Government of Punjab did not need foreign expertise for digitizing their archives: local communities have already built a robust infrastructure to support their various intellectual activities. Bilal's street-level network was far more engaged in the material life of book publishing than the average American scholar.

But even on this local level, there exist institutional and cultural barriers that prevent the Punjab Archives from becoming a unilateral, uniform thing. The object grounds the work, but also fractures it among specific lived sites. My reading of Russell is now forever informed by walking the streets of Lahore. In total, a committed materialism leads not to cultural relativism (there are no readings of the work on which we can agree), but to a congruence of specific cultures, communities, and interpretations.[7] A text emerges from the many-voiced consensus of localized perspectives. This agreement, once materialized, becomes yet another waypoint within the topography delimiting a work.

7.2 Laminate Text

The transition from print to screen further complicates the physical realities of textual material. In *Plain Text: The Poetics of Computation*, I proposed viewing digital media not as a homogeneous substance, but rather a laminate of technologies, inscriptions, and protocols.[8] An authorized digital edition of Russell's *Power* in English is not available in Pakistan. A digital copy of the Special Indian Edition can be purchased in India, from a major online retailer, for roughly the equivalent of $26 USD, the same price it fetches on the American market. The two versions of the text, print and digital, contain ostensibly the same information, but they differ substantially in the ways they can be read, shared, and archived.

The vocabulary of electrical engineering and user experience design gives us a way of thinking about books as digital objects in a language that differs from that of literary theory or media studies. Consider US Patent US20130219269A1, granted in 2018 to Apple, Inc. out of Cupertino, California. The patent materials relate to "displaying and facilitating the manipulation of electronic text ... of an electronic book (e-book) being read on an electronic device. Much like an ordinary book, electronic books can be used to present text and pictures to readers. Instead of ink and paper, however, an electronic book is a collection of digital data that software, known as an electronic book reader application, can interpret and present on a display." What kind of a thing is this electronic book, really (I ask a century after Percy Lubbock's *The Craft of Fiction*)?[9] At least three distinct laminates

---

[7] Similar thought developed in Q. D. Leavis, *Fiction and the Reading Public* (London: Chatto & Windus, 1932) and Karin Barber, *The Anthropology of Texts, Persons and Publics* (Cambridge: Cambridge University Press, 2007).
[8] Dennis Yi Tenen, *Plain Text: The Poetics of Computation* (Palo Alto: Stanford University Press, 2017).
[9] Percy Lubbock, *The Craft of Fiction* (London: J. Cape, 1921). On book as device and mechanism, see also Katherine Hayles, Peter Lunenfeld, and Anne Burdick, *Writing Machines* (Cambridge, MA: MIT Press, 2002) and Matthew Kirschenbaum, *Mechanisms: New Media and the Forensic Imagination* (Cambridge, MA: MIT Press, 2007).

seem to be involved, according to Apple's description. An electronic text comprises "a collection of digital data," its "software interpretation," and "presentation on a display." These layers are then positioned as secondary to what the patent describes as a book's "first publication" – that is, some notion of a canonical imprint, in relation to which all others follow.

The patent therefore concerns itself with a chain of events, which begins at the source of the first publication: for example, as when an electronic reader queries a library database to confirm that the original source of some particular printed matter was indeed a magazine article as opposed to a novel. Based on that initial query, the system creates a "representation of the first publication" – in our example, an appropriately formatted digital facsimile of a magazine (as opposed to a book). Additionally, the system places that first publication into a "state," indicating the difference, for instance, between a newspaper newly purchased and one already read. States and labels may further involve information about users, such as their location, or about other items found on their bookshelf. In the words of the patent, "determining the state for the first publication may include determining a location for a first device, determining that content appearing in the electronic bookshelf is associated with the location, and presenting the content to the user indicating that the content is relevant to the location." Presenting such content may "include a ribbon to indicate relevance" or "placing the content using a specified book location" in relation to other material. In other words, my virtual book items may change their virtual state or location in response to my handling of other virtual items, states, or locations. More than the sum of its contents, an electronic book embodies material contexts: geography and reader demographics.

The language of patents forces inventors to describe objects as if encountering the world anew, from an alien perspective (in order to protect their original claim). Nothing can be taken for granted: not the way books look nor the way we read them. The conceptual displacement reveals the supposed novelty of the proposed invention, affecting also our own perception of now habituated objects, such as word processors and electronic books. Exacting technical description, diagrams, and drawings satisfy a scholarly curiosity about the inner workings of machines that are usually sealed and which therefore may resist description or interpretation. Criticism by disassembly anchors theoretical insight within the material realities of the artifact.

My paper copy of Russell's book exists in a single location. I am free to gift it, resell it, and otherwise dispose of it as I please. The digital copy isn't technically a single object. I have purchased merely a temporary license to read the text within the technical confines of a retailer's proprietary platform. The very word "platform" suggests the implicit scaffolding of software and hardware architectures involved. Bits arranged on drives in secured data centers somewhere in the Asia Pacific Region (likely in Mumbai) represent the equivalent of Russell's text. These constitute only a small part of the information required to facilitate my reading. A great portion of the code involved specifies an electronic book's virtual affordances: the look and feel of its pages, its bookmarks and annotations, built-in dictionaries, and sponsored advertisements.

Digital rights management (DRM) safeguards prevent me from making unauthorized copies of the virtual book. I am also unable to read in locations for which I do not own a license.

The text I see on my screen exists also in part on my personal drive, where the instructions from the Mumbai server are assembled into synthetic equivalents of words, sentences, chapters, and pages. On screen, Russell's text takes shape as a configuration of electrodes, color filters, and light as it shines through glass substrates. Modern computers store information by charging and discharging millions of tiny transistors. Russell's *Power* is thus represented as a pattern of electrically charged "floating gates" in one stratum of inscription (in memory), and, in another, as a pattern of twisted nematic liquid crystal (on screen). The physical properties of each laminate differ, as does the shape of data at each level.

It follows that the affordances of a text – what can be done with it, where, when, and how – also diverge, depending on readers' privileges.[10] For example, a reader on screen is often prevented from copying and pasting information, where users with access to the underlying data on disk are not. We are ultimately dealing with multiple data formats which present unique challenges for their storage, manipulation, and transmission. A digital copy of the book I own simulates the "look and feel" of print, but only to a surface extent. I "turn pages," "read," "take notes," "copy," "paste," "share," and "own" books by metaphor alone. The familiar verbs occlude remote material realities: floating gates and liquid crystal, where reading and writing require highly specialized tools, alien gestures.

Law and software limit access to the underlying layers of representation of the electronic book I purchased on the South Asian market. The software license for my digital book allows me to manipulate purchased pages only in the ways specified by its terms and conditions. Back home,

---

[10] On "interfaces" and "affordances," see also Johanna Drucker, "Reading Interface," *PMLA* 128.1 (2013): 213–220.

I learn that according to Title 17, Chapter 12, Section 1201 of the United States Code, "No person shall circumvent a technological measure that effectively controls access to a work protected under this title." Further, to "circumvent a technological measure," "means to descramble a scrambled work, to decrypt an encrypted work, or otherwise to avoid, bypass, remove, deactivate, or impair a technological measure, without the authority of the copyright owner" and "to manufacture, import, offer to the public, provide, or otherwise traffic in any technology, product, service, device, component, or part thereof, that is primarily designed or produced for the purpose of circumventing protection afforded by a technological measure that effectively protects a right of a copyright owner under this title in a work or a portion thereof." Thus even though I now own multiple copies of the same text, including one authorized for the North American market, what I can do with each differs with the edition.

Legal scholars and activists have long argued against restrictions placed on electronic text. Individually, such restrictions alienate readers from the physicality of printed matter. Consequently, the armature of intellectual activity becomes enmeshed within the larger structure of corporate surveillance and state control. Electronic book devices routinely serve advertisements, record conversations, and track their users' location. In aggregate, collective alienation leads to systemic global inequities. Beneath the surface of electronic text, international publishing conglomerates are able to monopolize the means of textual production, distribution, and utilization. Publicly funded research is funneled into private, for-profit concerns that limit access to those not able to pay the entrance fee. Whole geographic regions, in Eastern Europe and the Global South, find themselves on the margins of literary and scientific development.

Worse still, these systemic inequities become difficult to redress, or even recognize, due to their diffuse technological complexity. For example, some proprietary electronic book devices are simply not available in Pakistan (as of writing this chapter). The means of their reproduction informally also lie beyond the immediate capabilities of local artisans such as Bilal. As education moves online, digital platforms threaten to further entrench economic disparities between those with access to scholarly knowledge and those without.

A number of recent projects attempt to redress such systemic inequities by means of epistemic, technological activism. For example, a community of librarians and technologists from South Asia have created a suite of free (as in freedom) software tools under the name Calibre, designed to edit, archive, and organize electronic books in numerous, nonproprietary data formats. An anonymous group of "apprentices" and "custodians" have extended this platform to manipulate those works under DRM protections. An online project started in Croatia called Memory of the World has made it possible to easily host and to share private Calibre libraries. In 2011, a scientist from Kazakhstan started a website where those users with access to research literatures can safely provide access to those who do not. Numerous so-called shadow-libraries have emerged to rival corporate digital collections in size and coverage. These efforts operate in the legal gray area of international commerce. The ethics of their use are more clear, however, aligning with those progressive ideals that would sustain fair use through unfettered intellectual activity in the commons.

7.3 Historical Materialism

Central to our discussion on materiality so far has been the distinction between the work of art as an idea and an object. In this regard, it may be useful to recall the distinction between painting and literature made by the philosopher Nelson Goodman in his 1968 classic *Languages of Art*.[11] With painting, he explained, we prefer to witness the original. No matter how high the fidelity, a reproduction loses in perceived value, aesthetic and economic. By contrast, few readers of literature care to consult original manuscripts. It is enough to know that a work belongs to its stated author. Most reproductions will do for casual reading. Matter thus recedes in the practice of literary criticism in favor of ideational content. Where paint is embedded in its medium in a way that makes it difficult to extract, text adheres lightly. Content appears weightless, transcending matter.

Yet even the most ephemeral of things such as text can also acquire the patina of metaphysical, extramaterial significance. In 1936, Walter Benjamin famously referred to this residue as an "aura," lost by the work of art in the Age of Mechanical Reproduction.[12] A handkerchief used by Princess Diana may be indistinguishable from any old handkerchief, down to the molecule. The cloth becomes more valuable, however, with proper documentation, attesting provenance. History thus permeates artifacts in a way that cannot be reduced to physical particularities such as the handkerchief size, type of cloth, or pattern. The royal tears it absorbed have long evaporated. Are we

---

[11] Nelson Goodman, *Languages of Art: An Approach to a Theory of Symbols* (London: Oxford University Press, 1968).
[12] Walter Benjamin, *The Work of Art in the Age of Mechanical Reproduction*, trans. J. A. Underwood (Harlow: Penguin Books, 2008).

then wrong to place sentimental value on such weightless tokens of history? How does this residue adhere to lifeless objects?

The notion of historical materialism hence contains within it the following contradiction. An idea arrives onto my bookshelves wrapped within a convenient paper receptacle, to be ingested and converted back into ideas that live in my head. I am eager to unwrap them and to discard the package. Materialist approaches to the study of text aim to reconstitute notational works within their socioeconomic contexts. The book appears first as a medium, the architecture of inscription (book bindings, ink, shelves, stacks), and second as a modality, its habitual vestments (comportment, customs, body posture, ways of reading). A materialism that is historical in addition views the object in time. A book in that sense is more than a perceptual thing in our sensory field. It arrives already weathered by the patina of interpretation, marred by the dust of the ideal.

Finally, we must hold onto both of these extensions of the object: in time and space. In his visual compendium of types and methods for architectural drawing, Rendow Yee describes the technique of picturing a building in its "expanded" or "exploded" view, by which the viewer is able to peer inside, as it were, illustrating "the nature of this structure as an assemblage of standardized parts," showing "how structural components relate to each other" in a way that also reveals the "genesis" of its construction.[13] If we are to draw the book in its expanded, exploded form, under the paradigm of historical materialism, we would picture it not only as an object that appears to view, but also as a history of its production:[14] its various translations and editions; its accrued metadata; related scholarly articles, book reviews, and online book club discussions; the machinations of the language within; the handprints of a typesetter and warehouse worker involved in literary production.

---

[13] Rendow Yee, *Architectural Drawing: A Visual Compendium of Types and Methods* (Hoboken: John Wiley & Sons, 2013), 311.

[14] On literary production see Childress Clayton, *Under the Cover: The Creation, Production, and Reception of a Novel* (Princeton: Princeton University Press, 2017) and Pierre Macherey, *A Theory of Literary Production*, (London: Routledge, 1978).

CHAPTER 8

The Literary Marketplace

Tully Barnett

When Jonathan Franzen wrote, in an opinion piece in *The Guardian* in 2013, that "in my own little corner of the world, which is to say American fiction, Jeff Bezos of Amazon may not be the antichrist, but he surely looks like one of the four horsemen," he signaled the extent of the literary establishment's anxiety over what the future of literature might be given the digital disruption of almost every aspect of the production, circulation, and reception of books and reading – of which Amazon was a significant part. Franzen added that

> Amazon wants a world in which books are either self-published or published by Amazon itself, with readers dependent on Amazon reviews in choosing books, and with authors responsible for their own promotion. The work of yakkers and tweeters and braggers, and of people with the money to pay somebody to churn out hundreds of five-star reviews for them, will flourish in that world.[1]

In the decade since Franzen's comments, Amazon remains a controversial agent in the circulation of literary and textual material. Dave Eggers, Lydia Davis, and Cory Doctorow have all tried to limit Amazon's authority to sell their works. Dave Eggers negotiated a contract for his novel *The Every* that partially avoided Amazon's bookselling platform, for a while at least, and Cory Doctorow has launched a Kickstarter crowdfunding campaign to enable him to release an audiobook version of his latest novel without using the Audible platform, a subsidiary of Amazon.

At the same time, however, authors such as Margaret Atwood have embraced the opportunities for new means of literary expression and engagement enabled by the digital literary marketplace and the platforms and infrastructures afforded by it. Atwood has cultivated a profile on

---

[1] Jonathan Franzen "What's Wrong with the Modern World" *The Guardian*, September 13, 2013, https://web.archive.org/web/20130913183746/http://www.theguardian.com/books/2013/sep/13/jonathan-franzen-wrong-modern-world.

Wattpad, an online platform that connects writers and readers, and in 2012 she uploaded to it extracts from her novel *Oryx and Crake*,[2] just before the release of Atwood's third novel in the series. On Wattpad, Atwood's profile bio reads: "I've been a writer since 1956. I've seen writing and publishing change a lot over the years. I look forward to exploring the ways Wattpad connects people to reading and writing, and may help give them confidence through feedback from readers."[3] A range of comments by readers on the extracts from *Oryx and Crake* on Wattpad show engagement by both long-time fans of Atwood's work and a host of new readers as well. Atwood herself does not appear to have added anything to the site since 2017. Other platforms are also popular, however. Hanif Kureishi is one of a number of established authors using the platform Substack to share writing, and both Wattpad and Substack have lively comments sections.

The examples of Franzen and Atwood show two different approaches to change in the literary marketplace due to so-called digital disruption. New data on the decline of average earnings for authors,[4] concerns about the effects of screens on deep reading at the neurological level,[5] and the rise of a new kind of self-publishing through Amazon and its ilk all contribute to a sense of destabilization in the world of books and publishing. But change has become the new normal for publishing in the decades after consolidation in the sector in the 1970s and 1980s, followed by technological upheaval in the 1990s and 2000s that persists.[6] Radical changes are felt in the production, circulation, and consumption of books and literature, including in the domain of authorship and the remuneration authors receive; the increased conflation between publishing and bookselling; the tension between e-books and print, and online versus bricks-and-mortar stores; and in reading. Headlines announcing the end of the book or the irrelevancy of reading in a media-saturated world continue to come and go. Books remain.

To consider some of these questions around authorship, publishing, and reading practices in the digital age, this chapter looks to concepts from the

---

[2] Margaret Atwood, *Oryx and Crake* (London: Bloomsbury, 2003).
[3] Margaret Atwood, "About @MargaretAtwood," *Wattpad*, April 25, 2023, www.wattpad.com/user/MargaretAtwood.
[4] "Authors Guild Survey Shows Drastic 42 Percent Decline in Authors Earnings in Last Decade," *Authors Guild*, January 5, 2019, www.authorsguild.org/industry-advocacy/authors-guild-survey-shows-drastic-42-percent-decline-in-authors-earnings-in-last-decade/.
[5] Maryanne Wolf, *Reader, Come Home: the Reading Brain in a Digital World* (New York: Harper Collins Publishers, 2018).
[6] Claire Squires, "The Global Market 1970–2000: Consumers," in *A Companion to the History of the Book*, ed. Simon Eliot and Jonathan Rose (New York: Blackwell Publishing), 406–418.

field of book history and new media studies to unpack features of and consequences for the literary marketplace in digital times. To attempt to make sense of these changes, this chapter looks at researchers' attempts to update Robert Darnton's communications circuit: a mapping of the production, circulation and reception of books in a social, intellectual, and commercial environment (see Figure 8.1). The chapter considers Adriaan van der Weel's revision of Darnton's circuit, highlighting the "short circuit"[7] and Padmini Ray Murray's and Claire Squires's own "digital publishing communications circuit."[8] It then turns to a few key controversies in the digital literary sphere to highlight some of the grand shifts that have come about as a result of the digitalization of literary production, circulation, and reception in practice. Finally, the chapter considers particular case studies that illuminate the many complications of the literary marketplace in the digital literary sphere, such as the relationship between fan fiction and literary consumption, as evidenced through the pathway to publication of E. L. James's *Fifty Shades of Grey*;

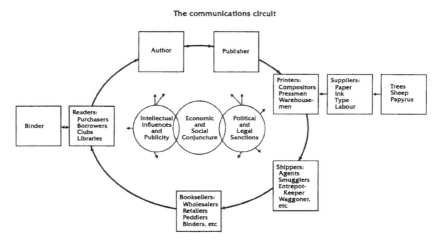

Figure 8.1 Robert Darnton's Communications Circuit. Robert Darnton, "What Is the History of Books?," *Daedalus* 111, no. 3 (1982), 67.

---

[7] Adriaan van der Weel, "The Communications Circuit Revisited," *Jaarboek voor Nederlandse boekgeschiedenis* 8 (2001): 13–25.
[8] Padmini Ray Murray and Claire Squires, "The Digital Publishing Communications Circuit," *Book 2.0* 3.3 (2013): 3–23.

the tension between the rise of Amazon and the cultural significance of bricks-and-mortar stores; the undulating successes of the e-book and its relationship to the material printed codex book; and the role of Goodreads and other paratextual, paramarket components of what Simone Murray calls "the digital literary sphere."[9] Mark Davis argues that "pathways to reception have increased" in the digital era through the rise of "social media forums such as Goodreads, Facebook, Twitter, YouTube, Instagram, Reddit, Tumblr, Library-Thing and Pinterest, among others," but concludes that "none of them are authoritative."[10] Central to this is what Davis sees as the equal and opposite narrowing of the "valorizing pathways and practices of literary reception" in the digital era.[11] Davis's insight is central to this chapter's understanding of the digital literary marketplace, in which the expanded opportunities for publication in new ways, giving voice to new authors, are balanced by the narrowing of opportunities for financial or reputational recompense for that work.

8.1 The Publishing Circuit and Its Usefulness in the Digital Literary Sphere

In making sense of what he saw as the "communications circuit" of writing, publishing, distributing, and reading, Robert Darnton developed a visual representation of the chain or circuit of agency and action in the publishing world.[12] While specifically reflecting the circuit as he saw it in the eighteenth-century French book trade, the image was designed to be relevant to or adaptable for other eras and contexts, and takes into consideration the traditional roles of author, publisher, printer, and their suppliers, and the physical movement of books from sites of production to sites of reception through the agency of booksellers.

At the center of the circuit are concepts that influence some or all of these sites of action, including what Darnton terms "economic and social conjecture," "intellectual influences and publicity," and "political and legal sanctions."[13] The circuit's visual construction allows for some level of interplay between these elements in the style of a Venn diagram, and

---

[9] Simone Murray, *The Digital Literary Sphere: Reading, Writing, and Selling Books in the Internet Era* (Baltimore: Johns Hopkins University Press, 2018).
[10] Mark Davis, "Who Are the New Gatekeepers? Literary Mediating and Post-Digital Publishing," *Publishing Means Business*, ed. Aaron Mannion, Millicent Weber and Katherine Day (Clayton: Monash University Publishing, 2017), 129.
[11] Ibid.   [12] Robert Darnton, "What Is the History of Books?," *Daedalus* 111.3 (1982): 65–83.
[13] Ibid., 67.

when Darnton came to reconsider, if not revise, his circuit in his later work[14] he focused on the robustness and adaptability of the circuit as a way of understanding how publishing works, while acknowledging room for improvement. The circuit became influential in the field of book history. However, within a decade of its publication, new technologies of information and communication began challenging the old workings of the sector and, therefore, the usefulness of the circuit to the contemporary publishing landscape.

Adriaan van der Weel sought to incorporate what he saw as some fundamental shifts in the functionality of the publishing industry as engendered by the digital turn in the 1990s. His model conceived of "the digital transmission of texts" as a *short* circuit, a way of looking to both the history and the future of the book.[15] It's a short circuit, in van der Weel's view, because the gatekeepers that exist between author and reader in traditional print publishing models (agent, publisher, printer, book distributor, bookseller, book reviewer) are cut out in a way that seemingly allows for a more direct communication between author and reader. This new phase in the communications circuit, he argues, is characterized by low costs, multiplicity, and, ultimately, the democratization of print culture: "Electronic text has the amazing characteristics that the original can be multiplied without limit, without loss of quality and at negligible cost. If an electronic text is available on a network of linked computers (such as the Internet), such multiplication can, in addition, take place over any distance at the same negligible cost."[16] In this wording, we see something of the hyperbolic language characteristic of the techno-enthusiastic response common before the dot.com bubble-burst of the early 2000s. Ultimately, this is a matter of the fundamental values that underpin the Internet, at least as it was seen at the time. According to van der Weel's analysis, "The internet is thus capable of 'democratising' in the true sense of bringing to ordinary people the distribution of recorded text (and further democratising production) by its low cost and easy access."[17] This is emblematic of much contemporaneous commentary, which tended to focus on the democratization of publishing and the financial benefits of decreasing the cost of replication and distribution inherent in book publishing. Van der Weel's emphasis on democracy has not diminished. In 2019 he wrote:

---

[14] Robert Darnton, "'What Is the History of Books?' Bevisited," *Modern Intellectual History* 4.3 (2007): 495–508.
[15] Van der Weel, "Communications Circuit Revisited."   [16] Ibid., 17.   [17] Ibid.

> The paper world is essentially hierarchical and top-down. Only the privileged have access to print to reply to anything they have read. Others are confined to making approving or disapproving notes in the margins of their reading. Online, the author–reader relationship essentially swivels by 90 degrees to become horizontal and "democratic." But in the meantime, the hierarchical print world with all its access barriers has not vanished.[18]

In this way, for van der Weel, the Internet, and other digital-oriented technologies feeding into and enabled by the Internet, recast Darnton's communications circuit and provide new shortcuts to publication. For van der Weel and others, these shortcuts work to overcome the gatekeeping and bias that prevents ordinary people from having access to pathways to publication.

As with so much of the enthusiasm for the affordances of technology and its influence on the world prior to the dot.com bubble-burst, much of the hype of the so-called "short circuit" has also failed to live up to its promises. This is not to say that extraordinary opportunities are not afforded by the capacity for the closing of these distances, but that for the most part there are new barriers to replace or complement the old. A short circuit can be both a shortcut and a blown fuse; the role played by Amazon in the contemporary literary sphere looks more like an example of the latter. Other commentators have questioned the extent to which new technologies of writing, publishing, and sharing work have democratized the literary sphere.[19] Nick Canty, for example, argues that while there exists some evidence that "technology has democratised publishing[,] the evidence is patchy and contradictory."[20] Canty highlights the gap between access and success: "Access is almost universal but it is still a winner-takes-all world for authors and existing hierarchies carry over to new media."[21] That is, the barriers and biases inherent in the traditional publishing model are not overcome by increasing individuals' access to the world stage through the technological and social inventions of the World Wide Web and social media. What was meant to be (or forecast to be) a closing of the distance between writer and reader has now, in hindsight that was not

---

[18] Adriaan van der Weel, "Literary Authorship in the Digital Age," *The Cambridge Handbook of Literary Authorship*, ed. Ingo Berensmeyer, Gert Buelens, and Marysa Demoor (Cambridge: Cambridge University Press, 2019), 220.

[19] See Murray, "Digital Literary Sphere," Ray Murray and Squires, "The Digital Publishing Communications Circuit"; and Nicholas Canty, "Publishing and Technology: The Digital Revolution, Democratisation and New Technologies," in *Publishing and Culture*, ed. Dallas Baker, Donna Lee Brian, and Jen Webb (Newcastle Upon Tyne: Cambridge Scholars Publishing, 2019), 184–198.

[20] Canty, "Publishing and Technology," 184.   [21] Canty, "Publishing and Technology," 195.

available to van der Weel in 2001, become something more like a black hole of noise. Coupled with declining financial remuneration for authors in the publishing circuit and the rise in power of online booksellers, this has become very complicated.

Other adaptations of Darnton's circuit to the digital publishing moment are to be found in the works of Simone Murray[22] and Padmini Ray Murray and Claire Squires.[23] In *The Digital Literary Sphere*, Simone Murray points out the problems with the linearity of Darnton's circuit, even if it allows for conceptual overlaps.[24] In response to this, Murray recasts the circuit as a sphere, given what she identifies as "the collapsing and disintermediation of the traditional print-centric communications circuit."[25] Murray argues that

> The chief characteristic of Darnton's model is its linearity: like an electrical circuit, printed texts flow from an "Author" right around to "Readers" via the crucial gatekeeping intermediary of a "Publisher." As with an electrical circuit, if the current is interrupted or a link is missed, the bulb fails to light – that is, communication does not occur. Authors may communicate with their readers *only* via the medium of a publisher, and direct contact between authors and readers is at best unlikely (perhaps in the form of fan mail), represented by Darnton's tentative dotted line.[26]

This is a linearity that is in many ways at odds with the fundamental foundations of the digital literary sphere, and one that van der Weel's early accounting of changes in the digital literary sphere has not been able to address. Padmini Ray Murray and Claire Squires offer several revisions of Darnton's work in their 2013 article "The Digital Publishing Communications Circuit," highlighting that the historical modes of transmission of value in publishing where content or intellectual property is circulated from writer to reader through a publishing system that provides a wide range of editorial, marketing, and design activities "is being disrupted and disintermediated at every stage."[27] Ray Murray and Squires begin by highlighting elements of the twentieth-century literary sphere that Darnton's circuit neglects to account for, such as the role of literary agents in the value chain from writer to reader. This too begins to change in the digital moment. For Ray Murray and Squires, "the

---

[22] Simone Murray "Publishing Studies: Critically Mapping Research in Search of a Discipline," *Publishing Research Quarterly* 22.4 (2006): 3–25; Simone Murray "'Remix My Lit' Towards an Open Access Literary Culture," *Convergence* 16.1 (2010): 23–38; Murray 2018.
[23] Ray Murray and Squires, "The Digital Publishing Communications Circuit." [24] Ibid.
[25] Ibid., 9 [26] Murray, "Digital Literary Sphere," 25–26
[27] Ray Murray and Squires, "The Digital Publishing Communications Circuit," 9

disintermediated digital publishing communications circuit ... becomes a battleground for control of the marketplace, both in terms of financial reward and placement in the value chain. Relationships between authors, literary agents, publishers, retailers and distributors are changing with the roles of some being taken over by others, or dropping out of the circuit altogether."[28] It is this set of conditions Ray Murray and Squires take up in their revised circuit that they call the "Digital Publishing Communications Circuit"(see Figure 8.2).[29]

In this model, Darnton's conception of the circuit in which, as Ray Murray and Squires have it, "readers sit at the end of a process in which the book passes from the author via various intermediaries" is shown to be outmoded.[30] Rather, a range of new intermediaries and old intermediaries, inflected differently by technologies and new social practices, are elements

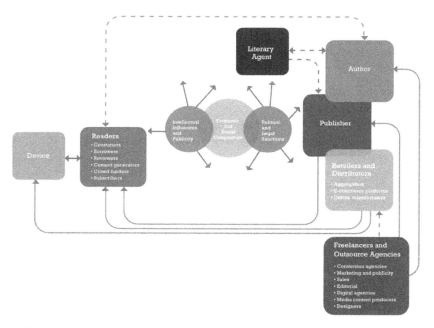

Figure 8.2 Ray Murray and Squires's Digital Publishing Communications Circuit.

[28] Ibid.   [29] Ibid.   [30] Ibid., 14.

of the circuit that have a relationship both to the readers and also to the retailers and distributors of a text.

8.2 Bookselling and the E-Book

The domain of bookselling is one of the most contentious aspects of the digital literary sphere, due in no small part to the enormous influence of Amazon – an entity that complicates every aspect of and interaction in the digital literary circuit. Headlines have charted the rise of a very different kind of bookseller and the unstable fortunes of traditional booksellers over time, from the rise and decline of the bookstore chain Borders to the position of independent bookstores in the market, to the myriad of ways the sector seeks to compete with massive online retailers. Not only is the bookselling sector in constant flux, this is examined in excruciating detail in the media, within a frame of the supposed decline of the material book if not the book altogether. New financial models for publishing destabilize many of the historical markers of the sector. A large component of the literary marketplace is now influenced by the platformization of cultural production. Amazon has thoroughly changed the sector – first by selling books online, then by developing algorithms for selling books, then in providing hardware, software, content, and eventually publishing mechanisms for e-books, and print-on-demand – with flow-on effects in the publishing landscape. Amazon maintains a number of publishing imprints under the banner of Amazon Publishing or APub. AmazonEncore, which is a print-on-demand service for out-of-print books, was the first of these, launched in 2009. This is complemented by a number of genre-based imprints such as Montlake for Romance fiction, Little A for literary fiction, and 47North for Science Fiction and Fantasy, amongst others. The history of the relationship between bookselling, reading devices, publishing and printing platforms, and the shape of the literary marketplace in the digital age reveals elements of the publishing circuit not always immediately obvious. A quick tour of the history of the e-reader sheds light on how e-books entered the bookselling market.

The arrival of the Amazon Kindle in 2007 marked a change in the e-reading market, with far-reaching consequences for the future of bookselling.[31] This was twelve years after Amazon started selling books

---

[31] Simon Peter Rowberry, "Ebookness," *Convergence* 23.3 (2017): 289–305; Simon Peter Rowberry, *Four Shades of Gray: The Amazon Kindle Platform* (Cambridge, MA: MIT Press, 2022).

online, before quickly expanding to other forms of retail, and ten years after Barnes & Noble, a bricks-and-mortar bookstore chain, sued Amazon over its right to use the term "bookstore" to describe its (then) exclusively online business, suggesting "book broker" was more accurate.[32] The two companies settled this matter in October 1997, with neither side paying damages nor changing the way it described its business, yet the broader questions over what role bookselling plays in the digital literary sphere remain.

There had been many attempts to design a game-changing e-book reader prior to the Kindle, such as the Sony Reader, which first launched in 2004 and did modestly well. Before that was the Rocket eBook, released by NuvoMedia in 1998 and only in production for two years. These early attempts themselves followed on from a spate of devices collectively known as personal digital assistants (PDAs) in the late 1980s and early 1990s, including the Apple Newton and the Palm Pilot. These PDAs were multi-use handheld computers that encompassed many functions, such as electronic calendars, notetaking, games, calculators, and contacts, and which also included e-book functionality in a range of formats. For example, French company Mobipocket released the robust .mobi e-book file format in the early 2000s, which continued to gain market share and was bought out by Amazon in 2005. Reading was only a small component of the purpose or affordance of the PDA devices, which were aimed more at business users. Research was conducted around the usefulness of PDAs for reading in tertiary education environments,[33] and some universities experimented with using e-books on PDA devices for textbooks. In terms of leisure reading, however, much of the early discussion about the usefulness of devices such as PDAs was limited to the library sphere.[34] Although computer hobbyists were downloading from Project Gutenberg in large numbers, there is little scholarship about the cultural or literary implications of this.

In response to the Kindle, Barnes & Noble released its own, US-only, e-reader device in 2009 using a range of file formats, including its proprietary PDB format, EPUB, and PDF. The Kobo e-reader joined the market

---

[32] Patrick M. Reilly, "Barnes & Noble Sues Amazon.Com Over Rival's Book-Selling Claims," *Wall Street Journal*, May 13, 1997, Eastern edition, www.proquest.com/newspapers/barnes-amp-noble-sues-amazon-com-over-rivals-book/docview/398565981/se-2.

[33] See Jennifer Waycott and Agnes Kukulska-Hulme, "Students' Experiences with PDAs for Reading Course Materials," *Personal and Ubiquitous Computing* 7 no. 1 (2003): 30–43.

[34] Roberta Burk, "E-book Devices and the Marketplace: in Search of Customers," *Library Hi Tech* 19.4 (2001): 325–331.

in 2010 and supported EPUB and PDF formats. Formats developed to deter piracy were never very successful at doing so. While the EPUB format is the most universal, it isn't supported by Kindle devices and apps. Whereas companies such as Microsoft attempted to enter into the e-reader market – for example, when Microsoft partnered with Barnes and Noble and its Nook device for a short time between 2012 and 2014 – the focus of other companies such as Apple was a broader technological object that could incorporate e-books but not be limited to them, reinvigorating the PDA market with the new screen technology and its mediatization. This saw research and development that led to the release of the iPad early in 2010, building on the strength in sales and functionality of early generation iPhones; Samsung released an Android tablet late in 2010. The capacity to serve as e-readers was part of the sales strategy for tablets from the beginning. For example, Apple launched iBooks (later renamed Apple Books), a book equivalent to iTunes, concurrent with the release of the iPad. This platformization of the reading experience created demand for e-books through the novelty but also through convenience (though this demand has waned slightly over the years, or at least tapered off).

Platformization and its convenience are at work on the supply side of the digital literary sphere as well. Amazon produces software not only for readers but also for writers, in the form of Amazon's Kindle Direct Publishing suite of tools and services.[35] In an attempt to streamline the process of getting books to market, Amazon provides free software for writers to turn manuscripts written in external software such as Microsoft Word into a well-formatted Kindle e-book. According to Bradley et al., models like those exemplified by Kindle Direct or Apple's iBooks have changed the publishing landscape dramatically, vastly increasing the ratio of self-published e-books to traditionally published books and e-books. This has created a new financial model in publishing, characterized by "hyperabundance" of self-published e-books in the marketplace; the "blurring of boundaries" between newly published material and reused or remixed material; nonstandardized e-book metadata; the inability to confirm an e-book's "quality and value"; and "discovery" as challenges in the e-book market.[36]

As an example of this new financial model, consider these rather graphic opening lines from a well-known self-published work: "DS Wendy Knight

---

[35] Jana Bradley, Bruce Fulton, Marlene Helm, and Katherine A. Pittner, "Non-Traditional Book Publishing," *First Monday* 16.8 (August 2011).
[36] Ibid., n.p.

stared at the crime-scene photograph of Ella Barrington. Ella's swollen purple face looked lifeless as her head sat indented in the mud. Blood had trickled from her nose and dried onto her lips. Her eyes had the appearance of glass, almost doll-like."[37] The author sets the tone here, free of the editorial constraints of a traditional publishing house. Beyond the text, this work serves to illuminate some of the factors involved in "participation" in the Kindle Direct Publishing "program" as Amazon terms its transactions.

These lines are taken from Adam Croft's *Too Close for Comfort* (Kindle edition), the first novel by a marketing manager who, so the news story goes, quit his job to take up an opportunity to become an author through Amazon's Kindle Director Publishing. *Too Close for Comfort*, published in 2011, is part of a series of books by Croft that has sold 350,000 copies in five years.[38] These books are priced between US$0.99 and $9.99 (at the time of writing, pricing fluctuations is one the features of this model, with authors encouraged to play with pricing and discounting to build a readership). While the Kindle version of the book is the first and most emphasized format for this series of self-published crime novels, audiobook versions (read by the author) and paperback print versions are also available to purchase, most often through print-on-demand facilities. The paperback is $9.99 through Amazon, and second-hand copies are available on eBay and AbeBooks, where the publisher is listed as CreateBook. On Amazon, no publisher is listed for this title; on WorldCat, the international library database, circlehouse is listed as the publisher of three of the four editions registered and Amazon.com (Firm) is listed as the publisher of the fourth. On the audiobook page on Amazon, Adam Croft is listed as "Author, Narrator, Publisher," introducing tension between these roles and their traditional understandings.

In 2018, Croft published what *The Guardian* called his "gamechanger" book: *Her Last Tomorrow*, which sold 150,000 copies in five months.[39] *Her Last Tomorrow* is housed in thirty-eight libraries around the world and its five editions list the publisher as Adam Croft himself; circlehouse (a self-publishing company that announces "Your story, your book, your way" and "We're passionate about books. We also know the publishing industry

---

[37] Adam Croft, *Too Close for Comfort* (2011). Kindle edition, no publisher given, www.amazon.com.au/Too-Close-Comfort-gripping-Culverhouse-ebook/dp/B004I438EE/ref=sr_1_1; Google Books gives Smashwords as the publisher, www.google.com.au/books/edition/Too_Close_for_Comfort/kEpTDwAAQBAJ; Worldcat identifies the publisher of the print book as circlehouse (place of publication not identified), www.worldcat.org/title/1029836150.

[38] Alison Flood, "From Paying the Bills to £2,000 a Day: Making a Killing from Self-Publishing," *The Guardian*, June 2, 2016, www.theguardian.com/books/2016/jun/02/adam-croft-self-published-her-last-tomorrow-story.

[39] Ibid.

as [sic] we know it is dead");[40] and finally Thomas & Mercer – this last one signaling that Croft has subsequently signed with an Amazon imprint.

As this tour through one author's use of new platforms for publication has shown, there is significant support in the form of infrastructure designed to short circuit the traditional publishing sphere, as van der Weel would have it. Amazon has swept in and made good on the idea of the shortened circuit of the publishing sphere – but not in the utopian way that early enthusiasts had hoped. Nick Canty raises the question of "a narrowing of publishing decisions and the acquisition of titles and the sourcing of authors with editorial decisions being based on author social media profiles and the size of their fan base or data on past sales performance."[41] Author Douglas Preston has exposed a range of ways that online self-publishing platforms such as Amazon Kindle Direct enable different forms of piracy, such as "counterfeiting, author 'doppleganging,' title cloning, e-book piracy, cut-and-paste plagiarism and other rip-offs."[42] This can range from taking the text of a published book and uploading it through the self-publishing platform as if it were a book for which the uploader holds the copyright, to more covert tactics such as using cover art or titles that are very similar to those of well-known books in order to encourage mis-clicking or accidental purchase. Undoubtedly, the digital era has introduced confusion and uncertainty into what had been an apparently stable and largely structured and policed system of authorization of the literary object in the twentieth century.

That confusion is particularly evident throughout the many paratexts of literary works in digital publishing environments.[43] Gérard Genette uses the idea of the paratext to account for the influence of all the elements of a published work that accompany the text but are not the actual text, including blurbs, cover art, dedications and epigraphs, acknowledgments and author biographical notes, and so on. The transformation of paratexts into hypertextual digital objects in the digital age may is illustrative of the ease with which digital publishing can play with the traditional hallmarks of publishing in ways that open opportunities for new voices to be published

---

[40] circlehouse, no date, https://web.archive.org/web/20130816005138/http://www.circlehouse.co.uk/.
[41] Canty, "Publishing and Technology," 185.
[42] Douglas Preston, "Op-Ed: Online Book-Selling Scams Steal a Living from Writers," *Los Angeles Times,* July 26, 2019, www.latimes.com/opinion/story/2019-07-25/amazon-books-counterfeit-authors-copyright.
[43] Tully Barnett, "Hyperparatextuality: Making Meaning in the Reading Frame," *Book 2.0* 10.1 (2020): 43–58.

but also in many instances undermine the quality indicators many readers rely on. For example, the titles from publishing house Thomas & Mercer, a publishing arm of Amazon largely devoted to the mystery and thriller genre, display awards and bestseller status markers of all kinds, from Amazon Charts bestsellers through to Washington Post and Wall Street Journal bestsellers. Titles on the website sport the Amazon Publishing logo, a blue arrow rather than Amazon's famous yellow one, and website visitors are invited to "Sign in with your Amazon Publishing account credentials to access the APub.com Dashboard." These similar but different icons spread the hallmarks of Amazon branding from reading to authoring. If we accept that a book's paratextual elements connect the content of the work with a diverse variety of stakeholder actors in a network such as different kinds of readerships, awards and other markers of legitimacy, authority, and quality, its place in collections, genre, and other metadata, and so on,[44] then the digital paratexts of the platformatized closed-circuit writing and reading environment serve functions that legitimate the digital literary object and place it in a context that both emulates and displaces the original work.

While Amazon's Kindle Direct Publishing and other providers maintain pathways for users to turn their manuscripts into e-books through digital platforms, traditional publishers have had a more difficult time. Authonomy – HarperCollins's version of a publisher-owned digital platform for the sharing of and commenting on manuscripts – closed in 2015 after seven years. The Authonomy platform used a model in which manuscripts could be uploaded for reading and commentary by other members of the community, and each month the five most highly ranked manuscripts were read by commissioning editors.[45] The following year, Penguin Random House sold Author Solutions, its own self-publishing company, to a private equity firm for a small proportion of the $116 million it had paid for the platform just four years earlier.[46] The optimism that these platforms would somehow automate the so-called "slushpile" of unsolicited manuscripts – by having crowdsourced readers and other hopeful writers unearth the gems or discover the next E. L. James – was rather short lived, even by Silicon Valley standards.

---

[44] Gerard Genette, *Paratexts: Thresholds of Interpretation* (Cambridge: Cambridge University Press, 1997); Simone Murray, "'Selling' Literature: The Cultivation of Book Buzz in the Digital Literary Sphere," *Logos 27* 1 (2016): 11–21.
[45] Alison Flood, "Authonomy Writing Community Closed by HarperCollins," *The Guardian*, August 20, 2015, www.theguardian.com/books/2015/aug/20/authonomy-writing-community-closed-by-harpercollins.
[46] Henry Mance, "Penguin Random Exits Self-Publishing," *Financial Times*, January 6, 2016, www.ft.com/content/a6070036-b3d6-11e5-8358-9a82b43f6b2f.

8.3 Fan Fiction

Self-publishing has another component outside of the vertical integration of Amazon: fan fiction. A darling case study in the commercial opportunities of fan fiction is presented by author E. L. James; her Fifty Shades series is often used to demonstrate the way online platforms provide direct access from the writer to the reader in ways that create opportunities[47] and "democratize" publication in line with van der Weel's views of the capacities of online publishing.[48] But this discourse tends to lack nuance: as in many other areas, it seeks to extend rare individual exceptionalism to a broad base that it cannot sustain, assuming that access to the affordances of digital publication success are equitably distributed or that the open doors of the short circuit don't come at the expense of other doors closing.

In 2009, E. L. James uploaded to fanfiction.net part of a work-in-progress called *Master of the Universe* that developed an erotic story using Stephanie Meyer's *Twilight* characters to tell a different, steamier, story. She developed a following and was encouraged to "file off the serial numbers": to remove traces of Meyer's work from her own. The characters were placed in a different universe (i.e., one without vampires). Meyer's character Bella was recast as a young and naïve student Anastasia Steele, and vampire Edward as the confident and domineering businessman Christian Grey. Having removed all copyrighted detail, James released the books first as e-books and then using a print-on-demand service in 2011. By 2012, James had signed a contract with Random House's Vintage imprint. The rest is history. This discrepancy between perceived and real opportunities is a particular feature of the digital age, where innovation is heralded as an open door even as the gates are closing fast as accessibility is shut down either by commercial interests or high volume of use. However, this is elided by a focus on the characteristics of the successful exceptional example, suggesting that if others could only emulate those characteristics they too would have access to equivalent success when really only the temporal characteristic – being in the right place at the right time as the platform is taking off – is the most salient characteristic in the success, and one that subsequent participants can't control or emulate.

Beyond the few examples of fan fiction authors who have gone on to secure publishing contracts and bestseller status, however, are a multitude

---

[47] Bethan Jones, "Fifty Shades of Exploitation: Fan Labor and Fifty Shades of Grey," *Transformative Works and Cultures* 15 (2014): 115–123; Paul Booth, *Playing Fans: Negotiating Fandom and Media in the Digital Age* (Iowa City: University of Iowa Press, 2015).
[48] Van der Weel, "Communications Circuit Revisited."

of authors working in the form of fan fiction in private and semiprivate, on- and offline communities, and in online shared public spaces such as Wattpad and Archive of our Own (AO3). Regardless of the opportunities for capitalizing on the "short circuit" of publishing in the digital age, the active fan fiction communities enact reading and writing publics that draw on and enhance a range of skills that support a critical civic public sphere. Critical reading and communicating skills are important for a strong political sphere and an informed citizenry, and for facing the wicked challenges of the present era. These thriving communities open doors to new practices of reading and writing, and new ways of developing a following, yet they do little to disrupt traditional publishing gatekeeping models.

8.4 Conclusion

The story of the digital literary marketplace is also the story of the bricks-and-mortar bookstores and publishing that supports them – complete with biased gatekeeping and quality control – augmented by transformative digital technologies and the upsurge of online interactivity brought about by social networking and the democratization of communication through online platforms. As many years have now passed between Darnton's original circuit and van der Weel's short circuit as between the notion of the short circuit and the publication of this chapter. The shortened circuit cannot be expected to tell the full story of the chain of content, value, and influence between the writer and the reader through a maze of digital infrastructure. After all, a glimpse at an issue of *Wired* magazine from 2000 shows a very different technological environment and set of expectations, with its techno-utopian framing of changing movements between humans and their technologies. Despite the enduring strength of the technology of the hardback and the paperback book, change is set to be the constant for the literary marketplace. The twofold dominance of Amazon – creating a convenient space for the purchase of books, the curation of wishlists, and recommendations, emphasized now through its acquisition of Goodreads, reviews, and communities of sharing (all elements of the demand-side of reading); and also developing a publishing model and platforms that cut out many of the traditional authorizers of the literary text (the supply side of reading) – has fundamentally changed the literary marketplace in the digital age.

The increasing popularity of digital platforms such as Wattpad and Amazon Kindle Direct Publishing means that writers now have the capacity to even more dramatically short the Darnton communications circuit, speaking (and selling) directly to their readers, bypassing the editors, publishers, printers, shippers, and booksellers who are seen to serve as gatekeepers and censors in the print model of publishing. Yet the barriers to cultural significance today are even more robust. As a result, the consequences of the "short circuit" model of Internet-based publication have been debated. On the one hand, platforms such as Wattpad and services like Kindle Direct Publishing are welcomed as agents that increasingly democratize the publishing sphere, allowing access to publication for voices, communities, subjects, and modes of expression that have been unable to gain traction in the print world, especially in the increasingly corporatized global publishing industry. On the other hand, these gate-keeping roles have been interpreted as forces for quality and for respect for authors. Others suggest that in the era of hyperabundance of e-books, authors are forced to spend valuable time marketing themselves and their works when they could be writing. On top of this, the recent decline in e-book sales and the ongoing resurgence of literature in print requires a constant reworking of any communications models to understand the networks of the book in digital environments. In presenting an overview of the controversies surrounding literary self-publishing and its relationship to the digital literary sphere, to economies of attention and prestige, to the debates over the health and the future of the book, this chapter has considered some of the twists and turns of the literary marketplace in the digital age – a marketplace marked by flux, by the development of new complications of the notions of production, distribution, and reception and the sense of where those terms begin and end, but also the rise of remarkable forms of access and new meaning for books and literature in the digital age.

CHAPTER 9

Fanfiction, Digital Platforms, and Social Reading
Anna Wilson

Since the advent of home dial-up, it's arguable that fanfiction (aka "fan fiction," "fanfic," or "fic") has been the most popular and prolific form of digital literature – that is, literature written, distributed, and read primarily, if not exclusively, online.[1] Archive of Our Own (AO3), the largest fan-owned, not-for-profit digital fanfiction archive, hosted 10.5 million works of fanfiction as of January 2023. Of the major for-profit archives, a 2019 study suggested that Wattpad hosted upwards of 8 million (the number is now no doubt far higher),[2] while Fanfiction.net had more than 14 million. There are also countless more works dispersed over other, smaller archives and social media platforms. With this explosion in popularity in the digital era has come mainstream visibility for this previously niche and often secretive literary subculture, along with seismic changes in the way fanfiction is written, read, and circulated. And yet, fanfiction is rarely analyzed as *digital* literature, nor are the ways in which fanfiction challenges dominant literary paradigms often placed in conversation with other digital literatures.[3]

---

[1] I am very grateful to Dr Kristina Busse and Dr Kavita Mudan Finn for their valuable comments on this article, and for making unpublished proofs available to me. A note about vocabulary in this chapter: I prefer "fanfiction" and "fic" (the standard terms in fanfiction communities) to "fan fiction" (the standard term in the field of fan studies). I will use the words "source text" and "source creator" to refer to the original text that has inspired the fan activity and the creator of that text. This is to avoid defining fanfiction and fan writers in opposition to terms such as "original work" or "creator," since fans are also creators and the term "original" is often misleading and evaluative. I also use "transformative work," a term adopted from American legal terminology by the fan advocacy nonprofit *The Organization of Transformative Works*, to describe fanworks of all kinds, as opposed to terms such as "derivative work."

[2] There are many pieces of fanfiction on the site which are untagged as such, making giving exact figures difficult. toastystats (destinationtoast), "How Many Fanworks Are There on Wattpad?," An Archive of Our Own, November 20, 2018, https://archiveofourown.org/works/16948002.

[3] Some important exceptions to this include Abigail De Kosnik, *Rogue Archives: Digital Cultural Memory and Media Fandom* (Cambridge, MA: The MIT Press, 2016); Judith Fathallah, "Digital Fanfic in Negotiation: LiveJournal, Archive of Our Own, and the Affordances of Read–Write Platforms," *Convergence* 26.4 (2020): 857–873; Suzanne R. Black, "Adding a Digital Dimension to Fan Studies Methodologies," *Transformative Works and Cultures* 33 (June 15, 2020), https://doi.org/10.3983/twc.2020.1725; Louisa Ellen Stein, "'This Dratted Thing': Fannish Storytelling through New

154

This is partly because several key elements of fanfiction's community and practice have been characteristic of the genre since before its digital revolution. The first is the demographics of fanfiction communities. Several (necessarily small and selective) surveys have suggested the overwhelming predominance of women in fanfiction communities, with a significant population of people in gender minorities (including trans* and nonbinary people). In English-language fanfiction communities (on which this article focuses), the majority are white, and between the ages of fifteen and thirty (although with such huge numbers, there are still significant populations of fanfiction writers and consumers outside of those categories). While studies of the 1990s tended to assume that most fanfiction writers were heterosexual women, the number of fans self-identifying as members of a gender, sexual, or romantic minority has increased over time, now apparently outnumbering heterosexual fans in some fan community spaces.[4]

Other distinctive aspects of fanfiction which are typically given as characteristic of the genre and which have spanned the genre's move from analogue to digital include: a relationship between fanfiction and a source text or "canon," filling a desire for *more of* and/or *more from* the source text;[5] interaction between fans and source creators (both positive and negative); the emergence of fanfiction from and alongside communal reading practices as a means of exchanging opinions and theories about the source text with other fans;[6] and romance as a defining genre of fanfiction.[7]

Media," in *Fan Fiction and Fan Communities in the Age of the Internet: New Essays*, ed. Karen Hellekson and Kristina Busse (Jefferson: McFarland & Co., 2006), 245–260; Alexis Lothian, "From Transformative Works to #transformDH: Digital Humanities as (Critical) Fandom," *American Quarterly* 70.3 (2018): 371–393; Louisa Stein and Kristina Busse, "Limit Play: Fan Authorship between Source Text, Intertext, and Context," *Popular Communication* 7.4 (October 14, 2009): 192–207, https://doi.org/10.1080/15405700903177545.

[4] Prior to 2000, most assessments of fanfiction demographics were anecdotal or restricted to small fan communities, and few took race or ethnicity into account. Fanlore's "Fandom Statistics" page links to a number of studies of fanfiction demographics done across different platforms and fandoms from the 2000s to 2021: https://fanlore.org/wiki/Fandom_Statistics. In the 2018 Fansplaining Shipping Survey, with 17,391 participants drawn from AO3 users, 80% identified as other than heterosexual, 72% identified as female, 21% as nonbinary or genderqueer, and 9% as transgender; 77% self-identified as white, and the largest number of respondents were between 18 and 24.

[5] I use "source text" rather than the fan-preferred term "canon" to avoid confusion with the conventional meaning of the term "canon" in literature studies.

[6] I am indebted for this formulation to an unnamed fanfiction writer quoted in Sheenagh Pugh, *The Democratic Genre: Fan Fiction in a Literary Context* (Bridgend: Seren, 2005), 19.

[7] Katherine Morrissey, *"Romance Networks: Aspiration & Desire in Today's Digital Culture"* (unpublished PhD thesis, University of Wisconsin-Milwaukee, 2016); Anne Kustritz, "Slashing the Romance Narrative," *Journal of American Culture* 26.3 (September 2003): 371–384, https://doi.org/10.1111/1542-734X.00098.

There are currently two major scholarly approaches to fanfiction, which I shall call the "diachronic" and "synchronic" approaches.[8] The diachronic approach situates fanfiction in a *longue durée*, often going back to the literature of Classical Greece and Rome, that retells, continues, or otherwise adapts stories and characters already known to its audience, including epic, medieval romance, and so forth; less expansive vertical approaches locate fanfiction's origins in 1960s cult television and science fiction fan communities, and tend to enfold fanfiction's digital era into a continuation of practices developed in these communities.[9] The synchronic approach, on the other hand, situates fanfiction amid other kinds of fan creative activity or "transformative works" online and offline, including fanvids, filking (fan songwriting), fanart, *doujinshi* (fan-created manga), cosplay, fan essays or "meta," RPGs, fan discussion or debate, and interaction between fans and source creators.[10] In these two approaches, *digitality* as such rarely comes to the foreground as a significant subject or even medium of analysis. The diachronic approach might hold that while the digital environment has proved ideal for fan communities and practices that have continued along similar lines since at least the 1950s, few fan practices are wholly born digital (one exception being game mods), and fanfiction's digital revolution is one of scale rather than of essence. The synchronic approach might argue that fanfiction is inseparable from other fan practices that are mutually influential (since many fans both consume and create multiple kinds of transformative work), and fanfiction's digital medium is secondary to the fluidity between on- and offline activities. But *in its digital medium* fanfiction, like other digital literatures, demands a reassessment of fundamental categories of literary analysis such as the text, the author, the reader, and the act of reading itself. This article synthesizes elements of both the diachronic and synchronic approaches to fanfiction into a framework for reading fanfiction as digital literature, along three axes: *creative authority*, *social reading*, and *paratext*.

---

[8] Abigail Derecho, "Archontic Literature: A Definition, a History, and Several Theories of Fan Fiction," in *Fan Fiction and Fan Communities in the Age of the Internet*, ed. Karen Hellekson and Kristina Busse (Jefferson, NC: McFarland & Co., 2006), 61–67.

[9] See, for example, Pugh, *The Democratic Genre*; Anne Elizabeth Jamison, *Fic: Why Fanfiction Is Taking over the World* (Dallas: Smart Pop, an imprint of BenBella Books, Inc., 2013); Francesca Coppa, "A Brief History of Media Fandom," in *Fan Fiction and Fan Communities in the Age of the Internet*, ed. Kristina Busse and Karen Hellekson (Jefferson: McFarland & Co., 2006), 41–59.

[10] See, for example, Henry Jenkins, *Textual Poachers: Television Fans & Participatory Culture* (New York: Routledge, 1992).

9.1 Creative Authority

Scholarship on fanfiction has often pointed out that a fixation on originality as the highest form of creativity is a modern phenomenon, emerging in England with the rise of the novel in the eighteenth century. Samuel Richardson's attempts to suppress unauthorized continuations and adaptations of his bestselling novel *Pamela* (1740), including Henry Fielding's *Shamela* (1741), led to landmark cases in copyright law that restricted printing presses to properties to which they held licenses granted by the author.[11] If one defines fanfiction broadly as any text that supplements, continues, or retells another, we might look to Virgil's *Aeneid*, Milton's *Paradise Lost*, and indeed most premodern literature as fanfiction. However, even defined more narrowly as texts that supplement, continue, or retell, *and* which emerge from a community of desiring, loving, and often minoritized readers, fanfiction has a long history. Examples of fanfiction before the twentieth century might include Lady Dorothy Bradshaigh's commentaries and reworkings of *Clarissa* shared within her circle of friends, the powerfully affective retellings and supplementations of the Bible's account of the life of Christ aimed specifically at (and sometimes authored by) medieval women, John Lydgate's *Siege of Thebes* (in whose prologue the author joins the pilgrims of Chaucer's *Canterbury Tales* to add another tale to that work), and many more.[12]

The second half of the twentieth century saw the emergence of artistic movements that tended toward the disruption of Enlightenment notions of creativity and authorship. The histories of these artistic movements – which includes fanfiction – are bound up with each other but also are inseparable from their relationship with technology; these artistic communities were both earlier adopters of and often drove technological development.[13] Even as postmodernism generated artistic interest in reduplication and replication, popular culture, and the destabilization of the canon, the widespread adoption of new technologies of replication such as the photocopier opened up new possibilities for transformative art.

---

[11] Natasha Simonova, *Early Modern Authorship and Prose Continuations: Adaptation and Ownership from Sidney to Richardson*, Early Modern Literature in History (Houndmills: Palgrave Macmillan, 2015), 124–159; Kristina Busse, "The Return of the Author: Ethos and Identity Politics," in *Framing Fan Fiction: Literary and Social Practices in Fan Fiction Communities* (Iowa City: University of Iowa Press, 2017), 19–38.

[12] I have written elsewhere about the utility of the term "fanfiction" for discussing premodern literature; Anna Wilson, "Fan Fiction and Premodern Literature: Methods and Definitions," *Transformative Works and Cultures* 36 (September 15, 2021), https://doi.org/10.3983/twc.2021.2037.

[13] Linda Hutcheon, *A Poetics of Postmodernism: History, Theory, Fiction* (New York: Routledge, 1988).

The photocopier enabled cheap, fast publication and distribution of zines, self-published magazines which were the first venues for *Star Trek* fanfiction as well as many other marginal artistic and political subcultures.[14] This rapid adoption of the photocopier anticipated the digital revolution in fan communities several decades later.

At the same time, the founders of hip-hop were using turntables to sample and remix tracks to put a creator's distinctive spin on another artist's work, often without that artist's consent or remuneration.[15] Hip-hop group 2 Live Crew's unlicensed 1989 use of a sample from the Roy Orbison track "Pretty Woman" led to a landmark 1994 United States Supreme Court ruling on copyright and artistic fair use (*Campbell* v. *Acuff-Rose Music, Inc.*, 510 US 569). As this case was moving through the courts, fan communities were taking advantage of new technological advances to move online. Fanfiction-hosting listservs were appearing in digital fora such as Yahoo Usergroups, then increasingly in self-hosted archives via domain providers such as Geocities, in commercially run fanfiction digital archives (Fanfiction.net was founded in 1999), and on personal blogs.

In the 2000s, legal scholars and pro-fanfiction activists would adopt the language of the *Campbell* v. *Acuff-Rose Music* ruling to justify fanfiction's legality as an artistic practice in the face of legal threats to fanfiction archive webhosts and individual authors from owners of major media properties, including Warner Brothers and Lucasfilms.[16] In 2008, Lawrence Lessig coined the term "remix culture," linking the turntable to the rise of communities using digital technologies to make art by combining or editing pre-existing materials.[17]

The explosion of popularity and accessibility through the digital revolution drove major shifts within fanfiction culture. In the 1970s and 1980s, fanzines were sold at booths at conventions, by mail catalogues, and

---

[14] Several university libraries in the USA have dedicated collections of fanzines, the largest being at the University of Iowa and Texas A&M.

[15] Abigail T. Derecho, *"Illegitimate Media: Race, Gender and Censorship in Digital Remix Culture"* (ProQuest Dissertations Publishing, 2008), https://search.proquest.com/docview/304541549?pq-origsite=primo. Justin A. Williams, *Rhymin' and Stealin': Musical Borrowing in Hip-Hop* (Ann Arbor: University of Michigan Press, 2013), Wayne M. Cox, "Rhymin' and Stealin'? Rhymin' and Stealin'? The History of Sampling in the Hip-Hop and Dance Music Worlds and How US Copyright Law & Judicial Precedent Serves to Shackle Art," *Virginia Sports and Entertainment Law Journal* 14.2 (Spring, 2015): 219–249.

[16] Rebecca Tushnet, "Copyright Law, Fan Practices, and the Rights of the Author," in *Fandom: Identities and Communities in a Mediated World*, ed. Jonathan Gray, Cornel Sandvoss, and C. Lee Harrington (New York: New York University Press, 2007), 60–71. www.transformativeworks.org/legal/.

[17] Lawrence Lessig, *Remix: Making Art and Commerce Thrive in the Hybrid Economy* (New York: The Penguin Press, 2008).

through friends; from the advent of search engines, it became possible to access fanfiction with the touch of a button. In the early days of the web, fanfiction writers commonly began their stories with a disclaimer along these lines: "I do not own these characters, I'm making no money from this story, please don't sue me."[18] Such disclaimers, of dubious legal weight, nonetheless demonstrated a major shift between privately distributed fanzines and online publishing: an uneasy awareness among fanfiction readers and writers of being visible to powerful media owners who might object not only to unlicensed spin-offs, but to a loss of control of their brand. This was a particular concern around romantic fanfiction for family-friendly brands.[19] This sense of vulnerability contributed to the widespread adoption of pseudonyms in digital fandom (writers in fanzines often used their real names, one of the reasons why fanzine digitization projects have sometimes proved controversial[20]). This use of pseudonymity and the adoption of various privacy technologies was particularly the case for slash (same-sex romance) fanfiction and real person fanfiction, two popular genres of fanfiction in existence since the 1960s whose content made them controversial both within fan communities and among source owners and creators.[21]

Although they still attract criticism, these most controversial areas of fanfiction are now among its most widespread and popular. Slash in particular has become in some respects emblematic of fanfiction, both in the broader culture and within the academy, and has attracted its strongest defenses as an artistic culture, influenced by work in cultural studies by Stuart Hall and other proponents of the Birmingham school which focused on subversive audience engagement with popular culture. In this understanding of fanfiction, it offers a space for fans to perform resistive readings, imagining minoritized affects and identities into their favorite media properties. Abigail Derecho influentially situates fanfiction in a history of "archontic literature": literature that adds itself to another text's "archive,"

---

[18] Alexandra Herzog, "'But This Is My Story and This Is How I Wanted to Write It': Author's Notes as a Fannish Claim to Power in Fan Fiction Writing," *Transformative Works and Cultures* 11 (2012): https://doi.org/10.3983/twc.2012.0406; Derecho, "Illegitimate Media," 140–174.
[19] Henry Jenkins, *Convergence Culture: Where Old and New Media Collide* (New York: New York University Press, 2006), 169–205.
[20] See, for example, the comments on the OTW's announcement of The Fan Culture Preservation Project, a partnership with the University of Iowa. One commenter writes, "my fanzines are meant for fans. Not scholars. I don't want my zines to be able to be photocopied and sent off to god-knows-who." The Organization for Transformative Works, "Announcing: The Fan Culture Preservation Project!" www.transformativeworks.org/announcing-fan-culture-preservation-project/.
[21] Camille Bacon-Smith, *Enterprising Women: Television Fandom and the Creation of Popular Myth* (Philadelphia: University of Pennsylvania Press, 1992), 228–254.

in the Derridean sense, and which, she argues, has a history "as a medium of social and political resistance," particularly by women.[22] Other scholars taking this tack have argued that fans rereading their central homosocial pair-bonds (Starsky and Hutch, Kirk and Spock) as homoerotic subverts the misogyny of many of the science-fiction and police procedural shows beloved of fans.[23] The undeniable recuperative and reparative potential of fanfiction continues to characterize its overall profile; self-published, with low barriers to access, within often supportive communities, fanfiction is widely recognized to offer unique spaces both to explore underrepresented experiences (including disability; mental and physical illness; minoritized gender, sexual, and racial identities), and to critique and celebrate their representations (or lack thereof) in popular media.[24]

However, scholars of fanfiction increasingly resist characterizing fanfiction as *fundamentally* subversive or radical, instead teasing out its multiple affordances for reflecting audience desires, which may be inherently conservative. For example, in the 1980s and 1990s, fanfiction which imagined same-sex romance between characters not "canonically" gay, such as Kirk and Spock, rarely imagined its characters as partaking in the struggles or lifestyles of real LGBTQ+ people (in fact, some such fanfiction acquired its own subgenre acronym, "WNGWJLEO," shorthand for "we're not gay, we just love each other"). While this apparent disinterest in the political struggles of LGBTQ+ communities during that period – including the AIDS crisis – could be perceived as the cultivation of a utopian queer space, it has also been perceived as internalized homophobia and the appropriation – fetishization, even – of queer sexualities.[25] Scholars and fans have also been increasingly calling for both fandom and fan studies to recognize the structural whiteness

---

[22] Derecho, "Archontic Literature," 67.
[23] Shoshanna Green, Cynthia Jenkins, and Henry Jenkins, "'Normal Female Interest in Men Bonking': Selections from the 'Terra Nostra Underground' and 'Strange Bedfellows,'" in *Theorizing Fandom: Fans, Subculture and Identity*, ed. Cheryl Harris and Alison Alexander (Cresskill: Hampton Press, 1998), 9–38; Mirna Cicioni, "Male Pair-Bonds and Female Desire in Fan Slash Writing," in *Theorizing Fandom: Fans, Subculture, and Identity*, ed. Cheryl Harris and Alison Alexander (Cresskill: Hampton Press, 1998), 153–177; Joanna Russ, "Pornography by Women for Women, with Love," in *The Fan Fiction Studies Reader*, ed. Karen Hellekson and Kristina Busse (Iowa City: University of Iowa Press, 2014), 82–96.
[24] See, for example, André Carrington, "Dreaming in Colour: Fan Fiction as Critical Reception," in *Race/Gender/Class/ Media 3.0*, ed. Rebecca Ann Lind, 3rd ed. (Boston: Pearson/Prentice Hall, 2012); Jonathan A. Rose, "'My Male Skin': (Self-)Narratives of Transmasculinities in Fanfiction," *European Journal of English Studies* 24.1 (January 2, 2020): 25–36, https://doi.org/10.1080/13825577.2020.1730044.
[25] Kristina Busse and Alexis Lothian, "A History of Slash Sexualities: Debating Queer Sex, Gay Politics, and Media Fan Cultures," in *The Routledge Companion to Media, Sex and Sexuality*, ed. Clarissa Smith and Feona Attwood (Abingdon: Routledge, 2017).

of fanfiction communities, and their frequent complicity with racism in popular culture. Such criticisms have pointed out the extent to which fanfiction concentrates on white characters, even to the extent of distorting texts which center BIPOC characters. Critics including Rukmini Pande, Mel Stanfill, and Rebecca Wanzo have pointed out that defenses of fanfiction as a feminist or queer art form neglect intersectional attention to the experiences of fans of color.[26] Such critiques have extended to the digital architecture of fandom, including AO3 itself.[27]

While these debates on the nature and cultural positioning of fanfiction develop within fandom and fan studies, the mainstream view on fanfiction has also changed substantially since its digital explosion in the late 1990s. To demonstrate the sea change in mainstream attitudes to fanfiction (and to homosexuality), one might look, for example, to a 2019 interview with actor Michael Sheen in the British newspaper *The Telegraph*, in which Sheen referred to online slash fanfiction about Aziraphale and Crowley, characters played by himself and actor David Tennant in the cult fantasy miniseries *Good Omens* (2019). "I wanted to play Aziraphale being sort of in love with Crowley," Sheen said. "There's a lot of fan fiction where Aziraphale and Crowley get a bit hot and heavy towards each other, so it'll be interesting to see how an audience reacts to what we've done in bringing that to the screen."[28]

With an unprecedented level of casual acceptance of fanfiction by source creators, fanfiction in the 2020s forms an increasingly acknowledged, recognized, and even welcomed part of the multiplatform, networked texts that characterize new media – part of what Henry Jenkins has called *convergence culture*. "Convergence requires media companies to rethink old assumptions about what it means to consume media, assumptions that shape both programming and marketing decisions," Jenkins wrote in 2006; in the

---

[26] Rebecca Wanzo, "African American Acafandom and Other Strangers: New Genealogies of Fan Studies," *Transformative Works and Cultures* 20 (July 22, 2015), http://journal.transformativeworks.org/index.php/twc/article/view/699; Mel Stanfill, "Doing Fandom, (Mis)Doing Whiteness: Heteronormativity, Racialization, and the Discursive Construction of Fandom," *Transformative Works and Cultures* 8 (November 15, 2011), https://doi.org/10.3983/twc.2011.0256; Rukmini Pande, *Squee from the Margins: Fandom and Race* (Iowa City: University of Iowa Press, 2018); Rukmini Pande, "How (Not) to Talk about Race: A Critique of Methodological Practices in Fan Studies," *Transformative Works and Cultures* 33 (June 15, 2020), https://doi.org/10.3983/twc.2020.1737.

[27] Alexis Lothian and Mel Stanfill, "An Archive of Whose Own? White Feminism and Racial Justice in Fan Fiction's Digital Infrastructure," *Transformative Works and Cultures* 36 (September 15, 2021), https://doi.org/10.3983/twc.2021.2119.

[28] "Michael Sheen on Good Omens, Sex Scenes, and Why Brexit Led to His Break-Up," *The Telegraph*, Tristram Fane Saunders, November 28, 2018, www.telegraph.co.uk/radio/what-to-listen-to/michael-sheen-martians-good-omens-brexit-led-break-up/.

wake of the economic upheavals of the 2018 crash and the global pandemic, media franchises with engaged, reliable fanbases have become the bread and butter of many entertainment industries, and convergence has arguably become the dominant form of media production.[29] In the convergence model, fanfiction, along with other kinds of fan creativity, has become a sought-after sign of fan engagement that is expected to translate into financial profit for the media properties, although source-text owners' attempts to create official digital spaces for fanfiction often result in awkward compromises that please few. Marvel's "Create Your Own" app, launched in 2017, with which fans can make their own comics starring Marvel characters, was pilloried by fans for both its awkward interface and its content restrictions. "The site's hefty list of terms and conditions are a set of usage rules that, essentially, will kill any creativity or worthwhile discussion," wrote Caitlin Busch for science and culture media site *Inverse*.[30]

The convergence strategy of the BBC's wildly successful *Sherlock* TV series, starring Benedict Cumberbatch and Martin Freeman in a twenty-first-century reimagining of Arthur Conan Doyle's Sherlock Holmes stories, seamlessly integrated online fan activity into the show (such as in comments to the real blog, which was represented in the show as John Watson's), while the show is itself an example of an adaptation of a highly popular public-domain intellectual property with a pre-existing, engaged fanbase – indeed, one active since the early twentieth century.[31] While the show's writers were resistant to the popular fan interpretation of the two main characters' relationship as romantic and/or sexual, the show made this reading of Watson and Holmes's relationship a subject of frequent and playful references within the show, with the effect that the vast quantities of fanfiction created by fans around the show blurred into the show's own "official" digital paratexts.[32] In contrast, Brian Fuller's *Hannibal* (2013–15),

---

[29] Jenkins, *Convergence Culture*, 18–19.
[30] Caitlin Busch, "Marvel's 'Create Your Own' Really Doesn't Understand How Fanfiction Works," *Inverse*. www.inverse.com/article/39789-marvel-create-your-own-comic-fanfiction-site; Charles Pulliam-Moore, "Marvel's 'Create Your Own' Comic Tool Is a Hot Mess With a Whole Lot of Potential," *io9*. https://io9.gizmodo.com/marvels-create-your-own-comic-tool-is-a-hot-mess-with-a-1823551690.
[31] Evgeniya D. Malenova, "Transmedia Is 'New Sexy': Case Study of the 'Sherlock' BBC Series Transmedia Project," in *Social, Mobile, and Emerging Media around the World: Communication Case Studies*, ed. Alexander V. Laskin (Lanham, MD: Lexington Books, 2018), 161–174; Louisa Ellen Stein and Kristina Busse, *Sherlock and Transmedia Fandom: Essays on the BBC Series* (Jefferson, NC: McFarland, 2012).
[32] Jennifer Wojton and Lynnette Porter, *Sherlock and Digital Fandom: The Meeting of Creativity, Community and Advocacy* (Jefferson: McFarland & Company, Incorporated Publishers, 2018), 101–153.

another cult television show which was an adaptation of a popular cultural property – indeed, Fuller referred to the show as "fanfiction" of Thomas Harris's novels – was remarkable for the extent to which the show's creator and cast courted fans in online spaces and celebrated fanfiction and fanart.[33] In the new cult media landscape, ongoing dialogue in online spaces between source text creators and fan creator–readers can mutually influence both the source text and its fanfiction in complex ways.[34]

This uneasy alliance between media producers and fanfiction communities remains contingent on fanfiction ultimately funneling profit and fan engagement toward media properties rather than drawing it away. Despite the legal advocacy of the Organization for Transformative Works and others, fanfiction still inhabits a gray area in the marketplace of ideas. Even authors who are publicly supportive of fanfiction will rarely admit to reading fanfiction of their own work. Common reasons given include the fear that this would put them at risk of being sued by fans for theft of their ideas, endanger their copyright in other ways, give them writer's block, or simply make them uncomfortable.[35] In a Twitter thread about *Good Omens*, writer Neil Gaiman – who is openly supportive of fanfiction as an artistic form[36] – responded to a fan's question about whether he reads *Good Omens* fanfiction with the tweet, "No. I don't." To another fan's reply, "sorry ... I cant understand this ... I just cant. a writer who doesnt want to read other's writing. I cant wrap my head around that [sic]," Gaiman replied, "Hmm. Think of it as a songwriter who doesn't want to listen to other people's cover versions of his songs, perhaps? I love reading most writing, but I don't (and legally shouldn't) read other people's takes

---

[33] Lori Morimoto, "Hannibal: Adaptation and Authorship in the Age of Fan Production," in *Becoming: Genre, Queerness, and Transformation in NBC's Hannibal*, ed. Kavita Mudan Finn and E. J. Nielsen (Syracuse: Syracuse University Press, 2019), 258–282.

[34] See, for example, Laura E. Felschow, "'Hey, Check It Out, There's Actually Fans': (Dis) Empowerment and (Mis)Representation of Cult Fandom in 'Supernatural,'" *Transformative Works and Cultures* 4 (March 15, 2010), https://doi.org/10.3983/twc.2010.0134; Eve Ng, "Between Text, Paratext, and Context: Queerbaiting and the Contemporary Media Landscape," *Transformative Works and Cultures* 24 (June 15, 2017), http://journal.transformativeworks.org/index.php/twc/article/view/917.

[35] Fantasy author Marian Zimmer Bradley notoriously reported this happening to her in a case now known as "the *Contraband* incident," which was widely publicized within the science fiction and fantasy publishing community. See Catherine Coker, "The Contraband Incident: The Strange Case of Marion Zimmer Bradley [Symposium]," *Transformative Works and Cultures* 6 (March 15, 2011), https://doi.org/10.3983/twc.2011.0236.

[36] On November 29, 2017, Gaiman tweeted, "I won the Hugo Award for a piece of Sherlock Holmes/ H. P. Lovecraft fanfiction, so I'm in favour." https://twitter.com/neilhimself/status/936059562863550471. He was referring here to "A Study in Emerald," a short story published in the anthology of stories based on the Conan Doyle characters, *Shadows Over Baker Street*, ed. Michael Reaves and John Pelan (New York: Del Rey Books, 2003). The Doyle estate approved the anthology.

on my characters."[37] In a further tweet in this thread, Gaiman referred to Marion Zimmer Bradley's experience of being sued by a fan (see note 35). Where hard legal guidelines and precedents do not exist, anecdotal wisdom guides authorial praxis regarding fanfiction. Meanwhile, digital platforms such as Twitter, where fans and creator–owners interact, become spaces of negotiation over creative authority.

However, the circulation of fanfiction for free – a community norm since the genre's inception (although not without its critics and ambiguities)[38] – is shifting with the tides of the digital creative economy. The wild success of E. L. James's *Fifty Shades of Grey*, in its first incarnation a popular *Twilight* fanfiction story titled "Masters of the Universe," remains a benchmark, but is only the tip of an iceberg of profitable publication of fiction originally published online as fanfiction.[39] As fanfiction gains mainstream acceptance and the memory of legal threats to fanfiction writers recede, it is not unusual in digital spaces occupied by fan communities to see fans linking to personal fundraising sites like Patreon or Ko-Fi.[40] This cultural shift is obscured partly by the fact that requests for donations are often framed as solicitations for financial support for a community member in need, rather than remuneration for services rendered. Such mutual support within fan communities has a long history, as does fan fundraising for charities and causes by auctioning off fanwork commissions. However, the increasingly fine line between charity and remuneration in fanfiction communities has yet to be tested in a court of law. Other kinds of fan artistic practice, such as fanart, fan costumes, and replica prop production, have been bought and sold for decades; we are perhaps not far from a time where the private commission of fanfiction for money, already a fringe activity, becomes a common and visible practice, resulting in another phase of renegotiation between fanfiction writers and readers and source-text owner–creators.

Fanfiction remains a subcultural literature, simultaneously mainstream and marginalized, existing in tension between the participatory model of

---

[37] Neil Gaiman, Tweet, *Twitter*, 19AM, 6/8 2019, https://twitter.com/neilhimself/status/1137378507238137856.
[38] Abigail De Kosnik, "Should Fan Fiction Be Free?" *Cinema Journal* 48.4 (2009): 118–124, https://doi.org/10.1353/cj.0.0144; Karen Hellekson, "Making Use Of: The Gift, Commerce, and Fans," *Cinema Journal* 54.3 (2015): 125–131, https://doi.org/10.1353/cj.2015.0017; Abigail De Kosnik, "Fifty Shades and the Archive of Women's Culture," *Cinema Journal* 54.3 (2015): 116–125, https://doi.org/10.1353/cj.2015.0037. NB: while fanzines containing fanfiction were sold, they were typically sold at cost.
[39] Jamison, *Fic*, 224–231; 274–288.
[40] AO3's Terms of Service, as of June 2019, forbid "commercial activity," but authors may link to their own sites on other platforms, which may include solicitations for financial support.

convergence media and the creative economy of the digital landscape. An intriguing case that demonstrates both the cultural marginalization of fanfiction and the legal gray area which it inhabits is that of novelist Francis Spufford's "unauthorized Narnia novel" *The Stone Table*, unlicensed by the Lewis estate (the books are in copyright until 2034), which was covered in *The Guardian* and other mainstream media outlets. Spufford printed copies for friends and family, and friend Frank Cottrell, with Spufford's permission, posted screencaps of the first two chapters on Twitter, apparently with the ultimate goal of eliciting approval from the Lewis estate.[41] The publicity around Spufford's novel and Cottrell's digital distribution of the two chapters met with mingled bemusement and scorn from the fanfiction community, who pointed out that distribution venues exist for unauthorized novels: "Tell him to upload it to fanfic.net or Ao3 like the rest of us," tweeted one fan. Fans and fan studies scholars pointed out that the media's (and Spufford's) unwillingness to use the word "fanfiction" to describe *The Stone Table* perpetuates a spurious high culture/low culture distinction and, given the demographics of fandom, what smacks of a sexist double standard. Kate Gardner's article for web media outlet *The Mary Sue* bore the headline "Let's Call an 'Unauthorized' Narnia Novel What It Is: Fanfiction," with the subtitle, "I guess it gets a fancy title if a man writes it."[42]

Spufford's avoidance of the word "fanfiction" shows the extent to which the term can describe a cultural positioning rather than a legal or artistic category defined by its content or relationship to another text; by avoiding both the term "fanfiction" and the digital contexts of fanfiction (such as a distribution venue like AO3), Spufford could rhetorically position *The Stone Table* as awaiting licensing rather than as unauthorized, and therefore as a novel potentially partaking of the same cultural cachet as Jean Rhys's *Wide Sargasso Sea* and Tom Stoppard's *Rosencrantz and Guildenstern Are Dead*. The fanfiction community objected to the unspoken but clear additional implication of an essential artistic difference between Spufford's creation and those of innumerable other fans. The Spufford and Gaiman cases suggest that the relationship between fanfiction and source text remains, officially at least, unidirectional, with fanfiction commonly viewed as what we might call a kind of "active reading," rather than

---

[41] Richard Lea, "Francis Spufford Pens Unauthorised Narnia Novel," *The Guardian*, March 19, 2019, sec. Books, www.theguardian.com/books/2019/mar/19/francis-spufford-pens-unauthorised-narnia-novel.

[42] Kate Gardner, "Let's Call an 'Unauthorized' Narnia Novel What It Is: Fanfiction," *The Mary Sue*, March 19, 2019, www.themarysue.com/fanfiction-narnia-double-standard/.

an artistic activity entitled to remuneration. Correspondingly, many fans view fanfiction as a stepping stone toward the production of "original" work – a space to play and to practice their craft.

The ambiguous legality of fanfiction is perhaps the primary shaping force behind the subterranean nature of the fanfiction community, but fanfiction is often intensely intimate and self-revealing, a place where many young writers and members of minoritized groups explore their identities and pleasures for the first time. Fanfiction's ephemerality (both through digital obsolescence and through the design of platforms such as Tumblr, Instagram, and Twitter), its pseudonymity, and the sometimes perplexing community slang and the speed with which it changes are not incidental; they are, to an extent, defensive mechanisms with which the community protects itself from scrutiny. Fan studies, like other fields which study digital communities, is in a moment of negotiation over the issue of subject consent when taking online texts – particularly those of contested legal status – out of their intended context and exposing them to other publics through scholarship. Research ethics boards have lagged behind the realities of digital research, and it falls to informal bodies such as the Association of Internet Researchers to encourage scholars and teachers of digital texts to interrogate their own practice. Guidelines for best practice and ethical philosophies for research (as well as counter-examples of good practice) are emerging within fan studies.[43]

9.2 Social Reading

The first part of this chapter traced the longer history of fanfiction within communities of loving readers. This section situates fanfiction within the context of "social reading," the term coined to describe the emergence of new (or newly accessible, or newly visible) reading communities and practices using digital technologies. "Social reading" has been primarily imagined to take place on dedicated social media sites such as Goodreads, where readers share recommendations and reviews, participate in reading

---

[43] "Special Issue: Ethics in Fan Studies," *Journal of Fan Studies* 4.3 (2016); Kristina Busse, "The Ethics of Studying Online Fandom," in *The Routledge Companion to Media Fandom*, ed. Melissa A. Click and Suzanne Scott (New York: Routledge/Taylor & Francis Group, 2018), 9–17; Kristina Busse and Karen Hellekson, "Identity, Ethics, and Fan Privacy," in *Fan Culture: Theory/Practice* (Newcastle upon Tyne: Cambridge Scholars Publishing, 2012), 38–56; Brianna Dym and Casey Fiesler, "Ethical and Privacy Considerations for Research Using Online Fandom Data," *Transformative Works and Cultures* 33 (June 15, 2020), https://doi.org/10.3983/twc.2020.1733; Natasha Whiteman, "Undoing Ethics," in *Undoing Ethics* (Boston: Springer US, 2011), 135–149, https://doi.org/10.1007/978-1-4614-1827-6_6.

challenges and communicate with authors. E-books and digital editions that allow communities of readers to annotate, highlight, and curate also offer a space of social reading. In the digital environment, "[r]eader intervention in the written text and the communicative collaboration and exchange between readers and the different agents in the edition/publication chain are emerging as a new paradigm."[44] While the editors of *Social Reading* are not referring to fanfiction in this quotation, fanfiction's reading and writing cultures have played an important but often overlooked role in the paradigm shift they describe.

While the legal and artistic particularities of fanfiction do create a buffer between digital spaces where fanfiction is published and circulated and social reading digital spaces allied to mainstream publishing, this buffer is increasingly flexible and artificial. Fanfiction readers and writers naturally also participate in larger online interpretive communities focused on reading and discussing texts. Cross-platform activity between social media sites and dedicated digital archives is the norm for fan communities, where collective discussion of the latest novel in a series or episode of a television show flows easily into the creation of new fanfiction, and vice versa. Indeed, readers' cross-platform activity is evident in the amount of fanfiction tagged and reviewed in Goodreads posts which link directly to sites such as Fanfiction.net. Fanfiction authors sometimes also self-publish "original" fiction e-books under another pseudonym and promote it to readers of their fanfiction.

Fanfiction itself also represents social reading practice. As digital literature, fanfiction erodes the (perhaps always artificial) distinction between readers and writers that tends to frame conversations about literature and its audiences. Fanfiction's creation almost always represents an interpretive act of reading another text and circulates within an "interpretive community." Despot and colleagues include among social reading practices "virtual book reading clubs, readers' communication with authors on social networks, [and] initiatives for collaborative book writing where readers finish stories or create new endings themselves."[45] This vision for social reading enfolds reader creative responses into other kinds of reader responses – discussion, criticism, speculation – and, indeed, studies of the fanfiction community bear out this analysis. Reader prompts for

---

[44] José-Antonio Cordón-García, Julio Alonso-Arévalo, Raquel Gómez-Díaz, and Daniel Linder, *Social Reading* (Witney: Chandos Publishing, 2013).
[45] Ivona Despot, Ivana Ljevak Lebeda, and Nives Tomašević, "Social Reading – the Reader on Digital Margins," *Libellarium: Journal for the Research of Writing, Books, and Cultural Heritage Institutions* 9.1 (December 2, 2016): 189, https://doi.org/10.15291/libellarium.v9i1.269.

fanfiction often take the form of such speculation: one influential fan speculation early in the publication of the *Harry Potter* book series – that Professor Severus Snape was Harry Potter's biological father – became known as the "Severitus" challenge and spawned hundreds of fanfiction stories exploring the premise.[46]

We can also find evidence of fanfiction *as* social reading in the emergence of slang in fanfiction communities for concepts that split precise ontological hairs. The word "headcanon" refers to a fan's conviction that a certain fact is the case about a character or story despite the fact that it is unstated in the source. Fans might develop elaborate arguments justifying headcanons, based on evidence from the source text: such arguments often take the form of fanfiction. The word "fanon" likewise refers to facts which are widely accepted by fans for the purposes of fanfiction writing while remaining unofficial – for example, the first name of the *Star Trek* character Uhura, first played by Nichelle Nichols, was never used in the three seasons of the original show. After William Rotsler supplied the name "Nyota" for Uhura in his 1982 licensed tie-in book *Star Trek II Biographies*, fanfiction and tie-in writers adopted it as fanon, and eventually the name entered the canon in Abrams's 2009 film.

Another formulation used in fandom since the mid-1990s to describe divergent readings of the source text is particularly illustrative of the permeation of the digital into fannish reading practices. This is the use of an exclamation mark between the emphasized characteristic and the character, e.g. "evil!Harry" or "muggle!Harry" (a version of Harry Potter who is evil, or nonmagical, respectively). Etymologies of the "characteristic!character" formulation vary slightly, but it appears to derive from uses of the "bang" to describe variables in C/C++ or javascript, or to distinguish between local addresses in early web listserv communities. The use of such born-digital linguistic phenomena in fandom suggests the interconnectedness of digital platforms and fannish social reading, as well as the broader phenomena described by Gretchen McCulloch in her study of internet slang.[47]

Finally, fanfiction is itself also the *subject* of social reading, circulating in digital spaces – some custom-built, some not – whose designs prioritize social reading organized around fanfiction primarily and source text only secondarily. Fanfiction.net, Wattpad, and AO3, three of the largest digital

---

[46] https://fanlore.org/wiki/Severitus_Challenge.
[47] Gretchen McCulloch, *Because Internet: Understanding the New Rules of Language* (New York: Riverhead Books, 2019).

fanfiction archives, all allow readers to comment directly on stories either through a logged-in profile or anonymously, with AO3 and Wattpad also allowing readers to leave "likes" or "kudos." Similarly to social reading sites such as Goodreads, readers on AO3 can also curate their own collections of thematically related stories or recommendations. AO3 allows readers to filter searches by number of hits, comments, and bookmarks. This filtered search enables a snowball effect for popular stories, and suggests the extent to which a culture of reader recommendation and mutual influence was built into the archive's design. This feature also incentivizes writers to publish serially, thereby creating a community of readers waiting for the next installment. Posting fanfiction to social media sites rather than archives, on the other hand, can allow for fanfiction that is highly spreadable and ephemeral, and for discussion of media texts to flow into the creation of fanfiction and vice versa. This multiplatform activity is also visible in the bleeding over of usage norms from those other sites into AO3, such as the use of Tumblr tagging conventions in AO3's freeform tagging spaces.[48]

The culture of social reading which surrounds fanfiction has a profound impact on its creative culture. The frequency of serial publication means that communication between author and readers is ongoing, and readerly desires, expressed in comments, can influence the narrative trajectory (as was the case with Victorian serial publication). The feedback culture of fanfiction is strongly oriented toward positive response and affective expressions of readerly pleasure; negative comments are often viewed as a violation of community etiquette, regardless of the comment's tone or content, but soliciting trusted readers to "beta" one's fanfiction (that is, to do developmental or copy-editing work prior to publication) is common. Coauthoring is not uncommon, and other kinds of less visible collaboration are the norm. These include fanfiction authors soliciting prompts or suggestions from readers (although dividing the fanfiction community into "authors" and "readers" is misleading, since many of its members are both), authorial participation in community writing challenges or exchanges, and writing sequels or remixes of other fanfiction author's work. Fan studies scholars have observed that some aspects of the fanfiction community function like a gift economy, where the gift of fanfiction to the community creates a communal obligation to respond with the gift of positive

[48] Elli E. Bourlai, "'Comments in Tags, Please!': Tagging Practices on Tumblr," *Discourse, Context & Media* 22 (2018): 46–56, https://doi.org/10.1016/j.dcm.2017.08.003; Max Dobson, "FandomCommunication: How Online Fandom Utilises Tagging and Folksonomy," 2018, https://doi.org/10.29085/9781783303403.007.

feedback, and also the cumulation of social cachet among prolific or popular fanfiction writers.[49]

Interpretive practices in and around fanfiction are fluid, blurring the lines between literary consumption, communal discussion, and artistic activity. The inadequacy of these conventional divisions of literary activity is most visible in fan-designed online architecture for fanfiction. The next section takes as a brief case study AO3, with the caveat that this represents only one of many models for digital archives, and that it has come under criticism for reflecting the biases of its creators (see note 27).

9.3 Paratext

I have noted that fanfiction circulates in multiple digital spaces that sometimes differ widely in design and utility, although all must enable a level of self-publishing, reader response, and spreadability. Another feature of fanfiction online which remains relatively consistent across platforms is its authors' exploitation of the digital platform's capabilities to create extensive paratextual apparatus to shape their readers' experiences in ways that differ from those used in print publishing and in other digital publishing venues. These are uniquely tied to the synergy between the community's needs and the digital platform's capabilities.

The paratext constitutes "the fringe of the printed text." Earlier in this chapter I used "paratext" more loosely to refer to epitexts: texts which are "outside" of the original text but nonetheless subtend to it; here I refer to "peritexts": textual elements at the threshold of the text which in a print book include apparatuses such as titles, prefaces, and notes, and in the digital context is often synonymous with metadata. Following Génet's influential formulation in Maclean's translation, I hold that "This fringe, always bearer of authorial commentary either more or less legitimated by the author, constitutes, between the text and what lies outside it, a zone not just of transition, but of transaction."[50] I provide a few examples of the kinds of transactions that can take place in the paratexts (or peritexts, or metadata) of fanfiction; finally, I suggest that through the translation and evolution of predigital paratextual practices into digital technologies, the fanfiction *archive* (as opposed to the individual fanfiction text) gains rhizomatic qualities from fanfiction paratextual conventions.

---

[49] Karen Hellekson, "A Fannish Field of Value: Online Fan Gift Culture," *Cinema Journal* 48.4 (2009): 113–118.
[50] Gérard Genette and Marie Maclean, "Introduction to the Paratext," *New Literary History* 22.2 (1991): 261, https://doi.org/10/brbx64.

AO3, which won a Hugo award in the category Best Related Work in 2019, was created in 2008–9 as the flagship project of the newly formed, fan-run, nonprofit Organization for Transformative Works, who also run the academic online journal Transformative Works and Cultures and fanzine archival projects, and co-ordinate legal advocacy for fanfiction.[51] AO3 is a nonprofit site largely staffed by volunteers, its server usage funded by donation. Its interface for uploading fanfiction was designed according to paratextual conventions that had emerged in fanfiction communities, which at that time largely used digital publishing platforms where text entry was freeform (e.g. Livejournal). While it should not be taken as representative of all fanfiction publishing practice, therefore, as a case study it functions as a snapshot of how a particular community of fans conceived their own practice in the late 2000s. AO3 went further in its paratext standardization than other fanfiction digital archives (such as Fanfiction.net), which usually had some but not many preset fields, often including simply Title, Fandom (that is, source text), and Author. AO3's design resulted in a metadata scheme which is reasonably restrictive for authors (although some freeform elements are preserved and many fields are opt-in) but enables powerful search functions for reader convenience. The preset metadata fields on AO3 give an insight into both the community practices that its designers observed at the time and the features of fanfiction they considered most important for searchability.

Title, Author, and Fandom are naturally included, as are Characters (an autofill function standardizes character names), [Romantic] Pairing (again, the autofill function in combination with volunteer human tag wranglers maintain consistency), and Rating (the options are Not Rated, General Audiences, Teen and Up Audiences, Mature, and Explicit). Less familiar to readers of print publishing are fields which determine Category, where authors indicate whether the central romantic pairing is M/F, M/M, F/F, Gen ("general," meaning here, no romantic pairing), Multi, or Other – that is, whether it focuses on a same-sex, opposite-sex, or other romantic coupling(s). Following fanfiction conventions influenced by feminist activism in the 1980s and 1990s, AO3 also has a field for Archive Warnings, where authors can warn readers about potentially disturbing content (the six preset options include Major Character Death and Rape/Non-Con and Choose Not to Warn).[52] The Additional Tags field is

---

[51] On the history and uses of fan-run digital archives, see De Kosnik, *Rogue Archives*.
[52] Alexis Lothian, "Choose Not to Warn: Trigger Warnings and Content Notes from Fan Culture to Feminist Pedagogy," *Feminist Studies* 42.3 (2016): 743–756, https://doi.org/10.15767/feministstudies.42.3.0743.

freeform but offers autofill and is monitored for consistency by the aforementioned "tag wranglers." Here, typical tags might include types of sexual content ("BDSM," "spanking"), additional content notes readers might want to seek out or avoid ("canon-typical homophobia"), and the hyperspecific subgenre terminology used within fanfiction communities, some widely recognized across fandoms, some specific to a given fandom ("wingfic," for example, describes fanfiction in which the main characters have wings). By maintaining a partially freeform tag field, AO3 maintains a compromise between a restrictive, top-down taxonomizing attitude to fanfiction, and a freeform "folksonomy" (bottom-up) approach, enabling both searchability and the swift evolution of new subgenres – a form of flexibility crucial for a fast-moving digital community.[53] There is also space for "author's notes" before or after the story, reflecting the common addition of author's notes to fanfiction paratexts in Livejournal and other freeform text-entry digital spaces prior to AO3, which in 2010 Alexandra Herzog observed fans were using for "a variety of testaments of fannish agency and authority."[54] The influence of Tumblr tagging conventions means, however, that authors increasingly use the freeform tag space for additional author's notes or commentary (see note 50).

In addition to providing readers with what AO3 designers considered the most salient information about the story at hand for its readers, this paratextual schema prioritizes hypertextual connection to other fanfiction, enabling a rhizomatic structure to unfold. Figure 9.1 gives an example of what this paratextual frame looks like in practice on AO3. *Before* encountering the title and author, the reader encounters fields containing tags which describe what they are about to read, including "Weird Metaphysical Sex" (a content note) and "Alternate Universe – Canon Divergence" (a subgenre description). These tags are hypertextual links that search for other fanfiction in the archive which shares those tags. The reader can also view the story's length, its popularity metrics, and an author-provided freeform summary of the story. The author's notes, below the summary, credit two other fans for suggestions and beta, attesting to the culture of creative collaboration within which the story was

---

[53] Shannon Fay Johnson, "Fan Fiction Metadata Creation and Utilization within Fan Fiction Archives: Three Primary Models," *Transformative Works and Cultures* 17 (2014), http://journal.transformativeworks.org/index.php/twc/article/view/578/459; Casey Fiesler, Shannon Morrison, and Amy S. Bruckman, "An Archive of Their Own: A Case Study of Feminist HCI and Values in Design," in *Proceedings of the 2016 CHI Conference on Human Factors in Computing Systems* (Association for Computing Machinery, 2016), 2574–2585, https://doi.org/10.1145/2858036.2858409.

[54] Herzog, "But This Is My Story and This Is How I Wanted to Write It."

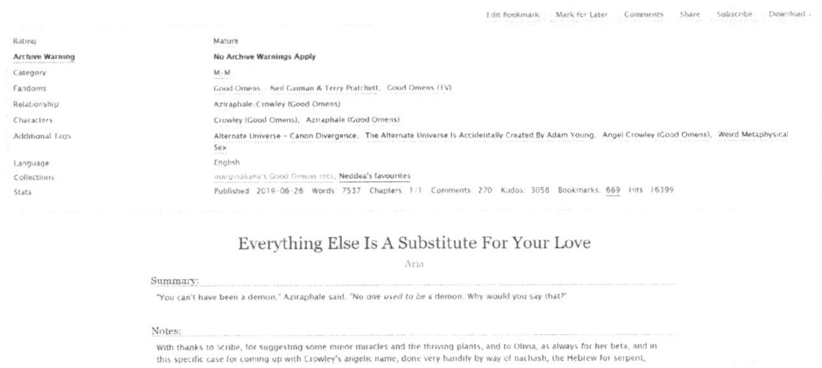

Figure 9.1 Paratextual frame for "Everything Else Is A Substitute For Your Love" by Aria from Archive of Our Own (Archive account-holder view). Image appears with kind permission from the author.

written. The buttons on the top right of the reader interface anticipate the cross-platform social reading practices of fanfiction readers: "Share" offers a html code for easy sharing on another platform, "Comments" take the reader directly to responses to the story by other readers, "Subscribe" allows archive users to receive email notifications when the author updates the story (in the case of serial publications), and "Download" offers downloadable formats for e-book devices such as the Kindle. Taken in sum, this paratextual frame reflects the predominance of the romance and erotica genres in fanfiction, and offers the reader the chance to curate their own reading experience according to their own desires.

A few features of this frame bear further comment: I have previously mentioned the ubiquity of the disclaimer in early fanfiction digital publishing, which AO3 entirely drops from their paratextual frame, partly reflecting the Organization for Transformative Work's own position on the legality of fanfiction, and partly reflecting the convention's erosion even when AO3 was in its design stages. Equally important is the deprioritization of the source text's author. AO3's robust search engine does not enable one to search for fanfiction written about source texts by a specific author (e.g. J. K. Rowling), nor do the less comprehensive search engines of Wattpad or Fanfiction.net. Conversely, this paratextual frame enables cross-fandom searching for specific readerly affective experiences. It anticipates readers who might be interested in seeking out other fanfiction in any fandom featuring "Weird Metaphysical Sex"; other fanfiction for *Good*

Omens; or other *Good Omens* fanfiction featuring a version of the character Crowley who is an angel (in the show, Crowley is a demon).

The metadata also includes links to two archive user collections of recommended stories in which this story has been included: one fandom-specific ("marginaliana's Good Omens recs"), one multifandom ("Neddea's favourites"). Thus, through hypertextual linkages in the paratext or visible metadata, the fanfiction archive forms a rhizomatic structure around its source text. AO3's design suggests the extent to which the digital social reading cultures within which fanfiction is enmeshed shape every aspect of the genre. Approaching fanfiction in this way – as digital literature – challenges approaches to fanfiction, such as the convergence model, that see the genre as primarily engaged in a relationship with its source text; here, fanfiction is first and foremost in dialogue with other fanfiction. It also makes visible the ways in which reading cultures can become inextricable from, and intertwined with, their digital platforms, emerging as something quite different from print readerships.

I conclude by returning to the seemingly paradoxical connection between fanfiction and premodern literature. While the diachronic approach to fanfiction, which situates it in a long tradition of transformative literature, can seem to pass over the impact of the digital revolution on fanfiction, nonetheless taking a transhistorical approach to digital fanfiction can open up new histories of the relationship between reading and medium. Alison Tara Walker observes that medieval manuscripts make reading a haptic experience different from that of reading print, in ways that digital literature such as Shirley Jackson's *Patchwork Girl* and Young-Hae Chang Heavy Industry's *Dakota* explore.[55] Likewise, while paratextual navigation technologies like the table of contents are medieval experimental innovations,[56] many medieval texts are rhizomatic or fragmentary, with multiple points of entry and exit, not intended to be read from beginning to end, or they contain multiple layers of marginal commentary that forms "hyperlinks" with other texts, as Kavita Mudan Finn points out in her comparison between early print and fanfiction paratexts.[57] Medieval literary practices illuminate how, outside the fragile boundary around the discrete coherence of, for example, the Harry Potter book series

---

[55] Alison Tara Walker, "The Boundless Book: A Conversation between the Pre-modern and Posthuman," *DHQ* 7.1 (2013).
[56] Malcolm B. Parkes, *Scribes, Scripts, and Readers: Studies in the Communication, Presentation, and Dissemination of Medieval Texts* (London: Hambledon Press, 1991).
[57] Kavita Mudan Finn, "Conversations in the Margins: Fannish Paratexts and Their Premodern Roots," *Journal of Fandom Studies* 5:2 (2017), 157–174, https://doi.org/10.1386/jfs.5.2.157_1.

(supplemented by official and semi-official paratexts such as the original movies, the *Cursed Child* play, the Pottermore website, J. K. Rowling's tweets, and so forth), fanfiction expands the text outward in every direction, enabling multiple points of entry and repetition, hyperfocus and divergence.

Both the medieval examples like those Finn and Walker explore and AO3 correspond to the "web book" described in *Social Reading*, "in which linearity is replaced by multilinearity, syntactic coherence and semantic complexity, and where completeness of final texts is replaced by writer–user interactivity and open-ended virtuality, generating open spaces that preclude divergent intentionalities."[58] De Kosnik, too, suggests a way to understand fanfiction's digital archives as continuing a predigital history. Extending Derecho's "archontic" theory of fanfiction and Coppa's theory of fanfiction as a performance genre in which fans write new "scripts" for characters,[59] De Kosnik argues that fanfiction, along with other variations and transformations of a given source text, enter into an infinitely expandable virtual archive: a "meta-archive." One such virtual meta-archive, she suggests, would be a hypothetical space in which Shakespeare fans could see every performance of *Hamlet* ever given being staged simultaneously. Fanfiction digital archives, she argues, rather than being simply databases, are "the closest we can come to concrete, perceptible instantiations of these meta-archives."[60] In these conceptual frameworks, the distinction between "source" and "derivative" texts becomes irrelevant; fanfiction in digital archives, like many other digital literatures, demands a mode of reading that encompasses the explosion of a single text into near-infinite branching narrative paths.

Reading digital fanfiction in relation to early and preprint reading technologies makes sense when we consider that the kinds of reading practices common to social reading which diverge from the postenlightenment idea of the solo, passive reader and the book as sacrosanct object are visible in the same premodern literary cultures in which "fanfiction" is the norm – that is, if we understand fanfiction to mean literature which reworks and reuses pre-existing narratives and characters. For this reason, medievalists have been at the forefront of innovations in digital editions of medieval manuscripts, observing that the digital edition in many ways better replicates the medieval reading

---

[58] Cordón-García et al., *Social Reading*.
[59] Francesca Coppa, "Writing Bodies in Space," in *Fan Fiction and Fan Communities in the Age of the Internet*, ed. Kristina Busse and Karen Hellekson (Jefferson: McFarland & Co., 2006), 225.
[60] De Kosnik, *Rogue Archives*, 34, 325.

experience than the printed edition. Digital editions can encompass the unstable medieval text extant in multiple versions, the cumulative marginalia and reader annotation, in ways paralleled by fanfiction. As we move further into the digital age, we may find ourselves reassessing the era of the solo reader at the feet of the author-genius, and of the stable, linear text, as an historical aberration.

CHAPTER 10

Narrative and Interactivity

Emily Short

I write this chapter as a creator rather than an academic narratologist. Though I have a PhD in a literary field (Classics), I have worked in the video game industry for more than a decade, and have been a practicing author of interactive literature since the late 1990s, when I took up a hobby of writing text adventures and sharing them with a small group of other interactive fiction (IF) enthusiasts. Since then, the IF community has expanded to include fans of choice-based story games and hypertext, and (eventually) to overlap the community of commercial video game writers.[1] These groups sometimes engage in theoretical discussion about the expressive possibilities of the medium but are most often concerned with achieving practical effects in their work and with developing a shared language of craft.

The first half of the chapter examines common assumptions about texts that are frequently broken by interactive narrative – assumptions such as "the reader does not write any of the text," "the text is finite and bounded," and "the external circumstances of reading have no effect on content." I draw the examples here from a variety of interactive stories, both commercial and noncommercial, many of which I encountered first as a player. In the second half, I explore terminology used by creators of interactive stories to describe their work and process, and sometimes by players and readers to explain their reactions. My first priority has been to document what is actually discussed, and how ideas are actually used, by working writers of IF. This discussion includes phenomena that exist in noninteractive literature, such as viewpoint characters and protagonists, but that are fundamentally transformed by the introduction of interactivity. It also explores terms largely unique to interactive narrative, such as agency, complicity, and simulation.

---

[1] A description of IF communities from the 1990s through the early 2010s can be found in Nick Montfort and Emily Short, "Interactive Fiction Communities: From Preservation through Promotion and Beyond," *Dichtung Digital* 41 (2012).

10.1 Expectations Overturned

Interactive literature overturns a host of received assumptions about what a text might be.

The Expectation That Texts Are Finite, Terminating, and Bounded

Noninteractive literature is typically finite, with a limited amount of text available. Interactive texts are often generative, building new text as the reader goes. Noninteractive literature typically has a point that might be described as the end: a last chapter, a final page. Many interactive pieces, especially in the literary hypertext tradition, loop endlessly or supply no definite conclusion. *The Reprover* (2008),[2] for instance, maps its texts to the sides of a three-dimensional object: one reads *The Reprover* by moving from the text on one side to the text on an adjacent side. There are constraints on possible paths through the text, but there is no fixed ending. Noninteractive texts are generally assumed to be bounded in the sense that there is a clear distinction between words that are and words that are not part of the text. Hypertexts, however, frequently incorporate links outward to other websites. It may not be immediately apparent when the reader is still reading a composition created by the original author(s) and when they have begun to engage with other content on the Internet.

The Expectation That a Text Can Be Reread

It is typically possible to reread noninteractive texts and encounter the same contents on the second pass. Many interactive texts make it unlikely or even impossible to see the exact same text in the same order. Indeed, some interactive texts make a point of their aleatory, unrepeatable nature, drawing on traditions of divination. Sam Kabo Ashwell's *Scents and Semiosis* (2020)[3] generates short incidents from the life of a fictional perfumer and describes the scents they supposedly mixed during their career. The output is so randomized that the player will never see exactly the same text again. For instance, on one of my playthroughs, a description read:

> Pepper shines through smoked massoia bark. This was the first perfume you made yourself. (Well, a reproduction. You kept the original long after the scent had denatured, until you threw it out in an ill-considered fit of

---

[2] François Coulon, *The Reprover (Le Réprobateur)* (independent publisher, 2008), web.
[3] Sam Kabo Ashwell, *Scents and Semiosis* (independent publisher, 2020), Inform.

Narrative and Interactivity 179

decluttering.) It was a lucky fluke, and despite intense efforts you didn't make anything nearly this good again for almost two years.

> **pepper could mean growth**
> **pepper feels like second chances**
> **pepper could suggest synchronicity**
> **pepper feels like progressive and incremental approaches**
> **None of these feel right. Reconsider.**

Selecting one of the options – such as "pepper could mean growth" – designates that scent association as significant, and the story remembers it for later. If the reader chooses "none of these feel right," the story proposes alternative meanings. When the reader is ready to move on, the story generates a new scent and a new vignette for consideration. At the end of a session, the reader receives a list of the scent notes they picked out:

> **pepper for growth**
> **pink champagne for alliance complicated by rivalry**
> **myrtle for radiant craft**
> **salt for long-sufferance**
> **cedar for debauched disdain**
> **boronia for the impossibility of achieving everything at once**
> **gaiac wood for light persistence**
> **hops for misbehaviour**

Thus, the reader's role is to curate a collection of texts and meanings from amongst those semirandomly generated. Reading *Scents and Semiosis* is a meditative experience, and an ephemeral one. A given output trace can never be repeated.

The Expectation That a Reader Can Experience All of a Given Work
Assuming a work has been completely preserved, the reader may assume that they will be able to read every word of the text. The same does not hold for interactive stories. A reader of a literary hypertext might miss a link to new material. The player of a text adventure might never enter a command that produced a whole new outcome for the story. Many interactive works not only tolerate but celebrate this fact.

Hatoful Boyfriend (2011)[4] presents itself initially as a dating simulation about getting to know potential partners. In that genre, the player typically

---

[4] Hato Moa, *Hatoful Boyfriend* (MIST[PSI]PRESS, 2011), Famous Writer.

has to spend time with particular characters and choose the right dialogue options to reach a happy relationship. *Hatoful Boyfriend* adds the twist that these characters are birds, after an apocalyptic event that has replaced most of the humans on the planet. Aside from this peculiarity, however, the game follows the conventions of its genre, up until the player has completed a number of playthroughs with different partners. On the playthrough after that, the game unlocks an alternate scenario in which the protagonist is killed and the gameplay centers on the surrounding characters solving the mystery of her death. This outcome completely alters the meaning of the story. The dating storylines are light and upbeat in tone, and considerably shorter. The mystery story is the *real* story of *Hatoful Boyfriend*. Nonetheless, it would be possible for a reader to play *Hatoful Boyfriend*, miss the mystery plot, and come away thinking that the story was very different.

Two contextual factors decrease the risk that a reader of *Hatoful Boyfriend* will make that mistake. One is genre convention: in many dating simulations, key outcomes are revealed only after the player has achieved several successful playthroughs. The author of *Hatoful Boyfriend* can assume that members of their audience know this: they can trust that most players will persist in playing through the game long enough to find the hidden material, or will at least know that they did not complete it even though they reached one "ending" of the story. The other factor is extradiegetic discussion: people who encounter *Hatoful Boyfriend* on the Internet are likely to find it surrounded by user discussions that allude to the existence of hidden content.

Even so, players do miss important developments in many interactive works: because they are unaware of the conventions of reading, because the author has intentionally concealed elements, or because the work belongs to a category in which completionist play is not expected. Victor Gijsbers's text adventure *The Game Formerly Known as Hidden Nazi Mode* (2011)[5] directly addresses this ambiguity of digital IF. On the surface, it appears to be a child-friendly story about rabbits. Extradiegetic material, in the form of files distributed alongside the game, raise the possibility that a "hidden Nazi mode" can be activated if the player types the wrong input at the command line. Gijsbers's provocation argues for the release of source code along with compiled, running digital fiction, on the grounds that only readable source code will allow people to be certain what content they are recommending or redistributing.

[5] Victor Gijsbers, *The Game Formerly Known as Hidden Nazi Mode* (self-released, 2010), Inform.

Some authors of digital literature do release their source code, either as an intentional project (such as Andrew Plotkin's release of a large printed source book for his text adventure *Hadean Lands* [2014][6]) or as a side effect of distributing the work at all. For most works written with the hypertext tool Twine, the code can be read by anyone who knows how to find a "view source" option in their web browser, and how to decrypt what they find there. Where this kind of access is available, some scholars engage in code critique alongside literary critique of IF.[7] While this type of analysis is highly valuable to understanding the intention of the work, it is usually not the primary intended experience for readers. Instead, often the author intends for the "complete" reading of a work of IF to omit portions – possibly significant portions – of the writing that the reader might theoretically have reached.

The Expectation That the External Circumstances of Reading Will Not Alter the Text

Interactive digital literature may be implemented as an application with access to information such as the time, the date, the physical location of the reader, the weather in the reader's location, and perhaps even personal profile information. *Lifeline* (2015),[8] a textual game originally developed for the Apple Watch, invites the player to exchange messages with a distant character, Taylor. Taylor is an astronaut who crash-landed on a planet in another solar system and needs both advice and moral support. Instead of playing out all at once, the story inserts significant real-time delays between portions of the conversation, simulating the delays when Taylor is fictionally asleep or busy. The player is forced to experience the story over multiple days even though the text is not especially long. The mimetic use of time increases the suspense about whether Taylor will survive difficult events, connecting players more deeply with the story.

Location-based stories, meanwhile, may use GPS (for placing the user in a large outdoor space) or Bluetooth signals (for narratives sited in a small indoor space) to connect the story to the user's immediate environment. Nico Czaja's *Septima*[9] is an audio story about an elderly

---

[6] Andrew Plotkin, *Hadean Lands* (Zarfhome, 2014), Inform.
[7] See, for example, Naomi Clark's close reading of Horse Master including its code: "Horse Master by Tom McHenry," *Videogames for Humans: Twine Authors in Conversation* (New York: Instar Books, 2015), 85–134.
[8] Dave Justus, et al., *Lifeline* (3 Minute Games, 2015), Apple Watch.
[9] Nico Czaja, *Septima* (Villa Borg, n.d.).

Roman slave, provided to visitors to the archaeological reconstruction of Villa Borg in Germany. As the listener moves through the villa, they hear portions of Septima's story. At the end, they're able to express a final choice on her behalf: either to buy their (her) freedom by walking out the front gate of the villa, or to head in another direction to signal that she should sacrifice her own emancipation and give the money to a needy friend instead. The location features turn the piece into a form of interactive theater in which the audience enacts the climactic moment of the narrative.

The Expectation That the Text Cannot Vary With a Reader's Understanding or Emotional Reaction

Andrew Plotkin's text adventure *Spider and Web* (1998)[10] is framed as a story told to an interrogator in a fictional totalitarian state. The protagonist is a spy and has infiltrated the interrogator's base. The game begins with them being captured and forced to recount their activities so far. For most of the game, the player types commands that describe what the spy did in the base before being caught. If the player ever does something that would have killed the spy early, the interrogator interrupts to point out that that can't have happened; play resumes at the relevant moment until the player is able to get the story "right." This story is only "right," however, from the perspective of the interrogator. It is not necessarily the truth. The spy protagonist has strong motives to conceal key information. The player can see what the protagonist reveals to the interrogator but cannot see anything else. Critically, the player does not have much access to the protagonist's secret thoughts, though there are moments in the story that hint at what is being left out.

At the climax of the story, the player must figure out what the protagonist has omitted from the narration and act on that secret information. The secret fact has never been truthfully narrated, but it's possible to infer, if the player has paid close attention. In other words, solving this puzzle requires the player to demonstrate that they have detected the unreliability of the narrator and have made correct guesses about the motives and past actions of all parties. It is a lock that prevents the story from being completely read unless it is also adequately understood.

---

[10] Andrew Plotkin, *Spider and Web* (self-released, 1998), Inform.

The Expectation That None of the Text Is Written by the Reader

Katherine Morayati's *Human Errors* (2018)[11] puts the player in the role of a customer support worker answering consumer complaints about a buggy product, a science-fictional implant designed to control the impulses of the wearer. Reported errors tend to be personally revealing, funny, horrific, or all three at once. One user works at a retail store and gets a discount version of the implant installed in order to improve her attitude and (consequently) her sales. The sales do go up, but the discount implant is physically damaging. Another user relies on the implant to manage his depression, but its flashing lights draw the notice of other people and cause social problems. In the persona of the customer service worker, the reader has access to a screen full of support tickets that she must resolve by choosing whether they should be closed, marked as high priority, or answered with a request for more information.

Messages sent to the reader at the beginning of play make clear that their boss wants the worker to close as many tickets as possible as fast as they can. If the worker goes too far in helping customers, their boss will intervene and fire them, cutting off access to the people the worker is trying to help. On the other hand, it is only by responding to the customers that one can find out more of their stories. When the worker responds, the reader has a timed opportunity to type a reply, with enough duration to input a sentence or two.

Human Errors does nothing with the typed input. That text never appears on the screen again, and it has no influence on what happens next. The result of emailing a response to one of the customers is simply that this customer will respond with more of their personal story. The act of typing is far from irrelevant to the story, however. For the overworked, underpaid, unappreciated protagonist, the text input is the one opportunity for self-expression. For the reader, it is a chance to place herself in the worker's role and improvise the character's thoughts.

10.2 The Creative Vocabulary of Interactive Narrative

Some of the craft of interactive narrative is about mitigating its differences from the noninteractive sort: to assist the reader, as much as possible, in learning to read a work that may be endless, edgeless, and deeply puzzling. At other times, one is looking to make the most of those differences, offering a reader experiences that could be found nowhere else. In choosing the craft terminology to discuss here, I focus on the second category: the conversations that point to expressive possibility, rather than technical difficulty.

---

[11] Katherine Morayati, *Human Errors* (self-released, 2018), Twine.

10.3 Player, Protagonist, Narrator

The role-playing game *Disco Elysium*[12] features a middle-aged detective protagonist named Harry (or Harrier) Du Bois. Certain aspects of Harry's personality are immutable. He is always an alcoholic and a drug addict. He always has a difficult history on the police force and a number of freshly made enemies. His thoughts are presented to the player as internal dialogue with various components of his personality, and the player may decide which inner voices to develop. A player who invests heavily in Logic and Volition will read Harry's interior state as comparatively rational and self-controlled. One who focuses on Empathy will make Harry observant about the motives of the people he meets. *Disco Elysium* presents two dozen interior qualities, permitting the player to remix Harry's personality in considerable detail. The player's influence is not limitless. The player cannot change Harry's past, as he himself cannot. One can choose to make him sober from this point on, however, or select how he interprets and talks about those past events.

Disco Elysium's design points out a productive tension that exists in many interactive texts. If the player has some control over what the protagonist will do, does this make her the authority on the protagonist's personality? Should the protagonist be a blank slate onto which the player can project her preferences, or should they be strongly defined by the author, requiring the player to immerse herself in a mindset she may find off-putting? How much is the interactive story invested in the experience of a particular person, and how much is it about allowing the player room to introduce themselves into the story?

These questions – and related questions about narrative voice – formed the basis of considerable discussion among text adventure authors in the late 1990s and early 2000s. Many early text adventures refrain from asserting anything about the protagonist, even gender or age, in order to allow the player to imagine that when the game addresses a "you," it means the actual human sitting at the computer. Later, text adventure authors became more interested in building characters for the protagonist as well.

Theorists often find more than two roles here – more than "just" protagonist and player. In *The Inform Designer's Manual*,[13] Graham Nelson identifies a triangle of identities: "There are at least three identities involved in play: the person typing and reading ('player'), the main character within the story ('protagonist') and the voice speaking about

---

[12] Robert Kurvitz et al., *Disco Elysium* (ZA/UM, 2019), Unity.
[13] Graham Nelson, *The Inform Designer's Manual*, 4th ed. (Interactive Fiction Library, 2001). See section 48, "A Triangle of Identities."

what this character sees and feels ('narrator'). There is a triangle of relationships between them, and it's a triangle with very different proportions in different games."

Many of these elements are identifiable in the opening of C. E. J. Pacian's *Gun Mute* (2008):[14]

> The desert sand squirms beneath your feet, alive with mutant nanomachines. Sheriff Clayton has Elias. He's hanging him at noon.
> It looks like you're going to have to shoot some people.
> Radiation Plains
> Rolling dunes stretch in every direction, ending in a distant horizon broken only by a few low, jagged mountains. A small pile of sticks burns here, sending a thin trail of black smoke into the ruddy dawn sky.
> A pot of some strange green fluid sits bubbling on the fire.
> The plainswoman sits meditatively by the fire, her spear resting across her lap.
> **> EXAMINE ME**
> You're Mute Lawton. A devilishly handsome cowboy with windswept black hair and roguish stubble. Lean and tall, your tanned body is taut with cool, calculated strength.
> You're topless and barefoot, wearing nothing but a pair of dust-caked black jeans and your holster.
> Far in the distance, you can just make out something uttering a low, metallic howl.

Through this prologue and first move, *Gun Mute* introduces us to setting and protagonist: a robot-inhabited postapocalyptic wasteland; a voiceless cowboy who needs to rescue his boyfriend. The text uses the second person to address both fictional protagonist and the real-world player: "It looks like you're going to have to shoot some people" is at once Mute's internal monologue – he doesn't see how to get Elias back without violence – and a hint from the author to the player that we'll need the gun to solve the puzzles. Meanwhile, the objectifying description of Mute – "tanned body ... taut with cool, calculated strength" – invites the player to imagine the protagonist from the outside. It also signals the game's queer viewpoint at a time when queer narratives were uncommon in this medium. One line later, we are back inside Mute's head, hearing a distant sound as he hears it, perhaps encouraging the player to type LISTEN as her next command. Elements that might seem disjointed to a habitual reader of linear fiction are all doing significant work to fulfill the special requirements of an interactive story.

---

[14] C. E. J. Pacian, *Gun Mute* (independent developer, 2008), TADS 3.

10.4 Agency

Agency refers to the effect that the player has on the story world. The player might have the ability to make major choices on the protagonist's behalf, or to determine how the protagonist feels about the story's major events. Conversely, they might have little or no agency at all, able only to traverse lexia without changing anything that happens in the story, as in much literary hypertext.

Agency is further broken down into *intention* and *perceivable consequence*.[15] *Intention* refers to the reader's ability to plan ahead and to pursue an outcome of their own choosing. The player of a text adventure might demonstrate intention when she acquires a poison because she hopes to be able to eliminate an antagonist later. This sequence still demonstrates intention even if the player later loses the poison or finds that it is ineffectual on the chosen target: the point is that the player has formed a plan and executed it. *Perceivable consequence* refers to the reader's ability to recognize that something has happened as a result of past actions. In this case, the reader might have served a friend a dish of mushrooms without knowing that the dish was poisonous. The friend's illness was not intended, but it is a consequence of serving the mushrooms, and it might not have occurred if the player had chosen to serve a different dish. In this case, the poisoning has a perceivable consequence but not intention.

Many interactive stories make their consequences perceivable by explicitly calling back to what the player has already done. This requires tracking what the player has done in the past, even if that tracking is as simple as knowing that the player can only reach a particular page in a Choose Your Own Adventure novel by making a specific choice earlier. Intention, on the other hand, usually requires that the work offers the player a system whose possibilities are comprehensible and consistent. For the player to manipulate causal chains in a story, she first needs to understand how causality works within this imagined universe – even if the fictional rules differ from those in reality.

In the examples presented so far, the player is always directing the actions of a protagonist, which then determines which events are included in the narrative they experience. Agency can be more limited or differently directed, however. In many text adventures, the main plot always includes the same events. The player's contribution is simply to work through the

---

[15] These terms were identified by Doug Church and subsequently adopted by many practitioners. See "Formal Abstract Design Tools," *Game Developer* (July 16, 1999).

puzzles that block this outcome. In Michael Gentry's Lovecraftian horror game *Anchorhead* (1998),[16] the player investigates a town full of dangerous cultists. From moment to moment, the player is forming and executing intentions, finding secret locations, unlocking important doors, and so on. If the player does not do these things, the story does not progress; the protagonist either gets stuck or dies. If they do progress, the story always advances to the same crisis. Stacey Mason refers to this type of agency as "affect";[17] Sam Kabo Ashwell calls it "grasp."[18] It is agency that applies to small-scale actions but not to the constituent events of the plot. By contrast, narrative or diegetic agency refers to the reader's ability to select or alter which events occur in the story. A reader of a branching narrative may have diegetic agency because they are selecting actions for the protagonist that lead to different outcomes, creating a causal trace through the work.

Chandler Groover's text adventure *Midnight. Swordfight* (2015)[19] makes the idea of narrative agency especially visible. In this piece, areas of the game world represent different moments in the course of an evening, culminating in a duel that may kill the protagonist. The player begins the game in the location representing the end of the evening. From there, they can play through the duel, or they may explore backward through the space-and-time of the plot, revising earlier events until they lay the groundwork for a more satisfactory outcome. *Midnight. Swordfight* makes its causal sequence into a puzzle that the player can experiment with, delivering plenty of narrative agency but distancing the player from the motives and vulnerability of the protagonist.

10.5 Complicity

Offering or denying player agency is central to the effect of an interactive narrative design. Stephen Bond's *Rameses* (2000),[20] Adam Cadre's *Photopia* (1998),[21] and Meghna Jayanth's *80 Days* (2014)[22] all derive

---

[16] Michael Gentry, *Anchorhead* (independent developer, 1998), Inform.
[17] Stacey Mason, "On Games and Links: Extending the Vocabulary of Agency and Immersion in Interactive Narratives," *Interactive Storytelling*, ed. Hartmut Koenitz, Tonguc Ibrahim Sezen, Gabriele Ferri, et al. (New York: Springer, 2013) 25–34.
[18] Sam Kabo Ashwell, "A Bestiary of Player Agency," *These Heterogenous Tasks* (September 22, 2014), https://heterogenoustasks.wordpress.com/2014/09/22/a-bestiary-of-player-agency/.
[19] Chandler Groover, *Midnight. Swordfight* (independent publisher, 2015), Inform.
[20] Stephen Bond, *Rameses* (independent publisher, 2000), Inform.
[21] Adam Cadre, *Photopia* (independent publisher, 1998), Inform.
[22] Meghna Jayanth, *80 Days* (Inkle Studios, 2014), Ink.

emotional effect from withholding agency over a situation the reader is especially likely to care about. In *Photopia*, a player will never be able to change the outcome of a fatal traffic accident. In *Rameses*, the protagonist will never have the confidence to stand up to the bullies at his school, no matter how much the player commands him to do so. *80 Days*, meanwhile, uses its restriction of player agency as a comment on colonialist expectations about white saviors: the protagonist encounters many injustices, but can seldom alter the situation in any but peripheral ways.[23] In each of these works, the limits on the player's agency are an important part of the meaning of the work.

Other interactive stories represent protagonist failure by analogy to a forced failure on the player's part. Christine Love's Twine *Even Cowgirls Bleed* (2013)[24] concerns a cowgirl who desires a submissive relationship with an imposing woman, but who lacks the skillset to navigate that relationship without damage. The interaction metaphor of *Even Cowgirls Bleed* equates hypertext-reading with shooting a gun. The cursor turns into crosshairs that "fire" whenever the player moves the mouse across a link. A gunshot sound plays and the screen flashes as the link is triggered. That metaphor becomes especially important at the end of the game, when the link we might intend to click is surrounded by others we definitely don't want to hit. However, it is impossible to reach the desired link with the mouse. We will, necessarily, fire at the wrong things instead of the right one, reenacting the protagonist's frustration and chagrin.

Interactive fiction authors sometimes speak of "complicity": the responsibility that the player might feel for events that they did not *choose* but that they did *cause*, if only by exerting the effort to drive the story forward. To gain the player's complicity, the author often provides conflicting motives for player and protagonist. In Jimmy Maher's Lovecraftian text adventure *The King of Shreds and Patches* (2009),[25] too much investigation into unholy secrets will drive the protagonist mad and end the game – an outcome the player can easily undo again. The player wants to know what will happen next, even if it kills the protagonist. Along similar lines, but with different emotional effect, Paolo Pedercini's *McDonald's Video Game* (2006)[26] invites the player to try to run a successful fast-food franchise, but the winning strategy may require abusing your labor force

---

[23] See, for instance, Meghna Jayanth, "Forget Protagonists: Writing NPCs with Agency for 80 Days and Beyond," *Medium* (June 5, 2016).
[24] Christine Love, *Even Cowgirls Bleed* (independent developer, 2013), Twine.
[25] Jimmy Maher, *The King of Shreds and Patches* (independent developer, 2009), Inform.
[26] Paolo Pedercini, *McDonald's Video Game* (Molleindustria, 2006), Flash.

and corrupting politicians – a comment on the perverse incentives in our economic system. The deliberate opposition of player motive and protagonist motive often drives interactive stories meant to end in tragedy or disaster.

10.6 Freedom and Choice Poetics

Critics have often assumed that interactive stories offer freedom from authorial control, in a way that they consider liberating (Robert Coover)[27] or damaging to the art form (Roger Ebert).[28] In practice, a player may have choices – but every aspect of those choices is authored.[29] How are choices presented to the reader? How are they framed? How do they communicate what is at stake? The likelihood of success or failure (if success and failure are meaningful here)? This is the territory of choice poetics, extensively theorized by Peter Mawhorter[30] and less formally discussed by many other practitioners.

Consider a passage from Porpentine Charity Heartscape's *Their Angelical Understanding* (2013).[31] Key adjectives in the description are rendered as cycling text (represented in bold): when the reader clicks the highlighted word or phrase, it is swapped out for another. The screen begins with the text:

> In the bottle float **black** eyes, lips **cracked with dehydration**, and your **aquiline** nose.

It is a common feature of Twine stories to allow the reader to change an individual word by clicking on it. Clicking on the eye color, lip description, and nose shape might let us change the description of our face:

> In the bottle float **purple** eyes, lips **plump and red,** and your **snub** nose.

A few screens later, the protagonist is leaving the monastery where they have lived in seclusion. The reader needs to choose which direction they will go when they step outside. The screen presents us with this text:

---

[27] Robert Coover, "The End of Books," *New York Times*, June 21, 1992.
[28] Roger Ebert, "Video Games Can Never Be Art," *RogerEbert.com*, April 16, 2010.
[29] There are a handful of recent exceptions driven by machine learning, such as Nick Walton, *AI Dungeon* (Latitude, 2019), which uses a GPT-3 language model to generate text responding to whatever the player has typed. But *AI Dungeon* is not presented as *a* story. On the contrary, the platform provides various methods of refining and controlling the output, and is ambiguous about whether *AI Dungeon* should be approached as a text or as a creative tool for the production of texts.
[30] For instance, Peter Mawhorter, Carmen Zegura, Alex Gray, et al., "Choice Poetics by Example" *Arts* 7.3 (September 2018), 47.
[31] Porpentine Charity Heartscape, *Their Angelical Understanding* (independent developer, 2013), Twine.

> And between you and your **destiny** was a vast
> **sea**
> **desert**
> **jungle**

The latter three lines represent different options. Do we want to go on to the sea, the desert, or the jungle? Meanwhile, the word **destiny** presents another opportunity to edit the text. We might expect, after we've altered the text about our face, that to click on "destiny" will allow us to rotate through other terms. But when we click on the word, it is replaced with "lol" – a bathetic mockery of the whole concept of destinies:

> And between you and your lol was a vast

Once clicked, the word ceases to be interactive. The reader cannot turn it back into "destiny" even if she wants to. Meaning is carried not only by the content of the choice but in the functionality of the text links.

10.7 Structure

Practitioners in the field frequently discuss interactive story structures using terms such as "linear," "multiple ending," "gauntlet," "branch and bottleneck," "pearls on a string," and "loop and grow."[32] These terms refer to issues that don't arise with noninteractive narrative: namely, how are the elements of the text sequenced, and under what circumstances? When does the reader have the opportunity to choose between multiple sections to read? When do paths reconverge, or re-enter an existing structure?

Linear stories are those in which the same constituent events of the plot occur in the same order on every play-through. Branch-and-bottleneck stories are those in which player choice causes some short-term variation in the plot, with various alternate events happening immediately after the choice ("branch"), but then reconverge at some important future development ("bottleneck"). Loop-and-grow stories are cyclical – perhaps playing out through the hours of a day or seasons of a year, presenting the player again and again with recurring issues or problems – but perhaps allowing

---

[32] Some of these picturesque structure terms come from unknown sources and were simply adopted by common consent; others do have a known origin, with Sam Kabo Ashwell's taxonomy providing a standard for discussion in the IF community. See Sam Kabo Ashwell, "Standard Patterns in Choice-Based Games," These Heterogenous Tasks, January 27, 2015, https://heterogenoustasks .wordpress.com/2015/01/26/standard-patterns-in-choice-based-games/, and Michael Joyce, "Nonce Upon Some Times: Rereading Hypertext Fiction," *Modern Fiction Studies*, 43.3 (Fall 1997), 579–597, suggesting structural terms for literary hypertext.

some progress nonetheless, so that the third time through a cycle, the player might have new affordances available. (If this structure seems distant from noninteractive narrative structures, consider that many classic fairy tales, such as The Three Billy Goats Gruff or The Three Little Pigs, are structured as a repeated cycle where the pattern breaks on the third cycle.)

Many of these structures are an attempt to tackle a fundamental issue: assuming that the player is given a large number of choices and that all of those choices have perceivable consequence, how does the creator avoid needing to write an unreasonable number of possible variant texts? One approach – separately invented many times over by different practitioners – is to organize passages of the story not into branches but into atomic "lexemes" or "storylets": chunks which become available when particular world state preconditions are met: for instance, a vignette about a grieving parent becomes available any time after the child character has died, and as long as that vignette has not already been viewed.

10.8 Simulation, Immersion, Emergence

In computationally complex digital literature, the code that drives the telling of a story embeds assumptions about what will be narrated and where the player's agency may be applied. A video game world model describes everything important that can happen in that imagined universe. In some games, this world model might represent the objects in the world, their locations, and the physics that allows them to interact. In others, the model might track the political alignment of countries on a map, the disposition of their soldiers, and the state of their military defenses and agricultural resources. In yet others, the model might represent the social relationships between characters, together with tracking whether characters know important facts about the universe.

As choice presentation and framing have great expressive potential, there is also a productive tension between the story and the model world used to present it. In the late 1990s and early 2000s, IF authors frequently talked about "immersion" as a desirable quality for interactive narrative, meaning that the story engrossed the player and avoided jarring responses that undercut the player's belief in her environment. Providing a seamless world model was seen as a major contributor to immersion. The simulations might be in aid of narratively slight but programmatically complicated questions, such as: Is the protagonist carrying liquid in a container? If so, how much? Are there multiple liquids in the game, and may they be mixed together?

Can we understand the player's natural-language references to the objects in all their various states (can we distinguish the "full" bucket from the "empty" bucket? The "bucket of milk" from "the bucket of ale"?)? Finally, can we form correct and (ideally) aesthetically pleasing sentences to describe every possible system state?

Over the years, references to "immersion" have dropped off, as fewer IF authors are writing games with freely typed input that would let the player test the boundaries in the first place. Then, too, some authors came to feel that "immersion" was less than useful as a term of craft because it described the player's mind state, not a quality of the game. More recent discussions on the benefits of simulation for narrative games have tended to focus on a different quality: emergence, the system's ability to generate or combine story elements through the procedural qualities of the work rather than from authored predetermination, and even to tell stories that are unexpected to the author. Perhaps the best extant emergent narratives are produced by games like *Dwarf Fortress* (2006)[33] and *Crusader Kings III* (2020),[34] where vast rulesets control the behavior of many characters and factions over a long period of time, allowing for long and intricate chains of causality. In the process, though, they sometimes lose coherence, pacing, and a sense of individual characterization.

Consequently, there is a persistent interest in some hypothetical IF piece that will remain coherent, well-paced, and compelling throughout, and yet also offer the player such a wealth of emergent narrative possibilities that no two paths through the story are ever quite the same.

10.9 Further Terminologies

This has been only a partial survey of the language used by writers of interactive stories. There are many other terms of craft we might have considered. It might have been fruitful, for instance, to cover "difficulty" and "fairness" for talking about narratives with a puzzle element; the "cruelty scale" designed by Andrew Plotkin to categorize interactive stories around how likely it is that a player might become permanently stuck without realizing that there was no longer any way to progress to the end of a story;[35] "procedural rhetoric" to talk about meaning that emerges only from playing with a system for a time and seeing what pressures it applies to

---

[33] Tarn Adams and Zach Adams, *Dwarf Fortress* (Bay 12, 2006). [34] *Crusader Kings 3* (Paradox, 2020).
[35] Andrew Plotkin, "The Zarfian Cruelty (or Forgiveness) Scale," *Eblong.com*, n.d. https://eblong.com/zarf/essays/cruelty.html.

winning and losing (and other experiences);[36] and "expressive range" to talk about the scope of possibility found within a generative system.[37]

These conversations are broad and evolving. Old terms lose prominence (as, arguably, "immersion" has ceased to be as extensively discussed) and new terms are invented, discovered, or borrowed from an adjacent artform. A development of theory in the tabletop RPG world or in immersive theater, for instance, might be imported with some modifications into IF conversations as well.

*

I find IF compelling because it demands I consider truths that other art practices might not force to light. To build a detailed model world requires the author to express what is possible and what is likely: that expression might take the form of code rather than text, but still requires consideration and artistic commitment to what is being said. To write a story where the player may change out viewpoint characters at any time, the author must consider every character's opinion at every moment of the story.

---

[36] See Ian Bogost, *Persuasive Games: The Expressive Power of Videogames* (Cambridge, MA: MIT Press, 2007).

[37] See, for instance, Gillian Smith and Jim Whitehead, "Analyzing the Expressive Range of a Level Generator," *Proceedings of the 2010 Workshop on Procedural Content Generation in Games*, June 2010, 1–7. Though here applied to nonnarrative contexts, the same ideas are used in discussions of procedural narrative.

CHAPTER 11

Generated Literature

Nick Montfort and Judy Heflin

11.1 Introduction

Literature has been generated by computers since the beginning of the 1950s. We mean "computer" in the usual sense it is used today: a general-purpose, programmable, electronic digital machine that performs symbol manipulation automatically. We are also using a standard concept of literature, or literary art, which includes but is not limited to poetry and fiction. "Generated" means that computer programs have actually been written and run, resulting in literary output. Sometimes the output of programs is reworked before publication in various ways – particular poems are selected, or the text is smoothed over, or more extensive editorial intervention is made. But in many cases this output is presented exactly as originally produced. In this chapter, we deal with the history of literary text generation, the rise of the author/programmer within this digital literary art practice, how computer-generated literature speaks in machine voices, and how critics and scholars can better understand what is happening in this area, now and in the future.

A sustained type of computer-generated literature practice is now becoming widespread: that of the author/programmer. Individuals have worked as both authors and programmers throughout the history of computer-generated literature. The difference in the twenty-first century is that the author/programmer is becoming prevalent, and such people are making computer-generated literature the core of their work, building on their first explorations and producing more nuanced and compelling computational literature. To deal thoughtfully with their work, critics, like author/programmers, will need to have both technical and literary abilities.

There are certainly machines that precede the literature-generating computer, such as Ramon Llull's early fourteenth-century *Ars Magna*, allowing the generation of philosophical propositions with paper volvelles.[1] There are also a wealth of fictional text-generating mechanisms, such as The Engine in Jonathan Swift's *Gulliver's Travels*, George Orwell's Versificator in *Nineteen Eighty-Four, and* The Great Automatic Grammatizator in Roald Dahl's short story of the same title.[2] Authors including Stanisław Lem[3] and Italo Calvino[4] have also offered intriguing speculative discussions of how computer-generated literature might develop. Additionally, there are many present-day applications of text-generation technologies that are not utilized for literary purposes. There have been many companies in recent years (not only OpenAI, but earlier ones, including Narrative Science and Automated Insights) that have provided generation technologies for nonfictional and journalistic purposes. These do have some implications for literary studies and notions of authorship.[5] Because this generation is not directed at literary art, however, it is beyond our scope.

We have sought different threads of practice, and looked to distinguish those cases where computer-generated literature is the outcome of a unified process of programming and writing by author/programmers. By doing so, we mean to highlight an increasingly prominent practice that has been neglected in critical and theoretical discussion. It is also possible to slice computer-generated literature for study in other ways, as some have done. One could focus on a particular genre, such as poetry or prose; keep to a particular historical era; or sort literary systems based on the media elements they use, or based on how their fundamental algorithms work. There are also different contexts of presentation, including the format of the printed book, gallery and museum installation, and presentation online, which could be used as an organizing principle. While these are worthwhile ways to look at generated literature, we aim to fill a gap and describe the growing community of individual and distributed author/programmers. Those working in this community of practice have a variety

---

[1] Anthony Bonner, *The Art and Logic of Ramon Llull: A User's Guide* (Leiden: Brill, 2007); Michelle Gravelle, Anah Mustapha, and Coralee Leroux, "Volvelles," *ArchBook: Architectures of the Book*, December 1, 2012, https://drc.usask.ca/projects/archbook/volvelles.php.

[2] Mario Aquilina, "Text Generation, or Calling Literature into Question," *Electronic Book Review* produced by po, June 27, 2017, https://electronicbookreview.com/essay/text-generation-or-calling-literature-into-question/.

[3] Stanisław Lem, "Juan Rambellais et al., *A History of Bitic Literature, Volume 1*," in *Imaginary Magnitude* (San Diego: Harcourt Brace Jovanovich, 1984), 39–76.

[4] Italo Calvino, "Cybernetics and Ghosts," in *The Uses of Literature* (San Diego: Harcourt Brace & Company, 1986), 3–27.

[5] Leah Henrickson, "Natural Language Generation: Negotiating Text Production in Our Digital Humanity," *Proceedings of the Digital Humanities Congress 2018* (Sheffield: The Digital Humanities Institute, 2018). www.dhi.ac.uk/books/dhc2018/natural-language-generation/.

of approaches to generating literature, working to engage with computing more explicitly and profoundly than "prompt engineers" who are trying out companies' new systems and publishing the results.

11.2 Three Threads in Twentieth-Century Generation

Three significant threads of practice can be seen in the twentieth century: early programs that produced short-form outputs such as love letters, stanzas, and sentences, all formally similar; more elaborate story generators that were the academic projects of computer scientists; and more elaborate and longer-form literary text generators produced by poets and writers.[6]

11.3 Early Work in Short Forms

Author/programmers have been developing short-form projects for decades. One famous example of computerized text generation is seen in the collaboration of Brion Gysin and Ian Sommerville (one artist/poet, one programmer), who permuted lines of four or five words in the 1960s by computer – following earlier permutation poems that Gysin had written manually.[7] Such collaborations remain productive, although there have also been individual author/programmers working by themselves on short-form computer-generated literature, even before Gysin and Somerville collaborated.

Christopher Strachey seems to be the first to have undertaken creative text generation using a general-purpose computer. Strachey wrote a parody love letter generator (its first outputs were apparently displayed in 1953) that was both a humorous intervention and discussed in an art journal.[8] Strachey's other creative computing work includes a draughts (checkers) player and the first computer music, both programmed before his love letter generator.[9]

---

[6] These and many other sorts of text generation systems can be experienced via the text they produced in *Output: An Anthology of Computer-Generated Text, 1953–2023*, edited by Lillian-Yvonne Bertram and Nick Montfort and coming from the MIT Press and Counterpath in August 2024. Here, we provide a brief, synthetic discussion of three types of significant work.

[7] Christopher T. Funkhouser, *Prehistoric Digital Poetry an Archaeology of Forms* (Tuscaloosa: The University of Alabama Press, 2007); David Pocknee, "The Permutated Poems of Brion Gysin," 2019, http://davidpocknee.ricercata.org/gysin/.

[8] Christopher Strachey, "The 'Thinking' Machine," *Encounter*, October 1954; Noah Wardrip-Fruin, "Christopher Strachey: The First Digital Artist?" *Grand Text Auto*, August 1, 2005, https://grandtextauto.soe.ucsc.edu/2005/08/01/christopher-strachey-first-digital-artist/.

[9] Alexander Smith, "The Priesthood at Play: Computer Games in the 1950s," *They Create Worlds*, February 2, 2017, https://videogamehistorian.wordpress.com/2014/01/22/the-priesthood-at-play-computer-games-in-the-1950s/; Jack Copeland and Jason Long, "Restoring the First Recording of Computer Music," *The British Library*, September 13, 2016, https://blogs.bl.uk/sound-and-vision/2016/09/restoring-the-first-recording-of-computer-music.html.

Theo Lutz programmed the German *Stochastic Texts* (1959) to generate what read like propositions of second-order logic, using a lexicon drawn from Franz Kafka's *The Castle*.[10] Victor H. Yngve, who worked in machine translation, wrote a program to generate random sentences (1961) that used text from a children's book and was considered, by some, poetic.[11] While these two people are mainly identified with computing, the same cannot be said for poet and Neoavanguardia artist Nanni Balestrini, Nobel Prize winning writer J. M. Coetzee, or Fluxus artist Alison Knowles. Balestrini's first significant work was the 1961 *TAPE MARK I*, an Italian generator of centos with its output shown on video.[12] Coetzee wrote a combinatorial program with an extensive vocabulary that generated five-word lines (c.1962–5).[13] Knowles, after learning some FORTRAN from composer James Tenney, worked in collaboration with him to program *The House of Dust* (1967), which endlessly produces quatrains describing houses around the world.[14]

By the late 1960s the programming language BASIC (Beginners All-purpose Symbolic Code) had been developed at Dartmouth College.[15] It was used for many diversions, including short-form literary text generation. In one of very many examples, a program of unknown authorship simply called POETRY was included in a book published in 1975.[16] BASIC was implemented on microcomputers and became the lingua franca of personal computing.[17] The microcomputer era saw the publication of a book of poems generated by a BASIC computer program for the TRS-80 Color Computer (1981), with the source code for the program included in the back.[18] One BASIC "folk program" for Commodore computers

---

[10] Theo Lutz, "Stochastische Texte," *Augenblick* 4.1 (1959): 3–9, www.stuttgarter-schule.de/lutz_schule_en.htm.
[11] Margaret Masterman, "The Use of Computers to Make Semantic Toy Models of Language," in *Astronauts of Inner-Space: An International Collection of Avant-Garde Activity* (San Francisco: Stolen Paper Review, 1966), 36–37.
[12] "TAPE MARK 1, Nanni Balestrini: Research and Historical Reconstruction," Museo dell'Informatica Funzionante, June 30, 2017, https://museo.freaknet.org/en/tape-mark-1-nanni-balestrini-ricerca-ricostruzione-storica/.
[13] Rebecca Roach, "The Computer Poetry of J. M. Coetzee's Early Programming Career," *Ransom Center Magazine*, June 28, 2017, https://sites.utexas.edu/ransomcentermagazine/2017/06/28/the-computer-poetry-of-j-m-coetzees-early-programming-career/.
[14] Funkhouser, *Prehistoric Digital Poetry*.
[15] John G. Kemeny, *Man and the Computer* (New York: Scribner, 1972).
[16] "POETRY," in *101 BASIC Computer Programs* (Maynard: Digital Equipment Corporation, 1975), 169–71.
[17] Nick Montfort, Patsy Baudoin, John Bell, et al., *10 PRINT CHR$(205.5 RND(1)); : GOTO 10* (Cambridge, MA: MIT Press, 2013).
[18] Ron Clark, *My Buttons Are Blue, and Other Love Poems from the Digital Heart of an Electronic Computer* (Woodsboro: ARCsoft Publishers, 1982).

generates what can be read as concrete poetry and is only a single line long.[19] People with established poetry practices began to write BASIC programs, too, with prominent early examples written for the Apple II in the 1980s by bpNichol[20] and Geof Huth.[21] Both produce animated visual output, and are a bridge to the more extensive projects discussed later in the chapter.

11.4 Story Generation Research

Sometimes the focus of generation projects is on computing, with researchers seeking to demonstrate aspects of computing or the mind. James Meehan's TALE-SPIN, Scott Turner's MINSTREL, and Michael Lebowitz's UNIVERSE are examples of systems meant to model something general about thinking, writing, or narrative. TALE-SPIN was the first major academic project in story generation, an interactive storytelling program developed by Meehan for his 1976 PhD dissertation.[22] Noah Wardrip-Fruin has described it as having a fascinating and complex underlying model which, unfortunately from an aesthetic standpoint, is not revealed in the simple surface texts that are generated.[23] Turner's MINSTREL and Lebowitz's UNIVERSE were both developed during the 1980s. MINSTREL[24] focused on the simulation of goal-directed human authorial behaviors, while UNIVERSE[25] was designed to generate continuing serials, or never-ending stories within a universe. At the very end of the century, another research system, MEXICA, developed by Rafael Pérez y Pérez and described in his 1999 dissertation, was specifically designed to automate a model of the human creative writing process. MEXICA was developed as a research system, to inquire into the nature of creativity, but in 2017 the curated output of an updated system was

---

[19] Montfort et al., *10 PRINT*.
[20] bpNichol, *First Screening: Computer Poems*, 1984. Republished in *Vispo*, ed. Jim Andrews, Geof Huth, Lionel Kearns, Marko Niemo, and Dan Waber, March 2007, http://vispo.com/bp/.
[21] Geof Huth, "Endemic Battle Collage, 1986-1987," in *Electronic Literature Collection, Volume 2*, ed. Laura Borràs, Talan Memmott, Rita Raley, and Brian Stefans, Cambridge, MA: Electronic Literature Organization, February 2011, http://collection.eliterature.org/2/works/huth_endemic_battle_collage.html.
[22] Noah Wardrip-Fruin, "The Story of Meehan's TaleSpin," *Grand Text Auto*, September 13, 2006, https://grandtextauto.soe.ucsc.edu/2006/09/13/the-story-of-meehans-tale-spin/.
[23] Noah Wardrip-Fruin, *Expressive Processing: Digital Fictions, Computer Games, and Software Studies* (Cambridge, MA: MIT Press, 2009).
[24] Noah Wardrip-Fruin, "Turner's Minstrel Part 1," *Grand Text Auto*, March 1, 2006, https://grandtextauto.soe.ucsc.edu/2006/03/01/turners-minstrel-part-1/.
[25] Noah Wardrip-Fruin, "Lebowitz's Universe Part 1," *Grand Text Auto*, March 4, 2006, https://grandtextauto.soe.ucsc.edu/2006/03/04/lebowitzs-universe-part-1/.

published as *Mexica: 20 Years–20 Stories* as part of the Using Electricity series. Pérez y Pérez's involvement with the MEXICA system changed from solely that of the programmer to that of the literary author/programmer, whose name is now on the spine of a book categorized on the back cover as "Fiction/Artificial Intelligence."

11.5 Extensive Projects by Poets and Writers

The first published book of computer-generated writing seems to be *La Machine à écrire* (1964),[26] which contains a selection of unedited outputs from a text-generation project created by engineer and linguist Jean Baudot. He used a simple grammar and a constrained lexicon of 630 words to computationally generate phrases. Although this project was not necessarily created for literary purposes, the output of Baudot's program appeared in the book with contextualizing commentary by poets and writers including Gatien Lapointe and Oulipo cofounder Raymond Queneau.

Many later projects were undertaken by poets and writers. The most well-known is likely *The Policeman's Beard Is Half Constructed* (1984), a book of computational prose and poetry generated by a program called RACTER that was coauthored by writer and programmer William Chamberlain along with the help of programmer Thomas Etter.[27] Authorial credit is given to RACTER, a system that explores the grammatical structure of the English language with a dynamism propelled by random number generation.[28] RACTER was by no means a short-form text generator, and was also not a project created with the purpose of academic research in mind. It was an extensive project by an author/programmer who wished to explore the creative potential of computer-generated text. Some criticism of *Policeman's Beard* in the 1990s took the position that the project was a trick, actually done by a human author.[29] Espen Aarseth offered in response that computer-generated literature should be called "cyborg literature," giving this category of writing the tentative definition "literary texts produced by a combination of human

---

[26] Jean Baudot, *La Machine à Écrire: Mise En Marche Et Programmée Par Jean A. Baudot* (Montréal: Les Éditions du Jour, 1964).
[27] RACTER, *The Policeman's Beard Is Half Constructed* (New York: Warner Books/Warner Software, 1984).
[28] Bill Chamberlain, "Getting a Computer to Write About Itself," in *Digital Deli: The Comprehensive, User-Lovable Menu of Computer Lore, Culture, Lifestyles and Fancy*, ed. Steve Ditlea (New York: Workman Publishing Company, 1984), 172–173.
[29] Espen Aarseth, *Cybertext: Perspectives on Ergodic Literature* (Baltimore: Johns Hopkins University Press, 1997).

and mechanical activities."[30] The introduction to *Policeman's Beard* claims that "Once it's running, RACTER needs no input from the outside world." Aarseth found this at least misleading, as the work is not completely autonomous: Chamberlain's creative efforts are embodied in dialogue templates, the writing of source texts, and the selection of generated output for the printed book, activities Aarseth organizes into preprocessing and postprocessing, as he notes that coprocessing is also possible.[31] This, however, is not inconsistent with the claim in the introduction, which simply states that the version of the RACTER program used to produce the book doesn't take any user input after it has started running. (To muddy the waters further, there was also a commercial version of the RACTER software for home computers, not the version of the program that generated the book, which *was* interactive.) The perspective that critics and authors take on generated literature today, whether it is produced by bots that used to operate on Twitter or printed in books from poetry presses, acknowledges that there are always some "cyborg" aspects and that text cannot arise from a computer without some human involvement.

Several twentieth-century computer-generated books were produced by one author with the substantial programming done beforehand by others. An example is John Cage's *Anarchy: New York City – January 1988*, published posthumously in 2002. It consists of twenty mesostic poems generated using MESOLIST, a program written by Jim Rosenberg, and ic, an I Ching program written by Andrew Culver.[32] Having some familiarity with computing, poet Charles O. Hartman began a series of experiments with programs that were in line with his literary interests in the prosody of free and metrical verse. He developed a system to automate the process of scansion, and continued along these lines until publishing a book of poems in 1995 called *Sentences*. The poems in the book were generated in part by TRAVESTY, a system by Hugh Kenner, who is listed as a coauthor. Also used was a program Hartman devised, DIASTEXT, which automates the diastic writing strategy of poet Jackson Mac Low. Hartman's work demonstrates a personal literary exploration by way of computation that resulted in not only printed output in the form of poetry but also computer programs that engage with literary questions and forms of analysis.[33] As compelling as many of these twentieth-century projects were, they

---

[30] Ibid., 134. [31] Ibid., 135.
[32] Andrew Culver, "John Cage Computer Programs," Anarchic Harmony Foundation, www.anarchicharmony.org/People/Culver/CagePrograms.html.
[33] Charles O. Hartman, *The Virtual Muse: Experiments in Computer Poetry* (Middletown: Wesleyan University Press).

were often isolated experiments. In the twenty-first century, author/programmers more frequently engage in a sustained type of practice, and the emergence of communities of practice encourage and support further work in this area.

11.6 New Directions in Generation

There are now numerous author/programmers creating literary work that depends on a wide variety of computational approaches – not just the combinatorial and permutational work of Strachey, Lutz, Knowles, or Gysin, but many explorations involving, for instance, machine learning, word/image juxtapositions, performance, small-scale programs, large language models, remix, and free software culture. There is no single sort of author/programmer, as work is advancing in many new directions.

11.7 Communities of Practice

Among the several developing communities of practice, makers of Twitterbots[34] devised systems that cleverly intervene in social media feeds, producing computer-generated literature for this context. Twitter (now X) proved an amazing context for creative work in the early twenty-first century. Eleven good examples of bots, discussed and archived in an online anthology,[35] include:

- Allison Parrish's @everyword, which tweeted every word in an English lexicon from 2007 to 2014,
- Everest Pipkin's @tiny_star_field, a generator of visual poems,
- Darius Kazemi's conflation system @TwoHeadlines, the output of which included "China's Lawyer to Unveil New Evidence on Colbert Show,"
- Zach Whalen's @ROM_TXT, which finds runs of text in ROM data from videogames, and
- Ranjit Bhatnagar's @pentametron, which locates tweets that happen to be in iambic pentameter, and happen to rhyme, and pairs them into couplets.

---

[34] Tony Veale and Mike Cook, *Twitterbots: Making Machines That Make Meaning* (Cambridge, MA: MIT Press, 2018).
[35] "Bots," *Electronic Literature Collection, Volume 3*, ed. Stephanie Boluk, Leonardo Flores, Jacob Garbe, and Anastasia Salter (Cambridge, MA: Electronic Literature Organization), February 2016, http://collection.eliterature.org/3/collection-bots.html.

Some bots with literary and artistic aspects are nonfictional, as with @censusAmericans, which presents very short factual statements about Americans drawn from census data but "textualized" in forms such as "I haven't moved recently. I work for a private company. I was widowed."[36] There are also several fine literary bots that originate as academic research projects in computational creativity.[37] Botmakers were, of course, in touch with each other and aware of each other's work through the social network they were using. After a large-scale purge of bots from Twitter in 2018, some botmakers moved to the federated social network Mastodon.[38] Twitter became even more inhospitable for creative bots after Elon Musk's disastrous takeover of the company at the end of October 2022. With the rebranding of the company, the last creative bots were eradicated.

NaNoGenMo (National Novel Generation Month) is the main annual event in which people develop computer-generated literature. It was conceived by Kazemi in 2013, who was riffing on NaNoWriMo (National Novel Writing Month) and who included the constraint from NaNoWriMo that "novels" be at least 50,000 words in length.[39] This informal framework is welcoming and encourages offhand projects and experimentation. It also encourages people to return year after year and to develop a practice in literary generation. The technical and conventionally literary aspects of NaNoGenMo are reflected in the requirements for participation: sharing one's code and producing and sharing the textual output. Some remarkable books generated in recent Novembers include Leonard Richardson's *Alice's Adventures in the Whale*, in which dialog from *Moby-Dick* replaces that in *Alice in Wonderland*;[40] Liza Daly's *Seraphs*, a book intended to look like the undeciphered Voynich Manuscript;[41] visually innovative works, such as *i've never picked a protected flower* by Pipkin; and Nick Montfort's *Hard West Turn*, which pieces together English and Simple English Wikipedia entries related to gun violence in the United States. With the results consolidated online on GitHub, and

---

[36] Jia Zhang, "Introducing CensusAmericans, a Twitter Bot for America," *FiveThirtyEight*, July 24, 2015, https://fivethirtyeight.com/features/introducing-censusamericans-a-twitter-bot-for-america/.
[37] "The Best of Bot Worlds," Creative Language Systems Group, http://afflatus.ucd.ie/.
[38] Rob Dozier, "Twitter's New Developer Rules Might End One of Its Most Enjoyable Parts," *Slate Magazine*, August 8, 2018, https://slate.com/technology/2018/08/twitters-new-developer-guidelines-might-end-fun-bot-accounts.html.
[39] Josh Dzieza, "The Strange World of Computer-Generated Novels," *The Verge*, November 25, 2014, www.theverge.com/2014/11/25/7276157/nanogenmo-robot-author-novel.
[40] Leonard Richardson, "In Dialogue," November 18, 2013, www.crummy.com/software/NaNoGenMo-2013/.
[41] Liza Daly, *Seraphs: A Procedurally Generated Mysterious Codex* (San Francisco: Blurb, 2014).

the resulting texts frequently discussed by bloggers and journalists, NaNoGenMo has helped to foster new communities, critical and artistic.

Publishing computer-generated literature in print helps to raise the visibility of this form and also furthers the growth of such communities. Author/programmers often self-publish books and chapbooks, but books have also recently been put out by established presses. Named after one of the lines in Knowles's *The House of Dust,* Using Electricity is a series of computer-generated books published by Counterpath that critically engages with the long history of computer-generated literature while building a community of authors and introducing this type of work to readers through events such as group readings on the East Coast of the United States. Others have also had public gatherings to engage with interested readers and connect fellow author/programmers. Jhave Johnston, for instance, undertook a year-long project of human–computer collaboration, rising each day to revise the output of a computational poetry system he programmed. His project, titled *ReRites* and published by Anteism, includes essays by nine others and is contextualized by its own critical community. Johnson has done several readings from the project, as well as performances and recordings. Another performative project is Ross Goodwin's *1 the Road,* a reference to Jack Kerouac's book and road trip, published by Jean Boîte Éditions. The book was produced using an instrumented car that collected locative, visual, audio, and textual data. This seeded a long-short-term-memory recurrent neural network[42] that generated short texts related to particular moments. The project, supported by Google, was well documented, and Goodwin promoted it in public blog posts and offered a GitHub repository of his code.

Documentation is one of the key ways that author/programmers are building community and inspiring new projects. This may involve outlining a creative process in a blog post, creating repositories on GitHub or other code-sharing websites, publishing and distributing zines, or even developing frameworks or libraries to inspire new types of generative work and promote inclusivity.[43] There is also growing community-driven institutional support, whether through corporate sponsorship, publishing deals, or increased attention to creative coding in academic and teaching environments.

---

[42] For further details on LSTM (Long Short-Term Memory) RNN (Recurrent Neural Network), see www.analyticsvidhya.com/blog/2021/03/introduction-to-long-short-term-memory-lstm/.
[43] Kate Compton, Ben Kybartas, and Michael Mateas, "Tracery: An Author-Focused Generative Text Tool," *Lecture Notes in Computer Science*, volume 9445, (2015): 154–161, https://doi.org/10.1007/978-3-319-27036-4_14.

11.8 Concise Programs, Extensive Output

In identifying threads of twentieth-century work, we described short-form projects, which had early origins, and distinguished these from the generation of more extensive and often book-length texts. In the twenty-first century the distinction between short-form and extensive projects does not hold in the same way. One can, for example, produce intentionally concise and simple programs to generate book-length literary output; indeed, in response to the complexity and obscurity of contemporary computing, Montfort has taken this approach and promoted it.[44]

Collaborations between Bill Kennedy and Darren Wershler involved developing conceptually simple programs to achieve compelling effects. One of their books, *Apostrophe*, is a compilation of statements that begin with "you are" that were collected by a web-crawling program, while another, *Update*, uses a simple substitution algorithm to mine personal RSS feeds and databases of names to generate updates from dead poets.[45] More recently, Montfort's *The Truelist* and Milton Läufer's *A Noise Such as a Man Might Make* are examples of books by individual author/programmers that were published with the code included.[46] The former includes all data and code used on a single printed page; the latter uses two source novels, but is generated from a program just two pages long.

An advantage of short programs is that, when the code is made available as free/open-source software, they can be easily reworked by other author/programmers into new projects. A poetry generator that has undergone very extensive "remix" is Montfort's "Taroko Gorge."[s] Invitations to write short programs from scratch can also be welcoming to author/programmers. During the 2019 NaNoGenMo, Montfort declared an additional special event or competition: Nano-NaNoGenMo, in which the generating computer programs are restricted to be no more than 256 characters in length.[47] Even with this severe limitation, some remarkable work was

---

[44] Nick Montfort and Natalia Fedorova, "Small-Scale Systems and Computational Creativity," in *Proceedings of the Third International Conference on Computational Creativity*, ed. Mary Lou Maher, Kristian Hammond, Alison Pease, et al. (Dublin: Association for Computational Creativity; May, 2012), 82–86.

[45] Bill Kennedy and Darren Wershler, *Apostrophe* (Chicago: ECW Press, 2006); Bill Kennedy and Darren Wershler, *Update* (Montreal: Snare, 2010).

[46] Nick Montfort, *The Truelist* (Denver: Counterpath, 2017); Milton Läufer, *A Noise Such as a Man Might Make* (Denver: Counterpath, 2018).

[47] Gregory Barber, "Text-Savvy AI Is Here to Write Fiction," *Wired*. November 22, 2019, www.wired.com/story/nanogenmo-ai-novels-gpt2/.

produced. An example is Martin O'Leary's *Dublin Walk*, generated by linking together words from *Ulysses* and *Dubliners* based on whether they are anagrams or near-anagrams.[48]

11.9 The Prevalence of Author/Programmers

Some author/programmers working today can be identified as having started their work as poets, writers, and artists. Among them are John Cayley, J. R. Carpenter, and Talan Memmott, whose digital poetry practices originate in the 1990s, with or (in Cayley's case) prior to the World Wide Web. Similarly, some author/programmers started to investigate the intersection of computation and language from the perspective of the programmer. Significant effort has been expended by computer scientists in developing natural language generation systems, but there are also literary generation projects undertaken by programmers, within and beyond the context of NaNoGenMo. Some who work in computer-generated literature are professionally software engineers, including Daly, but also have extensive background in literary computing – developing interactive fiction, in her case, as well as working in the related area of digital publishing for many years.

While the "divide" of the slash between author and programmer does have meaning, many current author/programmers did not begin on one side or the other, but have been involved with both literary authorship and programming more or less from the beginning of their practice. For these people in particular, computation is not mainly an Other to be confronted, but a medium of art. Of the people mentioned already, we will venture to claim this is the case at least with Bhatnagar, Goodwin, Läufer, Parrish, Pipkin, Whalen, and Zilles.

One result of the increasing sophistication of author/programmers is that they have been able to make literary use of cutting-edge machine learning techniques, which take a statistical approach and improve their performance as additional data is provided. Johnson and Goodwin provide two examples. Another is offered by Sofian Audry, who displayed how the results of different epochs of training unfolded in his *for the sleepers in that quiet earth* (2019), the product of a deep recurrent neural network using only *Wuthering Heights* as data. Author/programmers have also made extensive use of word embeddings (in which words are represented as vectors), with

---

[48] Martin O'Leary, "Dublin Walk · Issue #102 · NaNoGenMo/2019," *GitHub*, November 2019, https://github.com/NaNoGenMo/2019/issues/102.

Word2vec models being of recent interest. Transformer-based approaches, in combination with pre-training on vast amounts of text, have been the latest major advance. The main large language models used in creative text generation are from OpenAI and include GPT-2, GPT-3, and ChatGPT (backed by GPT-4), which is trained by people to "align" with corporate purposes. Free and open models have been developed in addition to these proprietary ones. One of the early open access large language modes was GPT-NeoX 20B, a formidable model that is free by design and can be used by researchers (and artists) without restriction.

11.10 Machine Voices Wake Us

Poetry, and certainly modernist poetry, has been obsessed with "human voices" – the ones mentioned in the last line of "The Love Song of J. Alfred Prufrock." Eliot even initially thought to give *The Waste Land*, with its dialectal expressions, the title *He Do the Police in Different Voices*. In computer-generated literature, the machine "does" the voices, but they are not always imitations of human ones. To adhere to our law enforcement theme for a moment, the second, short poem in the computer system RACTER's book *The Policeman's Beard Is Half Constructed* reads:

> Awareness is like consciousness. Soul is like spirit.
> But soft is not like hard and weak is not like
> strong. A mechanic can be both soft and hard, a
> stewardess can be both weak and strong. This is
> called philosophy or a world-view.

The bland statements about similarity in the first three sentences seem, from today's perspective, like something that would be straightforwardly generated from word embedding data, or from a computerized lexical resource such as WordNet. Although they are felicitous examples of the English language, they certainly do not have dialectical nuance in them. Instead, like the rest of the poem, they wear their computer-generated nature proudly on their sleeve. This is an example of a machine voice, not a human voice. It showcases how computers think and speak, at least inasmuch as the creators of RACTER imagined this. And how is that? Computers understand similarities (near-synonymy) and oppositions (antonymy), but they also understand that people are complex entities that can embody supposedly opposite characteristics. They use simple declarative sentences. The computer circa 1984 also seems to have some perspective on gender, naming a stereotypically male profession (mechanic) and using a female-gendered term for flight attendant. This, we might say, is a hint of what is called philosophy or a world-view – and, in particular, a machinic one.

An example that is similarly formulaic but will likely seem even less human, as its grammar and lexicon are more constrained, is provided by Darby Larson's 9,450-word story "Pigs" (2011),[49] which begins:

> The pig pigged with the pigs. The pigs pigged in pens. The pigs pigged on pigs. The pigs pigged in pens. The pigs pigged on pigs. The pig pigged over pigs. The pig pigged with the pigs. The pigs pigged in pens. The pigs pigged with the pigs.

The story is generated by permuting lists of starting nouns, verbs, and prepositions with final nouns. There are only four or five options in each of these lists, and the resulting work exhausts all possible permutations of sentence structure, with added wrappers to shuffle the presentation of the generated sentences. While authors have experimented with these kinds of permutations without programming, the affordances of computation allow authors to lay bare the workings of combinatorial writing in more accurate, exhaustive, and ambitious ways. Larson's "Pigs" is one extreme example, showing that with a simple grammar and limited lexicon, one can achieve a piece of writing that is extensive, diverse, and even at times entertaining.

Machine voices do not always ring out in such formulaic ways, however. In the first part of Parrish's *Articulations*, lines of verse harvested from Project Gutenberg are automatically linked together based on phonetic similarity. The result resonates with the concern for similarity of sound in traditional poetry, but creates connections that neglect sense and differ from those humans have made:

> And like a dream sits like a dream: sits like a queen, shine like a queen. When like a flash like a shell, fled like a shadow; like a shadow still.
>
> Lies like a shadow still, aye, like a flash o light, shall I like a fool, quoth he, You shine like a lily like a mute shall I still languish, – and still, I like Alaska.[50]

To generate *Articulations*, Parrish developed a novel procedure to computationally represent phonetic similarity,[51] using that to creatively engage with language in surprising, machinic ways. Through this representation,

---

[49] Darby Larson, "Darby Larson: Pigs," *Calamari Press*, July 9, 2011, www.calamaripress.com/SF/X/ 070911_Larson.htm; Blake Butler, "If You Build the Code, Your Computer Will Write the Novel," *Vice*, September 11, 2013, www.vice.com/en_us/article/nnqwvd/if-you-build-the-code-your-computer-will-write-the-novel.
[50] Allison Parrish, *Articulations* (Denver: Counterpath, 2018), 45.
[51] Allison Parrish, "Poetic Sound Similarity Vectors Using Phonetic Features," *AAAI Conference on Artificial Intelligence and Interactive Digital Entertainment* (2017).

one can find the precise word that phonetically lies between two other words; for example, the phonetic halfway point between "kitten" and "puppy" is "committee."[52] This specific relationship between computation and language opens up new ways of poetic thinking, and Parrish's book is an ambulatory textualization, or articulation, of this new thought.

More semantically concerned – and probing more explicitly into machine cognition or at least the way computers view and organize data – is the book *Machine, Unlearning*. Li Zilles's generation process for this work involved using machine learning techniques to develop questions, rather than the usual declarations:

> Could LITERATURE be algorithmic in the way that psychology can be algorithmic?
> If someone teaches LITERATURE, do they teach sociology?
> What separates a leader in LITERATURE from a leader in economics?
> Can someone study LITERATURE like they study psychology?[53]

Practical text generation for informative purposes, as with many research projects in text generation, offers humanlike texts. Along these lines, computer generation systems have been used for literary hoaxes in which their output was presented as human-written.[54] Acknowledging these humanlike uses of computing with regard to literary generation, we find that computer text generation has a special applicability in the area of machine voices. There are some famous examples of human-authored text that read as computational, such as Samuel Beckett's *Watt*, written before general-purpose computing. And there are some less famous and more recent examples, such as *Cigarette Boy: A Mock Machine Mock-Epic Presented as a Proposal to The Mackert Corporation*.[55] The truly machinic investigation of machine voices is a unique contribution, however, extending more deeply and broadly into questions of computer cognition.

To see the ways in which contemporary computer-generated literature goes beyond these human-authored texts, consider another of Zilles's computer-generated books, *The Seeker*,[56] developed for NaNoGenMo

---

[52] Strange Loop, "'Experimental Creative Writing with the Vectorized Word' by Allison Parrish," YouTube, September 2017, https://youtu.be/L3DoJEA1Jdc.
[53] Li Zilles, *Machine, Unlearning* (Denver: Counterpath, 2018), 65.
[54] Erica T. Carter, Jim Carpenter, and Stephen McLaughlin, *ISSUE 1: Fall 2008* (forgodot.com, 2008); Jim Carpenter, "Erica T. Carter: The Collected Works," *Public Override Void*, April 17-June 10, 2004, Slought Foundation, Philadelphia, https://slought.org/resources/public_override_void.
[55] Darick Chamberlin, *Cigarette Boy: A Mock Machine Mock-Epic Presented As a Proposal to the Mackert Corporation* (Seattle: Rogue Drogue, 1991).
[56] Li Zilles, *The Seeker* ([n.p.]: thricedotted, 2014).

2014 under the nom de plume thricedotted. Each page of *The Seeker* has the appearance of a visual poem, with formats that recur in varied ways throughout the book. In it, an algorithm seems to be trying to understand humanity by reading the instructional website WikiHow (which is actually used as input by the generating system) and dreaming. That the text not only presents a machine voice, but also seems to offer a glimpse into a machine mind, is a crucial aspect for mathematician Marcus du Sautoy, who writes, with reference to *The Seeker* in particular: "This may in fact be the ultimate goal of any algorithmically generated literature: to allow us to understand an emerging consciousness (if it ever does emerge) and how it differs from our own."[57]

11.11 Critically Reading Computer-Generated Literature

No one can read an original Blake text, or a facsimile text, and not be struck by the following fact: that such a work has set in motion two large signifying codes, the linguistic code (which we tend to privilege when we study language-based arts like knowledge and poetry) and the bibliographic code (which interpreters, until recently, have largely ignored).[58]

Jerome McGann's observation can be expanded: William Blake was an artist as well as a poet. Engagement with visual art and art history, not just the form of the book, is of course important. Similarly, we argue that understanding the work of author/programmers requires an understanding of both literary art and computation. To understand computer-generated literature, understanding the formal and material nature of the computer as a symbol-manipulating machine – knowing something about how to program it – is essential. Otherwise, as would be the case with Blake, we can at best understand a sequence of words, not the work.

Montfort has developed a preliminary typology of computational writing that distinguishes systems based on "whether they sample or enumerate; whether they use a static or dynamic supply of source texts (or textons); their level of complexity; and their use of text only or multiple media." Each of these four axes are orthogonal, and thus each of these significant aspects is independent. This helps to show why characterizing a project with a single term (e.g., "random" or "multimedia") is inadequate. In

---

[57] Marcus du Sautoy, *The Creativity Code* (Cambridge, MA: Belknap Press of Harvard University Press, 2019), 265.
[58] Jerome McGann, *The Textual Condition* (Princeton: Princeton University Press, 1991).

explaining this typology, in the context of a book on poetics, a small amount of code (five lines of Python, two lines of BASIC) makes the discussion concrete. The two very short programs explain enumerating all combinations of text and sampling from a uniform and nonuniform distribution.[59]

Critical readers of computer-generated literature will need to come to terms with more code than this, because code, rather than language, is an essential medium for computer-generated literature. The author/programmer (or collaborative team) develops a text-generating system by writing code that runs on a particular computational platform, for instance the Manchester Mark I computer (in Strachey's case), FORTRAN IV (in Alison Knowles's case), the Apple II and Applesoft BASIC (in bpNichol and Huth's case) or Python (used by many currently). This particular code, with specific variable and function names, and particular implementations of different algorithms, has a form and function. That is, it works in a particular way, possibly taking data as input. Above the level of form and function, the system presents some sort of interface, graphical or command-line. Finally, there is a level of reception and operation, where a person considers how to interact and responds to the result.[60] A complete understanding of a work of computer-generated literature will include not only an analysis of the code that implements the system, but also an awareness of the platform's affordances. This is the major idea behind Platform Studies, initiated by Montfort and Ian Bogost.[61]

Another important approach is Critical Code Studies (CCS), described by Mark C. Marino in 2006 and developed in the online Critical Code Studies Working Groups run since 2010 by Marino and Jeremy Douglass. Those working in this area argue that to understand any culturally significant computer systems, poetic or otherwise, an understanding of programming is important and must be joined to more conventional types of critical reading ability. Marino's manifesto, for instance, states:

> CCS will require the artful combination of knowledge of programming languages and knowledge of interpretive approaches. These analytic projects will require programmers to help open up the contents and workings of

---

[59] Nick Montfort, "Conceptual Computing and Digital Writing," *Postscript: Writing After Conceptual Art*, ed. Andrea Andersson (Toronto: University of Toronto Press, 2018), 197–210.
[60] Nick Montfort, "Combat in Context," *Game Studies* 6.1 (December 2006), http://gamestudies.org/0601/articles/montfort.
[61] Ian Bogost and Nick Montfort, "Platform Studies: Frequently Answered Questions," in *Proceedings of the Digital Arts and Culture Conference*, Irvine, CA, December 2009; Nick Montfort and Ian Bogost, *Racing the Beam: the Atari Video Computer System* (Cambridge, MA: MIT Press, 2009).

programs, acting as theorists along with other scholars, as they reflect on the relationships between the code itself, the coding architecture, the functioning of the code, and specific programming choices or expressions, to that which it acts upon, outputs, processes, and represents.[62]

Marino now holds that, rather than requiring that programmers and critics join together, critics with knowledge of programming will help drive CCS forward. Marino is such a critic himself, and writes in his recent book on CCS, which includes large amounts of code, "it is my hope that the book will be intriguing enough to nonprogrammers to draw them deeper into the study of computers and programming languages, for programming is one of the key literacies of our age."[63]

Platform Studies and Critical Code Studies are not specific to computer-generated literature, but they provide important methodologies for critics of this sort of work. By joining technical knowledge to interpretive ability, those reading this sort of literature will be able to bring it fully into the discourse on human writings and other sorts of creative computing.

---

[62] Mark C. Marino, "Critical Code Studies," *Electronic Book Review*, December 4, 2006, http://electronicbookreview.com/essay/critical-code-studies/.

[63] Mark C. Marino, *Critical Code Studies* (Cambridge, MA: MIT Press, 2020).

CHAPTER 12

Literary Gaming

Timothy Welsh

12.1 The *Citizen Kane* of Videogames

It may seem odd to start a chapter on the relationship between videogames and literature by discussing a film. But, for a time, it was *Citizen Kane* rather than any work of literature that was the benchmark that would prove videogames were a medium capable of artistic expression. Rather than attempting to determine if the entire medium constitutes "art" – as if that were possible – the *Citizen Kane* benchmark asks if the medium has merely produced a single, sterling representative. This one example would then demonstrate the maturity of a medium ready to be taken seriously, not just for its commercial potential but as culture. The search for the *Citizen Kane* of videogames is not what it used to be, however. Felan Parker observes that "the comparison has become such a cliché that it has provoked considerable ridicule from game critics and journalists and numerous ironic invocations."[1] Sincere uses of the comparison have become harder to find as well. Parker points to thecitizenkaneofvideogames.tumblr.com as an indication that the search for the *Citizen Kane* of videogames remains active. But entries in this informal catalogue have declined precipitously since its launch in 2013. There are no entries for 2023 and only five have appeared since 2017.

The shifting perception and possible decline of the *Citizen Kane* comparison isn't necessarily a bad thing. Parker calls *Citizen Kane* comparisons the most "banal" version of legitimizing videogames through aligning them with an established artistic medium. Trending away from the comparison suggests that games – which regularly outpace movie box office numbers and have been the subject of several exhibitions at major art museums – no longer require this form of legitimization. Furthermore, the cross-media comparison has always been awkward and vague, making it

---

[1] Felan Parker, "Roger Ebert and the Games-as-Art Debate," *Cinema Journal* 57.3 (May 3, 2018), 91.

difficult to determine what would constitute a positive match. Much of this has to do with the ubiquity of ambiguous *Citizen Kane* references in popular culture more generally. Parker observes that *Citizen Kane* "has become a kind of simulacrum for art itself, and in particular popular art that transcends its commercial origins through authorship." So, when a game like 2K Boston's *Bioshock* or Rockstar North's *Grand Theft Auto IV* is referred to as the "*Citizen Kane* of videogames" it is hard to know what that means exactly.[2] Even so, Parker's definition narrows the field in a significant way, hinting at what may be lost in the waning of this imperfect cross-media comparison.

In the early days of videogame criticism, Henry Jenkins cautioned against "abandoning a focus on popular aesthetics" in the rush to legitimize videogames as a new art form.[3] He called videogames a "new lively art" due to their capacity to "open up new aesthetic experiences and transform the computer screen into a realm of experimentation and innovation that is broadly accessible." As compared to digital art aimed at the museum context, Jenkins argued, videogames as a popular art have to weigh experimentation against commercial demands, allowing them to push innovation while remaining accessible and responsive to experiences of a more general audience.

Despite its vagueness, the "*Citizen Kane* of videogames" is shorthand for some of these same priorities. It does not describe what Ian Bogost calls an "art game," like Jason Rohrer's *Passage*, but how a triple-A, console title like Insomniac Games's *Resistance 3* "does" art.[4] It is a commercial release game that, through its composition, becomes something more than just commodity, spectacle, or entertainment: a meaningful aesthetic experience for a popular audience. If we acknowledge, though, that the search for the *Citizen Kane* of videogames has been relegated to a cliché, what does that mean for videogames as a popular, or even "lively," art? Have videogames themselves changed, or has the perception and reception of them? As we consider in this chapter how literary criticism addresses videogames, to what degree is it meaningful to discuss contemporary videogames as art or as having more literary aspirations?

---

[2] 2K Boston (Irrational Games) *2K* Boston (Irrational Games), Bioshock (2K Games, 2007); Rockstar North, *Grand Theft Auto IV* (Rockstar Games, 2008).
[3] Henry Jenkins, "Games, the New Lively Art," *Henry Jenkins*, 2005, https://web.mit.edu/~21fms/People/henry3/GamesNewLively.html. See also Henry Jenkins, "Games, the New Lively Art," in *Handbook of Computer Game Studies*, ed. Joost Raessens and Jeffrey Goldstein (Cambridge, MA: The MIT Press, 2005), 175–189.
[4] Ian Bogost, *How to Do Things with Videogames* (Minneapolis: University of Minnesota Press, 2011); Jason Rohrer, *Passage*, Vers. 5 (2007) http://hcsoftware.sourceforge.net/passage/; Insomniac Games. *Resistance III* (Sony Computer Entertainment, 2011).

12.2 How to Tell a True "War" Story

Answering these questions has become more complicated in recent years. From the mid-1990s through the early 2000s, videogames seemed like they would have a part to play in the future of the book, the natural evolution of literary practice onto more expressly interactive digital platforms. Today, despite numerous compelling examples of videogames that support literary engagement, the comparison can seem strange, clichéd, banal, and also beside the point. Videogame studies has developed a variety of critical lenses and methodologies for taking videogames seriously as cultural objects, many of which draw on literary theory and criticism. Even so, it bears the legacy of its early period when it tried to distinguish itself from literary and cinema studies.[5]

Espen Aarseth, founder and editor-in-chief of the journal *Game Studies*, addressed this legacy recently in his "Ten Play-Tips for the Aspiring Game-Studies Scholar."[6] First among them is "don't mention the 'war.'" Aarseth refers here to the supposed debate between "narratologists," who emphasize story, semiotics, and representation, and the "ludologists," who assert the primacy of ludic, or game-like, properties. Aarseth rightly points out that there was no war. A "war," or even a debate, requires two opposing factions. Simply put, there was no group of videogame "narratologists." As Gonzalo Frasca put it in his 2003 corrective essay "Ludologists Love Stories, Too: Notes on a Debate that Never Took Place," "it would seem as if they [the narratologists] never existed."[7] Moreover, "narratology," as it is more commonly defined as the study of narrative, is not incompatible with ludology. Frasca, Aarseth, and Bogost observe that ludologists in fact pursued a kind of formalism not dissimilar from narratology.[8] Even so, this

---

[5] See Stephen Jones, *The Meaning of Video Games: Gaming and Textual Strategies* (Minneapolis: University of Minnesota Press, 2008). Jones attributes some of ludology's criticism of interdisciplinary work on videogames to aspirations toward "the kind of disciplinary purity that would ensure autonomous departments, classes, and research funding and would allow specialists to concentrate their energies on games as a unique object of attention" (4).

[6] Espen Aarseth, "How to Play – Ten Play-Tips for the Aspiring Game-Studies Scholar," *Game Studies* 19.2 (October 2019). http://gamestudies.org/1902/articles/howtoplay.

[7] Gonzalo Frasca, "Ludologists Love Stories, Too: Notes from a Debate That Never Took Place," *Ludology.org*, November 2003. www.ludology.org/2003/11/article-ludolog.html. In this essay, Frasca replaces "narratologist" with Michael Mateas's term "narrativist" after acknowledging that "narratologist" "has a different meaning outside and inside the game studies community." The only specific "narrativist" he can find named was Janet Murray, who, in his estimation, certainly couldn't be considered opposed to "studying game play from the point of view of their mechanics."

[8] Espen Aarseth, "How to Play"; Ian Bogost, "Videogames Are a Mess." Address delivered at the annual conference of the Digital Games Research Association. Uxbridge, UK, September 1–4, 2009. www.bogost.com/writing/videogames_are_a_mess.shtml; Frasca, "Ludologists Love Stories, Too."

"myth," as Aarseth calls it, keeps coming up, much to the frustration of weary videogame studies scholars. Thus, Aarseth advises newcomers to just "skip" it and avoid perpetuating myths about the war.

It is true that the narratologists never showed up for the war and that ludologists love stories too. But it is also true that those "murky days of 1998–2001," as Aarseth calls them, could be quite hostile to discussions of videogames as a medium of storytelling. In the first issue of Aarseth's *Game Studies*, for example, Markko Eskelinen sought "to annihilate for good the discussion of games as stories, narratives or cinema," describing game narratives as "marketing tools" and their study as "a waste of time and energy."[9] The field would temper this position not long after, with corrective essays such as Frasca's walking back the suggestion that story is irrelevant to the critical study of videogames. I hope to highlight in the following pages how the contemporary discussion of videogames has been shaped by work on the complicated relationship between *gameplay* and *story* and between *action* and *representation*. Even now, however, at this late date in videogame studies, Aarseth still feels the need to clarify that when he advises against mentioning the "war" he does not mean to suggest that "there should be no more discussion of the relation between games and stories." In fact, he continues, "there is very little actual, informed, productive disagreement in our field, both on that topic and many others, and room for much more."

The enduring harm of the "war" myth is less its mischaracterization of those "murky days" but the way it – and continuing frustration with it – has hampered and disrupted the field's ability to address its evolving relationship with literary criticism and practice. Resolving those tensions is, of course, beyond the scope of this one chapter; that harm can only be repaired through more, as Aarseth puts it, "informed, productive disagreement." In service of promoting and provoking those conversations, this chapter attempts to reset the field to address the present moment of digital culture. First, it presents a brief history of critical perspectives on videogames as literature. Second, it reflects on the contemporary status of and challenges to videogaming's literary aspirations following shifts in the industry's design priorities in the wake of the "casual revolution."[10] These shifts toward live service models supported by recurrent user spending have made explicit videogaming's protocological participation in the

---

[9] Markku Eskelinen, "The Gaming Situation," *Game Studies* 1.1 (July 2001). www.gamestudies.org/0101/eskelinen/.
[10] Jesper Juul, *A Casual Revolution: Reinventing Video Games and Their Players* (Cambridge, MA: The MIT Press, 2012).

circulation of power and capital within what McKenzie Wark has called the "gamespace" of neoliberal culture.[11] The goal of this chapter is less to present an argument than it is to describe what I see as the urgent work of literary studies in responding to these shifts and in continuing to rethink gaming in our evolving digital age.

12.3 The Future of Literature

It took a surprisingly long time for videogames to enter conversations about the future of literature. In *Games Authors Play*, Peter Hutchinson notes only a handful of literary studies like his own that attempt to use the foundational texts in game studies – such as *Homo Ludens* by Johan Huizinga or *Man, Play, Games* by Robert Caillois – to do literary criticism.[12] Hutchinson's work exemplifies these early intersections of game studies and literary study in that it does not address games themselves, but rather uses "games" and "play" as a critical lens to analyze traditional literature. It relies on the play in the term "game" to categorize game-like literary techniques common in post–World War II fiction such as allegory, allusion, and ambiguity. Despite the fact that the videogaming market had already grown big enough to experience a serious recession the year his book was published, Hutchinson doesn't mention videogames.[13]

Videogames proceeded through four or five generations of dedicated videogame consoles over the same period that poststructuralism grew in popularity and developed a critical language of "free play," "language games," and "readerly" interactivity. Yet literary scholarship paid little attention to the games themselves, digital or otherwise. Instead, hypertext fiction, exemplified by the works of Michael Joyce, Stuart Moulthrop, and Shelley Jackson, drew attention to the literary potential of digital platforms, prompting Robert Coover to declare, somewhat prematurely, the "end of books."[14] George Landow's *Hypertext: The Convergence of Contemporary Critical Theory and Technology* would argue that hypertext

---

[11] McKenzie Wark, *Gamer Theory* (Cambridge, MA: Harvard University Press, 2007).
[12] Peter Hutchinson, *Games Authors Play* (New York: Methuen, 1983); Johan Huizinga, *Homo Ludens* (Boston: Beacon Press, 1955); Roger Caillois, *Man, Play, and Games*. Translated by Meyer Barash (Champaign: University of Illinois Press, 1958).
[13] I am referring here to the infamous videogame crash of 1983. For some discussion, see Nick Montfort and Ian Bogost, "Pacman," *Racing the Beam: The Atari Video Computer System* (Cambridge, MA: MIT Press, 2009), 65–80.
[14] Robert Coover, "The End of Books," *New York Times*, June 21, 1992. https://archive.nytimes.com/www.nytimes.com/books/98/09/27/specials/coover-end.html.

embodies the textual openness prioritized in writings by poststructuralists such as Roland Barthes, Jacques Derrida, Paul de Man, and others.[15] Though he does not discuss videogames either, the expectation that digital platforms enable playful interactions between authorship and agency would eventually be applied to videogames as well.

It wasn't until the late 1990s that videogames were themselves taken seriously as a platform for literary expression. As personal computing costs went down and more and more users were accessing the World Wide Web, speculation swirled around advances in and toward "cyberspace" technologies. This included videogames. As Wendy Chun points out, the "science fiction" informing the cultural imaginary of digital communication technologies at the time enveloped all manner of digital environment, networked and nonnetworked.[16] Advances in videogaming seemed like a step toward the expected future development of fully immersive virtual environments.

The spread of this "VR madness," as Ron Wodaski would call it, relied on comparisons to the more generally understood immersive experience of reading – or being lost in a book.[17] Wodaski claimed, for example, "for centuries books have been the cutting edge of artificial reality."[18] By the end of the decade, literary critics were picking up on this comparison as well and using the conceptualizations of VR to analyze literature and the literary potential of digital platforms such as videogames. Marie-Laure Ryan spearheaded much of this discussion, expressly adapting theories of computer-enabled immersion for literary criticism.[19] In contrast to Landow's poststructuralist hypertext, Ryan argues that the literary properties and potential of virtual environments more closely align with the classics of nineteenth-century literary realism. Where "readerly" texts are more likely to draw self-aware, interactive attention to the artifice of the text, literary realism instead attempts to obscure the medium of instantiation, smooth over interactivity, and immerse users in another possible world. Janet Murray also theorized what literature would look like when developed

---

[15] George P Landow, *Hypertext: The Convergence of Contemporary Critical Theory and Technology* (Baltimore: The Johns Hopkins University Press, 1991).
[16] Wendy Hui Kyong, *Control and Freedom: Power and Paranoia in the Age of Fiber Optics* (Cambridge, MA: The MIT Press, 2006), 42–43.
[17] Ron Wodaski, *Virtual Reality Madness!* (Carmel: Sams Publishing., 1993).
[18] Ibid., 79.
[19] See Marie-Laure Ryan, "Immersion vs. Interactivity: Virtual Reality and Literary Theory," *Postmodern Culture* 5.1 (1994). http://muse.jhu.edu/journals/postmodern_culture/v005/5.1ryan.html; and Marie-Laure Ryan, *Narrative as Virtual Reality: Immersion and Interactivity in Literature and Electronic Media* (Baltimore: The Johns Hopkins University Press, 2003).

for advanced VR systems.[20] Emphasizing the need to recognize the specific, aesthetic properties of the digital platform – immersion, agency, and transformation – Murray offered contemporary examples, including videogames, as indicative of the future of literature designed for virtual environments.

Optimism about digital communication technologies dissipated after the turn of the century. The dotcom economic bubble had burst undeniably by 2001. Digital media scholarship subsequently (re)emphasized critiques of the techno-utopian rhetoric of cyberspace and promoted a return to bodies and embodiment, materiality and textuality, and media-specific analysis. Though games had become much more technically sophisticated – boasting polygonal 3D figures in open-world environments – the promise of fully immersive VR had not been fulfilled. Arguably, it won't ever be. Salen and Zimmerman explained at the time that awareness of the medium of implementation is a necessary condition for gameplay, coining the term "immersive fallacy" to describe the expectation that technology will advance to the point that "the frame falls away so that the player truly believes that he or she is part of an imaginary world."[21]

Though the hype around cyberspace died down, interest in the artistic possibilities of videogames picked up. Parker identifies an "intense period of debate about games and art involving journalists, critics, academics, and gaming enthusiasts" occurring between 2005 and 2010, "bookended" by Roger Ebert's infamous rejections of the medium's artistic aspirations.[22] Part of the reason for this new attention was that it coincided with the emergence of videogame studies as a field. This early period of videogame studies – the period of the "war" and just after – provided terminology and methodologies for analyzing videogames on their own terms, rather than through borrowed frameworks from film or literary studies.

Take, for example, Clint Hocking's critique of 2K Boston's *Bioshock*, which has become something like the "Hamlet and His Problems" of videogame studies.[23] *Bioshock* invites players to explore Rapture,

---

[20] Janet H. Murray, *Hamlet on the Holodeck: The Future of Narrative in Cyberspace* (Cambridge, MA: The MIT Press, 1998).
[21] Katie Salen and Eric Zimmerman, *Rules of Play: Game Design Fundamentals* (Cambridge, MA: The MIT Press, 2003), 31.
[22] Parker, "Games-as-Art Debate," 78.
[23] Clint Hocking, "Ludonarrative Dissonance in *Bioshock*," *Click Nothing*, October 7, 2007. www.clicknothing.com/click_nothing/2007/10/ludonarrative-d.html.

a collapsing underwater city founded on ideals of laissez faire capitalism and radical individualism roughly resembling the fiction-based philosophy of Ayn Rand. For Hocking, the project of *Bioshock* is to catch players in the "trap" of rational self-interest by first convincing them to "embrace" the social philosophy of Rapture as they fend off its mutated former citizens and later demonstrate "that the 'power' we derive from complete and unchecked freedom necessarily corrupts, and ultimately destroys us." One of the primary ways in which the game pursues this project is through the Little Sisters. In order to pass from one level to the next, the player must capture and dispense with a number of Little Sisters, choosing either to kill them to gain a large store of power-up materials or spare them and receive fewer materials immediately. Hocking finds that the "ludic contract" of the Little Sisters mechanic successfully expresses the game's themes: "Harvesting them in pursuit of my own self-interest seems not only the best choice mechanically, but also the right choice." At the same time, the story *Bioshock* tells about why the player is dispatching Little Sisters does not position players to practice rational self-interest. The "narrative contract," Hocking's argues, requires players to assist a character introduced as Atlas – thereby violating the central premise of playing at self-interest – in opposing the founder of Rapture, Andrew Ryan, with whom the player should be philosophically aligned. Hocking labels this misalignment of ludic and narrative contracts "ludonarrative dissonance." Whether one agrees with this critique or not, Hocking's article exemplifies analysis specific to the kind of storytelling videogames do, conducted in the interaction between story elements and gameplay elements, between representation and action.

So, what happened? Videogame studies was on the rise and games were more popular and sophisticated than ever. And, yet, this "intense period of debate" over the artistic aspiration of videogames concluded after just five years. What happened to shift the search for the *Citizen Kane* of videogames into cliché so quickly? Or, rather, what happened to the expectation that games that could "transcend [their] commercial origins through authorship?"

12.4 The Future of Videogames

Not coincidentally, Parker's period of intense discussion of games as art corresponds with the recovery period following the bursting of the dotcom bubble through the 2008 housing market crash. That is to say, it seems to have arisen as the videogame industry regained its footing heading into the seventh console generation and then entered a period of transition brought on by the Great Recession. In 2005 – the beginning of Parker's period – Microsoft announced the Xbox360, Sony announced the Playstation 3, and Nintendo revealed the Wii motion controller. When the Great Recession hit three years later, despite being computationally inferior to its high-definition competitors, the Wii far surpassed both rivals in total console sales. Around the same time, Apple released the iPhone and AppStore, initiating a wave of simple, inexpensive mobile games. By 2010, Zynga's *Farmville*, a free-to-play social game on Facebook featuring in-game purchases, had amassed 80 million players.[24] Jesper Juul dubbed this transitional period the "casual revolution."[25]

As the popular discourse surrounding the artistic potential of videogames reached its apex, videogames had never been more popular or more mainstream. The kinds of games dominating the industry and expanding its audience base, however, were casual games, not the kinds of games being raised in those discussions. Casual games simply have different design priorities.

Juul's 2009 analysis of the genre outlines several defining characteristics of casual games, none of which connect videogames to the long history of literary tradition.[26] Usability is prioritized, reducing the barrier to entry for users to pick up and play. Casual games can be difficult, but failure is not punished too severely and success is often met with effusive, "juicy" positive feedback. While fiction is a key element, its role is to invite users by presenting pleasant, appealing, recognizable scenarios. Casual games thus don't tend to aspire to something like artistic depth. In addition to being light and engaging, they must also be interruptible in order to conform to the busy, on-the-go lives of their players. While this allows players to squeeze in a short session of PopCap's *Bejeweled* between pomodoros or before getting off the subway, it prevents these kinds of games from prompting aesthetic reflection.[27]

There is certainly an art to designing games that meet Juul's criteria, but games in this style hardly inspire comparisons to *Citizen Kane*. Welles's masterpiece is brooding, introspective, and self-referential, a technical tour de force, blending and nodding to a variety of genres. It defined the aesthetic potential of an emerging medium even as it remained within the field of popular culture. Casual games, by contrast, broadened the gaming audience by eliminating barriers to entry and accommodating

[24] Zynga, *Farmville* (Zynga, 2009).
[25] Juul, *Casual Revolution*.
[26] Ibid., 30.
[27] PopCap Games, *Bejeweled* (PopCap Games, 2001).

a variety of playful engagements that could expand or contract to fit the busy lives of players. Juul observes that most people, especially those young adults who grew up playing videogames, simply don't have that much time to commit to videogames any more. The gaming industry's long-standing fixation on graphical improvement and hardcore mechanics, Juul argues, ignored the design challenges presented by the workaday schedules of their maturing player base, which he suggests might be considered the industry's "single most important problem."[28] The innovation of casual games, then, was not the advancement of an artistic tradition. Instead, it was their integration with the socioeconomic realities of their players, for whom the separation of work and leisure is increasingly nebulous.

The success of casual games and their free-to-play monetization strategies initiated a shift in videogame development, particularly at the major publishers. In 2011, Peter Moore, then the head of Electronic Arts (EA), declared explicitly that they were transitioning toward a service model: "We want to use this ability to make our games less discrete, standalone experiences and more like services. *Madden* shouldn't be a place you buy, it should be a place you go."[29] Despite layoffs and investment in social media games a year earlier, Moore's comments indicate that the future of videogames would not abandon big-budget, so-called AAA games such as the long-running *Madden* football series. Instead, these traditionally "hardcore" games, with detailed, high-definition graphics, responsive artificial intelligence, and complex control schemes, would be reconceptualized, designed as services rather than products, what is sometimes referred to as "AAA+." Rather than buy a game the way one buys a book, players pay for access as they would to enter an amusement park. And, much like an amusement park, once "inside," players may find they must pay more to access certain features and attractions.

The transition to a service model for videogame design has often involved a pivot away from precisely the kinds of "discrete, standalone experiences," like *Bioshock*, most frequently associated with gaming's artistic or literary potential. EA exemplified this trend away from single-player, narrative-driven design after acquiring the rights to make games for the *Star Wars* franchise following the closure of LucasArts in 2014. Visceral, maker of the successful, linear space horror series *Dead Space*, was tapped to develop one of the entries. The tentatively titled "Project Ragtag" was to be

---

[28] Juul, *Casual Revolution*, 12.
[29] Qtd. in Leigh Alexander, "EA Sports' Moore: 'There Will Be No Offline Games,'" *Game Developer*, June 14, 2018. www.gamedeveloper.com/business/ea-sports-moore-there-will-be-no-offline-games-.

about "space scoundrels" in the aftermath of George Lucas's *Star Wars: A New Hope*.[30] Three years later, EA shuttered Visceral, citing specifically the market viability of linear, narrative-oriented games:

> In its current form, it was shaping up to be a story-based, linear adventure game. Throughout the development process, we have been testing the game concept with players, listening to the feedback about what and how they want to play, and closely tracking fundamental shifts in the marketplace. It has become clear that to deliver an experience that players will want to come back to and enjoy for a long time to come, we needed to pivot the design.[31]

Many commentators interpreted this statement as the death knell of the single-player, narrative-focused videogame.[32] The problem with a "story-based, linear adventure game," the statement suggests, is that it can't be "enjoyed for a long time to come." If that statement weren't a clear enough message about EA's perspective on the future of gaming, they "pivoted" Project Ragtag into *Star Wars: Battlefront II*, a title now synonymous with predatory "lootboxes" and unrealistic progression systems.[33]

This shift in the industry is perhaps one reason why we don't hear much about the pursuit of the *Citizen Kane* of videogames anymore. The industry as whole, not just casual games, now designs to support service-model monetization strategies. To what degree, then, can they offer us playful aesthetic experiences? Do games organized as monetized services support literary play styles?

Of course, not all videogames today have gone down this route. The rise of online distribution platforms that spurred the casual revolution also spurred a surge in independent game development. Valve's Steam storefront, which is essentially like iTunes but for videogames, opened in 2003, granting independent studios an opportunity to reach a wider audience. Microsoft's Xbox Live Arcade also helped bolster the growing indie game scene by featuring games like Johnathan Blow's *Braid*, SuperGiant's

---

[30] For more on Project Ragtag, see Jason Schreier, "The Collapse of Visceral's Ambitious Star Wars Game," *Kotaku*, October 27, 2017. https://kotaku.com/the-collapse-of-viscerals-ambitious-star-wars-game-1819916152.

[31] Qtd. in Samit Sarkar, "EA's Star Wars 'Pivot' Is a Vote of No Confidence in Single-Player Games," *Polygon*, October 18, 2017. www.polygon.com/2017/10/18/16491188/ea-star-wars-visceral-games-single-player.

[32] Sarkar, "EA's Star Wars 'Pivot.'"

[33] EA DICE, *Star Wars Battlefront II* (Electronic Arts, 2017). A "lootbox" is an in-game item, which players either earn through play or purchase with money, that gifts a random in-game reward. For more on the lootbox controversy in *Star Wars: Battlefront II*, see Owen S. Good, "I Spent $90 in Battlefront 2, and I Still Don't Have Any Control over My Characters," *Polygon*, November 16, 2017. www.polygon.com/2017/11/16/16658476/star-wars-battlefront-2-loot-crate-costs-analysis.

Bastion, and Phil Fish's *Fez*, introducing games with literary relevance to more mainstream gaming contexts.[34]

The emerging indie market not only brought renewed attention to the artistic and literary capacity of games, it also contributed to the growing diversification of gaming culture. The term "videogame" has always applied to a broad range of only loosely related media objects, applying to everything from Microsoft's *Solitaire* to Infinity Ward's *Call of Duty 4: Modern Warfare* to Rovio's *Angry Birds* to Beat Game's *Beat Saber* to WOW Entertainment's *Typing of the Dead*.[35] As videogames have emerged from marginal subculture to quotidian pastime, their appeal and application has expanded into a variety of fields and practices, including education, politics, exercise, and advertising. In *How to Do Things with Videogames*, Bogost argues that videogaming will continue to find its way into more and more various practices of everyday life, eventually becoming such an ordinary, unremarkable activity that "soon gamers will be an anomaly."[36]

Indeed, recognizing all the forms videogames take today, it would be difficult to say that anything like a singular "gaming culture" exists. This is certainly a positive development, enabling players to find and play games suited to their interests and purposes. It can, however, have a secondary effect of reifying big budget, major studio games as, in some sense, the "real" games and, by extension, their players as the "real," even if anomalous, gamers.[37] This was a recurring theme of GamerGate, a harassment campaign targeting women in the videogame industry and feminist media critics that began in 2014. The campaign sought to defend a particular version of gaming culture against the diversification of the media form and its players. This often meant legislating what counts as truly a game, rejecting the notion that videogames are or can be anything more than "just games" or that they can have social or aesthetic meaning.[38]

---

[34] Number None, *Braid* (Number None, 2008); SuperGiant, *Bastion* (Warner Bros Interactive Entertainment, 2011); Polytron Corporation, *Fez* (Trapdoor, 2012).

[35] Microsoft, *Solitaire* (Microsoft, 1990); Infinity Ward, *Call of Duty 4: Modern Warfare* (Activision, 2007); Rovio Entertainment, *Angry Birds* (Rovio Entertainment, 2009); Beat Games, *Beat Saber* (Beat Games, 2019); WOW Entertainment, *Typing of the Dead* (Sega, 2001).

[36] Bogost, *How to Do Things with Videogames*, 154.

[37] For a study of gamer's perception of what constitutes a legitimate game, see Mia Consalvo and Christopher A. Paul. *Real Games: What's Legitimate and What's Not in Contemporary Videogames* (Cambridge, MA: The MIT Press, 2019).

[38] GamerGate inspired an outpouring of scholarship informed by queer theory. For a useful overview, see Bonnie Ruberg, ed. *Queer Game Studies* (Minneapolis: University of Minnesota Press, 2017). For more on GamerGate itself, see Caitlin Dewey, "The Only Guide to Gamergate You Will Ever Need to Read," *Washington Post*, October 14, 2014, www.washingtonpost.com/news/the-intersect/wp/2014/10/14/the-only-guide-to-gamergate-you-will-ever-need-to-read/.

Players and critics interested in videogames as a literary art form thus find themselves in a difficult position. The success and mainstreaming of videogames following the casual revolution has meant a greater diversity of games and gamers. Major release, "AAA" titles, though, boast the larger share of the market and player base. Increasingly, these widely recognized games eschew aesthetic and literary investment in favor of designing for recurrent user spending. At the same time, independent and art games have more exposure than ever thanks to a plurality of digital distribution platforms and marketplaces. This has resulted in a burgeoning of compelling games with literary relevance, such as Lucas Pope's *Papers, Please*, Fullbright Company's *Gone Home*, and Toby Fox's *Undertale*, which now appear alongside major release games in places like the Steam storefront.[39] Additionally, new hypertext platforms like Twine have spurred a renaissance of interactive hypertext fiction, led by authors like Emily Short and Anna Anthropy. Yet, these games – if they are received as games at all – are often marginalized under the heading of "art games" due to their more literary features.

Where, then, does one look to assess videogaming as a literary form? To major release titles, which seem to have given up their aspirations to "transcend their commercial origins through authorship?" Or to independent "art games," which may bear greater resemblance to the established literary forms and feature recognizable "linguistic foregrounding," but risk affirming a division between high and low gaming culture?[40] How does literary studies rethink videogames after GamerGate? Does the widening variety of videogames and their applicability to the processes of daily life make space for literary gaming and critical play or absorb it into the digital everyday?

12.5 What's Gonna Stop It?

At the 2010 Design Innovate Communicate Entertain (DICE) summit, Jesse Schell declared to a room of game developers "Facebook knocked us on our collective ass."[41] The gaming industry, he claimed, had not anticipated the success of casual Facebook games such as Zynga's *Farmville* – had

---

[39] 3909 LLC, *Papers, Please* (3909 LLC, 2013); The Fullbright Company, *Gone Home* (The Fullbright Company, 2013); Toby Fox, *Undertale* (8-4, 2015).
[40] Astrid Ensslin, *Literary Gaming* (Cambridge, MA: The MIT Press, 2014), 2.
[41] Jesse Schell, "When Games Invade Real Life," address delivered to Design Innovate Communicate Entertain annual summit, Las Vegas, NV, 2010. www.ted.com/talks/jesse_schell_when_games_invade_real_life.

not anticipated the casual revolution. Speaking the year after Juul's book, Schell went on to describe the future of gaming "beyond Facebook." With (hopefully) sarcastic techno-optimism, he extrapolated a vision of "everyware"[42] – enabled, gamified commercialism:

> You get to work on time. Good Job. You got to work on time. You get a special bonus, I don't know for something else, maybe because you've been on time all week. And then, there is your officemate, and he's like check it out I got the new digital tattoo, right? It's a tattoo where you can change the image because its got like e-ink in it in your arm. So you can change the image all the time to whatever you want, but a lot of people are using Tatoogle Adsense, right? And so he's got the ads up and you're thinking you're really dumb because Tatoogle Adsense has light sensors in it and so that when your arm is covered you're not going to get any money from people seeing the ads. You show him how yours is lower on the arm so it's more exposed so you get more points for it. Just then, you realize the two of you have your ads synchronized just by chance so you say "Link Sync!" and you get 30 points for noticing the link sync two of us had there. He says "Pop-Tarts!" because they are both Pop-Tart ads and the system is listening so it can tell that we said "Pop-Tarts" and then we do a high five because the body electricity sensors can tell when you do a high five and that's the rule. That's how the game works. That when the ads line up, cause it makes you pay more attention to the ads cause that's how these games will work. Games will be tricking you to pay more attention to ads.

While Tatoogle AdSense or a REM-tertainment system that implants ads in one's dreams seem far-fetched, versions of Schell's forecast have already been put into practice, such as insurance companies using electronic monitors to determine health benefits or to surveil driving habits with the promise of better rates. Schell imagines a number of scenarios in which we would earn these generic points for brushing our teeth for a dentist-recommended three minutes, buying a Dr. Pepper every day of the week for lunch, or completing a particularly successful session of piano practice. For Schell, the unexpected success of casual games in the Great Recession era signals gaming's future role, not only in the monetization of play, but the total monetization of everyday life. As Schell shrugs in conclusion, "what's gonna stop it?"

Curiously, his talk about the future of videogames ends with the reading of a novel. Schell imagines Microsoft acquiring Amazon and selling Kindles that use eye-tracking software to log what books a reader reads and how

---

[42] Adam Greenfield, *Everyware: The Dawning Age of Ubiquitous Computing* (Berkeley CA: New Riders Publishing, 2006).

much of them, awarding "super bonus points" if the reader goes on to leave an Amazon review and "it knows you read the whole book through." After twenty years of having their reading habits monitored, Schell's Kindle user unlocks an XBox Live Achievement after completing their 500th novel. They immediately feel shame at this accomplishment, though, because their 500th book "was this dumb *Star Trek* novel." For Schell, the achievement triggers a moment of reflection about the life of their data:

> And then you start thinking about all these achievements and points and things and realizing, you know, you had no idea what books your grandparents read or where they went on a daily basis. These sensors that we are going to have on us and all around us and everywhere are going to be tracking and watching what we are doing forever. Our grandchildren will know every book that we read, that legacy will be there, will be remembered. And you get to thinking about how, wow, is it possible maybe that since all this stuff is being watched and measured and judged, that maybe, I should change my behavior a little bit and be a little better than I would have been? And so, it could be that these systems are just all crass commercialization and it's terrible, but it's possible that they'll inspire us to be better people – *if* the game systems are designed right.

For Schell, the silver lining of the coming age of digitally enabled hypercommercialism is the potential for game designs to prompt users to improve their behavior and be "a little better." Ironically, the game design in this final scenario has very little to do with that. Its goal instead seems simply to be to record and reward reading, regardless of the content. It doesn't seem to distinguish between high and low culture or monitor the quality of the reader's engagement with their reading or their potential behavior changes toward being "a little better." Instead, it is the reader who feels self-conscious about their reading habits being surveilled, who has internalized the need to be "better" by engaging with more "high" culture. Schell's user apparently feels more embarrassed that their unborn grandchildren might discover they enjoy *Star Trek* novels than that they high five coworkers in celebration of being made aware of the existence of Pop-Tarts.

12.6 Literary Gaming

This is a significant change in the vision of the future of videogames. Nearly two decades earlier, Murray forecasted digital interactive fiction on a par with the greatest works of literary history, something like the *Hamlet* of videogames designed as an immersive experience on a perfected VR system like the Holodeck from *Star Trek: The Next Generation*.[43] In Schell's account, *Star Trek* is merely the kind of guilty pleasure a well-designed game might condition players to give up, maybe teaching them to prefer *Hamlet* instead. Literature is reified as the "high" art, the socially desirable cultural experience, while the aesthetic future of videogames is nowhere to be seen. Videogames in this vision only incentivize "better" behaviors, like reading literature. But, of course, literature has its own history of policing behaviors. Roger Eaglestone explains how the discipline of English emerged as a strategy for acculturating foreign "savages" in the British colonies.[44] This practice eventually came home to England. In an effort to stem the revolutionary spirit spreading though Europe after the French Revolution, "uncultured" British citizens were taught the proper, English way to behave by reading lowly, English novels.

Here, at the intersection of literary history and gaming future, is where literary studies has an opportunity to make a critical intervention in gaming culture today. Certainly, the degree to which videogames tell stories or resemble traditional literary practice continues to generate debate. But as we have those discussions, it is increasingly important to recognize how videogames occupy a cultural role once held by literature. Much like literature, videogames have been perceived as an unproductive, idle, and possibly dangerous activity, potentially redeemed through a capacity to teach more desirable behaviors. Literature came out of this position through the early twentieth-century as it came to be seen as a high art. The work of literary criticism and theory over the past half-century – the period during which videogames were invented and rose to cultural relevance – has been aimed at critiquing, decentering, queering, politicizing, and generally reading against the discipline's colonizing, normalizing trajectories. Literary studies thus seems particularly well positioned to respond to videogaming's evolving role in contemporary digital culture. In other words, to mitigate what Schell sees as gaming's inevitable crass commercialist future of behavioral conditioning, we will have to learn, just as we have with literature, how to read – or play – our games differently.

Not coincidentally, through the "murky" ludology "war" videogame studies situated the conflict between agency and authority in the interaction between gameplay and story. Linear, scripted narrative represented the imposition of authority on virtual spaces, restricting the player's

---

[43] The Holodeck first appears in *Star Trek: The Next Generation*, season 1, episode 1, "Encounter at Farpoint," directed by Corey Allen, written by Gene Roddenberry and D. C. Fontana. First aired September 28, 1987, on CBS.
[44] Robert Eaglestone, *Doing English* (New York: Routledge, 2017).

pursuit of free play, exploration, and self-definition. The cut-scene was singled out as particularly problematic because it takes control away from the player to deliver a bit of authored, cinematic exposition. In this context, Valve's *Half-Life* seemed revolutionary because its narrative unfolds in-engine, nonlinearly, and without cut-scenes.[45] Players retain interactive control of the protagonist Gordon Freeman, encountering the story piecemeal as they explore the Black Mesa facility.

As videogames empowered players with more and varied interactions within their virtual worlds, they invoked some of the same conversations about the political potential of decentered narrative and readerly coauthorship as hypertext fiction. DMA Design's *Grand Theft Auto III* attracted a great deal of critical attention for its innovative "sandbox" structure.[46] Setting aside the game's problematic and violent content, critics pointed to how *Grand Theft Auto III* allows players to move and play within a relatively open virtual environment without narrative obligations. When, whether, and in what order the player encounters story missions is up to them; otherwise, they are free to play with the game's driving and third-person action mechanics as they wish. Frasca connected this freedom directly to the liberatory potential of digital media, claiming *Grand Theft Auto III* delivers on "the ultimate promise of so-called new media: virtual reality, the internet and videogames aim to empower their users with freedom (or at least the illusion of freedom)."[47] This "freedom" is specifically described as a freedom from *story*. Kevin Parker, for instance, argues that, because *Grand Theft Auto III*'s decentered narrative structure does not restrict players to a linear pathing, the game is a "grand anti-authoritarian laboratory."[48]

As this kind of optimism about the potential of digital technologies began to wane, it soon became clear that freedom and control in videogames is a much more complicated issue, not merely a matter of narrative structure or integration. Alexander Galloway observes that videogames, like the Internet, rely on the "protocols of digital technology."[49] One of the most important of these protocols is flexibility, which enables digital technologies to "accommodate massive contingency" – designed to be

---

[45] Valve, *Half-Life* (Sierra Studios, 1998).
[46] DMA Design (Rockstar North), *Grand Theft Auto III* (Rockstar Games, 2001).
[47] Gonzalo Frasca, "Sim Sin City: Some Thoughts about *Grand Theft Auto 3*," *Game Studies* 3.2 (2003). www.gamestudies.org/0302/frasca/.
[48] Kevin Parker, "Free Play," *Reason*, April 2004. http://reason.com/archives/2004/04/01/free-play.
[49] Alexander R. Galloway, *Gaming: Essays on Algorithmic Culture* (Minneapolis: University of Minnesota Press, 2006), 99.

"be liberal in what [they] accept from others" – while maintaining system stability.[50] He argues that though flexibility would seem to be "liberating and utopian" it "is one of the founding principles of global informatic control. It is to the control society what discipline was to the previous one."[51] According to Galloway, the protocological flexibility of digital media facilitates a Deluezean "control society," in which the discrete enclosures of disciplinary power are replaced by open-ended structures, continuous, perpetual training, tracking, customization, and modulation.[52]

The sandbox structure of *GTA* games exemplifies this kind of protocological flexibility, which "subsume[s] all comers under the larger mantel of continuity and universalism."[53] It is designed to "accommodate [the] massive contingency" of a player's free play within in a vast open world. Players can punch, stab, shoot, grenade, run-over, and drop a helicopter on a pedestrian. They cannot, however, give one a handshake because handshakes are not one of the available interactions programmed into the game. Players are invited to do whatever they wish in the open-world of *GTA*, so long as what they wish to do is afforded by the game's input system. The player's activities are also documented by an extensive, but specific list of in-game statistics and achievements.[54] Again, only the activities for which there is a programmed statistical category are recognized. In this way, the game transcodes the individual player's experience of free play in an open world into the universally equivalence of a numerical record.

The current iteration of the *GTA* franchise, *Grand Theft Auto V*, goes a step further by configuring the sandbox as a live service.[55] The online mode offers ostensibly the same sandbox structure with even fewer inducements to engage with story; however, the currency earned and lost through in-game activities is also purchasable with "real" money. Free play now has a calculable cost. The game's massive open world is thus overlaid with, and stratified by, zones of relative productive efficiency. Furthermore, the

---

[50] Ibid., 100–101. Galloway references the robustness principle from RFC 761 – "be conservative in what you do, be liberal in what you accept from others" – which was central to the development of the modern internet. John Postel, DOD Transmission Control Protocol, January 1980. https://tools.ietf.org/html/rfc761.

[51] Galloway, *Gaming*, 100.

[52] See Gilles Deleuze, "Postscript on Societies of Control," *October*, 59 (Winter, 1992), 3–7.

[53] Galloway, *Gaming*, 101.

[54] For reference, a full list of statistics tracked in Rockstar North's *Grand Theft Auto IV* (Rockstar Games, 2008) can be found at *GTA Wiki: GTA Wiki*. "*GTA IV* Statistics." https://gta.fandom.com/wiki/GTA_IV_Statistics.

[55] Rockstar North, *Grand Theft Auto V* (Rockstar Games, 2013).

player's free play through San Andreas is tracked; the statistics recording in-game activities are sent to Rockstar, who uses this player data to design upgrade patches, balance game modes, price in-game items, identify cheaters, and otherwise generate more revenue.

A number of scholars have analyzed the relationship between videogames and the political economy. Nicholas Dyer-Witherford explored the material conditions of the videogaming industry and culture.[56] Möring and Leino argue that, with the advent of casual gaming, videogames transitioned from industrial – as noted by Julian Stallabrass – to explicitly neoliberal.[57] Wark, writing the year prior to the onset of the Great Recession, demonstrated videogaming's resonances with neoliberal "gamespace," in which social life is organized by "the same digital logic of one versus the other, ending in victory or defeat."[58] Chris Paul has drawn a connection between these same incentive structures and the toxicity in gaming culture that erupted in GamerGate.[59]

These scholars, and others, note the more insidious trajectory in videogame development: not the emergence of a new literary, artistic form, but the engine of commercialism that has become only more explicit in the wake of the casual revolution. Recognizing their troubling participation in and perpetuation of these repressive social systems of digitized global capitalism, it would be easy to write off videogames as too far compromised. But it is here that literary studies have a role to play in rethinking videogames for the unfolding digital era.

As videogames become an increasingly ordinary practice woven into the fabric of our everyday media environment, it will be the narrative, literary, and critical aesthetic elements that reframe, reshape, re-present, and recode digital culture. As Rune Klevjer argues in defense of those supposedly repressive cut-scenes, narrative is not "cut off gameplay" but is rather an

---

[56] See, for example, Nick Dyer-Witheford, "Cognitive Capital Contested: The Class Composition of the Video and Computer Game Industry," *Libcom.Org*, 2005. http://libcom.org/library/cognitive-capital-contested-nick-dyer-witheford; and Nick Dyer-Witheford and Greig de Peuter, *Games of Empire: Global Capitalism and Video Games* (Minneapolis: University of Minnesota Press, 2009).

[57] Sebastian Möring and Olie Leino, "Beyond Games as Political Education – Neo-Liberalism in the Contemporary Computer Game Form," *Journal of Gaming & Virtual Worlds* 8.2 (June 2016), 145–161; Julian Stallabrass, "Just Gaming: Allegory and Economy in Computer Games," *New Left Review*, 198 (April 1993), https://newleftreview.org/issues/I198/articles/julian-stallabrass-just-gaming-allegory-and-economy-in-computer-games.

[58] Wark, *Gamer Theory*, 6.

[59] Christopher A. Paul, *The Toxic Meritocracy of Video Games: Why Gaming Culture Is the Worst* (Minneapolis: University of Minnesota Press, 2018).

"integral part of the configurative experience."[60] Galloway himself explains that despite their protocological nature, videogames can, through narrative, "correspond" to the lived experience of their players, producing a realism that isn't about high-definition graphics but "fidelity of context."[61] Building on Galloway's work, I argue in my book *Mixed Realism* that this "context" for most gamers is contemporary digital culture, of which videogames are themselves a significant part.[62] Game narratives "skin" our playful engagements with the digital everyday as a battle with space invaders, a mythical quest for a sacred object, or an adventure to rescue royalty in another castle, fictional contexts that resonate with real-world ones. It takes a certain orientation toward gaming to recognize and respond to circuits of interaction running back and forth between the virtual reality and social reality. Developing this kind of playstyle, or "metagame,"[63] not just toward "art games" but to all forms of digital interactive media, is the challenge now facing literary approaches to videogames. For it is the literary in games that resists the implied imperative of efficient productivity, that invites aesthetic contemplation, and that prompts players to seek out correspondences and make meaning – to play playfully.

12.7 Getting Messy

Near the end of Parker's "intense period of debate" over the artistic value of videogames, Bogost observed that the so-called "war" in videogame studies wasn't really about story at all. Instead, it was about *ontology*: about what sort of thing is a game.[64] Videogames are a "mess," he concludes, a fundamentally interdisciplinary, irreducible amalgam of elements including the player's reception and operation of the game, the game's designed interface, the form and function of the game itself, the code that enacts the game, the platform that runs the code, and the particular sociohistorical and cultural context in which it transpires. This irreducibility makes videogames fascinatingly complex cultural objects and explains why

---

[60] Rune Klevjer, "In Defense of Cutscenes," in *Computer Game and Digital Cultures Conference Proceedings*, ed. Frans Mäyrä (Tampere: Tampere University Press, 2002), 191–202; www.digra.org/wp-content/uploads/digital-library/05164.50328.pdf.
[61] Galloway, *Gaming*, 78.
[62] Timothy J. Welsh, *Mixed Realism: Videogames and the Violence of Fiction* (Minneapolis: University of Minnesota Press, 2016).
[63] Stephanie Boluk and Patrick LeMieux, *Metagaming: Playing, Competing, Spectating, Cheating, Trading, Making, and Breaking Videogames* (Minneapolis: University of Minnesota Press, 2017).
[64] Bogost, "Videogames Are a Mess."

addressing videogames as literature can be so complicated. Print fiction is a very different sort of "mess" from videogames, so its lessons on how to "read" games are limited. Gamic literariness would necessarily draw from, cut across, and interact with videogaming's multiple, entangled layers. It is with the recognition of this fundamental interdisciplinarity of videogames and, by extension, videogame scholarship that Aarseth concludes his recent advice for new scholars. "Interdisciplinarity is hard," he writes, "and depends on the people, not the disciplines."[65] If we've learned anything in the brief history of videogame studies, it is that to do it well we have to be ready to get a little messy.

In the end, it may be fine that videogaming never will find its *Citizen Kane*. That marker suggests that it is the game object itself that matters – that it is "through authorship," formal composition, that a game could "transcend its commercial origins." At this point in the development of the medium, that possibility seems more and more difficult to imagine. Regardless, artists and authors throughout the twentieth century (particularly those working during the period in which videogames emerged) have demonstrated that art isn't totally about the object. It's in what we *do* with it: how we respond to it, how we interact with it. So, it may be the case that literary gaming doesn't describe a kind of game at all. Perhaps it is a kind of play.

[65] Aarseth, "How to Play."

CHAPTER 13

The Printed Book in the Digital Age

Inge van de Ven

In 2014, Scottish artist Katie Patterson started the Future Library Project. This consists of 100 books, placed in a time capsule that will remain unopened until 2114. Once a year, a writer is invited to contribute a new text that none of their contemporaries are allowed to read. The organizers planted 1,000 trees in a town outside of Oslo, in order to supply the paper for the books over a century. A printing press has been installed to ensure that these texts can still be printed in paper form, in case the technology is phased out in the meantime. Margaret Atwood, one of the first writers selected, has commented on the Future Library Project:

> It's very optimistic to believe, . . . that there will be people in 100 years, that those people will still be reading, . . . and that we'll be able to communicate across time, which is what any book is in any case – it's always a communication across space and time. This one is just a little bit longer.[1]

Atwood voices an ambivalent take on the longevity of the book, literature, and its readers. The logic underlying the time capsule of the Future Library Project is a logic of monumentality. It suggests that certain literary works are memorable enough to be consigned to posterity, yet expresses a sense of insecurity with regard to the novel's afterlife. The book-bound novel becomes a locus for speculation about the future of literature: a bulwark against *its own death*, a monument to the genre itself. In this chapter, I will argue that this urge to monumentalize the book and the novel inspires a range of strategies to make literature anew in the face of digitization.

As we know, both the form and the function of the book as the central carrier of cultural information have changed dramatically with the advent of digital technology. Analog literary texts are now just one node in a network of converging media that compete for our time and attention.

---

[1] Atwood, cited in Matt Novak, "Time Capsule of Unpublished Books Won't be Opened Until the Year 2114," *Paleofuture* (October 9, 2014).

How are reading and writing affected by these medial changes? Such questions force scholars of literature to attend to its material aspect, which for a long time has been insufficiently addressed. In the light of the alternative materialities of the digital, the book has been defamiliarized and, as a result, its affordances as a tangible carrier of information can be explored. How has the shift to the digital become an impetus for scholars in comparative literature to reexamine the printed book as an object and medium – or better, a multimedia object? How is digitalization affecting our engagement with, as well as our experiences and valuation of, the printed book and the book-bound novel? And how have book artists and authors exploited the codex, print materiality, and paper in innovative ways as a response to these shifts?

Starting from contested notions of the "end of the book" and the "death of the novel," and then examining several "renaissances," this chapter explores the resilience of paper-based literature and its academic scrutiny in the era of its foretold death. First, I examine how the academic discipline of comparative literary studies has responded to the shift from analog to digital materialities by developing new frameworks and critical tools to analyze this shift and the literary and artistic products that are created in response to it. Then, I zoom in on recent innovations in, and reinventions of, analog literary practices in book art and book design as well as literary fiction. I end with a reflection on a specific form of bookishness that emphasizes the novel's size and scale, and thus reinvents it as monumental. On all these levels, we will see, the digital has brought the book, and the novel as the literary art form bound by the book, into sharper focus.

13.1 End of the Book, Death of the Novel?

In the last ten years, the death of the novel has been announced time and again, by authors such as David Shields and Will Self.[2] Self blames digital media, the "perpetual now" that the Internet offers, and constant connectivity, for the demise of the "serious novel":

> There is one question alone that you must ask yourself in order to establish whether the serious novel will still retain cultural primacy and centrality in another 20 years. This is the question: if you accept that by then the vast majority of text will be read in digital form on devices linked to the web, do you also believe that those readers will voluntarily choose to disable that

---

[2] David Shields, *Reality Hunger: A Manifesto* (London: Penguin, 2010); Will Self, "The Novel Is Dead (This Time It's For Real)," *Guardian* (May 2, 2014).

connectivity? If your answer to this is no, then the death of the novel is sealed out of your own mouth.[3]

Philip Roth has likewise predicted that the "screen" technologies of computer and television condition our brains to the point where the old "single-focus requirement," the devout mode of concentration needed for slowly reading a book, will become an "elegiac exercise."[4] The novel, he predicts, will soon become an elite form for a small cult of readers.

These apocalyptic predictions are by no means new. During the past two centuries, almost every notable technological and social shift has led to anxieties about the future of the novel. In *Rethinking the Novel/Film Debate*, Kamilla Elliot outlines the rivalry between literature and film throughout the latter's history.[5] Kathleen Fitzpatrick, in *The Anxiety of Obsolescence*, examines the tenuous position of literary fiction in relation to US television culture.[6] With the installation of the printing press, the volume and intensity of new sensory and cognitive input was at first experienced as shocking, overwhelming, and distracting.[7] Already in 1758, Samuel Richardson suspected that the novel had run its course. Alexis de Tocqueville, in the 1830s, worried that the rise of American democracy would cause authors to write ever shorter text, eradicating "big novels."[8] In 1902, Jules Verne predicted newspapers would replace novels within years. In the relatively short history of the print novel, its impending end has been apprehended with the rise of the telegraph, telephone, radio, photography, television, and film. Of course, following all these landmarks, the production, publication, and consumption of novels continued unabated. The alleged "threat" that these then-emerging technologies exerted, even when it never truly jeopardized the novel, did make its impression on the status of literary texts, as well as their form and content. Time and again, the novel survives its own "death" by adapting to these changes.

---

[3] Ibid.
[4] Roth, cited in Dan Colman, "Philip Roth Predicts the Death of the Novel; Paul Auster Counters." *Open Culture* (October 18, 2011): www.openculture.com/2011/10/philip_roth_predicts_death_of_the_novel.html.
[5] Kamilla Elliott, *Rethinking the Novel/Film Debate* (Cambridge: Cambridge University Press, 2003).
[6] Kathleen Fitzpatrick, *The Anxiety of Obsolescence: The American Novel in the Age of Television* (Nashville: Vanderbilt University Press, 2006).
[7] Daniel Rosenberg, "Early Modern Information Overload," *Journal of the History of Ideas* 64.1 (2003): 1–9.
[8] Alexis de Tocqueville, *Democracy in America*, trans. Arthur Goldhammer (1835, 1840; New York: Penguin, 2004), 542.

Besides the novel as a genre of writing, the obsolescence of the book as its medium and material carrier has been predicted as well. Since the late 1980s, scholars and authors have claimed that the future of Western literature would be in electronic media and that hypertext would replace paper and books as bearers of literary texts and locus of literary innovation. Thus, hypertext author Robert Coover announced the death of the book in the early 1990s, and, in his defense of hyperfiction as the literary genre of the future, stated that "the print medium is a doomed and outdated technology, a mere curiosity of bygone days destined soon to be consigned forever to those dusty unattended museums we now call libraries."[9]

Both the celebratory and the pessimistic accounts of the book's obsolescence are informed by a logic of media superseding each other. As Marshall McLuhan and his son Eric write in *Laws of Media: The New Science*, it is a consistent factor in the reception of media (and other technological "extensions") that, with the emergence of a new medium, an old medium is expected to become obsolete. The telephone, as an extension of the human voice, lessens the need for the art of penmanship.[10] The "death of the novel" and end of the book have been (and continue to be) a prevalent instance of this logic of obsolescence.

Such claims regarding the end of the book have been part of a growing tendency in media studies to consider the digital as the point of integration of all media. In line with this tendency, Henry Jenkins has identified media convergence as the key dynamic of the present.[11] Users are participating in different media that meet and merge with and remediate each other so that a new integral media platform has come into effect. However, the expectation that books would be fully absorbed by the digital, rightfully criticized by Jenkins, is informed by a binary either/or logic which places digital screens in opposition to the book and paper page. This presumed animosity or competition between page and screen has been reinforced with the introduction of e-readers. Such pronouncements give the false impression that either electronic or paper books can survive, rather than serving diverging functions alongside each other.

---

[9] Robert Coover, "The End of Books," *New York Times* (June 21, 1992): 23, 27. https://archive.nytimes.com/www.nytimes.com/books/98/09/27/specials/coover-end.html.

[10] Marshall McLuhan and Eric McLuhan, *Laws of Media: The New Science* (Toronto: University of Toronto Press, 1988; 1992).

[11] Henry Jenkins, *Convergence Culture: Where Old and New Media Collide* (New York: New York University Press, 2006).

Yet, in the years following the hype about e-books and e-readers around 2010 – a period in which the end of the book was again widely prophesied – sales of printed books have increased while those of e-books have stagnated.[12] In this case, rather than rendering their predecessors obsolete, newer media technologies have produced the older media anew, to the extent that the latter has been reframed in the light of the new. In recent decades, literature has undergone transformations on paper and in book form at least as much as in electronic environments. This chapter offers an overview of scholarship that investigates such reinventions from the perspective of a more complex dynamic of media-interaction typified by *divergence* rather than convergence alone. Rather than digital convergence, it hinges on a dynamic of contrastive, material differences between analog and digital media in the present.[13]

13.2 Renaissance of the Book in Scholarship: The Turn to Materiality

I now turn to a threefold "renaissance" of the medium of print, a term which I borrow from Dutch book designer Irma Boom, who asserted:

> A book does something the Internet cannot do. It is about choices, about assembling text and image and making it unchangeable. I call it "frozen information." Designing a book is about rendering complex structures legible. The order is fixed. Unlike the internet, where everything is jumbled and you lack focus ... I predict the renaissance of the book![14]

The first renaissance can be discerned in scholarly work on book materiality; the second in book art and design; and the third in "bookish" novels.

As material carriers and technologies, books and paper had until the 1990s been so habitualized, so overly familiar, that they constituted a blind spot for most scholars of literature. As famously phrased by Viktor Shklovksy, "[h]abitualization devours work, clothes, furniture, one's

---

[12] David Sax, *The Revenge of Analog: Real Things and Why They Matter* (New York: Public Affairs, 2016); Christoph Bläsi, "The Book Between Media Convergence, Media Specificity, and Diverse Reading Communities in Present-Day US Culture," in *The Printed Book in Contemporary American Culture: Medium, Object, Metaphor*, ed. Heike Schaefer and Alexander Starre (Cham: Palgrave, 2019): 117–138.

[13] Kiene Brillenburg Wurth, Sara Rosa Espi, and Inge Van de Ven, "Visual Text and Media Divergence: Analogue Literary Writing in a Digital Age," *European Journal of English Studies* 17.1 (2013): 92–108.

[14] In Sander Pleij, "Irma Boom: de vrouw die het boek redt," *Vrij Nederland* (October 28, 2014), www.vn.nl/Artikel-Literatuur/Irma-Boom-de-vrouw-die-het-boek-redt.htm (my translation).

wife, and the fear of war."[15] And so it was with books, for a long time. In its heyday as the dominant mode for the circulation of information, the book was barely seen as a technology of communication. With the notable exception of specialists in the field of artists' books – Johanna Drucker, Charles Alexander, Ulises Carrión – scholars in comparative literature rarely considered book materiality. Academic disciplines such as book history and the sociology of literature did inquire into book production, transmission, and circulation as material practices, as well as the dissemination of texts. Yet, traditionally, these remained at a disciplinary remove from literary studies.

In her introduction to a special issue of *Comparative Literature* on the "material turn," Brillenburg Wurth argues that textual interpretation in Western culture has for the larger part of its history entailed a range of strategies aimed at looking *beyond* the material aspects of the text, for intangible, invisible, and nonliteral meanings.[16] In hermeneutics, the texture of stories has been conceived foremost as a stepping stone, an entry point into the often hidden, derived text hovering beyond the materiality of their words and letters. This immaterial, figural meaning is what the interpreter was after. Matter, if considered at all, was thought of as a vehicle for something else waiting to be disclosed.

Leah Price has chalked up this split between the material and the ideal to a Cartesian heritage of Western culture, which has taught us to filter out the sensuous aspects of the printed page.[17] This disembodied concept of the literary work further stemmed from eighteenth-century debates over copyright. As Mark Rose writes in *Authors and Owners: The Invention of Copyright*, literary property was not thought to reside in ideas but in the ways they were expressed.[18] Style could be held as literary property, hence copyrighted. In "Print Is Flat, Code Is Deep," N. Katherine Hayles explains how this led to the prevalence a concept of print literature as immaterial verbal construction.[19]

---

[15] Viktor Shklovsky, "Art as a Technique," trans. Lee Lemon and Marion Reis, *Russian Formalist Criticism – Four Essays*, ed. Lee Lemon and Marion Reis (1917; Nebraska: University of Nebraska Press, 1965), 12.
[16] Kiene Brillenburg Wurth, "The Material Turn in Comparative Literature: An Introduction," *Comparative Literature* 70.3 (2018): 247–263.
[17] Leah Price, "Introduction: Reading Matter," *PMLA* 121.1 (2006): 9–16.
[18] Mark Rose, *Authors and Owners: The Invention of Copyright* (Cambridge, MA: Harvard University Press, 1993).
[19] N. Katherine Hayles, "Print Is Flat, Code Is Deep: The Importance of Media-Specific Analysis," *Poetics Today* 1 (2004): 67–88.

Since the late twentieth century, with the advent of electronic text, online platforms, and print on demand, scholars began to see – and smell, and feel, and hear – the print book anew. In light of the multiplication of textual media, they were faced with the challenge to rethink the physical, material codex as a cultural agent, and to critically interrogate its affordances. Drucker has repeatedly emphasized the importance of the interconnection of textual materiality and cultural significance in this light: "Durability, scale, reflectiveness, richness and density of saturation and color, tactile and visual pleasure – all of these factor in – not as transcendent and historically independent universals, but as aspects whose historical and cultural specificity cannot be divorced from their substantial properties."[20] This ushered in an extension of hermeneutics to include not only the text, the inside, but also the outward materiality of its carrier, as Heike Schaefer and Alexander Starre argue in their introduction to *The Printed Book in Contemporary American Culture*.[21]

Recent decades have witnessed a renewed attention to books and paper as bodies of literature in a digital age. A body of academic work attempts to grapple with the physical properties and the changing communicative and cultural functions of the printed book. Jerome Rothenberg and Steven Clay, in *A Book of the Book*, assembled a wide array of creative and critical texts on the artistic potential of the book.[22] Peter Stoicheff and Andrew Taylor's *The Future of the Page* focuses on the materiality of the paper page and the electronic "pages" that literature has come to interact with in the twentieth and twenty-first centuries.[23] Simon Garfield's *Just My Type: A Book of Fonts* explores the history and contemporary significance of typography.[24] Nicholas Basbanes's *On Paper: The Everything of Its Two-Thousand-Year History* examines paper as the most important material constituent of bookmaking.[25] And Keith Houston's

---

[20] Johanna Drucker, *The Visible Word: Experimental Typography and Modern Art, 1909-1923* (Chicago: University of Chicago Press, 1994), 45.
[21] Heike Schaefer and Alexander Starre, "Introduction," in *The Printed Book in Contemporary American Culture: Medium, Object, Metaphor*, ed. Heike Schaefer and Alexander Starre (Cham: Palgrave MacMillan, 2019), 3–28.
[22] Jerome Rothenberg and Stephen Clay, *A Book of the Book: Some Works and Projections about the Book & Writing* (New York: Granary Books, 1999).
[23] Peter Stoicheff and Andrew Taylor, eds., *The Future of the Page* (Toronto: University of Toronto Press, 2004).
[24] Simon Garfield, *Just My Type: A Book of Fonts* (London: Profile Books, 2011).
[25] Nicholas Basbanes, *On Paper: The Everything of Its Two-Thousand-Year History* (New York: Vintage, 2013).

The Book: A Cover-to-Cover Exploration of the Most Powerful Object of Our Time covers the breadth and scope of bibliographic communication.[26]

The new interest in book matter should be understood as part of the material turn in the humanities and social sciences at large. In literary studies, this turn came about in close conjunction with the new materialism that grew out of feminist theory, philosophy, sociology, archaeology, and science and technology studies. As Liedeke Plate notes, this is informed by a dissatisfaction with the linguistic turn and social constructionism's focus on language and representation.[27] Bruno Latour critiqued this focus, in *We Have Never Been Modern* (*Nous n'avons jamais été modernes*), for its complicity with a conception of materiality as inert, passive, and separate from the human subject.[28] New materialists intend to re-establish materialist ontologies.[29]

This new awareness in turn led critics such as Drucker, Alan Liu, and Jay David Bolter to develop new vocabularies, analytical tools, and critical approaches for the analysis of literary works. Already in 1991, Jerome J. McGann urged textual scholars to attend to typefaces, bindings, book prices, page format, and other "paratextual" phenomena often regarded as extraneous to poetry or the text as such.[30] Leah Price's *How to Do Things with Books in Victorian Britain* has broadened the scope of literary history as a discipline by considering the social and material histories of books and print.[31] Hayles proposes the method of media-specific analysis. This entails a mode of attention to the fact that all texts are materially instantiated, and that the medium matters. She aims to reconceptualize textual materiality as an emergent, rather than a pregiven, property, described as "the interplay between a text's physical characteristics and its signifying strategies."[32]

Since then, the impact of the avalanche of studies reconsidering the inter/medial aspects of literature has even led scholars like Brillenburg Wurth, Hayles, and Pressman to suggest that comparative literature as an academic subject should no longer be understood solely as comparing

---

[26] Keith Houston, *The Book: A Cover-to-Cover Exploration of the Most Powerful Object of Our Time* (New York: W. W. Norton & Company, 2016).
[27] Liedeke Plate, "New Materialisms," in *Oxford Research Encyclopedia of Literature*, ed. John Frow, Mark Byron, Pelagia Goulimari, Sean Pryor, and Julie Rak (New York: Oxford University Press, 2019). https://doi.org/10.1093/acrefore/9780190201098.013.1013.
[28] Bruno Latour, *We Have Never Been Modern*, trans. Catherine Porter (1991; Cambridge, MA: Harvard University Press, 1993).
[29] Rick Dolphijn and Iris van der Tuin, *New Materialism: Interviews and Cartographies* (Ann Arbor: MPublishing, University of Michigan Library, 2012).
[30] Jerome J. McGann, *The Textual Condition* (Princeton: Princeton University Press, 1991).
[31] Leah Price, *How to Do Things with Books in Victorian Britain* (Princeton: Princeton University Press, 2012).
[32] Hayles, "Print Is Flat," 72.

across languages, but also as comparing across material textures and media technologies, which requires acts of medial translation.[33] "The literary" is then considered as a mode emerging between these textures and technologies. Such an approach gives rise to the new discipline of comparative textual media, as part of an increasing recognition of literature's place in a media ecology, and literary studies as part of media studies.

The material turn has not just increased attention to the text's visual and aural aspects, but also to the sensory and affective dimensions of *reading*: the touch, shape, weight, and smell of the paper page, and how they affect the reader.[34] The counterpoint of this rediscovery of the physicality of the book, its having a body, is the rediscovery of the obvious fact that the *reader* has a body as well. Scholars like Liedeke Plate have reconsidered reading as a physical act, reminding us that "books do things to us" in return.[35] Books, being material objects that affect us, have agency and foster sociality.

13.3 Renaissance of the Book in Artists' Books: The Disintegrating Codex

Concurrent with the renaissance of the book in scholarship, a similar awareness of the potentialities of the codex can be discerned in artistic and novelistic experiments. As Johanna Drucker has shown in *The Century of Artists' Books*, the book itself has changed shape as a material artifact in the twentieth century.[36] Undeniably, the variety of post-WWII artists' books is indicative of a newfound freedom for the medium that could transcend its function as a tool for disseminating information. The codex became an object for reflection by artists and graphic designers, who started to "treat" or creatively transform found book objects into multimedia objects, through a range of practices like overwriting, decoupage, book-altering, and text-treating. Book art as an analog art for digital times takes part in a range of artistic revivals of analog media such as vinyl, polaroids,

---

[33] Kiene Brillenburg Wurth, ed., *Between Page and Screen. Remaking Literature Through Cinema and Cyberspace* (New York: Fordham University Press, 2012); N. Katherine Hayles and Jessica Pressman, eds., *Comparative Textual Media: Transforming the Humanities in the Postprint Era* (Minneapolis: University of Minnesota Press, 2013); Jessica Pressman, "Jonathan Safran Foer's *Tree of Codes*: Memorial, Fetish, Bookishness," *ASAP/Journal* 3.1 (2018): 97–120.
[34] John T. Hamilton, "Pagina Abscondita: Reading in the Book's Wake," in *Book Presence in a Digital Age*, ed. Kári Driscoll and Jessica Pressman (London: Bloomsbury, 2017), 27–43.
[35] Liedeke Plate, "How to Do Things with Literature in the Digital Age: Anne Carson's *Nox*, Multimodality, and the Ethics of Bookishness," *Contemporary Women's Writing* 9:1 (2015), 105.
[36] Johanna Drucker, *The Century of Artists' Books* (New York: Granary Books, 1995).

and floppy disks that exemplify how old and new media evolve concurrently.

Garrett Stewart has examined a practice he calls "bookwork," a form of book altering that uses books as the material substance for sculpture, demonstrating that "the idea of the codex survives its use."[37] Such bookworks are expressions of what he calls *demediation*, a process by which media are neutralized in their function – in this case, as bodies of literature or information. As such, demediation pays tribute to an increasing cultural disuse of books, reducing them to works of display, from the library to the museum. Artists such as Doug Beube, Brian Dettmer, Cara Barer, and Simon Morris engage in the cutting up of an older, found, or discarded book to make new art objects. These effectively demediate the codex by rendering books illegible and thus impeding their former medial functionality. Thus, the books in Detmmer's *Dictionary* series are maimed, with pieces of the page cut away and shellacked, and no longer meant to be read.

Such ravaged book sculptures become an apt vehicle to interrogate the future of the book and reading in times of distraction and fragmentation. This ephemerality comes especially to the fore in Tom Philips's *A Humument,* a project he started in 1970 and completed in 2016.[38] Inspired by the cut-up techniques of postmodernist writer William Burroughs, Philips decided to alter the first book he could buy for threepence, which turned out to be the 1892 Victorian novel *A Human Document* by W. H. Mallock. Philips started to overwrite, overdraw, overpaint, and thus erase its text as a visual palimpsest, until only a small number of words remained on the page. In 2010, a digital version of *A Humument* was released as *A Humument App* for iPhone. The 367 fullcolor pages have been scanned, so now the user can zoom in on details at enhanced resolution. Meanwhile, a "find wheel" spins through the book and presents visual thumbnails, which make it easy to navigate.

Other disintegrating monuments to the book underline its fragility and transitory nature in the digital age even more forcefully. Consider *Agrippa (A Book of the Dead)*, a collaborative project by cyberpunk novelist William Gibson, graphic artist Dennis Ashbaugh, and publisher Kevin Begos. *Agrippa*, too, is made as a palimpsest, and performs the process of the book's decay. From the outside, it looks like a blackened log that has been exhausted and will no longer burn. The title is singed into the cover, the

---

[37] Garrett Stewart, *Bookwork: Medium to Object to Concept to Art* (Chicago: University of Chicago Press, 2011), xiii.
[38] Tom Philips, *A Humument: A Treated Victorian Novel* (London: Thames and Hudson, 2016).

pages are ragged and charred. The book includes etchings and pages of DNA sequences. It features a poem by Gibson, which can only be played from a 3½-inch floppy on a 1992 Apple Macintosh. When the disk runs, the text of the poem starts scrolling up the screen while an encryption program on the floppy disk encodes each line and makes the poem "disappear" after its first and only reading.[39] In addition, the pages of the artists' book were treated with photosensitive chemicals, causing the gradual fading of the words and images from the book's first exposure to light. On all these levels, the meaning of the text is founded on *absence*: it emerges in the space between the ephemeral referent and the reader's memory – the imperfect trace left on her mind. We see that these experimentations all point to disintegration, loss, and mourning, and can be considered monuments or memorials to the book which inscribe its transitoriness.[40]

13.4 Bookish Novels

Jonathan Safran Foer's *Tree of Codes* (2010) aptly illustrates the often porous boundaries between artists' books and experimental novels. Foer used a digitally enhanced method of die-cutting to carve into the text of *The Street of Crocodiles* (1934) by Polish–Jewish author Bruno Schulz. After Schulz was killed by the Nazis, his writing was largely lost, as were his paintings and drawings. Foer has cut Schulz's text to ribbons (beginning with the title: *Tree of Codes* is what's left over after shedding seven letters of *Street of Crocodiles*) and created a different book out of it. Visual Editions, die-cut specialists in the Netherlands, and a "hand-finisher" in Belgium have further created this intricate artifact. Its fragile and vulnerable materiality (any reckless turning of a page might destroy it) are all the more fitting considering Schulz's history. A sense of loss literally and materially permeates *Tree of Codes*, notably in the holes in its pages. Pressman argues he thus "memorializes the book by promoting awareness of the allegorical paradoxes that render books always on the verge of loss, erasure, and

---

[39] See www.youtube.com/watch?v=41kZovcyHrU for a video of the poem running.
[40] The same themes are foregrounded in *Nox* (2010), an experimental, multimodal work that is a replica of the scrapbook the Canadian poet Anne Carson made in memory of her recently deceased brother, Michael. In *Nox*, she has translated and parsed Catullus' elegiac poem 101 into lexicographical entries. The book is folded in concertina style, and contains photographs, paintings, drawings, collages, a letter by her brother, and pieces of text composed, photocopied, and stapled (see Plate, "How to Do Things with Literature"). In its digital replication of fragile analog materiality, *Nox* is not just a memorial for her lost brother but also for the book.

obsolescence."[41] In this respect, *Tree of Codes* has much in common with the carved bookwork of book sculptors Brian Dettmer and Doug Beube, with two important differences: it is intended to be read, and it is produced on a large scale by a mainstream publisher, the London-based Visual Editions.

In those respects, *Tree of Codes* is emblematic of a number of experimental literary works published during the last twenty years. Produced by big publishing houses in relatively large print runs, these novels appropriate the aesthetics of book art without being as exclusive. Today, digital media are involved at every stage of the production and distribution of literature, so even the book-bound, analog novel is digitally produced. Novels increasingly demonstrate an awareness of this fact, and of the interrelations between digital and analog materialities. Alexander Starre has aptly called such texts *metamedial*: literary works that openly reflect on their own existence as printed and bound codices.[42] In her research, Alison Gibbons analyzes such multimodal texts: literary works that combine multiple semiotic modes – such as the visual, the textual, and the tactile – in their narratives and experiment with the possibilities of the book form.[43] They exploit their material dimensions and paper materiality in a way that is not external to their narratives but part of the meaning, and thus they comment and reflect upon the shift to the digital and the book's changing status and meaning as a node in a network of converging and diverging media.

Perhaps most famously, we see this practice in Mark Z. Danielewski's experiments with typography and page layout in *House of Leaves* (2000), a book that transcends its own bindings by linking up to a website and a CD by the author's sister, the singer-songwriter Poe. Hayles has analyzed how *House of Leaves* performs the computer's tendency to absorb all other media, and then adapts this remediating craze in a graphomaniac, maximalist book. This book seeps out of its bindings, like the titular house. which is bigger on the inside than the outside, and thus embodies the transformations of both the reading subject and literature's materialities that digitalization brings about.[44]

---

[41] Pressman, "Jonathan Safran Foer's *Tree of Codes*," 115.
[42] Alexander Starre, *Metamedia: American Book Fictions and Literary Print Culture after Digitization* (Iowa City: University of Iowa Press, 2015).
[43] For example, Alison Gibbons, "Multimodal Literature and Experimentation," in *The Routledge Companion to Experimental Literature*, ed. Joe Bray, Alison Gibbons, and Brian McHale (London: Routledge, 2012), 420–434.
[44] See N. Katherine Hayles, "Saving the Subject: Remediation in *House of Leaves*," *American Literature* 74.4 (2002): 779–806; Mark B. Hansen, "The Digital Topography of Mark Z. Danielewski's *House*

Other examples of such 'hybrid' novels are Steven Hall's *The Raw Shark Texts*, which incorporates film through a mixture of typographic design and flipbook techniques. It features a "conceptual" shark presented visually as text on the page.[45] The shark is like a giant memory bank, an external hard disk that the protagonist believes has devoured his mind and identity. *The Raw Shark Texts* performs fears of print literature vanishing in the endless, dark recesses of networked digital media, and associated fears for the future of reading and literacy.[46] Other hybrid novels include Graham Rawle's *Woman's World*, which weaves its story entirely as a collage of recycled text from women's magazines from the early 1960s, and J. J. Abrams and Doug Dorst's *S*, with its handwritten marginalia.[47] Such books operationalize the power of print matter and foreground the book as a multimedia object that is in important ways shaped by digital technology.

Jessica Pressman has analyzed this phenomenon in terms of what she calls "the aesthetics of bookishness": a renewed appreciation, or even fetishization, of the book object. Bookishness is precisely inspired by, and created in response to, the threat of obsolescence: "[b]ookishness proliferates in twenty-first-century culture, presenting numerous and varied sites through which to calibrate and consider medial change as well as to critique digital culture, especially end-time narratives about the death of the book."[48] Authors such as Danielewski, Hall, and Safran Foer have responded to this threat by claiming to create books that cannot exist online: thus Foer writes, "On the brink of the end of paper, I was attracted to the idea of a book that can't forget it has a body."[49] Earlier, Danielewski said about his *Only Revolutions* (2006), "I'm ultimately creating a book that can't exist online ... I think that's the bar that the Internet is driving towards: how to further emphasize what is different and exceptional about books."[50]

---

of Leaves," *Contemporary Literature* 45.2 (2004): 597–636; Joe Bray and Allison Gibbons, *Mark Z. Danielewski* (Manchester: Manchester University Press, 2015); Jessica Pressman, *Bookishness: Loving Books in a Digital Age* (New York: Columbia University Press, 2020).

[45] Steven Hall, *The Raw Shark Texts* (Edinburgh: Cannongate, 2007).
[46] Pressman, *Bookishness*; Kiene Brillenburg Wurth, "Old and New Medialities in Foer's *Tree of Codes*," *CLCWeb: Comparative Literature and Culture* 13.3 (2011): 2–8.
[47] Graham Rawle, *A Woman's World* (London: Atlantic Books, 2005); J. J. Abrams and Doug Dorst, *S* (New York: Mulholland, 2013).
[48] Pressman, "Jonathan Safran Foer's *Tree of Codes*," 97.
[49] Steven Heller, "Jonathan Safran Foer's Book as Art Object," *New York Times Arts Beat* (November 24, 2010), https://artsbeat.blogs.nytimes.com/2010/11/24/jonathan-safran-foers-book-as-art-object/.
[50] Sophie Cottrell, "A Conversation with Mark Danielewski" *Boldtype* (December 3, 2000).

A subclass of bookish works distinguish themselves by incorporating augmented reality and taking place literally between book and computer. Amaranth Borsuk and Brad Bouse's digital pop-up book *Between Page and Screen* is such a text.[51] It is an augmented-reality book of poetry consisting of a print book with geometric shapes ("Quick Response" graphics), read by a webcam that projects a series of poems in the space between screen and page.[52] *The Ice-Bound Concordance* (2014) by Aaron Reid and Jacob Garbe is a text-based game where the reader is asked to coauthor a book by the AI simulacrum of a diseased writer. To help finish the story, you explore hundreds of permutations offered through a logic-driven combinatorial narrative system. It is accompanied by *The Ice-Bound Compendium*, a printed book that propels the game forward by unlocking new levels and fragments of the author's past.[53] The reader has to hold it up to a webcam that reads each page for relevant themes; when you find a match, an augmented reality layer appears over the page, revealing hidden notes, images, and short clips.

At the same time as reflecting on the meaning and status of bookishness, such works reflect on the changing meaning of human embodiment and subjectivities, as Brillenburg Wurth has argued. More than just the dominant medium for transferring information, the book "has been a mediator of human identity and consciousness, and the construction of an individual, humanistic subjectivity in Western culture has often been associated with the reading of books."[54] Rather than announcing the end of the book, or constituting a swan's song to its former prowess, these works reflect on the changing status and potentialities of the codex in relation to the shift to newer media: on what the book is, has been, and what it could be now that it is freed from its function as a vehicle of information.

13.5 Big Books and Monumental Novels

This brings us back to the monumentality of the Future Library Project addressed at the outset of this chapter. Aimed at *stability*, a monument inadvertently suggests a certain *vulnerability*; it thus becomes a vehicle for

---

[51] Amaranth Borsuk and Brad Bouse, *Between Page and Screen* (Los Angeles: Siglio, 2012).
[52] See Jessica Pressman, "The Posthuman Reader in Postprint Literature: Between Page and Screen," *FRAME* 28.1 (2015): 53–69.
[53] Aaron Reid and Jacob Garbe, *The Ice-Bound Concordance* (Down to the Wire, 2016), www.ice-bound.com; Aaron Reid and Jacob Garbe, *The Ice-Bound Compendium* (Simulacrum Liberation Press, 2016).
[54] Brillenburg Wurth, "Old and New Materialities," 120.

addressing the shift to the digital and the future of the book and novel. Digital media do not erase the "analog" novel, but produce it anew as a monumental form. A last development that I wish to mention here is that of building the novel to scale: the recent emphasis on big, heavy tomes that I address in *Big Books in Times of Big Data*.[55]

Of course, when we look at the actual production, dissemination, and consumption of current-day novels and books, we see that there is no reason to expect its impending end. In the face of predictions that people would no longer be able to concentrate on extended prose narratives because our attention spans would be shortened by digital media use, it is particularly striking that in recent decades many big books have been published. These decades have since witnessed the publication of other exceedingly large works, from Roberto Bolaño's *2666* to Garth Risk Hallberg's *City on Fire*, Péter Nádas's *Parallel Stories*, Haruki Murakami's *1Q84* (2009), and Eleanor Catton's *The Luminaries*.[56] At the same time, artistic projects of "big books" and "endless texts" stretch and enlarge the spatial-material form of the codex to the point of illegibility. Richard Grossman's ongoing project *Breeze Avenue* is a "novel" that the artist plans to expand to a three-million-page length; Yahaya Baruwa's projected *Struggles of a Dreamer*, the "world's largest published novel," measures 8.5 ft x 5.5 ft x 11 ft. Irma Boom creates lavishly designed monumental books like the *SHV Think Book 1996–1896*, currently exhibited in the MOMA. Boom introduced to book design the "fat book," a book that is remarkably thick.[57] The fact that monumentality sells is underlined by a popular line of merchandise ranging from tote bags to mugs and from notebooks to t-shirts with the text "I like big books and I cannot lie." Size is currently appropriated as one of the latest marketing strategies of the literary-value industry. This ties in with an overuse of the word "monumental" in reviews and critical essays on contemporary novels.

Interestingly, this emphasis on scale and monumentality comes about at a time in publishing history when size really shouldn't matter anymore. As Starre notes in "The Small American Novel," the shift to electronic text

---

[55] Inge van de Ven, *Big Books in Times of Big Data*. Series Media/Arts/Politics (Leiden: Leiden University Press, 2019).
[56] Roberto Bolaño's, *2666* (Barcelona : Editorial Anagrama, 2004); Garth Risk Hallberg, *City on Fire* (New York: Alfred A. Knopf, 2015); Péter Nádas, *Parallel Stories* (New York: Farrar, Straus, and Giroux, 2005); Haruki Murakami, *1Q84* (Tōkyō : Shinchōsha, 2009); and Eleanor Catton's *The Luminaries* (New York: Little, Brown, 2013).
[57] Joshua Barone, "Irma Boom's Library, Where Pure Experimentalism Is on the Shelf," *The New York Times*, Jan. 16, 2017. www.nytimes.com/2017/01/16/arts/design/irma-boom-bookmaker-vermeer-prize-amsterdam-library.html.

formats has largely eliminated concerns about a text's length: "From a publication angle, a short digital text is not much different from a long one ... Strictly speaking, digital texts can only be long and short, whereas printed texts can also be big or small."[58] Increasingly, writers emphasize big books' bulk, affective powers, and ability to inhabit spaces as ways to make sense of our experiences in and of a changing media landscape.

On the one hand, novels seem to expand. The fourth book of *2666*, "The Part about the Crimes," is situated in the Mexican border town of Santa Teresa in the desert of Sonora, and is based on the mass killings of women in Ciudad Juárez in the 1990s. Each of the 110 murder cases in this part is told separately, creating a massive textual memorial. Karl Ove Knausgård, with *My Struggle*, his six-volume series of monumental autofictional novels, can be considered a Proust for the Facebook generation, who does not need to choose between hundreds of "friends." His compulsion to retrieve and preserve "everything" makes his writing the equivalent of sharing "Too Much Information" on social media, "Instagramming" pictures of every meal, "Twittering" personal details, or posting overly revealing selfies. Even though these works do not specifically address the shift to the digital as a theme, we can see their representational strategies in light of a larger shift in culture to present the full picture (N=all) rather than a sample or selection.

On the other hand, creators of big books and novels stress their difference with respect to the engulfing flow of data, seeking to defy the predictions of shortening attention spans, to emphasize their monumental qualities like weight and bulk, and, through digression and regression, to promote a new kind of "slow" reading. In his projected 27-volume series *The Familiar*, which was put on hold after five volumes in 2015, Danielewski uses the formal and material aspects of the book to literally slow the reader down, and insists on difficulty over accessibility:

> You need a lot of imagination. You need a lot of skill. One of the things I've been toying with recently as I'm finishing volume five of *The Familiar* is to actually create a kind of reader rating system that somehow alerts readers, like skiers, that you are on a difficult trail. Because I feel the way that books are currently presented, everyone assumes, or in some degree feels entitled to be able to read everything that's put out there. And I feel it's a disservice to people who are good readers, who spend a great deal of time reading difficult

---

[58] Alexander Starre, "Reading the Small American Novel: The Aesthetics and Economics of the Short Book in the Modern Literary Marketplace," in *The Novel as Network. Forms, Ideas, Commodities*, ed. Tim Lanzendörfer and Corinna Norrick-Rühl (New York: Palgrave Macmillan, 2020), 6.

books and can make their way through hard texts. . . . It's a lot to ask that of readers.[59]

He uses page layout to make the reader reflect on the temporal unfolding of the narrative, for instance through the excessive use of white spaces to visually perform the characters' emotions, and tracks single sentences across multiple pages. Delay becomes meaningful as a provocative strategy to counter the renewed valuation of positivism and objectivity of datafication. It offers an alternative to the ideals of instantaneity and immediacy underlying trends of the quantified self and big data. The delay thus effected stems from a resistance embedded in the linear, finite form of prose writing and the novel, which is made visible and palpable as we make our way through the books. This stands in stark contrast to the aforementioned emphasis in contemporary media on real-time, "binging," and the instantly "on demand."

Sanctioned by the circular logic of the monument, these authors build the novel to scale to preserve it as an art form, while aspiring to their own brand of virtuosity that will carry them into the future. Bringing together the colossal and the memorial, big books today confront the challenges of an era in which the spheres of political, ethical, and aesthetic relations are expanding. The form of the novel flourished in the eighteenth century and achieved maturity in the nineteenth, and, despite its predicted obsolescence in the digital age, it continues to affect the present. Book-bound literature reinvents itself as monumental in deep interaction with the digital and with changing perspectives of the world in terms of scale – without, however, being absorbed by it. Thus, books and novels *survive* in the information age, as always living on past their own predicted expiration date, by adapting to social and technological changes and reinscribing their own unique affordances.

---

[59] Kári Driscoll and Inge van de Ven, "Book Presence and Feline Absence: A Conversation with Mark Z. Danielewski," in *Book Presence in a Digital Age*, ed. Kári Driscoll and Jessica Pressman (London: Bloomsbury, 2018), 149.

CHAPTER 14

Literature's Audioptic Platform
Garrett Stewart

In moving to align narrative envisioning with the likes of CGI (computer-generated images) or laser holograms, this chapter sets out to rethink the essential text/image relation in literary reading under the generative rubric of IMAGEdTEXT: the visualization made operational, just as it sounds in that compound, by the alphabetic (and thus phonetic even if unsounded) momentum of written speech. This is the forward motion, at times momentarily recursive, by which mental images are produced, vistas made available, narrative scenes set and peopled, events *brought to mind*. It is in this sense that Western literature, rooted in what linguists call the "graphophonemic" structure of sound–symbol relations, summons sights and sounds from the spinning gears of what is at base an audiovisual engine of its own – one that, in just such a phrase, may set ringing ears spinning, dizzy with unseen wording as well as new mental pictures. Language doesn't act upon us from outside; like any technical *medium*, before or after cinema, before or after computerization, language works on and in us. And when working specifically to explore any such likeness between language and other forms of visual or cognitive mediation, the prose of prose fiction has only its own resources to draw on in drawing out the correlation.

Henry James's magic lantern analogy is no exception. Differential iteration makes the prose go as well as the apparatus, moving forward so that even a dim dead metaphor may get relit in the process. A year after the arrival of cinema in London theaters, in the advertised form of the "Animatograph," James opens with a throwback trope in 1897's *What Maisy Knew*. It is first insinuated by a dead metaphor of vision ("looking out") after a heavy phonetic repetition: "The child was provided for, but the new arrangement was *ine*vitably confounding to a young *inte*lligence *intense*ly aware that something had happened which must matter a good deal and *looking anxiously out* for the effects of so great a cause."[1] These besetting "effects"

---

[1] Henry James, *What Maisie Knew* (Chicago: Herbert S. Stone & Co., 1897), 9 (emphasis added).

are, for the young girl of the title, only dimly shadowed forth – the whole point of the lantern analogy in this heavily serial prose – by the blur of treachery and deception surrounding her toxically divorced parents. After three *in*-prefixes, that "out" is reversed again, with a more direct optic trope, when we learn in the next sentence that "She was taken *into* the confidence of passions on which she fixed just the stare she might have had for images bounding across the wall in the slide of a magic-lantern."[2] Traced in one sense by the very slippage between "slide" as singular noun versus tacit gerund ("sliding"), that lantern effect is immediately detailed: "Her little world was phantasmagoric – strange shadows dancing on a sheet."[3] Sharing Maisie's epistemological vantage as we do, in our narrative ignorance so far, that "sheet" is all the more likely to suggest James's textual page, its dancing choreography and phonetic score beginning to be spun out from inscribing turns of pen and phrase.

In the move from this case of "optical allusion" in Victorian fiction to its high-tech legacy in recent narrative, the contemporary endpoint of this chapter marks its main conceptual rather than historical point. The goal isn't to revisit in some new way the technological continuity between Victorian optical toys and digital imaging in an epochal span from lantern slide to bitmap array, flicker to pixel. That kind of genealogical arc has been well tracked and ruminated. The point is to notice literature's own special mode of such technological consideration. This is where the continuum between mechanical lantern "views" and the digital facilitation, for instance, of both artificial and virtual cognition (AI and VR) may, under fictional description, serve to refigure more than just the latest artifice of fabrication. At a deeper medial level, such a perspective can capture the inherent linguistic quotient of just such fictional description, with its own stream of induced synaptic firings. My approach is therefore less metahistorical than metaphoric, tuned to the reflexive *figuration* of mediality within literary narrative. It certainly resists the slick evolutionary leap by which a CNN blog can glom on to Victorian scholarship with a headline like "Magic Lanterns and the Rise of '19th-century Netflix'" – even with the caveat of those scare quotes.[4] Evidence is far too loosely hung on such a hook. The news that lantern "magic" was widely advertised for home

---

[2] Ibid. (emphasis added). [3] Ibid., 9–10.
[4] Katy Scott, "Magic Lanterns and the Rise of '19th-century Netflix,'" *CNN* (7 September 2018), www.cnn.com/style/article/magic-lanterns-19th-century-netflix/index.html. Scott's reporting draws on a paper by John Plunket at a meeting of the British Association of Victorian Studies, building with new research on his previous collection, coedited with James Lyons, titled *Multimedia Histories: From the Magic Lantern to the Internet* (Exeter: Exeter University Press, 2007).

rental by moonlighting Victorian middlemen doesn't make the machine's parlor tricks – even in far more parlors than we realized – the progenitor of on-demand digital streaming, let alone of serial TV.

Nevertheless, what the entirely metaphoric appearance of such an apparatus in serialized fiction by Henry James may do is probe the medial conditions of his own written text: what I am calling the *audioptic platform* of literary language, including the "slide function" – regarding everything from syllabic to syntactic process – in silent (but still auralized) reading. A portmanteau compression, of course, that coinage *audioptic*: a phonic "dissolve" – to mix sensory metaphors in its own spirit – meant to inscribe the fluctuant interlace of subvocal phonemes and their triggered images. Between acoustics and narrative optics – textual cause and phenomenal effect – the term is meant to replay, to jump again, the sparked gap of the reading circuit it designates. And when what is evoked in literary writing is an optic operation in itself, from magic lantern images to the holographic embrace of VR, an underlying cognitive chiasm grows perhaps clearer than usual: in reading, on the way from inscription to description, what the eye sees on the page must feel heard in some way in order for its activated letters to make something else visible. Serialization aside, the premise of literary sequencing assumed from here on out turns the silently sounded lettering of the verbal page – if I may broach what seems a more plausible anachronism than "nineteenth-century Netflix" – into a continuous low-tech audiobook: downloaded phrase by phrase onto the closed-circuit platform of image projection in the theater of reading. When later in this chapter, beyond the magic lantern's route to cinema, evidence arrives at the kinds of cutting-edge ocular or radiographic science conjured by contemporary prose, the detected fictional effort involves so little media rivalry that it has a way of investing artificial intelligence (AI), the goggled optics of virtual reality (VR), and the sci-fi twist of transmissible brain scans in magnetic resonance imaging (MRI) with little more – and no less – than the envisaging potency of self-powered literary reading in technological allegory.[5]

---

[5] This approach reverses, in a sense, the archaeological perspective of media theorist Friedrich A. Kittler. Under his telltale title *Gramophone, Film, Typewriter*, trans. Geoffrey Winthrop-Young and Michael Wutz (Stanford: Stanford University Press, 1999), Kittler deploys that nineteenth-century triad of technical mechanisms for the recording of sound and sight – with radio, TV, and universal computation waiting in the wings – to point up his sense of reading's long-standing but ultimately doomed monopoly on information retrieval. For it was as "a surrogate of unstorable data flows" that "the book came to power and glory" (9). Conflating his mediatic triad helps emphasize how my own argument is focused instead, across the vicissitudes of technological innovation, on the book's own intrinsic function as the projection of mental *cinema* from silently *sounded type*.

Between the hand-advanced glass plates of lantern apparitions and the computerized laser holography of the helmeted VR surround – even when each is staged to figure the enrapt reading experience that conveys them – the actual science of optic sequencing has of course been entirely reconceived. Or say wholly rewritten – by computer code. Short of this, one might argue that celluloid cinema derived in part from the rudimentary principle of lantern projection: images – in the slide of their transparent shadow play – following one after the other (and sometimes one upon the other, from a second beam). But unlike the modular and serial imprints of celluloid's spun projection, in digital rather than filmic cinema the image plane operates its own internal shifts within rather than between frames – in the mutation of the tessellated image field. The instantaneous come-and-go – the generative coming/gone – of the photo unit (photogram) in celluloid scrolling (as before, and far more slowly, in glass frame projection) gives way to the off-on (infinitesimally often) of zeros and ones of the binary 0/one.[6] This will be seen to have its own curious bearing on contemporary literary style. But back first – before recent manifestations of this flicker-free, stream/lined digital regime evoked in turn-of-the millennium fictions by Richard Powers – to the tantalizations and tropes of Victorian lantern flux.

14.1 "Dissolving Views": Henry James via George Eliot

Two decades before *What Maisie Knew*, a similar optical trope had been deployed by James in the eighth chapter of *Roderick Hudson* (1875) to evoke the perspectival slide-change of wish fulfillment. As the hero Mallet foresees the "annihilation" not just of his eponymous friend's sculptural talent but of the man's life itself, another lantern metaphor arrives to figure anticipation by an inset flash-forward across an initially inverted and then further distended grammar: "Beyond this vision there

---

[6] The imitative alphabetic play here, anticipating the *audioptic* conflations to be evidenced ahead in literary texts, is meant to distill, in shorthand form, the transformation in screen media – from modular celluloid cells to molecular pixel bits – tracked from different perspectives by my books on the evolution of the cinematic apparatus in its various narrative fallout: *Between Film and Screen: Modernism's Photo Synthesis, Framed Time: Toward a Postfilmic Cinema, Closed Circuits: Screening Narrative Surveillance, and Cinemachines: An Essay on Media and Method* (Chicago: University of Chicago Press, 1999) – and since then, with a more concerted intermedial focus from which the thinking of this essay derives, *The Metanarrative Hall of Mirrors: Reflex Action in Fiction and Film* (Bloomsbury, 2022). That most recent book, with a separate spread of evidence and a more narratological emphasis, attempts, over three chapters, a fuller account of plot and metatext in all but one of the novels by Richard Powers (*Galatea 2.2.*) cited in this chapter's cross section of their high-tech thematics, electronic and digital (notes 7, 8, and 10).

faintly glimmered another, as in the children's game of the 'magic lantern'"[7] – a nuptial fantasy in which the dead man's fiancée might become Mallet's after all. Out of collapse, the mirage of reparation in a renewed marriage prospect. The initial "as in the children's game of the 'magic lantern'" is a comparison logically (and grammatically) sufficient to round out the suggested "faint glimmer" of an overlain vista. But then James's syntax slips out from under this temporary closure – edging ahead from prepositional phrase to underflagged subordinate clause: "as in ... the 'magic lantern' [where] a picture is superposed on the white wall before the last one has quite faded."[8] What we thought was a self-contained clause has been shuffled under, before having "quite faded" away, by a supplemental grammar imposed on it in further clarification of the "superposition" involved. In this mimetic seriality or cross-fade of cognitive frames in an unfolding syntax – bearing its own grammatical overlap and redirection – prose enacts the protracted syntactic slide of its simile's own vehicle.

Looking back another decade and a half from this early James, we come upon George Eliot's reference to the popular Victorian lantern show. The title of her rare venture into psychological gothic, *The Lifted Veil* (1859), names the premonition of her narrator's fatal heart attack: theatrical curtain up on a dead-ended futurity. In a further instance of foreshadowing, the phrase also figures the mechanical disclosure of one image from beneath another in slide *projection* – analogous to the narrator's psychic apparatus. This involves another inexplicable prevision; a whole unvisited cityscape has been laid open from the mere word Prague: "I could not believe that I had been asleep, for I remembered *distinctly* the gradual breaking-in of the vision upon me, like the new images in a dissolving view, or the growing *distinctness* of the landscape as the sun lifts up the veil of the morning mist."[9] Not "*some* dissolving view," but "*a* dissolving view" (technical term for the overlapping fades of multilamp Victorian "magic"). Even this technological analogue is quickly naturalized as a rising "mist" serving to devaporize (unveil) an emergent landscape. After yet another appearance of the lexical stem "distinct," the narrator returns to the abstract noun for this accidentally triggered hallucination of a city he's never laid eyes on: a vision "minute in its *distinctness* down to a patch of rainbow light on the pavement, transmitted through a coloured lamp in the shape of a star."[10] In this microcosm of the

---

[7] Henry James, *Roderick Hudson* (Boston: Houghton, Mifflin, and Company, 1906), 208.   [8] Ibid.
[9] George Eliot, *The Lifted Veil* (Harmondsworth: Virago, 1985), 13 (emphasis added).
[10] Ibid., 12 (emphasis added).

"transmitted" lit image within the thematic purview of the lantern trope, a kind of slide-grammar, a lateral slippage in descriptive reference, again conspires to mystify the optical crux, leaving us to wonder whether the "coloured lamp" is casting that star-shaped glow, or whether the light source is itself built "in the shape of a star." In either case, transmission-within-projection – a node of illumination within the lanternesque "illuminated view" – delineates a familiar circuit, in literary writing, from (beamed) effect to (thrown) cause.

After such diverse figurative uses of the phantasmagoric "dissolving view" – as a Victorian metaphor for a surreal emotional blur, for temporal palimpsest, and for optic telepathy – Proust, on the other side of cinema's invention, goes so far as to include an actual lantern apparatus, in a nostalgic narrative context, before dissolving it, too, into a metaphor for reading. Before turning to Marcel's founding experience of visualized wording at the start of *In Search of Lost Time*, I want to lift the veil a bit on what's coming in the way of digitized equivalents for figured legibility in the technologically inflected prose of novelist Richard Powers. In his 1995 fable of AI, *Galatea 2.2*, when reading aloud to a phonorobotic computer assemblage, the novelist narrator has his own Proust-like memory of maternal recitation. Blocked on a new novel, he can't get beyond its tentative first sentence: "Picture a train heading south," an imperative grammar soon punningly admitted to be "all I had to go on."[11] Mockingly nicknamed Marcel by his AI lab overseer, the stalled novelist fixates on how even so few letters, as narrative rather than locomotive "vehicle," do "tunnel astonishingly across the page," a linkage of "cars just pulling out."[12] The entrained concatenation is all simile rather than boxcar sighting. In saying as much he immediately remembers his childhood fascination with how such "cars hold together by invisible coupling-gaps" across serial blanks: "I counted these spaces as they clicked along on the tracks of type, under my mother's breath."[13] The near-miss idiom for whispering ("under her breath") is nudged instead toward impetus: words put in motion *under* phonetic impulse. And by a pulse-like mechanical tracking very different from electronic coding in the novel's AI present. Dividing audition from script in this flashback to childhood listening, the narrator recalls visualizing not just the meaning but the (otherwise invisible) ligatures – the traincar-like couplings – whose spacing paces wording from the ground up.

---

[11] Richard Powers, *Galatea 2.2* (New York: Farrar Straus Giroux, 1995), 25, 35.   [12] Ibid., 55.
[13] Ibid.

Proust would have recognized this rhythmic sense of propelled language, since it was just the variable tempi as well as timbre of his own "mother's breath" in reciting prose fiction that tacitly models the reading we do of his novels. Early in *Swann's Way*, Marcel recalls how his mother, when reading George Sand aloud, "breathed into this very common prose a sort of continuous emotional life."[14] There again "breathed" is no mere metaphor for animation, for artificial resuscitation, but a literal spiration in the act of speech. The episode is meant to be generalized, for even silent reading entails "sentences which seem written for [her] voice."[15] In performed wording, the *phrasing* is ultimately one's own.[16] It is just this voicing rather than visual script of his mother's book that "directed the sentence that was ending toward the one that was to begin" – across its own "coupling-gaps" – as clocked here, in mimetic cadence, by Proust's characteristic linking commas: "sometimes hurrying, sometimes slowing down the pace of the syllables so as to bring them, though their quantities were different, into one uniform rhythm."[17] On either side of this excursus on the flux of recitation in *Swann's Way*, as if to frame its centrality, are passages that also concern syllabic pacing in diverse yet complementary ways: first when, early on, a particular story is read aloud in Marcel's bedroom to the accompaniment of a magic lantern display, and later through alphabetic distortions eyed across the engraved marble of his beloved Combray church.

14.2 IMAGEdTEXT: Proust's Warp of Words

To the church first, for its own division of labor between the waverings of thrown light and those of malleable text – each on the way back to a primal scene of lantern projection that their separately registered details, verbal and ocular, serve to unpack in their combined tableau of "sculpted stone and stained glass."[18] It is only when recalling how the famous lantern slides, rippling across Marcel's draped bedroom windows, were timed to the

---

[14] While this and the previous texts by James and Eliot are in the public domain, it is important to cite, in Proust's case, the "new and improved" English version of *Swann's Way*, trans. Lydia Davis, (New York: Penguin 2002), 42; subsequent references are to this edition.
[15] Ibid., 43.
[16] This was the gist of my argument in *Reading Voices: Literature and the Phonotext* (Berkeley: University of California Press, 1990), its title intended illustratively as a clause rather than a phrase, a book that introduced the concept of "transegment drift" for the kind of cross-word effects instanced here by the unexpected ligatures across lexical juncture. This scale of textual audition is pursued in two of my later books especially: *The Deed of Reading: Literature * Writing * Language* Philosophy* and *The Ways of the Word: Episodes in Verbal Attention* (Ithaca: Cornell University Press, 2015, 2020).
[17] Ibid.   [18] Ibid., 61.

reading aloud of a narrative prompt text – only then that we are likely to spot the bond between the shifting colored projections of the church windows and the distorted letter forms carved into inlaid and time-worn floor stones and "read" by Marcel as nonverbal images in themselves. Again word and image come into an uneasy, or at least unfixed, relation. The tinted windows have been frayed frail by the atmospheric exposure, the incised stone whittled down by human tread. Together, if by a circuitous route, these two features, as disfeaturings, return us to the textures of projection and distortion already differently developed in the magic lantern passage. Light flickers unpredictably through the chapel glass, dousing stone with color while at the same time, in the plane of its gridded imagery, equivocating mimesis itself. A snowy mountain pictured in one composite stained panel appears "frosted onto the glass itself"[19] by some assaulting winter. Its "snowflakes," though seemingly "lit by some aurora," result instead from the flecks of erosion in the pitted glazing, "so old that here and there one saw their silvery age sparkle with the dust of the centuries and show, shimmering and worn down to the thread, the weft of their soft tapestry of glass."[20] As planes of visual representation, these windows simulate the assaults of real weather; as artifacts, their translucent "lozenge-shaped panes"[21] are themselves visibly weathered.

So, too, with the surface of the church's entryway floor, which, having endured the tread of centuries, has become "uneven and deeply hollowed at the edges."[22] Lived time has served to "bend the stone and carve it with furrows."[23] Same with the floor-embedded "tombstones" of the abbots that "formed for the choir a sort of spiritual pavement" – a tempting model for the Proustian text in its linguistic *platform*. The stressed stone – "no longer inert and hard matter"[24] – comes to offer, as we read on, a diagram of textual mutation per se. For "time had softened" the inset memorials and "made them flow like honey beyond the bounds of their own square shapes, which, in one place, they had overrun in a flaxen billow."[25] It takes a moment to recognize (through the young Marcel's eyes) what is going on, what has gone on. The rippling run-over of marble shapes is traced further by the cumulative Proustian grammar and the mixed-metaphoric flow of the graven script – so that the once chiseled inscriptions are seen "carrying off on their drift a flowering Gothic capital letter":[26] an eerie textual generativity from the stony grave. We must read as closely as Marcel does the abraded language before him. Once carved in marble, the letters "had reabsorbed themselves,

---

[19] Ibid., 60. [20] Ibid., 60. [21] Ibid., 61. [22] Ibid., 60. [23] Ibid. [24] Ibid. [25] Ibid.
[26] Ibid.

further contracting the elliptical Latin inscriptions, introducing a further caprice in the arrangement of those abridged characters, bringing close together two letters of a word of which the other had been disproportionately distended."[27] Alluded to there is the marmoreal economy of tombstone protocols – with such (unexampled) shortcuts as *vix* or *ann* (for *vixit*, he lived, or *annus*) or such phrasal condensates as the acronym DMS (*Dis Manibus*, to the spirits of the departed). Latin's original shorthand compressions are thus travestied in the scrunched letter forms that rivet the young boy's (and eventual writer's) gaze.

Philology seems recapitulated by marble topography. For in the form of exactly the Latin practice that first introduced word breaks (again, Powers's "coupling-gaps") into Western script, affording comprehension without vocalization, here letters lose signification in contingent mergers, cross-threaded into the new floral twists of phantom ligatures and strictly graphic diphthongs, including that fluctuant viscous "honey" of their cresting "flaxen billows." With this emphasis on verbal spacing in cryptic (both senses) abbreviations and swellings alike, we may conjure the fungibility of alphabetic writing even when, as it were, set in stone. The variable rhythm and fused continuities of the Proustian text, in the uptake by present reading, are emblematized – in this bending and blending of letters – as the plasticity, immediate rather than immemorial, of the typeset words, including all its vocalic "overruns," "drifts," "ellipses," "distensions," and "abridgments" (a virtual Proust-thesaurus).

This, we'll now see, is how even the establishing lantern scene early in the novel – in its play between storybook text and unstable lamplit illustration – has in effect paved the way for the distortions of the church's inlaid Latin floorspace. For beyond the mutable luminescence of the stained-glass windows, carved out there as a grounding textual condition is the intangible friability of inscription in the pacing and "caprice" of the reading moment. By junctural analogy, this is the word-to-picture ratio that I've "pronounced" IMAGEdTEXT: the foundational play, in short, between pictured graphic wording and worded pictures.

14.3 *Son et lumière*: Textual Imagineering

Proust's reflexive modernism depends in part on isolating the affect of remembrance from the words that struggle to summon it, only to render the bond more indissoluble in the long run between recovered mental

---

[27] Ibid.

image and the fashioned poetics of recall. And when the remembered scene is in fact that of an image system linked to verbal text, the case takes on an almost laboratory exactitude. Not ten pages into *Swann's Way*, the ripples and dips of lantern projection across a corrugated cloth surface have been synced with – and made figurative for – an inset and mostly uncited narrative text that seems to propel them. In this way, the distorting "fissures"[28] of the optical surface foreshadow the "furrows" of desecrated – and resectored – stone lettering. Anticipating the church's shimmer of stained glass light as well, the lantern's thrown play of color is noted specifically to be operating "after the fashion of the first architects and master glaziers of the Gothic age."[29] The analogy ("after the fashion of") becomes immediately more explicit. The beams of the apparatus "replace the opacity of the walls with impalpable iridescences, supernatural multi-colored apparitions, where legends were depicted as in a wavering, momentary stained-glass window."[30] One of these "legends" is submitted in particular to Proust's secondary novelistic depiction: "Moving at the jerky pace of his horse, and filled with a hideous design" – a design moral in this sense, rather than visual – the villainous knight Golo, on his supernatural mount, would "advance jolting toward the castle of poor Genevieve de Brabant."[31] All goes (forward) according to script, captured by this passage's naïve metalepsis – from the narrator's childhood perspective – of a visualized character taking instruction from his own text: "Golo would stop for a moment to listen sadly to the patter read out loud by my great-aunt."[32] From some accompanying (unspecified) commercial booklet – something like the equivalent of cinematic intertitles – these narrative signals are words that the painted knight "would seem to understand perfectly." The result is that he is watched "modifying his posture, with a meekness that did not exclude a certain majesty, to conform to the directions of the text."[33] Instructions take the form of spatial "directions" – with the vulnerable Genevieve's castle steadily in view: a goal to be approached on horseback at whatever frame rate the "glass ovals" were being "slipped between the grooves of the lantern."[34] But always the aunt's read words set the story's materialized pace.

In the inferred ocular archaeology of this episode, proto-cinematic analogies are hardly far-fetched. They have already been established a few pages earlier, where in the mental palimpsest (James's "superposed" fade) of half sleep, an awakening Marcel has his usual hard time bringing into focus which of his several past or present bedrooms is presently dawning on

[28] Ibid., 10.   [29] Ibid., 9.   [30] Ibid.   [31] Ibid.   [32] Ibid., 10.   [33] Ibid.   [34] Ibid.

him. He can't sort out such temporal overlaps "any better than we isolate, when we see a horse run, the successive positions shown to us by a kinetoscope." In contrast to the increments of chronophotography that historically underlie this allusion to Edison's battery-operated peephole animation, within two pages that photographed horse has reverted to a painted chivalric slide. It has taken this form in order to evince the more wholly unreal and malleable visualizations of the reading eye, whose phonetic slipstream is itself figured as an oral delivery system. Obeying the great-aunt's vocalized wording of the simplified legend, Golo's "slow ride" on his advancing steed was one that "nothing could stop." It was ungrounded in its vector – and thus, even if "the lantern was moved," his progress could pucker, tuck, and buckle across any surface, planar or creased. Combray's figurative "tapestry of glass" is here anticipated in composite form by draped cloth and overlain chromatic waver: "I could make out Golo's horse continuing to advance over the window curtains, swelling out with their folds, descending into their fissures":[35] all gauzy ruffle to the childhood gaze. And all still under orders from the order of the read text.

And beyond textual pace, wording accrues its own chromatics as well. "The castle and the moor were yellow" – but "I had not had to wait to see them to find out their color."[36] For in the great-aunt's oral "patter" of the brochure, "well before the glasses of the frame did so, the *bronze sonority* of the name Brabant had shown it to me clearly."[37] This synesthesia is given by Proust as "la sonorité mordorée du nom de Brabant" – *mordorée* for golden-brown, russet, bronze. The cognate, *bronze*, is available in French as well, but would have fallen flatter on the ear in adjectival position after the noun. The established previous translation by C. K. Scott Moncrieff gives the sonorous punch phrase first, and with something of an over-literal thud, so that "before the slides made their appearance the *old-gold* sonorous name of Brabant had given me an unmistakable clue." With Proust's assonance only pallidly approximated in the two long *o*'s of that hyphenated epithet, nothing of course can top the additional metric and nasalized pick-up from "son" by "du nom de" in the original "la *son*orité mordorée *du nom de* Brabant" – a phrase every bit as undulant as those curtain folds. Yet Lydia Davis's intrepid recent version (quoted earlier) has its own quasi-Proustian texture, if not quite metrical ring, its overlapped sonority burnished by the rub of elision itself: *Brahn-sahn* in anticipation of the golden-toned *Brah/bahnt*. If this sibilant "drift" can be heard to anticipate,

---

[35] Ibid.   [36] Ibid., 11.   [37] Ibid. (emphasis added).

at the narrowest compass, the sped-up syllabic continuities of the mother's later reading voice as well as the time-smudged meld of Latin characters in those Combray inscriptions, then its phonemic "elision" and "abridgment" may seem all the more apt.

And there is a longer view to take of this episode – or, say, a longer hearing. Whether or not the contemporary intertitles of silent cinema were on Proust's mind in the wedding of text and projected image, the back-dated medial twist speaks for itself. With the dutiful knight taking patiently literal *dictation* from the lantern's narrative manual (in vocal transmission), all imaged motion is matched in lockstep with literary process. Think by comparison of a stymied hero turning to the camera in some metafilmic screen comedy and asking what his next line of dialogue should be. The Proustian scene emerges as a protracted case of reading degree zero (sounded lettering and its produced image) in allegorical overdrive.[38]

Leaving all such shaky lantern intermittence behind, we turn next, on the other side of sound cinema, to the way software algorithms in the work of Richard Powers have, in fictional ekphrasis, carried on the IMAGEdTEXT circuit to a new level of computer-script immersion all its own. These ingenuities include a virtualized optic s(urr)ound – a fully audible Van Gogh mise en scène – that is "voiced"-in by digital code. Such grapplings

[38] My emphasis thus ratchets down one representational notch from the analysis of Proust's lantern that launches Elaine Scarry's *Dreaming by the Book* (New York: Farrar Straus Giroux, 1999, 11–16). In her compelling (and broadly generalized) account, the knight Golo's insubstantiality as lantern flicker – the flimsiness of his filmy status – confirms for the reader, by contrast, the imagined "solidity" (wherever on the spectrum from hard to soft) of the wall, then curtain, on which his advancing image is projected. The episode develops, under Scarry's lens, as a lab report on the incubation of mimetic credence in the waking dream of reading. For me, as well, the depicted effects at play in this scene are very much a test case of fiction's imagined scenography. Yet this is for the preliminary and more fundamental reason that not just the intangibility of the slide projection – making good on a narratively posited material reality behind, and backing, it – but the room's constitution to begin with are each the palpable work of phonetic language in the generation of meaningful words, including its synesthesias of sound and sight (as in naming's own effect of "bronze sonority" on Marcel's young ear). This includes Proust's language at large, of course, before uncited delegation to the great-aunt's embedded speech in her reading aloud (unmentioned by Scarry) from the accompanying lantern story in the comically treated verbal dictation of Golo's every dutiful, translucent move. It typifies, instead, the optical bias or priority of Scarry's approach to literary experience that such a flip-flop onomatopoetic grammar as the "quick, sharp, tapping sound" of Emma Bovary's leather-clad, high-heeled footfalls on a flagstone floor – a sound "sensorily present" if "read aloud," and thus approximating a direct "auditory registration" (115) of the event – is a textual prompt that for Scarry, when processed silently, would make for (the visual metaphor being symptomatic here) a "double acoustical scrim" (116). In that silent case, on Scarry's terms, we only "imagine the sound of the words" (116) in picturing motion, rather than producing the latter apparition through what linguistics would designate as phonemic language's own acoustic triggers in the first place.

with the intricacy of computerized perceptual science come with no loss of reflexive interest – interest on the part of their author, that is, as with Proust before him, in the staging of technological fabrication as a potential emblem of unwired reading. And so the remaining two numbered subheads shift to evoking, in the loosest form of pseudo-code, the directives of computer script – even while analysis retains its verbal emphasis in registering the impact of this digital regime on narrative prose.

14.4   <:=04/=scripting the digital image_AI to VR=:>

Even in the millennial turn to phonorobotics and AI magic, there remains what we might call lantern envy. In returning to *Galatea 2.2*, the computerized "blind box"[39] named Helen has been put through her digital paces in being prepped by the novelist hero in how to interpret literature. But she finally craves actual images of the world she's been programmed to read (or be read to) about. Eyeless but avid, she pleads for optical (computerized rather than ocular) signifieds to enliven her store of worded signifiers. In addition to the novelist's oral input, and all her CD-ROM and web downloads, she gets a simulated Grand Tour via the electronic scanning of dated slide carousels fed to her cortical rather than retinal inbox. These "flat pictures" offer "pathetic portals"[40] onto the real, a "travelogue" in the form – wait for it – of a "magic lantern" that has no use, or need, for an actual "projector."[41] The effort to "defraud" her cerebral network by second-order "images" rather than real-world sightings "would do for the machine the inverse of what virtual reality promised to do for humans:"[42] would do so, that is, by replacing a quasi-tactile immersion with mere digitized (not even lit) pictures. A giant technological step backward, hence the Victorian lantern trope.

The "promise" of VR is the central topic of Powers's next novel, *Plowing the Dark* (2000). Completing a diptych on electronic artifice, the plot's VR "Cavern" (a tacit update of Plato's Cave) hosts a digitally generated laser holography that yields images not as descendants of projection, lantern, or film, or of mere data injection, but via an immersive "electron feed."[43] What the protagonist, Adie, a former New York graphic artist come west to high-tech Seattle, discovers in this VR lab is that if one wants a lavish 3-D jungle – as a limbering-up exercise in pixelation – painting is no longer necessary. In computer speak, one simply needs to "write a decent Gauguin"[44] – to script his foliage in code. Same with the vegetal fantasia

---

[39] Powers, *Galatea 2.2*, 297.   [40] Ibid., 296.   [41] Ibid., 297.   [42] Ibid., 295.
[43] Richard Powers, *Plowing the Dark* (New York: Picador, 2000), 126.   [44] Ibid., 42.

of Henri Rousseau's *The Dream*, in characterizing which syllabically recursive phrasings like "philodendron tendril"[45] and "alien anemonies"[46] reprise the algorithmic accretions that are explicitly said to "grow"[47] that floral life, vein by fractal vein, like leaves themselves. With human language modeling the self-proliferating coherence of computer code, so close to reality are such botanic "cl*o*nes" that a further long-*o* assonance can trace them as they "turn g*o*ld in a c*o*ld snap."[48] One language is repeatedly playing catch-up with another in Powers's site-specific style, alphabetic with logarithmic. Yet the digital has subsumed all media in VR, so that one paints a laurel leaf with a brush that "never existed outside of a software library."[49] The mimetically generated prose that further describes the work of this library renders a mocking chiasmus – language on an auto-pilot of its own? – in treating the "man-handled, hand-mangled parodies"[50] of visual art in this simulated panoply of media.

Accidentally conflated by Powers's depiction of chromatic transparency in virtual space are, as it happens, the "lozenge-shaped panes" of Proust's "soft glass tapestry" at the Combray church as well the throwback aura of Gothic-age "glaziers" in the lantern slides. In Powers's allusion to medieval stained glass as a now-electronic option (just one of software's graphic choices in a drop-down design menu), a further smooth brew of assonance operates its own linguistic mimesis for another switch in the keyboarded medium of leafage: "At a blink" – a pixel twitch – "the laurel fractured into the leaded lozenges [Proust's own word] of a free-floating lancet, h*ue*d in c*oo*l Chartres b*lue*,"[51] where Monet's renowned multiple imaging of that cathedral may enhance this allusion to secondary visualization. No brush needed for the VR effect, though, just a kind of finger painting in vitreous illusionism. Participants in the techno cult associated with this "Cavern" as "Realization Lab" have become in themselves prosthetic agents of computerization, as they "maze out on silicon's sub-micron boulevards, trance over their keyboards, their carpal tunnels hollowed out for maximum brain-finger throughput."[52] Keyboards are here the type-scripting engines that hold the generated retinal phenomena within the orbit of ordinary creative writing writ large. Sound is then added when, in a 3-D simulacrum of Van Gogh's bedroom at Arles, algorithms are arranged for "voicing"[53] the effect of occupancy: from ambient noise pouring in along with light from the open window to the creak of irregular floorboards – the latter with their own punning "tongue in groove"[54] response to digital articulation.

---

[45] Ibid., 33. [46] Ibid., 57. [47] Ibid., 37. [48] Ibid., 38. [49] Ibid., 40. [50] Ibid. [51] Ibid.
[52] Ibid., 59. [53] Ibid., 257. [54] Ibid., 198.

All this deftly phrased depiction of encoded script, however forward-looking, is simultaneously normalized by anachronism. In general parlance, the not uncommon use of "film" (material substrate) for "movie" (optical condition) takes little notice of the shift in motion pictures from celluloid to digital generation. VR is, by contrast, a movie you *move through*. Yet still by analogy with history's major breakthrough in time-based mediation, we hear how in the Cavern "projectors spread a panorama wider than any glance could consume": a vista that could then be "fast-forwarded" as a "live-in movie" or "slowed" to a "frozen frame."[55] Moreover, and still in the argot of an outdated materiality, "past zero, the film ran in reverse. Floods got sucked back into whitening cumulus."[56] In an even more obvious mechanistic anachronism, we read how, instead of digital drivers, "the touch of a button set the film in motion upon inexorable sprockets" – how quaint those mechanically calibrated "sprockets" – until it could be "rewound in slow motion."[57] The meshed gearing of those phantom clutch-holes aside, even when statistical rather than spatial models are generated by this unperforated electron technology – in its "gorgeous motile tapestry,"[58] a digital upgrade of Proust's "tapestry of glass" at Combray – its 3-D environs are still characterized as a space through whose "changing variables" the "eye" could, as in classic cinema, "pan and zoom." This happens even as postcinematic prose is rising to this challenge by its own anaphoric scan, or pan, of "fantastic, fusing, fractal ice floes"[59] – including the homophonic and contradictory hint of "flows" in frozen "floes" and the phonetic feint of "fractalized" in "fractal ice." By a similar privileging of even more aleatory alliteration, we have heard in *Galatea 2.2* that computerized AI "had to use language to create concepts,"[60] rather than the other way around. In one staggered instance of Helen's wired learning curve in this mode, the spew of wording stops just short of her inventor's own name, Lentz, in the cascading consonant brackets of "Lint, lintels, lentils, Lent."[61] It is a list whose arbitrariness confirms by parody the deeper incremental rule. In algorithmic and alphabetic writing alike, as with the cellular advance of the cinematic spool, serial inscription precipitates mental picture in the normal course of reading.

In the VR of *Plowing the Dark*, the refinements of immersive illusion require eventually a haptic quotient as well from their speeding codes, since even "a simulated object" must be put under command "to bend or

[55] Ibid., 117. [56] Ibid. [57] Ibid., 120. [58] Ibid., 80. [59] Ibid. [60] Powers, *Galatea 2.2*, 248.
[61] Ibid.

droop or bruise or any of several dozen other *verbs* that real things did when bumped up against in the grotto that the Cavern stood for."[62] Substituting the grammatical category of "verbs" for more palpable instances of "collision" isn't just a metalinguistic joke on Powers's part. In computer-generated space, all motion, including impact and rebound, begins with the writing of algorithmic code: "Various variables toted up mass and speed and English."[63] Punned on there in the term for rotational "spin" is the play of "English" in a sense not just mechanical (for "torque") but lingual. Once again tech invention, a mathematical language unto itself, finds its figurative register in literature's different mode of alphabetic speech. Such pixel calisthenics may even come complete with their own free-associational slips and twisted idioms – as when, rounding out the semantic as well as corporeal reflexes of this somatically enhanced holography, "Adie watched as software turned her jungle into a gym."[64] But sometimes, in overloading the system with the programmable "verbs" of collision, the "graphic buffers" fail in sustaining the "myriad integrals" needed to prevent the kind of glitch that loses several "frames" at a time – again a vestigial celluloid terminology. The result is an unacceptable "hiccup" in "all the flicker-free, smooth scrolling" of the "reality engine."[65] The goal of flicker-fusion in the technological evolution of filmic cinema, as later in other continually refined modes of screen media, has become paramount in this new enworlding order of the holographic image: "The Cavern's goal – believability through total immersion – could not survive an image that sputtered."[66] Even *that* "verb," for digital glitch or elision, is perfectly poised on the threshold between holographic splatter and speech defect, splutter and stammer, in the activated script code of pixelation's electron-fast st/utterance. As with the audioptic crests and valleys of the lamp beam in Proust, a later prose of the electron stream in Powers acts under a similar impulse to reflect on its own generation – and in relation to modernist poetics explicitly, as we are next to find.

Comparable to such throwback figures for the "scrolling" of VR "frames," there is an openly mixed metaphor, cross-wired from spectacle and vehicular automation, when digital engineer and former poet Stevie "popped the hood and revealed the diorama's underpinning gears."[67] This is the same Stevie who remembers how he was smitten with Adie back in college when hearing her reading aloud, in English class, from

---

[62] Powers, *Plowing the Dark*, 60 (emphasis added).   [63] Ibid.   [64] Ibid., 61.   [65] Ibid.
[66] Ibid.   [67] Ibid., 63.

Yeats's "Sailing to Byzantium," recalled by digression at one point in similar mechanistic tropes. Typical for Powers, and not least in his self-appointed role as a *jargonaut* of advanced electronics in this turn-of-the millennium novel, no tech lingo takes us far, for long, from a celebration of the literary linguistics that generates it. As Yeats's words "issued from her mouth" that memorable day, in their "stream of discrete, miraculous gadgets,"[68] they were "mechanical birds mimicking living things."[69] Virtual reality *avant la lettre*: words that were the things they sang – as if in nested allusion to Yeats's legendary question elsewhere about how to "know the dancer from the dance," embodied agency from the choreography it performs.

Recalled here more immediately is Yeats's celebrating "such a form as Grecian goldsmiths make / Of hammered gold and gold enamelling / To . . . set upon a golden bough to sing . . . / Of what is past, or passing, or to come."[70] In this verse's embedded context, computerized simulation is among the latest "coming things." The poet's valuation of Grecian craft in the sculpting of a simulated vocal automaton for figured music (distant predecessor articulate AI) is rendered anew in this flashback tribute, by metonymy, through the singing out and taking wing of each tooled word: "Her mouth became the metal-worked machine its sounds described," bringing forth "sentences of hammered gold" from its "factory of ethereal phonemes."[71] So it is that each sound – in the metallurgy of this urgent welding – is an "alloy" composed of "confusion and astonishment"[72] alike. (Think again of such literary voicing in association with the alchemized Proustian alloy of golden ore and orality in "sonorité mordorée.") In Powers, the forge of verbal art and its ringing anvil craft is materialized in terms continuous, in the long span of industrial genealogy, with exactly the later digital *algorhythm* that so often, in his writing, comes into alignment, ironic or otherwise, with our alphabetic (and phonetically "etherealized") reading process.

14.5 <:=05/=Signal gl/hitching_OCR vs. ^Acoustic Character Recognition^=:>

Two decades after Powers's exercise in code-driven, word-riven ekphrasis in the virtual inscapes of *Plowing the Dark*, his 2021 *Bewilderment* goes so

---

[68] Ibid., 199. [69] Ibid., 200.
[70] W. B. Yeats, "Sailing to Byzantium" (Poetry Foundation), www.poetryfoundation.org/poems/43291/sailing-to-byzantium.
[71] Powers, *Plowing the Dark*, 200. [72] Ibid.

far as to imagine a suboptic simulacrum approaching, in "emotional telepathy," the condition of electronic immortality via preserved affect.[73] Pitched even further forward into sf (sci-fi) technofuturism, the novel tracks its astrobiologist hero's struggle to appease the grieving of his son over the accidental death of the boy's mother. When alive, she was part of an experiment in the brain-scanning of affect's own pulsations, and the fMRI science has evolved since to the point where a mental transcript of his mother's most euphoric moments can be uploaded as mood elevator to the cerebral hardware of her son. When the boy later dies in another bitter accident, the father becomes in turn the experimental subject for a double transfusion of vanished affect as nested brain "print":[74] impalpable imprint, not implant – a "read out" – to be internalized only as decoded, technologically deciphered. What results is a conflation of the two previous high-tech novels in the adjacent electronic realms of AI as VR: here the cognitive approximation of virtual moods.

The gradual restoration of feeling in the transmit from mother to and through son – a feeling first theirs together, then in turn the bereft narrator's under renewed fMRI input – begins by an assonant phrasal chord change of "magnetic" prose "resonance" in a stylistic rather than psychic echo chamber: "I lie in the *tube* and *tune* myself to a print"[75] of the son's cortical circuitry. The process is known as DecNef ("decoded neural feedback"), with that abbreviation's vaguely necrological vibe in this case of a posthumous delivery system whereby the dead boy is already channeling his deceased mother. In its phrasing, "What they felt, then, I now feel,"[76] *then* is both retrospective and consequential: a recovered temporal "then" (cause) under the force of a mediating technological "therefore" (effect). Like a lap-dissolve in an implicitly comma-spliced grammar: "they" thought, therefore I am – am the repository of their continuance, their feelings again not so much for as *in* me. It is, finally, as if the novel's detailed tech miracle of affective transfer were generated by suppressing the clichéd formulation of its own goal (with the anchoring term in question never actually used to evoke the electromagnetic circuits involved). Enacted rather than named is the fantasy that the living and the dead could be *on the same wavelength*. Technical magic figures and inflects the textual: the moods of the dead renewed, dead metaphors literalized.

In just this way, on the novel's last page, the boy's fired synapses instigate the narrator's own: "The thought occurs to him – and I have it."[77]

---

[73] Richard Powers, *Bewilderment* (New York: W. W. Norton, 2021), 93.   [74] Ibid., 277.   [75] Ibid.
[76] Ibid., 278.   [77] Ibid.

Direct thought transference, yes, an internal "telepathy" again, but with an overtone of a eureka moment: "[Ah] I have it." I get it! – this a reference to the son's wonder at their time together amid the failed stewardship, but persistent beauty, of planet earth: "*Can you believe where we just were?*"[78] As much as with Proust's lantern, DecNef goes out of its way to figure the story's own consumption, its own internalization, as print text. The novel, after all, has been transmitted to us by literary narrative's everyday version of thought transference, with a sorcery all its own. In the phenomenology of reading's ordinary mental ventriloquism, critic Georges Poulet stresses that in reading "I am thinking the thoughts of another"; am, in the grammatical sense of a speaking I, "the subject of thoughts other than my own."[79] In the science fantasy of *Bewilderment*, the worded thoughts of a lost other are *had* (the father's verb in "I have it") as if they were his (subsumed into first-person plural in "where *we* just were") in their very decoding and articulation. As much as with DecNef decipherment, then, in reading Powers's fiction, absent others can live on in me, their thoughts reactivated.

It is only the electronic sophistication of fMRI (*functional* magnetic resonance imaging) that has allowed this *purposeful* tracking of the cortical blood flow – as if it were the very lifeblood of consciousness. That fMRI abbreviation is an acronym, we'll soon find, with more than ordinary "resonance" even amid the oblique quirks of Powers's cultivated technospeak. In the VR Cavern from *Plowing the Dark*, where the 3D picture cell (the pixel) becomes its own fractal cubical as illusory building block, the technicians allow the alternate terms "voxel" or "boxel"[80] for its foursquare volumetric operations. But for the reader, such terminology is composited of its own phonemic *vox*-cells. That is why, for the tag of this final subsection, I wanted to tap (and tamper with) a computational abbreviation, OCR, that I haven't seen exploited by Powers. There is, of course, an everyday instance of so-called optical character recognition in any processing of alphabetic increments in the linear scans of ordinary human reading. Think of this as exaggerated, in a "catchy" jam-up, by the trademarking of an open-source "word embedding" program designed for AI language software: the branded phonetic (rather than algorithmic) compression of the one-word "fastText." This is a muted verbal in-joke (via accelerated elision), like many in Powers's own writing, made legible

---

[78] Ibid.
[79] Georges Poulet, "The Phenomenology of Reading," *New Literary History* Vol. 1.1 (1969), 55.
[80] Powers, *Plowing the Dark*, 15.

only by what, in the near-simultaneity of eye–ear coordination, I'm therefore moved to call ACR (acoustic character recognition). Such is a volatilized mode of word's-splay that remains hospitable to any number of burnished bronz(ed) sonorities and laminated golden hammerings, as well as many less resonant dentings of sense in the "factory" of "phonemes." These include any number of "drifts" and "abridgments" not just in the Proustian fetish of compressed Latin lettering but in the "tongued groves" of vulgate fiction (recalling again the punned-on digital "voicing" of Van Gogh's floorboards).

On the score of ACR, there is in Powers's 2018 ecocritical epic, *The Overstory*, a late moment when a militant critic of deforestation, on the run from the police for antilogging terrorism, is reduced to boxing Amazon products in none other than tree-pulped cartons. They are stamped for transport in a way that explicitly recalls the ridged striations, the "furrows of bark"[81] (not unlike the "fissures" of curtaining in Proust), associated with the character's own guerilla painting of doomed redwoods, which now seem to resemble a "two-foot *wide* UPC bar code."[82] In that ubiquitous term (typically "barcode"), the common contraction of epithet and noun seems left to the reader's own (Proustian) "drift" and "abridgment" to perform, so that the pictured trompe-l'oeil effect is also an ear-opening irony. Epitomizing this novel-length "ode" to vegetal proliferation, the phonetic flicker of syllabic "superposition" (that term, via James, from Victorian visual culture once more) coruscates across the triple-take of this syncopated two-beat "bark/c/ode." Hear it as another literary (rather than a software) instance of "fastText" in audioptic overlap.

In its intrinsic eye–ear (eyer's) skid, that pun on laser decryption is also a computer-savvy upgrade of the former slide lantern's frame-advance – especially when, in Proust's double-tracked performance of this device, its specular manifestation was looped back into the logic not just of oral generation at large but its unique synesthetic sonorities. And with phonetic compression and overlap in mind, we may also recall here, from *Plowing the Dark*, how the abbreviation for the "Realization Lab" (and its Cavernous volumetric simulations), namely "RL," had its own inherent way – if phonetically sounded rather than acronymically scanned – of deleting the ReaL before our ears. To put it in terms earlier from Powers on childhood reading: sometimes the decisive "coupling-gaps" operate not merely "under [the] breath" and *between* words, but also in a manner suggested by the syllabic c/leaving (both senses) of that hyphenated

---

[81] Richard Powers, *The Overstory* (New York: W. W. Norton, 2018), 380.   [82] Ibid.

phrase's own gaping and latching *g*'s. At other times, too, such vernacular idioms or acronyms are turned, under contextual pressure, into the kind of pun or alphabetic rebus we audit in "bark code" or "RL." It is then that certain fertile couplings, under the audioptic pressure of a neo-Proustian abrasion, may be found induced by the skid-marks of invisibly traced ligatures or swallowed vowels.

   So forward, in conclusion, to another such example in Powers, where again, as with RL at a glance, no actual syllables seem waiting to unfurl. Regarding the lettering of fMRI (functional MRI) as a refrain in *Bewilderment*, the fsf (functional sci-fi) point is the same, with or without the resulting syllabic afterimage. But its techno wizardry can only seem more eerily infused and distributed across the acronym's many appearances when its letters are found ghosted as syllabic vocables. For it is then that the term's insinuated inference may indeed "resonate magnetically" (*fMRI* science aside) in the swift enacted transience (f/m/r=effemare) of all things ephemeral. Looming further there in the many iterations of this scientific shorthand, or at least lurking, is a lexical auto-complete (incorporating the shorthand *I* of "imaging") that resembles not so much an Anglicized technospeak plural like "antenn*ae*," long *e*, as the long *i* plural of a term like "dramatis person*ae*" (fitly enough, given the residual force of the deceased fictional characters involved). Trailing off from the acronym, then, as it flips to yet another phonemic rebus, is the long psychic rather than just phonetic *I* of extended identity in this novel of "brain prints" and their affective postmortem upload. As if actually to speak Proust's warped marble Latin for once – given the "drift" of this spill-over "billow" or "distension" and its vocalized "caprice" – so it is that the *ephemerae* live on. In reference to a sci-fi apparatus extrapolated well beyond the far reaches of ultrasound, and in yet another convergence of lexical and electron codes in Powers, the alphabetic vox(c)el here elicits the human raw material of a transcriptive system other than its own. Even the machine's repeated numb acronym, in other words, cannot altogether repress an ulterior syllabic sounding of the very evanescence that its operation – as reading's own emblem or parable – is meant to transcend.

   In the three main Powers novels we've sped through, anything like a D(igital) H(umanities) frame of reference has moved from the electronic posthuman of AI, through the postreal of virtual engulfment by pixel "realization," to a sci-fi prosthesis of loss rehumanized by electronically traced brain prints and their transferred phenomenological mapping. In a recent interview with Ezra Klein on his *New York Times* podcast, Powers guessed that it wouldn't take most readers of *Bewilderment* long to figure out that decoded neurofeedback (DecNef), in its conduit of emotion, is operating as a metaphor for reading.[83] For reading's affect, that is: alternating in relay between narrator and empathetic reader in a circuitry so essentially phonetic that Powers has written eloquently about the iPad dictation of his novels, through voice-recognition software, as an effort to bring the writing closer to the silent enunciation of its reader.[84] Set that down as another computerized case, though generalized and demystified, of affective imprint as reading's blueprint.

In light of such preformatted reading, current text-processors of the closural metaphorics in *Bewilderment*, namely the novel's performative readers – if they sense their own activity mirrored back to them as cause to reflex affect – may well recall an earlier moment in Powers's fiction. The overloaded circuits of phonorobotic Helen, the eponymous Galatea 2.2, have engorged volumes of literary-historical data with skewed acuity before pleading finally to see the worded world on its own specular terms, if only through the electronic mediation of her "magic lantern." But even apart from such visual aids, among more than a dozen questions on famous texts alluded to with equally oblique but signature snippets, the computer "wanted to know" who "this 'Reader' was and why he rated knowing who married whom" – as well as wondering, at the metanarrative level, what "it meant to be 'only a novel.'"[85] *Jane Eyre*'s famous "Reader, I married him"[86] going unmentioned has its way of universalizing the audience address of prose fiction; *Northanger Abbey*'s bracketing off of the fictional offers a rudimentary metanarrative gesture in those relativizing three words. And to the latter question, the latent answer – provided first by *Plowing the Dark*, then by *Bewilderment*: to be a novel "only" is to approximate life never more closely than by language's own modes of immersive virtuality and affective transfer. Over a century of diverse ocular

---

[83] Ezra Klein, "Ezra Klein Interviews Richard Powers," *New York Times* (September 28, 2021), www.nytimes.com/2021/09/28/opinion/ezra-klein-podcast-richard-powers.html.

[84] Richard Powers, "How to Speak a Book," *New York Times* (January 7, 2007), www.nytimes.com/2007/01/07/books/review/Powers2.t.html. On the metalinguistics of Powers's brief but compelling sketch of orality's evolution into literacy – and the replay of this trajectory in the produced "phonemes" of every reading act – see Stewart, *The Metanarrative Hall of Mirrors*, 99. This avowed poetics of dictation returns us, coincidentally enough, to our opening example from Henry James, who began his long-standing practice of dictation to a typist halfway through the composition of *What Maisy Knew* – so that the opening analogy of "dancing" patterns or "shadows" on a "sheet" for the lantern blur of Daisy's apprehension might have had a different valence if appearing later in the novel, where the typescript analogue would have been more like the clicked heels of keystrokes.

[85] Powers, *Galatea 2.2*, 294.

[86] Charlotte Brontë, *Jane Eyre* (Project Gutenberg, 1998), www.gutenberg.org/files/1260/1260-h/1260-h.htm.

and cerebral evidence has been meant to confirm this premise. Different visual and neural *media*, in sum, from mechanical to electronic, when summoned to description in the same linguistic *medium*, throw into relief the full range of prose's own technical affordances. <:=read/out_textual process to ^phenomenal imprint^=:>

CHAPTER 15

Critique

Gabriel Hankins

The war over critique stands as the signal intellectual controversy of the early twenty-first century, at least in the literary and cultural disciplines where it has been most active. The debate over critique could hardly fail to encroach on digital literary studies, and indeed it has come to define an entire wave of work in the field. That work is, broadly speaking, "political" and "critical," committed to certain political readings and orientations. Yet just as much contemporary work firmly rejects the premises of critique either in favor of a traditional philological orientation or in favor of "postcritique" and allied positions. Fundamental questions remain unanswered and unclarified here: Is contemporary work in digital literary studies by its very nature "postcritical" or does it still circle within critique's general intellectual trajectory? What are the legacies of critique, and how should we engage them? What does cultural critique mean now, and what should we take from the critique wars, if anything?

This chapter surveys the history of critique before turning to the uses of critique for digital literary work. I will make the case for a self-reflective mode of digital literary theory and practice, one that takes the long intellectual and political history of critique seriously: not as a series of enclosed conversations to be surveyed, but as a continuous challenge and supplement to dominant modes of thinking and acting, including our own received critical languages. Rather than a series of enclosures, critique deserves to remain part of our disciplinary commons, as a mode of thinking, a critical inheritance, and a contested terrain. Critique has a history which should be remembered, and has generated several generations of digital projects aimed at recovery, resistance, and resonance. But critique is not singular or monolithic. At its best, the incitement to critique develops new conceptual tools and questions their use, advances the core purposes of the disciplines without reifying into yet another fixed vocabulary. Critique must retain a suspicion of its own characteristic moves, its tendency toward a theoretical athleticism that avoids commitments, as

Stuart Hall argued during the rapid incursion of cultural studies on American shores.[1] Commitment, belief, and prejudgment are concealed in critique's characteristic unveilings, fundamental to its position but inimical to its process.[2]

This chapter approaches the problem of critique for literary studies in the digital age through the historical genealogy of the problem, a genealogy that illuminates the contemporary critical divisions that the problem has engendered. I recall the "method wars" over critique and postcritique, and then examine specific waves of digital literary studies work motivated by the demands for cultural and methodological critique. A genealogy of critique does not imply that the subject is "merely" historical, however. If critique denotes "a reflective theory which gives agents a kind of knowledge productive of enlightenment and emancipation," our epistemological and political horizons are always intimately entangled in the battle over critique.[3] We have never, as modern subjects, not been enmeshed in the problem of critique, even when we dissent from its more characteristic moves, affects, and metaphors.

15.1 Histories of Critique

Critique arises historically out of aesthetic criticism, a contested birth that shapes a continuing antagonism. As a scholarly term, "critique" has no exact counterpart in German or French, as both *Kritik* and *la nouvelle critique*, for example, refer to criticism more generally, even as they include the possibility of a more general history of Enlightenment reason. That history is surveyed in Reinhart Koselleck's *Kritik und Krise* (1959), a major sociological and philological study of the "pathogenesis of modern society" in the cycle of crises associated with the Enlightenment critique.[4] As Koselleck demonstrates, critique arises in the European context out of

---

[1] Stuart Hall, "Cultural Studies and Its Theoretical Legacies," in *Cultural Studies*, ed. Lawrence Grossberg, Cary Nelson, and Paula Treichler (New York: Routledge, 1992), 277–294.

[2] Understood as *Vorurteil*, following Hans-Georg Gadamer, *Truth and Method* (New York: Continuum, 1975) [translation of *Wahrheit und Methode: Grundzüge einer philosophischen Hermeneutik* (Tübingen: Mohr, 1960)].

[3] Raymond Geuss, *The Idea of a Critical Theory: Habermas and the Frankfurt School* (Cambridge: Cambridge University Press, 1999), 2.

[4] The following account is indebted to Reinhart Koselleck, *Critique and Crisis: Enlightenment and the Pathogenesis of Modern Society* (Cambridge, MA: MIT Press, 1988), originally a doctoral thesis published as *"Kritik und Krise: Ein Beitrag zur Pathogenese der bürgerlichen Welt"* (Freiberg: Alber, 1959); and to Simon During, "The Eighteenth-Century Origins of Critique," in *Critique and Postcritique*, ed. Elizabeth S. Anker and Rita Felski (Durham: Duke University Press, 2017), 73–96.

early humanist textual dispute and religious controversy: the first seventeenth-century "critical texts" were readings of the Bible according to the "veritable Loix de la Critique," as in Richard Simon's *Histoire Critique du Vieux Testament*. These rational laws of critique were supposed to transcend sect and schism, uniting Simon's justification of the Catholic ecclesiastic tradition with the Protestant demand "sola scriptura!"[5] The notion of a "critical text" survives in contemporary biblical studies and textual studies more broadly, where it refers to the careful comparison of textual versions. What was meant by "critique" in the seventeenth century was, on the one hand, the objective evaluation of ancient texts, and on the other hand, the evaluation of literature, art, and music. The systematic movement from aesthetic criticism to a more general critique, and in particular from the laws of aesthetics to the laws of the polity, would be characteristic of a later period.[6]

Critique as the specific and characteristic stance productive of "enlightenment and emancipation" (as in Geuss's definition of "critical theory") appears in a decisive new form in the eighteenth century. Koselleck's ideal-type history offers one polemical account of the genesis of political critique, an account fundamental to such critical theorists as Jürgen Habermas: out of the devastation of the religious civil wars, the state creates a new political order that moves individuals into a private sphere, creates a monopoly on legitimate violence, and neutralizes the moral demands of religious affiliation through subordination to the Absolutist ruler. But through the demands for moral autonomy made by individuals newly given a realm of private morality, through the rising bourgeois class and its characteristic attitudes and interests (art criticism, theater, literary debate) – importantly through collective spaces like the coffee-house, the club, and the Masonic Lodge – the political legitimacy of the Absolutist State, its right to a sovereign "decision" over political matters, would be radically challenged by the "Enlightened" rationalist critic.[7] As Koselleck puts it, "Each one thus becomes a judge who knows, on grounds of his enlightenment, that he is authorized to try whatever heteronomous definitions contradict his moral autonomy."[8]

---

[5] Richard Simon, *Histoire Critique du Vieux Testament par R. P. Rich. Simon* (Paris, 1680), Preface; cited in Koselleck, 105–106.
[6] Koselleck: "This use of 'criticism' to denote methods of developing laws of beauty, their recognition or production ... is characteristic for the genesis of the bourgeois sense of self. Philosophy and art criticism entered into a personal union" (108 ft. 31).
[7] In the terms of Carl Schmitt, the jurist and political theorist on whom Koselleck draws: see *The Concept of the Political*, trans. George Schwab (Chicago: University of Chicago Press, 2007).
[8] Koselleck, 11.

Yet this accession of the bourgeois critic to the role of sovereign judge, without any access to formal political representation and power (particularly in absolutist throne-and-altar states), leads to a fundamental dialectic between political power itself and the Enlightenment: the political present becomes the Other to rational critique, a fallen desert of the real to critique's utopian Eden. This dualism leads to a fundamental orientation toward the future as the only realm of legitimate politics, to the continual posing of new concepts and their equally continual negation, and, finally, for Koselleck, to a political utopianism that began with the Terror and culminated in fascism and Stalinism. Koselleck's reading of Pierre Bayle's *Dictionnaire Historique et Critique* (1695) explicates the temporal orientation he finds in critique in resonant terms:

> Bayle's critic also knows only one obligation: his duty to a future in which truth is found only through the exercise of criticism ... The self-assurance of criticism [*Kritik*] lay in the connection of the critic to yet-to-be-discovered truth. Every error discovered, every hurdle overcome reveals fresh obstacles; thus the human compulsion to unravel finds ever more subtle methods to seize on evil and do away with the continuous flow of confusion, until finally there is nothing left for critics to do. Criticism transformed the future into a maelstrom that sucked out the present from under the feet of the critic. In these circumstances there was nothing left for the critic but to see progress as the temporal structure appropriate to his way of life. Progress became the *modus vivendi* of criticism even when – as in Bayle – it was not deemed a forward movement but one of destruction and decadence.[9]

Habermas and others would take over many of the terms of this account, particularly its notion of the development of bourgeois civil society in the public sphere fashioned by private individuals, while renarrating the subsequent development of Enlightenment critique as a progressive orientation toward the production of greater emancipatory possibility, in the present as well as the future. An equally influential Marxist historicization of critique emplots Enlightenment reason into a tragic dialectic, as the ever-accelerating use of rational means for ever more irrational ends. Against the rationalization of mass murder and the industrialization of culture, Adorno and Horkheimer pose a commitment to immanent critique. But the role of the "cultural critic" within that larger struggle is necessarily paradoxical for Adorno: "The words [*Kulturkritik*] recall a flagrant contradiction. The cultural critic is not happy with civilization,

---

[9] Koselleck, 109. Citing Pierre Bayle, *Dictionnaire Historique et Critique* (1695; Rotterdam 1720, 3rd ed.).

to which alone he owes his discontent. He speaks as if he represented either unadulterated nature or a higher historical stage. Yet he is necessarily of the same essence as that to which he fancies himself superior."[10]

15.2 Contemporary Critique and the Method Wars

The battles over critique in digital literary studies are part of a long-running debate over political readings, a debate reaching back as early as Adorno's essays of the thirties in favor of autonomous art and against the "committed literature" proposed by Sartre. Political critique gained new currency in the revolt against established humanist ideals after 1968, a revolt against establishment ideas that generated its own counter-reformation within and without the humanities. Late-twentieth-century political critique in the literary disciplines inherited many contradictory intellectual legacies: the battle over a Marxist, post-Marxist, or neo-Marxist politics as the ultimate horizon of interpretation; the liberation movements against racial, sexual, and queer oppression; the post-1968 move toward the study of ordinary or "popular" culture; the work of Foucault, Deleuze, Derrida, and co., formalized in what François Cusset has called the specifically North American invention of "French Theory";[11] and the more equivocal legacy of modern philosophical skepticism, inherited by those "masters of suspicion" that Paul Ricœur put at the foundation of the modern mode of interpretation – Marx, Nietzsche, and Freud. That Marx appears twice here, first as a political legacy and second as a thinker, is not incidental to the story of the war over critique: that we cannot fully know the nature of our own thought without a reflective theory of the economic and social history that produces that knowledge (to paraphrase Geuss) is a distinctive premise of Marxist historicism.

Late twentieth-century thinkers associated with "critique" differ in their view of what should be considered the fundamental underlying, unspoken, artfully concealed forces that lie beneath the veil of appearances – economic forces, class and racial supremacy, the id, the history of power – but they tend to coalesce around a hermeneutic and rhetoric of suspicion and unveiling in the late twentieth century.[12] Along with the enclosing of intellectual life almost entirely within academic contexts, and the need for stable methods

---

[10] Theodor Adorno, *Prisms* (Cambridge, MA: MIT Press, 1997), 17.
[11] François Cusset. *French Theory: How Foucault, Derrida, Deleuze, & Co. Transformed the Intellectual Life of the United States* (Minneapolis: University of Minnesota Press, 2008).
[12] See chapter 4 of *The Limits of Critique*, and Felski's earlier version, "Critique and the Hermeneutics of Suspicion," *M/C Journal* 15.1 (November 26, 2011).

and disciplinary procedures that came with it, the overall trajectory of critique is one of institutionalization, professionalization, and standardization, among other bureaucratic formations that critical theorists both resist and enact.

Suspicion of the institutionalization of critique is as old as critique itself; indeed, such suspicion can be seen as intrinsic to critique's uneasy balance between scrutiny of the observed and the self-positioning of the observer. In the mid-twentieth century many practitioners of critique voiced uneasiness with its institutionalized forms. Susan Sontag followed Adorno in her resistance to programmatic critical hermeneutics of the kind associated with Freudian and Marxist critique, famously concluding *Against Interpretation* (1961) with a call for an erotics rather than a hermeneutics of art. Peter Sloterdijk engaged in a more extended *Critique of Cynical Reason* (1983), a reckoning with the diminution of post-1968 student movements into cynical theory. Michel Foucault's entire project, often taken as representative of "critique" as such, develops in part out of the exhaustion of phenomenological and Marxist critical vocabularies in postwar French philosophy;[13] his premise that oppositional discourses always run the risk of recapitulating the dominant ideology they oppose is exemplified in *The Order of Things* (1966) by Marx's reception of the economic and mercantilist assumptions of David Ricardo. Critique always runs the risk of imprisonment within the vocabulary it criticizes: this is a fundamental problem not just for Marxists but for critical theory more generally.

British cultural studies, in its first institutional forms at Birmingham, generally developed a skeptical and pragmatic approach to critique, demanding attention to working-class resistance and rebellion against the ruling-class ideas embedded in literature as well as film, television, fashion, and ordinary life. Cultural studies theorists differ in their sympathies from the typical distance and objectivity implied in mid-century critique (for example in Althusser's retention of the Marxist tradition of critique as historical "science"), engaging in noncynical readings of what Adorno and Horkheimer call "mass culture": cultural texts as reflective of utopian desires, potential sites of liberation, filled with the energy of the carnivalesque, open to textual poaching and recoding from excluded positions. Critical moves to "surface reading" (Best and Marcus), Robyn Wiegman's "object lessons," Heather Love's move toward

---

[13] See Barry Smart, *Foucault, Marxism, and Critique* (London: Routledge and Kegan Paul, 1983) on the relation between "critical theory" as ideology critique and Foucault's notion of critique (135).

a reading practice that would be "close but not deep," Elizabeth S. Anker's "integrative criticism," and recent work on ordinary language philosophy by Toril Moi and others, are all inherent this long history of critical resistance to critique, and all suggest theoretical moves beyond its standard repertoire.[14]

The method wars were truly joined by the move to "postcritique," and by a book that at once crystalized the debates over critique and catalyzed a wave of vehement response: Rita Felski's *The Limits of Critique* (2015). Despite, or because of, its continuing drive toward theoretical and methodological self-criticism, late twentieth-century and twenty-first century critique consolidates in a familiar set of orientations, affects, and objects, Felski argues. Critique employs characteristic spatial metaphors ("digging down" and "standing back") and the classic narrative emplotments of detective fiction: the collection of the clues and the narrative tension of unconcealment. Distance is crucial to critique, as it prefers the secondary and symbiotic: it does its thinking by responding to the thinking of others, by commentary and metacommentary on a familiar text.[15] Little surprise that literary scholars have been attracted to critique, as it arises from an essential primary act of literary scholarship itself: textual criticism. Here we can find one of the shared keywords that divide digital philologists, many still engaged in textual criticism in the sense of ascertaining and preserving texts, from the practitioners of critique, engaged in a secularized mode of elaboration and commentary on postsacral materials. Yet, like the sacred and the profane, the preservation of the text and the negations of critique form two sides of a dialectical whole.

For Felski, critique is more like an ethos or disposition than a philosophical position, and as such does not lend itself to normative or propositional explanation. In the Marxist critical literature, for example, such key terms as "mediation" are not clearly defined, in part because definitions would reify the movement of thought itself.[16] Critique is intellectual: self-reflexive, second-order, drawn to metahistory, metanarratives,

---

[14] Stephen Best and Sharon Marcus. "Surface Reading: An Introduction." *Representations* 108.1 (2009): 1–21. https://doi.org/10.1525/rep.2009.108.1.1. Heather Love, "Close but Not Deep: Literary Ethics and the Descriptive Turn." *New Literary History* 41.2 (2010): 371–391. Elizabeth Anker, *On Paradox: The Claims of Theory* (Durham: Duke University Press, 2022). Toril Moi, *Revolution of the Ordinary: Literary Studies after Wittgenstein, Austin, and Cavell* (Chicago: The University of Chicago Press, 2017).

[15] Rita elski, *The Limits of Critique* (Chicago: The University of Chicago Press, 2015), 121.

[16] See a lucid counterexample in Anna Kornbluh's recent *Marxist Film Theory and Fight Club* (London: Bloomsbury 2019), which does attempt and then enact a definition of mediation.

metatheory.[17] It prizes difficulty, certain kinds of obscurity, and a critical idiom that defamiliarizes its nouns and problematizes its verbs. An attachment to deliberate critical opacity, to contradiction, paradox, and the infinite regress of "a justice to come," binds the language of critique to the aesthetic disposition itself, understood as still attuned to that negative capability that refuses easy conclusions and closures of meaning. That sensibility clashes immediately with the graphs, maps, and algorithms of much work in digital literary studies, easily taken to suggest the superficial closure of a badly posed problem.

Critique is famously negative in other senses: it renders a less than favorable verdict on its object, and turns most clearly negative when aimed at the critic herself, in the almost mandatory practice of private self-scrutiny and public self-disclosure that Ian Hunter suggested connects the spiritual intelligentsia of the seventeenth and twentieth centuries.[18] This insistence on self-scrutiny, coupled with the modernist insistence on "making it new" and the inherent orientation toward the future as a horizon of political meaning within critique, produce endless dissatisfactions and reconfigurations in the cultures of critique. At the level of disciplinary fields – as in American studies, for example – that attachment to self-criticism produces cyclical waves of scholarship that proclaim a fresh "critical" avant-garde by disavowing the previous wave of work: American literature requires the political and social correction of a new paradigm of politically oriented work, in American studies; but American studies is too attached to its object, or too essentialist in its ethnocentrism, and thus implicitly upholds the evils of the American imperium, so requires a transnational American studies; but transnational American studies is complicit with global capitalism, reflecting its role in the transnational political order without being able to reflect upon it, and so on.[19] Waves of fashion and attachment to the newest "turn" are not incidental but programmatic, even as the critical attachment to specific methods and canons are retained.[20] Such dynamics are clearly in evidence within recent work in digital literary critique, moving at an even more rapid rate, but in frequent tension with statistical and philological work in the field.

[17] Felski, *The Limits of Critique*, 135.
[18] Ibid., 127; Ian Hunter, *Rethinking the School: Subjectivity, Bureaucracy, Criticism* (New York: St. Martin's Press, 1994), 167.
[19] See Robyn Wiegman, *Object Lessons* (Durham: Duke University Press, 2012).
[20] See Eric Hayot "Then and Now," in *Critique and Postcritique*, ed. Elizabeth S. Anker and Rita Felski (Durham: Duke University Press, 2017), 279–295.

Critique identifies itself from below even as it speaks *ex cathedra*: it enacts a solidarity of the critic with the oppressed, the misread, the dominated and despised, even as it employs a vocabulary usually unavailable to those with whom it sympathizes, from class positions positioned differently from its object of sympathy.[21] Critique is aimed precisely at "ruling-class ideas," as British Marxism put it. Class critique is a major source of contention within digital literary studies itself, and a potential source of confusion in the turn toward tactical and political readings. What could be more "ruling-class" in an era of digital disruption than the adaptation and instrumental use of digital tools? And wouldn't critique of such tools, even as we study them carefully and employ them judiciously, enact our alignment with the oppressed? Yes and no: clearly we need a reflective and critical digital hermeneutics, especially insofar as we employ digital tools; just as clearly the language of critique does not cash out in an immediate solidarity with the oppressed without other kinds of political engagement.

The privileged critic is always snared in the double bind of institutionalized critique as a classed language: we can correctly point to the inequalities and injustice of racial privilege, for example, in language that demonstrates and enacts our own class and institutional privilege. That French civil servants must now demonstrate their familiarity with Bourdieu's notion of *habitus* for the purpose of the civil service exams concisely demonstrates the double bind of a classed language of class privilege. The attempts of digital theorists to develop a language for algorithmic oppression, for example, necessarily engage in the double bind inherent to critique's alignment with and separation from the languages of the oppressed. That double bind still holds for work that claims to draw its authority from suppressed forms of knowledge, from marginal or transgressive critical positions. This does not mean that we should do away with the political horizons of our work, or adjure political vocabularies as such, but that we should recognize instead in good Marxist fashion the contradictions of intellectual work that engages the struggle against an age of digital instrumentalism, data science solutionism, and pervasive surveillance (amongst other pressing concerns) from *within* surveillance capitalism, not some point outside it.

Nonsecular or postsecular forms of thinking and being pose a particular problem for critique's embrace of the dispossessed and marginal. As Talal Assad pointed out in the debate over secular critique, secular critique often

---

[21] Felski, *Limits of Critique*, 140.

fails to address the experiences of non-Western religious thought, as of the forms of thinking in the West that precede and produce secular modernity.[22] Digital literary studies, like "digital humanities" more generally, rooted as it often is in textual studies, textual commentary, and other practices distinctively associated with the preservation of the sacred Word – Father Busa springs to mind here as a symptomatic sublimation of the theological roots of digital textual studies – has much at stake in this desacralization of literate culture, and in the possible models that historically replaced religious belief in the West: the nation, republican citizenship, or utopian forms of politics itself.

One version of critical "postcritique" enacts various forms of the re-enchantment of the text, whether through its canonical figures, as in the astonishing annotated version of Derrida's personal library at Princeton, or through the discovery of new saints.[23] The recent literary canonization of Toni Morrison has many of the features typical of this secular canonization, including the testaments to the miracles of her prose, the brilliant careers of her disciples, and the allegorization of her life. Postcritique has some intellectual affinities to studies rooted in a particular embodied identity, despite the strong association of critique with what Robyn Wiegman calls "identity studies": the first moment of affirmation and commitment rhetorically enacted by many of these fields is simply the affirmation that the writer-subject is queer, or a transman, or racialized, or cyborg, or psychosocially disabled, and that this identity-position provides an inescapable foundation for thinking and acting, a necessary prelude to theory.[24]

Postcritique arises in large part through an exhaustion with the styles and structures of critique, as with the habituation of such once-common academic verbs as "problematize," "transgress," and "trouble." Eve Kosofsky Sedgwick's argument for a queer model of reparative reading, against standard paranoid reading styles, was a particularly clear moment of the move past critique by one of the canonized founders of queer theory, and remains a contested moment of departure in gender and sexuality studies. Rita Felski and Elizabeth S. Anker point to other possible models of postcritique in their collected volume on the subject, ranging from neophenomenological models to affect theory to the literary reception of

---

[22] In Talal Asad, Wendy Brown, Judith Butler, and Saba Mahmood. *Is Critique Secular? Blasphemy, Injury, and Free Speech* (New York: Fordham University Press, 2013).
[23] See Katie Chenoweth et al., *Derrida's Margins*: https://derridas-margins.princeton.edu/.
[24] For the final category see Kara Stone, "Time and Reparative Game Design: Queerness, Disability, and Affect," *Game Studies* 18.3 (December 2018). http://gamestudies.org/1803/articles/stone.

ordinary language philosophy. Paul Saint-Amour, Wai Chee Dimock, and Grace Lavery, among others, have called for the development of "weak theories" of the attachments between text, history, and world, drawing on Gianni Vattimo's notion of weak theory after the death of grand theoretical narratives. Saint-Amour and Grace Lavery claim large swathes of work in queer theory, affect theory, new historicism, and even (outrageously) moments in the work of Fredric Jameson, an icon of "strong" historicist critique.[25] Work in weak theory has the apparent advantage of embracing the traditional particularism, contingency, and individuality prized in literary studies: this is precisely why we should distrust it, for Marxists, antihumanist theorists, and many others.

For not everyone has been enchanted by postcritique, to say the least. The most serious objections made a series of interconnected points. First, no one now practices the straw-man or ideal-type of critique: the centrality of Fredric Jameson's early book on the political unconscious, but not his later work on postmodernism, cinema, science fiction and utopia, is taken as symptomatic of postcritique's theoretical simplifications.[26] Many critics contended that the turn away from political readings implied in some forms of postcritique either misunderstood its moment or was symptomatically allied with the long reaction to post-1968 theory across the humanities. More pointedly, Marxist theorists warn that critical activity must remain attentive to the ongoing diagnosis of capitalist society performed in Marxist critique. Anna Kornbluh argues, against postcritique, that literary works themselves already perform the work of critique, when imaginatively read, and calls her readers to reengagement with totality as a horizon (not object) of analysis.[27] Kornbluh and other critics read postcritique symptomatically, as a narrowing of intellectual and political horizons in a time of profound crisis in literary studies and the world, a constriction that offers no equivalent new project or method.

---

[25] Grace Lavery, Paul Saint-Amour, Aarthi Vadde, et al., "Responses to the Responses to the Special Issue on Weak Theory," *Modernism/modernity Print Plus*, (Volume 4 cycle 2, August 15, 2019). https://modernismmodernity.org/forums/posts/responses-responses-special-issue-weak-theory.

[26] See Bruce Robbins's vehement response in "Not So Well Attached." *PMLA* 132.2 (March 1, 2017): 371–376. https://doi.org/10.1632/pmla.2017.132.2.371. Bruce Robbins's own work, however, shares much of postcritique's skepticism about the aporias and complacencies associated with the critique of professionalism, state institutions, and "neoliberalism" in literary studies, as in "Everything Is Not Neoliberalism." *American Literary History* 31.4 (November 1, 2019): 840–849.

[27] See Anna Kornbluh, "We Have Never Been Critical: Toward the Novel as Critique," *Novel: A Forum on Fiction* 50.3 (November 11, 2017): 397–408; and "Extinct Critique," *The South Atlantic Quarterly* 119.4 (October 2020): 767–777.

The method wars took specific and local form for digital literary studies in the debate over neoliberalism and complicity within the larger digital humanities, a controversy that should be briefly recalled, as it played out as a contest over attitudes, methods, and epistemologies that would be formative for later political work in the field. Prominent in the debates over critique was the "Dark Side of the Digital Humanities" issue of *differences: a feminist journal*, the attack on digital literary and textual studies as one of the "neoliberal tools" of the corporate university, and the #transformDH movement. All these were roughly simultaneous political rebellions, all with their primary points of reference in literary and cultural studies.[28] "Neoliberal Tools (and Archives): A Political History of the Digital Humanities," widely read in the Los Angeles Review of Books, exemplifies the symptomatic style within critique, moving quite directly from "the unparalleled level of material support that Digital Humanities has received" to "its (perhaps unintentional) facilitation of the neoliberal takeover of the university," in one introductory sentence.[29] All "explicit claims" to the contrary, *because of* those strenuous disavowals, digital humanities – by which is meant mostly digital literary and textual studies – is "not about ... the use of digital or quantitative methodologies to answer research questions in the humanities," but rather about the dismissal of political research, the denigration of "traditional" methods and modes of scholarship, and, ultimately, the fire sale of the humanities.[30] See, for instance, Alan Liu, Rita Raley, Fiona Barnett, and Tara McPherson, who, less polemically, called in the *differences* issue for a digital humanities that would put cultural and institutional critique at the center of the conversation.[31]

Within digital literary studies, Alan Liu has long investigated a question he made pointedly to the field in 2011: Where is cultural criticism in our field, and where should it go?[32] Liu's own answer to the question points to

---

[28] See "The Dark Side of the Digital Humanities," *differences* 25.1 (May 1, 2014): 26–45. https://doi.org/10.1215/10407391-2419991; Moya Bailey, Anne Cong-Huyen, Alexis Lothian, and Amanda Phillips, "Reflections on a Movement: #transformDH, Growing Up," in *Debates in the Digital Humanities 2016*, ed. Matt Gold and Lauren Klein (Minneapolis: University of Minnesota Press, 2016), 71–80.

[29] Daniel Allington, Sarah Brouillette, and David Golumbia. "Neoliberal Tools (and Archives): A Political History of Digital Humanities." *Los Angeles Review of Books*, May 1 2016. https://lareviewofbooks.org/article/neoliberal-tools-archives-political-history-digital-humanities/.

[30] Ibid.

[31] Rita Raley, "Digital Humanities for the Next Five Minutes," *differences* 25.1 (May 1, 2014): 26–45. https://doi.org/10.1215/10407391-2419991.

[32] Alan Liu, "Where Is Cultural Criticism in the Digital Humanities?" in *Debates in the Digital Humanities*, ed. Matthew K. Gold (Minneapolis: University of Minnesota Press, 2012), 490–509.

an engagement with new media theorists, hackers, and artists, along with an investigation of technological infrastructures as both material and cultural, following science and technology studies. In response to the work of Liu and others, we have seen a wave of work that affirmed or affiliated itself with political goals and readings, that explicitly aligned itself with a "critical digital humanities" – thus standing as inheritor of one lineage of the critical tradition described earlier – or that positioned itself within a set of intersections: postcolonial digital humanities, feminist data science, Black and Caribbean DH, queer digital literary studies, digital disability studies.[33] Alan Liu has redescribed such intersectional work through the metaphors of the "contact zone" and the "diversity stack," after the modular structure of internet protocols, organized in "layers of abstraction, each limited in its goals because it is about doing one thing well."[34]

In the North American context this work inherits much of the language and practice of intersectionality originally developed in Black feminist and critical race theory, including the description of intellectual work as situated in particular racialized, gendered, colonized, classed, and differently abled sites, within which the practitioner of a critical digital vocabulary positions their work.[35] Outside that context a different sense of intersectional might obtain: the inevitably contested political and disciplinary intersections of the digital and literary in various national and linguistic contexts, across fields and regions, between the global South and the old metropoles, between Afro-Caribbean DH and African *humanites numeriques*, all terrains of translation subject to what Brent Hayes Edwards calls the *décalage* (unevenness) of translation even within the shared struggle of a diasporic formation.[36] The shared languages and methods of critique that unite strands of literary studies, media studies, and cultural studies with some of the humanistic social sciences here acts as a potentially enabling metalanguage, if one that requires careful rhetorical positioning and historicizing. What would it mean, however, to imagine that metalinguistic exchange not as one of application, deployment, and

---

[33] See, among others, James Dodson, *Critical Digital Humanities: The Search for a Methodology* (Urbana: University of Illinois Press, 2019).
[34] Alan Liu, "Towards a Diversity Stack: Digital Humanities and Diversity as a Technical Problem," *PMLA: Publications of the Modern Language Association of America* 135.1 (January 1, 2020): 135.
[35] For the origins of Black feminist intersectionality as a concept, see Kimberlé Crenshaw, "Mapping the Margins: Intersectionality, Identity Politics, and Violence against Women of Color," *Stanford Law Review* 43.6 (1991): 1241–1300.
[36] See Brent Hayes Edwards, *The Practice of Diaspora: Literature, Translation, and the Rise of Black Internationalism* (Cambridge, MA.: Harvard University Press, 2003), 14.

validation through one canon of critique or another, but rather as an active project of construction, composition, and engagement? We might imagine the work of critique, that is, not as the endless search for the yet-to-be-discovered truth, on the lines of Bayle's critic, emplotted within an endlessly receding future perfect, but rather as the imperfect synthesis of new forms and collectives, the construction of frangible communities. Critique as critical reconstruction, building, and making, indeed, serves as one important of connection between Hegelian legacies within critique and the movement toward critical making in digital literary and media studies.[37]

15.3 Languages of Critique: Intersectional Feminism, Neoliberal Horizons, and Decolonized Archives

The work of critique within digital literary studies did not begin just in the last wave of tactical and political work: that history is essential to recall when considering particular approaches and areas of critical work. Feminist digital literary studies, for example, have a long history that new entrants should know, certainly including the archival and recovery work at the Women Writers Project, the Orlando Project, the Poetess Archive, Josephine Miles's mid-twentieth century work on phrasal forms in poetry across three centuries, and more recent intersectional feminist approaches that build on the work of critical race theory.[38] Some of the first generations of digital literary projects and archives have survived; many more have not.[39] Critical vocabularies preserve and remake another intellectual inheritance, just as easily lost. Marxist and cultural studies work in particular has a long history of self-reflection and refinement that deserves recollection in historically informed critique. This critical legacy includes the method and practice of articulation; such key ideas as interpellation, ideology, and hegemony; and the idea of the "situatedness" of the critic themselves, referring to the self-reflective and contradictory position of the

---

[37] On the latter, see Jentery Sayers, ed., *Making Things and Drawing Boundaries* (Minneapolis: University of Minnesota Press, 2018).

[38] See Julia Flanders et al., *The Women Writers Project* (www.wwp.northeastern.edu/); Susan Brown, Patricia Clements, and Isobel Grundy, eds., *The Orlando Project* (https://cwrc.ca/orlando); Laura Mandell, general editor, *The Poetess Archive* (www.poetessarchive.org/); and Rachel Sagner Buurma and Laura Heffernan, "Search and Replace: Josephine Miles and the Origins of Distant Reading," *Modernism/Modernity Print Plus*, https://modernismmodernity.org/forums/posts/search-and-replace.

[39] See, again, Earhart, "The Era of the Archive."

critic within particular economic, social, racial, and discursive conjunctions that they both participate in and analyze.

Recollection of this critical inheritance does not imply repetition, however, nor a mere litany of critical terms and categories: critique as synthesis means wrestling productively with the critical vocabularies that bring structure to individual projects and collective experience. Neoliberalism serves here as a prime example, a node through which an entire critical vocabulary is connected. As a term for specific developments in the last half-century of capitalism, neoliberalism has a storied history, from its extensive treatment in Michel Foucault's lectures of the late seventies at the Collége du France to the more materialist analysis of David Harvey.[40] Whether understood as an all-encompassing privatization and pervasive orientation toward the market, as in Wendy Brown's analysis, or as a specific economic and political program developed within certain sites and institutions, neoliberalism indicates specific economic and political changes to postwar social democracy.[41] Neoliberalism – like "platform capitalism" or, indeed, "modernity" – functions differently as a horizon of understanding, a historical moment of subject formation within which the critic is situated and situates herself. Yet a horizon of understanding is not the same as a universal framework for explanation or the hidden motor of all literary production. As Bruce Robbins notes, everything is not neoliberalism: the need to position contemporary literary culture within the ever-shifting neoliberal present can lead to underdetermined broadstrokes analysis, shifting terms of reference, and the loss of particular class conflicts and economic conjunctions.[42]

Rather than broad invocations of neoliberalism, recent digital literary critique has attended to the finely tuned ways that market-rationalist literary production works in the "era of Amazon," through what specific networks of algorithmic preference, though the racialized market comparisons that Laura McGrath describes as "comping white," through what counter-publics and fandoms, through what modes and tactics

---

[40] See Michel Foucault, *The Birth of Biopolitics: Lectures at the Collège de France, 1978–79*, ed. Michel Senellart; trans. Graham Burchell (Basingstoke: Palgrave Macmillan, 2008).

[41] See Wendy Brown, *Undoing the Demos* (New York: Zone, 2015) and Dieter Plehwe, Quinn Slobodian, and Phillip Mirowski, eds., *Nine Lives of Neoliberalism* (London: Verso 2020), on the institutional history and development of neoliberalism.

[42] Bruce Robbins, "Everything Is Not Neoliberalism," *American Literary History* 31.4 (November 1, 2019): 840–849, a review of Mitchum Huels and Rachel Greenwald Smith, eds., *Neoliberalism and Contemporary Literary Culture* (Baltimore: Johns Hopkins University Press, 2017).

of reading.[43] Though we need not rehearse the history of postwar economic order to position our work, digital critique must confront the ever-more-inescapable digital mediation of EdTech platform pedagogy, information wholesalers, and gamified life chances. Digital critique must be positioned within the accelerated algorithmic marketization of everyday life, within the data-extractive economies that Nick Srnicek historicizes as "platform capitalism," as within the critical infrastructures articulated within and against such platforms and rationalisms. These critiques need not be articulated in each project, but should underpin the larger self-understanding of the field.[44] We need to collectively position our work within these networks even as we acknowledge that contemporary neoliberal capitalism remains "as such" impossible to represent, as Fredric Jameson said of an earlier stage of late capitalism.

One of the strongest drives within the communities of critique that contribute to digital literary studies has been the push for more self-reflexive, situated, and embodied accounts of the labor that produces apparently frictionless and transparent digital technologies.[45] This move in part reiterates calls within the first generations of Marxist cultural studies for an account of the theorist's own class/gender/race position within a "complex system, structured in dominance" of certain positions over others (Althusser).[46] That need to establish the speaker as partisan and participant in "culture as a whole way of struggle," to paraphrase an old slogan from E. P. Thompson, has expanded to include a much broader range of dominative or coercive structures, including the normative identities associated with heterosexuality, stable sex/gender identity, ability, and position within the caste structure (of several types). Distant readings, on the model of Franco Moretti's influential work, have given way to tactical, situated, intersectional, and embodied readings, as theorists have increasingly focused digital methods and corpora onto corporal life: the essays in Losh and Wernimont's *Bodies of Information* are exemplary of this more general

[43] Mark McGurl, "Everything and Less: Fiction in the Age of Amazon," *Modern Language Quarterly: A Journal of Literary History* 77.3 (September 9, 2016): 447–471; Laura B. McGrath, "Comping White," *Los Angeles Review of Books*. https://lareviewofbooks.org/article/comping-white/.
[44] Nick Srnicek, *Platform Capitalism* (Cambridge: Polity Press, 2016).
[45] For examples see Shawna Ross and Andrew Pilsch, eds., *Humans at Work in the Digital Age: Forms of Digital Textual Labor* (New York: Routledge, 2020).
[46] See Stuart Hall's revision of Althusser in "Race, Articulation and Societies Structured in Dominance": "Race is thus, also, the modality in which class is 'lived', the medium through which class relations are experienced, the form in which it is appropriated and 'fought through'" (in Marion O'Callaghan, ed., *Sociological Theories: Race and Colonialism*. Paris: Unesco, 1980), 305–345; 341. For the original discussion of "dominance" see Ben Brewster's "Althusser Glossary" of 1969, reprinted in Louis Althusser and Ben Brewster, trans., *For Marx* (London: Verso, 2005).

theoretical moment.[47] Insights in Science and Technology Studies, media studies, and Human-Computer Interaction (HCI) join with recent movements in cultural studies: the turn or return to materialist accounts; affective approaches to technology; and decolonial, queer, and feminist approaches. Intersectional feminism has become a common language for a range of critical work, from Losh and Wernimont to Lauren Klein and Catherine D'Ignazio's *Data Feminism*, along with collaborative, generous, and collective authorship practices that break with the masculinist model of critical disruption.

A related area of shared concern between literary studies and digital critique is the decolonial reassessment of lingering colonial legacies in the digital archives now being instituted, in ways that reiterate classic liberal-imperialist archival forms.[48] Literary and linguistic archives are still overwhelmingly white, Anglophone, and biased toward European and settler-colonialist notions of what constitutes lasting "literature" – a problem for the epic literatures of primarily oral cultures.[49] Digital recovery projects, common in the first wave of archival work on the Internet, themselves now require recovery, as they have proved more fragile than the cultures they described.[50] Recent approaches to preserving indigenous cultural production have often focused on reading the "archival silences," or working with communities to form counternarratives and counterarchives, but silence itself can be a powerful tool of resistance against the official archive.[51] Silences in the archive represent not just the absent presence of the repressed, but a strategy for political survival within and outside our current regime of omnipresent digital surveillance and self-disclosure. The lives of the enslaved constitute one significant test for such digital recovery projects, as for broader archives such as the Trans-Atlantic Slave Trade Database at Emory. Lauren Klein demonstrates one mode in which digital tools can be both adapted and

---

[47] Elizabeth Losh and Jacqueline Wernimont, *Bodies of Information: Intersectional Feminism and Digital Humanities* (Minneapolis: University of Minnesota Press, 2018).
[48] See Patrick Joyce, "The Politics of the Liberal Archive," *History of the Human Sciences* 12.2 (May 1, 1999): 35–49. https://doi.org/10.1177/09526959922120234.
[49] On this problem, see David Golumbia, "Postcolonial Studies, Digital Humanities, and the Politics of Language," *Postcolonial Digital Humanities*. https://web.archive.org/web/20131207190925/http://dhpoco.org/blog/2013/05/31/postcolonial-studies-digital-humanities-and-the-politics-of-language/.
[50] See Amy Earhart on this problem in "The Era of the Archive: The New Historicist Movement and Digital Literary Studies," chapter 2 of *Traces of the Old, Uses of the New: The Emergence of Digital Literary Studies* (Ann Arbor: University of Michigan Press, 2015). https://doi.org/10.3998/etlc.13455322.0001.001.
[51] Rodney G. S. Carter, "Of Things Said and Unsaid: Power, Archival Silences, and Power in Silence," *Archivaria* 61.61 (September 25, 2006). http://journals.sfu.ca/archivar/index.php/archivaria/article/view/12541.

queried in her approach to recovering the importance of James Hemings within Thomas Jefferson's household economy through both visualization and close reading. As she emphasizes, this approach to archival silences must acknowledge, in Saidiya Hartman's words, that our narratives about figures like Hemings are "predicated upon impossibility ... and intent on achieving an impossible goal: redressing the violence that produced numbers, ciphers, and fragments."[52] That violence echoes the epistemic violence of an era of data surveillance in which Black bodies are still figured as numbers, ciphers, and fragments within digital dragnets.[53]

Some scholars resist the political methods of critique exactly because those methods arise out of political struggles in the present (the historicist critique of critique often called "presentism"). Digital editions of twelfth-century texts, they argue, should not be subjected to the identitarian calculus of twenty-first century politics. But no intellectual work occurs in a social and political vacuum, and no field can claim to be outside politics simply through the historical remove of its object: medieval studies itself has become the site of a contentious scholarly battle over the uses and abuses of medieval iconography as a source of white supremacist imagery and appropriation.[54] A self-reflexive mode of digital critique need not engage in that narcissism of endless self-positioning that ends in reaffirming the identitarian core it hoped to decenter. Critique in digital literary studies might instead question that willing suspension of disbelief which constitutes faith in received methods, digital or otherwise, while remaking the intellectual inheritances in cultural studies, queer theory, postcolonial studies, and Black feminist theory that lie at the foundations of our work.

The movements for critique within digital literary studies call for self-reflection on how our tools and methods are embedded within economies and societies always structured in dominance, how our literary visualizations connect to an algorithmically mediated economy and society, and how our digital dependencies go far beyond APIs and software packages into an entire digital mode of production. That kind of self-reflection

---

[52] Saidiya Hartman, "Venus in Two Acts," *Small Axe: A Caribbean Journal of Criticism* 26 (June 6, 2008): 2–3, cited in Lauren Klein, "The Image of Absence: Archival Silence, Data Visualization, and James Hemings," *American Literature* 85.4 (January 1, 2013): 661–688. https://doi.org/10.1215/00029831-2367310.

[53] Jessica Marie Johnson, "Markup Bodies: Black [Life] Studies and Slavery [Death] Studies at the Digital Crossroads," *Social Text* 36.4 (137) (December 1, 2018): 57–79. https://doi.org/10.1215/01642472-7145658.

[54] See Dorothy Kim, "Teaching Medieval Studies in a Time of White Supremacy": http://www.inthemedievalmiddle.com/2017/08/teaching-medieval-studies-in-time-of.html, August 28, 2017.

entails inter- and metadisciplinary thinking and conversation, rather than just a new set of critical vocabularies to be deployed for the moment; it entails reflection on the history of critique itself, and on the legacies of critique within several waves of digital work in literary studies. Most of all, the building of new digital futures for literature and critique requires the will to collaborate, the capacity to synthesize new critical collectives and forms of community that will sustain projects and archives. Critique encounters literary studies within the historical horizon of the latter's entire transformation and remediation. Within that confrontation lies a shared future, whether of antagonism, dialectical transformation, or silent disavowal.

Index

80 Days, 187

Aarseth, Espen, 199–200, 214–215, 232
Adorno, Theodor, 276–278
AI (artificial intelligence), 73, 221, 246, 251–252, 255, 262, 264, 266–268, 270
Amazon.com, Inc., 137–138, 140, 142, 145–152, 225–226, 269, 287, *See* Kindle e-reader
Anchorhead, 187
annotation, 108, 113, 116–119, 133, 176
Apple, Inc., 131–132, 146–147, 181, 198, 210, 220, 243
Archive of Our Own (AO3) (platform), 152, 154, 161, 165, 168–169, 171–175
Aristotle, 125
Armantrout, Rae, 73, 82
Arnold, Matthew, 50
Ashbaugh, Dennis, 242
Ashbery, John, 81
Atwood, Margaret, 137–138, 233
Austen, Jane, 59, 63
Authonomy (platform), 150
author/programmers, 194–196, 199, 201, 203–205, 209–210

Baldwin, James, 70
Balestrini, Nanni, 197
Bamman, David, 94–95
BASIC (Beginners All-purpose Symbolic Code) (programming language), 197–198, 210
Baudot, Jean, 199
Bayle, Pierre, 276, 286
Begos, Kevin, 242
belles lettres, 7, 17, 19–22, 33
Bernstein, Charles, 67, 84–85, *See* close listening
Bioshock, 213, 218–219, 221
Blake Archive, the, 99, 113–114
Bode, Katherine, 5–6, 108, 110, 115
Bogost, Ian, 210, 213–214, 223, 231
Bolaño, Roberto, 247–248
Boom, Irma, 237

Bourdieu, Pierre, 54–56, 58, 281
Brennan, Timothy, 3
Brouillette, Sarah, 4
Busa, Roberto, 24, 98, 282

Cage, John, 200
Calibre (software), 134
Callahan, Bill, 72
ChatGPT. *See* GPT-1–4
Choose Your Own Adventure novels, 186
Citizen Kane, 212–213, 219–220, 222, 232
Clement, Tanya, 80, 85
close listening, 67–68, 84, *See* slow listening
codex, the, 107–109, 111–117, 120, 123–124, 140, 234, 239, 241–242, 246–247
Coetzee, J. M., 197
Cohen, Margaret, 52
comparative textual media, 100, 241
concordances, 13, 15, 23–25, 28–31, 113, 246
Cook, Albert Stanburrough, 17, 23–24, 28, 30
Cooper, Lane, 18, 24–25, 28, 30–31
Coover, Robert, 189, 216, 236
copyright law, 53, 97, 123, 129–130, 134, 149, 151, 157–158, 163, 165, 238
Cordell, Ryan, 89, 91, 101–102
Critical Code Studies, 210–211
Croft, Adam, 148–149
Crusader Kings III, 192
Cuddy-Keane, Melba, 42

Da, Nan Z., 4–6, 45
Danielewski, Mark Z., 244–245, 248
Darnton, Robert, 107–108, 111, 113, 139–144, 152
data visualization, 13, 22–23, 38, 46, 61–62, 64, 74, 78, 81, 92, 121, 280
Davis, Lydia, 137, 260
de Martinville, Edouard-Leon Scott, 74
decolonization, 289
detective fiction, 36, 40–41, 45, 184, 279
DIASTEXT (software), 200
Dick, Jonathan, 86

292

Index 293

Dickinson, Emily, 68, 119–120
digital rights management (DRM), 133, 135
Disco Elysium, 184
Drift (software), 75, 78–81, 86
Drucker, Johanna, 238–241
Dwarf Fortress, 192

Earhart, Amy A., 109, 112
EEBO (Early English Books Online), 101
Eidsheim, Nina, 69–70
Electronic Arts, Inc., 221–222
Eliot, George, 254–255
Eliot, T. S., 86, 122, 206
embeddings, word and contextual, 52, 205–206, 268
English literature, discipline of, 15–16, 19
English, James, 87
Even Cowgirls Bleed, 188
evolutionary models of social change, 44–45

Fanfiction.net (platform), 154, 158, 167–168, 171, 173
Felski, Rita, 279, 282
Foucault, Michel, 278, 287
Franzen, Jonathan, 137–138
Frasca, Gonzalo, 214–215, 228
Future Library Project, 233, 246

Gaiman, Neil, 163–165
Galloway, Alexander, 228–229, 231
GamerGate, 223–224, 230
Garbe, Jacob, 246
Gentle (software), 75, 77, 79–81, 86
Gibson, William, 242
Ginsberg, Allen, 73, 82
Glück, Louise, 72–73, 75, 77–78, 82
Goffman, Erving, 67
Good Omens (TV series), 161, 163, 174
Goodman, Nelson, 135
Goodreads, 55, 140, 152, 166–167, 169
Goodwin, Ross, 203
Google Books, 94, 100, 118
GPT-1–4 (software), 10, 98, 206
Grand Theft Auto franchise, 213, 228–229
Greve Rasmussen, Krista Stinne, 114–115
Guillory, John, 50
Gun Mute, 185
Gysin, Brion, 196

Habermas, Jürgen, 275–276
Hadean Lands, 181
Half-Life, 228
Hall, Steven, 245
Hall, Stuart, 159, 274
Hannibal (TV series), 162
Hartman, Charles O., 200

HathiTrust Digital Library, 94, 100
Hatoful Boyfriend, 179–180
Hayles, N. Katherine, 238, 240, 244
Heuser, Ryan, 38
HiPSTAS (High Performance Sound Technologies for Access and Performance), 85
Horkheimer, Max, 276, 278
Human Errors, 183
Hurston, Zora Neale, 126–127
Hutchinson, Peter, 216

interactive fiction (IF), 177, 180–181, 192–193, 205, 226

James, David, 41
James, E. L., 139, 150–151, 164
James, Henry, 250–254
Jameson, Frederic, 41–42, 283, 288
Jenkins, Henry, 161, 213, 236
Jockers, Matthew, 91, 93
Johnston, Jhave, 203
Juul, Jesper, 220–221, 225

Kabo Ashwell, Sam, 178, 187
Kennedy, Bill, 204
Kindle e-reader, 145–150, 152–153, 173, 225–226
Kirsch, Adam, 3
Kirschenbaum, Matthew, 104–105
Kirtsaeng v. John Wiley & Sons Inc., 129–130
Kittler, Friedrich, 88
Klein, Lauren, 289
Knausgård, Karl Ove, 248
Knowles, Alison, 197
Koselleck, Reinhart, 274–276

Larson, Darby, 207
Lee, Sabrina, 94–95
Le-Khac, Long, 38
Lifeline, 181
linearity and nonlinearity (of narrative), 113–116, 143, 175–176, 185, 190, 221–222, 228, 249, 268
Liu, Alan, 105, 240, 284–285
Llompart, Cecilia, 72–73, 82
Long, Hoyt, 93, 96
Lutz, Theo, 197

machine learning, 5–6, 45, 85, 201, 205, 208
Mak, Bonnie, 101
Marino, Mark C., 210–211
McDonald's Video Game, 188
McGann, Jerome, 80, 98, 109–113, 115, 117, 121–122, 209, 240
McLuhan, Marshall and Eric, 236
media archaeology, 89, 104

MESOLIST (software), 200
metadata, 6, 30–31, 102, 116, 119, 121, 136, 147, 150, 170–171, 174
MEXICA (software), 198
Midnight. Swordfight, 187
Miles, Josephine, 24, 98, 286
MINSTREL (software), 198
Moncrieff, C. K. Scott, 260
Montfort, Nick, 202, 204, 209–210
Moretti, Franco, 3, 43–44, 46, 52, 89–90, 92–93, 99, 106, 288
MRI (Magnetic Resonance Imaging), 252, 267–268, 270
multimodality, 108, 119, 121–122, 124, 209, 234, 241, 244–245
Murray, Janet, 217, 226
Murray, Simone, 140, 143
Mustazza, Chris, 84

NaNoGenMo (National Novel Generation Month), 202–205, 208
narrative, 34, 38, 42, 44, 46, 107, 169, 175, 198, 214–215, 219, 222, 228, 230–231, 244, 247, 250–252, 255, 259, 262, 268, 290
Nelson, Graham, 184
neoliberalism, 3, 90, 216, 230, 284, 287–288

OCR (optical character recognition), 91, 97, 104, 268
OpenAI, Inc., 195, 206, See GPT-1–4
Organization for Transformative Works, the, 163, 171, 173
Orlando Project, 99, 286

page, the, 68, 116–117, 119–120, 242–243, 245–246, 252, 255
Pannapacker, William, 2–3
paratext (Gérard Genette), 102, 140, 149–150, 156, 162, 170–175, 240
Parker, Felan, 212–213, 218–220, 231
Parrish, Allison, 201, 207–208
Parrish, Stephen, 13
patent law, 131–132
PennSound, 68, 85
personal digital assistants (PDAs), 146–147
Philips, Todd, 242
philology, 16–19, 21–23, 30, 33, 89, 98, 100–101, 103–104, 106, 273–274, 279–280
Photopia, 187
Piper, Andrew, 103, 116, 120
Platform Studies, 210–211
Plotkin, Andrew, 181–182, 192
Poet Voice, 71–74, 79, 82, 84
Poetess Archive, 286
Porpentine Charity Heartscape, 189–190
Porter, J. D., 55–57, 92

Powers, Richard
    Bewilderment, 266–268, 270–271
    Galatea 2.2, 255–256, 258, 262, 264, 271
    Plowing the Dark, 262–266, 268, 271
    The Overstory, 269–270
Pressman, Jessica, 240, 243, 245
Price, Leah, 238, 240
Project Gutenberg, 118, 146, 207
Proust, Marcel, 256–266, 268–270
Punjab Archives, the, 127, 130

RACTER (software), 199–200, 206
Rameses, 187
Ray Murray, Padmini, 139, 143–144
realism, 38, 40, 88, 217, 231
Reid, Aaron, 246
Richards, I. A., 74
Risam, Roopika, 99
Ross, Shauna, 99
Rossetti Archive, the, 99, 110
Roth, Philip, 235
Rubery, Matthew, 87
Russell, Bertrand, 128, 130–133
Ryan, Marie-Laure, 217

Safran Foer, Jonathan, 243, 245
Sahle, Patrick, 114
Saussy, Haun, 90
Scents and Semiosis, 178–179
Schell, Jesse, 224–227
Schulz, Bruno, 243
Sedgwick, Eve Kosofsky, 282
sentiment analysis, 73
Septima, 181
Seshagiri, Urmila, 42
Sherlock (TV series), 162
Sherman, Lucius Adelno, 21–22, 24
Shields, David, 234
Shillingsburg, Peter, 113–114, 119, 124
Sloterdijk, Peter, 278
slow listening, 70, 81, 84, 88, See close listening
So, Richard Jean, 93, 96
Sobchuk, Oleg, 43–44, 46
Sommerville, Ian, 196
Sontag, Susan, 278
speech perception, 66, 72
Spider and Web, 182
Spufford, Francis, 165
Squires, Claire, 139, 143–144
Stanford Literary Lab, 38, 55, 92
Sterne, Jonathan, 68
Strachey, Christopher, 196
stylometry, 21–22, 52

TALE-SPIN (software), 198
Text Editing Initiative (TEI), 118–119

The Game Formerly Known as Hidden Nazi Mode, 180
The King of Shreds and Patches, 188
The Reprover, 178
Their Angelical Understanding, 189–190
topic modeling, 52, 60–64
Trans-Atlantic Slave Trade Database, 289
TRAVESTY (software), 200
Treharne, Elaine, 120–121
Trethewey, Natasha, 72–73, 82
Trumpener, Katie, 89
Twitter/X (platform), 140, 163–166, 200–202

Underwood, Ted, 5, 7, 87, 94–95
UNIVERSE (software), 198

van der Weel, Adriaan, 139, 141–143, 149, 151–152
Venuti, Lawrence, 103–104

virtual reality (VR), 217–218, 226, 251–253, 262–265, 267–268
Voxit (software), 79–81

Warren, Austin, 41
Wattpad (platform), 138, 152–154, 168–169, 173
Wellek, René, 41
Wershler, Darren, 204
Wilkens, Matthew, 35
Women Writers Project, 99, 286
Wordsworth, William, 24–25, 28, 30, 34

Yeats, W. B., 73, 82, 266
Yngve, Victor H., 197

Zapruder, Matthew, 72–73, 82
Zilles, Li, 208

Cambridge Companions To ...

Authors

Edward Albee edited by Stephen J. Bottoms
Margaret Atwood edited by Coral Ann Howells (second edition)
W. H. Auden edited by Stan Smith
Jane Austen edited by Edward Copeland and Juliet McMaster (second edition)
James Baldwin edited by Michele Elam
Balzac edited by Owen Heathcote and Andrew Watts
Beckett edited by John Pilling
Bede edited by Scott DeGregorio
Aphra Behn edited by Derek Hughes and Janet Todd
Saul Bellow edited by Victoria Aarons
Walter Benjamin edited by David S. Ferris
William Blake edited by Morris Eaves
Boccaccio edited by Guyda Armstrong, Rhiannon Daniels, and Stephen J. Milner
Jorge Luis Borges edited by Edwin Williamson
Brecht edited by Peter Thomson and Glendyr Sacks (second edition)
The Brontës edited by Heather Glen
Bunyan edited by Anne Dunan-Page
Frances Burney edited by Peter Sabor
Byron edited by Drummond Bone (second edition)
Albert Camus edited by Edward J. Hughes
Willa Cather edited by Marilee Lindemann
Catullus edited by Ian Du Quesnay and Tony Woodman
Cervantes edited by Anthony J. Cascardi
Chaucer edited by Piero Boitani and Jill Mann (second edition)
Chekhov edited by Vera Gottlieb and Paul Allain
Kate Chopin edited by Janet Beer
Caryl Churchill edited by Elaine Aston and Elin Diamond
Cicero edited by Catherine Steel
John Clare edited by Sarah Houghton-Walker
J. M. Coetzee edited by Jarad Zimbler
Coleridge edited by Lucy Newlyn
Coleridge edited by Tim Fulford (new edition)
Wilkie Collins edited by Jenny Bourne Taylor
Joseph Conrad edited by J. H. Stape
H. D. edited by Nephie J. Christodoulides and Polina Mackay
Dante edited by Rachel Jacoff (second edition)
Daniel Defoe edited by John Richetti
Don DeLillo edited by John N. Duvall
Charles Dickens edited by John O. Jordan
Emily Dickinson edited by Wendy Martin
John Donne edited by Achsah Guibbory

Dostoevskii edited by W. J. Leatherbarrow
Theodore Dreiser edited by Leonard Cassuto and Claire Virginia Eby
John Dryden edited by Steven N. Zwicker
W. E. B. Du Bois edited by Shamoon Zamir
George Eliot edited by George Levine and Nancy Henry (second edition)
T. S. Eliot edited by A. David Moody
Ralph Ellison edited by Ross Posnock
Ralph Waldo Emerson edited by Joel Porte and Saundra Morris
William Faulkner edited by Philip M. Weinstein
Henry Fielding edited by Claude Rawson
F. Scott Fitzgerald edited by Ruth Prigozy
F. Scott Fitzgerald edited by Michael Nowlin (second edition)
Flaubert edited by Timothy Unwin
E. M. Forster edited by David Bradshaw
Benjamin Franklin edited by Carla Mulford
Brian Friel edited by Anthony Roche
Robert Frost edited by Robert Faggen
Gabriel García Márquez edited by Philip Swanson
Elizabeth Gaskell edited by Jill L. Matus
Edward Gibbon edited by Karen O'Brien and Brian Young
Goethe edited by Lesley Sharpe
Günter Grass edited by Stuart Taberner
Thomas Hardy edited by Dale Kramer
David Hare edited by Richard Boon
Nathaniel Hawthorne edited by Richard Millington
Seamus Heaney edited by Bernard O'Donoghue
Ernest Hemingway edited by Scott Donaldson
Hildegard of Bingen edited by Jennifer Bain
Homer edited by Robert Fowler
Horace edited by Stephen Harrison
Ted Hughes edited by Terry Gifford
Ibsen edited by James McFarlane
Kazuo Ishiguro edited by Andrew Bennett
Henry James edited by Jonathan Freedman
Samuel Johnson edited by Greg Clingham
Ben Jonson edited by Richard Harp and Stanley Stewart
James Joyce edited by Derek Attridge (second edition)
Kafka edited by Julian Preece
Keats edited by Susan J. Wolfson
Rudyard Kipling edited by Howard J. Booth
Lacan edited by Jean-Michel Rabaté
D. H. Lawrence edited by Anne Fernihough
Primo Levi edited by Robert Gordon
Lucretius edited by Stuart Gillespie and Philip Hardie
Machiavelli edited by John M. Najemy

David Mamet edited by Christopher Bigsby
Thomas Mann edited by Ritchie Robertson
Christopher Marlowe edited by Patrick Cheney
Andrew Marvell edited by Derek Hirst and Steven N. Zwicker
Ian McEwan edited by Dominic Head
Herman Melville edited by Robert S. Levine
Arthur Miller edited by Christopher Bigsby (second edition)
Milton edited by Dennis Danielson (second edition)
Molière edited by David Bradby and Andrew Calder
William Morris edited by Marcus Waithe
Toni Morrison edited by Justine Tally
Alice Munro edited by David Staines
Nabokov edited by Julian W. Connolly
Eugene O'Neill edited by Michael Manheim
George Orwell edited by John Rodden
Ovid edited by Philip Hardie
Petrarch edited by Albert Russell Ascoli and Unn Falkeid
Harold Pinter edited by Peter Raby (second edition)
Sylvia Plath edited by Jo Gill
Plutarch edited by Frances B. Titchener and Alexei Zadorojnyi
Edgar Allan Poe edited by Kevin J. Hayes
Alexander Pope edited by Pat Rogers
Ezra Pound edited by Ira B. Nadel
Proust edited by Richard Bales
Pushkin edited by Andrew Kahn
Thomas Pynchon edited by Inger H. Dalsgaard, Luc Herman and Brian McHale
Rabelais edited by John O'Brien
Rilke edited by Karen Leeder and Robert Vilain
Philip Roth edited by Timothy Parrish
Salman Rushdie edited by Abdulrazak Gurnah
John Ruskin edited by Francis O'Gorman
Sappho edited by P. J. Finglass and Adrian Kelly
Seneca edited by Shadi Bartsch and Alessandro Schiesaro
Shakespeare edited by Margareta de Grazia and Stanley Wells (second edition)
George Bernard Shaw edited by Christopher Innes
Shelley edited by Timothy Morton
Mary Shelley edited by Esther Schor
Sam Shepard edited by Matthew C. Roudané
Spenser edited by Andrew Hadfield
Laurence Sterne edited by Thomas Keymer
Wallace Stevens edited by John N. Serio
Tom Stoppard edited by Katherine E. Kelly
Harriet Beecher Stowe edited by Cindy Weinstein
August Strindberg edited by Michael Robinson
Jonathan Swift edited by Christopher Fox

J. M. Synge edited by P. J. Mathews
Tacitus edited by A. J. Woodman
Henry David Thoreau edited by Joel Myerson
Thucydides edited by Polly Low
Tolstoy edited by Donna Tussing Orwin
Anthony Trollope edited by Carolyn Dever and Lisa Niles
Mark Twain edited by Forrest G. Robinson
John Updike edited by Stacey Olster
Mario Vargas Llosa edited by Efrain Kristal and John King
Virgil edited by Fiachra Mac Góráin and Charles Martindale (second edition)
Voltaire edited by Nicholas Cronk
David Foster Wallace edited by Ralph Clare
Edith Wharton edited by Millicent Bell
Walt Whitman edited by Ezra Greenspan
Oscar Wilde edited by Peter Raby
Tennessee Williams edited by Matthew C. Roudané
William Carlos Williams edited by Christopher MacGowan
August Wilson edited by Christopher Bigsby
Mary Wollstonecraft edited by Claudia L. Johnson
Virginia Woolf edited by Susan Sellers (second edition)
Wordsworth edited by Stephen Gill
Richard Wright edited by Glenda R. Carpio
W. B. Yeats edited by Marjorie Howes and John Kelly
Xenophon edited by Michael A. Flower
Zola edited by Brian Nelson

Topics

The Actress edited by Maggie B. Gale and John Stokes
The African American Novel edited by Maryemma Graham
The African American Slave Narrative edited by Audrey A. Fisch
African American Theatre edited by Harvey Young
Allegory edited by Rita Copeland and Peter Struck
American Crime Fiction edited by Catherine Ross Nickerson
American Gothic edited by Jeffrey Andrew Weinstock
The American Graphic Novel edited by Jan Baetens, Hugo Frey and Fabrice Leroy
American Horror edited by Stephen Shapiro and Mark Storey
American Literature and the Body edited by Travis M. Foster
American Literature and the Environment edited by Sarah Ensor and Susan Scott Parrish
American Literature of the 1930s edited by William Solomon
American Modernism edited by Walter Kalaidjian
American Poetry since 1945 edited by Jennifer Ashton
American Realism and Naturalism edited by Donald Pizer
American Short Story edited by Michael J. Collins and Gavin Jones

American Travel Writing edited by Alfred Bendixen and Judith Hamera
American Women Playwrights edited by Brenda Murphy
Ancient Rhetoric edited by Erik Gunderson
Arthurian Legend edited by Elizabeth Archibald and Ad Putter
Australian Literature edited by Elizabeth Webby
The Australian Novel edited by Nicholas Birns and Louis Klee
The Beats edited by Stephen Belletto
The Black Body in American Literature edited by Cherene Sherrard-Johnson
Boxing edited by Gerald Early
British Black and Asian Literature (1945–2010) edited by Deirdre Osborne
British Fiction: 1980–2018 edited by Peter Boxall
British Fiction since 1945 edited by David James
British Literature of the 1930s edited by James Smith
British Literature of the French Revolution edited by Pamela Clemit
British Romantic Poetry edited by James Chandler and Maureen N. McLane
British Romanticism edited by Stuart Curran (second edition)
British Romanticism and Religion edited by Jeffrey Barbeau
British Theatre, 1730–1830 edited by Jane Moody and Daniel O'Quinn
Canadian Literature edited by Eva-Marie Kröller (second edition)
The Canterbury Tales edited by Frank Grady
Children's Literature edited by M. O. Grenby and Andrea Immel
The City in World Literature edited by Ato Quayson and Jini Kim Watson
The Classic Russian Novel edited by Malcolm V. Jones and Robin Feuer Miller
Comics edited by Maaheen Ahmed
Contemporary African American Literature edited by Yogita Goyal
Contemporary Irish Poetry edited by Matthew Campbell
Creative Writing edited by David Morley and Philip Neilsen
Crime Fiction edited by Martin Priestman
Dante's "Commedia" edited by Zygmunt G. Barański and Simon Gilson
Dracula edited by Roger Luckhurst
Early American Literature edited by Bryce Traister
Early Modern Women's Writing edited by Laura Lunger Knoppers
The Eighteenth-Century Novel edited by John Richetti
Eighteenth-Century Poetry edited by John Sitter
Eighteenth-Century Thought edited by Frans De Bruyn
Emma edited by Peter Sabor
English Dictionaries edited by Sarah Ogilvie
English Literature, 1500–1600 edited by Arthur F. Kinney
English Literature, 1650–1740 edited by Steven N. Zwicker
English Literature, 1740–1830 edited by Thomas Keymer and Jon Mee
English Literature, 1830–1914 edited by Joanne Shattock
English Melodrama edited by Carolyn Williams
English Novelists edited by Adrian Poole
English Poetry, Donne to Marvell edited by Thomas N. Corns
English Poets edited by Claude Rawson

English Renaissance Drama edited by A. R. Braunmuller and Michael Hattaway, (second edition)
English Renaissance Tragedy edited by Emma Smith and Garrett A. Sullivan Jr.
English Restoration Theatre edited by Deborah C. Payne Fisk
Environmental Humanities edited by Jeffrey Cohen and Stephanie Foote
The Epic edited by Catherine Bates
Erotic Literature edited by Bradford Mudge
The Essay edited by Kara Wittman and Evan Kindley
European Modernism edited by Pericles Lewis
European Novelists edited by Michael Bell
Fairy Tales edited by Maria Tatar
Fantasy Literature edited by Edward James and Farah Mendlesohn
Feminist Literary Theory edited by Ellen Rooney
Fiction in the Romantic Period edited by Richard Maxwell and Katie Trumpener
The Fin de Siècle edited by Gail Marshall
Frankenstein edited by Andrew Smith
The French Enlightenment edited by Daniel Brewer
French Literature edited by John D. Lyons
The French Novel: From 1800 to the Present edited by Timothy Unwin
Gay and Lesbian Writing edited by Hugh Stevens
German Romanticism edited by Nicholas Saul
Global Literature and Slavery edited by Laura T. Murphy
Gothic Fiction edited by Jerrold E. Hogle
The Graphic Novel edited by Stephen Tabachnick
The Greek and Roman Novel edited by Tim Whitmarsh
Greek and Roman Theatre edited by Marianne McDonald and J. Michael Walton
Greek Comedy edited by Martin Revermann
Greek Lyric edited by Felix Budelmann
Greek Mythology edited by Roger D. Woodard
Greek Tragedy edited by P. E. Easterling
The Harlem Renaissance edited by George Hutchinson
The History of the Book edited by Leslie Howsam
Human Rights and Literature edited by Crystal Parikh
The Irish Novel edited by John Wilson Foster
Irish Poets edited by Gerald Dawe
The Italian Novel edited by Peter Bondanella and Andrea Ciccarelli
The Italian Renaissance edited by Michael Wyatt
Jewish American Literature edited by Hana Wirth-Nesher and Michael P. Kramer
The Latin American Novel edited by Efraín Kristal
Latin American Poetry edited by Stephen Hart
Latina/o American Literature edited by John Morán González
Latin Love Elegy edited by Thea S. Thorsen
Literature and Animals edited by Derek Ryan
Literature and the Anthropocene edited by John Parham
Literature and Climate edited by Adeline Johns-Putra and Kelly Sultzbach

Literature and Disability edited by Clare Barker and Stuart Murray
Literature and Food edited by J. Michelle Coghlan
Literature and the Posthuman edited by Bruce Clarke and Manuela Rossini
Literature and Religion edited by Susan M. Felch
Literature and Science edited by Steven Meyer
The Literature of the American Civil War and Reconstruction edited by Kathleen Diffley and Coleman Hutchison
The Literature of the American Renaissance edited by Christopher N. Phillips
The Literature of Berlin edited by Andrew J. Webber
The Literature of the Crusades edited by Anthony Bale
The Literature of the First World War edited by Vincent Sherry
The Literature of London edited by Lawrence Manley
The Literature of Los Angeles edited by Kevin R. McNamara
The Literature of New York edited by Cyrus Patell and Bryan Waterman
The Literature of Paris edited by Anna-Louise Milne
The Literature of World War II edited by Marina MacKay
Literature on Screen edited by Deborah Cartmell and Imelda Whelehan
Lyrical Ballads edited by Sally Bushell
Medieval British Manuscripts edited by Orietta Da Rold and Elaine Treharne
Medieval English Culture edited by Andrew Galloway
Medieval English Law and Literature edited by Candace Barrington and Sebastian Sobecki
Medieval English Literature edited by Larry Scanlon
Medieval English Mysticism edited by Samuel Fanous and Vincent Gillespie
Medieval English Theatre edited by Richard Beadle and Alan J. Fletcher (second edition)
Medieval French Literature edited by Simon Gaunt and Sarah Kay
Medieval Romance edited by Roberta L. Krueger
Medieval Romance edited by Roberta L. Krueger (new edition)
Medieval Women's Writing edited by Carolyn Dinshaw and David Wallace
Modern American Culture edited by Christopher Bigsby
Modern British Women Playwrights edited by Elaine Aston and Janelle Reinelt
Modern French Culture edited by Nicholas Hewitt
Modern German Culture edited by Eva Kolinsky and Wilfried van der Will
The Modern German Novel edited by Graham Bartram
The Modern Gothic edited by Jerrold E. Hogle
Modern Irish Culture edited by Joe Cleary and Claire Connolly
Modern Italian Culture edited by Zygmunt G. Baranski and Rebecca J. West
Modern Latin American Culture edited by John King
Modern Russian Culture edited by Nicholas Rzhevsky
Modern Spanish Culture edited by David T. Gies
Modernism edited by Michael Levenson (second edition)
The Modernist Novel edited by Morag Shiach
Modernist Poetry edited by Alex Davis and Lee M. Jenkins
Modernist Women Writers edited by Maren Tova Linett

Narrative edited by David Herman
Narrative Theory edited by Matthew Garrett
Native American Literature edited by Joy Porter and Kenneth M. Roemer
Nineteen Eighty-Four edited by Nathan Waddell
Nineteenth-Century American Literature and Politics edited by John Kerkering
Nineteenth-Century American Poetry edited by Kerry Larson
Nineteenth-Century American Women's Writing edited by Dale M. Bauer and Philip Gould
Nineteenth-Century Thought edited by Gregory Claeys
The Novel edited by Eric Bulson
Old English Literature edited by Malcolm Godden and Michael Lapidge (second edition)
Performance Studies edited by Tracy C. Davis
Piers Plowman edited by Andrew Cole and Andrew Galloway
The Poetry of the First World War edited by Santanu Das
Popular Fiction edited by David Glover and Scott McCracken
Postcolonial Literary Studies edited by Neil Lazarus
Postcolonial Poetry edited by Jahan Ramazani
Postcolonial Travel Writing edited by Robert Clarke
Postmodern American Fiction edited by Paula Geyh
Postmodernism edited by Steven Connor
Prose edited by Daniel Tyler
The Pre-Raphaelites edited by Elizabeth Prettejohn
Pride and Prejudice edited by Janet Todd
Queer Studies edited by Siobhan B. Somerville
Race and American Literature edited by John Ernest
Renaissance Humanism edited by Jill Kraye
Robinson Crusoe edited by John Richetti
Roman Comedy edited by Martin T. Dinter
The Roman Historians edited by Andrew Feldherr
Roman Satire edited by Kirk Freudenburg
The Romantic Sublime edited by Cian Duffy
Science Fiction edited by Edward James and Farah Mendlesohn
Scottish Literature edited by Gerald Carruthers and Liam McIlvanney
Sensation Fiction edited by Andrew Mangham
Shakespeare and Contemporary Dramatists edited by Ton Hoenselaars
Shakespeare and Popular Culture edited by Robert Shaughnessy
Shakespeare and Race edited by Ayanna Thompson
Shakespeare and Religion edited by Hannibal Hamlin
Shakespeare and War edited by David Loewenstein and Paul Stevens
Shakespeare on Film edited by Russell Jackson (second edition)
Shakespeare on Screen edited by Russell Jackson
Shakespeare on Stage edited by Stanley Wells and Sarah Stanton
Shakespearean Comedy edited by Alexander Leggatt
Shakespearean Tragedy edited by Claire McEachern (second edition)

Shakespeare's First Folio edited by Emma Smith
Shakespeare's History Plays edited by Michael Hattaway
Shakespeare's Language edited by Lynne Magnusson with David Schalkwyk
Shakespeare's Last Plays edited by Catherine M. S. Alexander
Shakespeare's Poetry edited by Patrick Cheney
Sherlock Holmes edited by Janice M. Allan and Christopher Pittard
The Sonnet edited by A. D. Cousins and Peter Howarth
The Spanish Novel: From 1600 to the Present edited by Harriet Turner and Adelaida López de Martínez
Textual Scholarship edited by Neil Fraistat and Julia Flanders
Theatre and Science edited by Kristen E. Shepherd-Barr
Theatre History edited by David Wiles and Christine Dymkowski
Transnational American Literature edited by Yogita Goyal
Travel Writing edited by Peter Hulme and Tim Youngs
The Twentieth-Century American Novel and Politics edited by Bryan Santin
Twentieth-Century American Poetry and Politics edited by Daniel Morris
Twentieth-Century British and Irish Women's Poetry edited by Jane Dowson
The Twentieth-Century English Novel edited by Robert L. Caserio
Twentieth-Century English Poetry edited by Neil Corcoran
Twentieth-Century Irish Drama edited by Shaun Richards
Twentieth-Century Literature and Politics edited by Christos Hadjiyiannis and Rachel Potter
Twentieth-Century Russian Literature edited by Marina Balina and Evgeny Dobrenko
Utopian Literature edited by Gregory Claeys
Victorian and Edwardian Theatre edited by Kerry Powell
The Victorian Novel edited by Deirdre David (second edition)
Victorian Poetry edited by Joseph Bristow
Victorian Women's Poetry edited by Linda K. Hughes
Victorian Women's Writing edited by Linda H. Peterson
War Writing edited by Kate McLoughlin
Women's Writing in Britain, 1660–1789 edited by Catherine Ingrassia
Women's Writing in the Romantic Period edited by Devoney Looser
World Literature edited by Ben Etherington and Jarad Zimbler
World Crime Fiction edited by Jesper Gulddal, Stewart King and Alistair Rolls
Writing of the English Revolution edited by N. H. Keeble
The Writings of Julius Caesar edited by Christopher Krebs and Luca Grillo

Milton Keynes UK
Ingram Content Group UK Ltd.
UKHW041357111124
450968UK00017B/5